W9-APX-758

Meaning and Moral Order

BL
60
. W87

Meaning and Moral Order

Explorations in Cultural Analysis

Robert Wuthnow

APR 2 5 1988

UNIVERSITY OF CALIFORNIA PRESS
Berkeley · Los Angeles · London

476371

University of California Press
Berkeley and Los Angeles, California

University of California Press, Ltd.
London, England

©1987 by
The Regents of the University of California

Library of Congress Cataloging-in-Publication Data

Wuthnow, Robert.
  Meaning and moral order.

  Bibliography: p.
  Includes index.
  1. Religion and sociology. 2. Ethics.
3. Social ethics. 4. Ideology. 5. Culture.
I. Title.
BL60.W87 1987 306 86–14668
ISBN 0–520–05950–6 (alk. paper)

Printed in the United States of America

1 2 3 4 5 6 7 8 9

For Robert N. Bellah and Charles Y. Glock

Contents

Preface

In a previous volume (*Cultural Analysis*, 1984), several colleagues and I argued that some promising new directions in social scientific approaches to the study of culture were becoming evident. In surveying the work of four prominent theorists representing four quite different approaches—the American phenomenological sociology of Peter L. Berger, the British cultural anthropology of Mary Douglas, the French historical neo-structuralism of Michel Foucault, and the German philosophical critical theory of Jürgen Habermas—we suggested that several potentially converging tendencies could be identified in current theories of culture. Among these were tendencies away from subjectivist conceptions of culture, toward more objectivist conceptions, toward innovative resolutions of the problem of sociological reductionism, and toward analyses of the internal relations and patterns among components of culture. These, we suggested, provided some hopeful signs for the analysis of culture to be placed on a more systematic empirical footing.

Reviewers of that volume took various stances toward our suggestions. Some agreed with us; others thought we had been overly pessimistic in suggesting a need for new directions in the study of culture; still others saw us as being overly optimistic and argued that the differences in the traditions we had surveyed were still far more interesting than any of the potential convergences we had sought to identify.

Some of these criticisms seemed more plausible than others. What we ourselves saw as the major limitation of that project was the need to put into practice some of the ideas that had been distilled. That is, only by attempting to work with some of the general theoretical orientations that had been outlined did it seem possible to extend, clarify, modify, and assess the utility of these ideas.

The present volume represents a modest effort to move in that direction. It is not a sequel to the earlier volume in that it does not in any way attempt to create a full-blown synthesis from the four theoretical traditions previously examined (that possibility still seems less useful than drawing eclectically from each tradition). Nor is this volume an effort to "make good" on the claim that an emerging framework with which to orient research on culture might be evident. The present aim is considerably less ambitious than that. It is to contribute to the advancement of cultural analysis by addressing several of the theoretical and conceptual issues that seem particularly important to the study of culture and by wrestling with various methodological approaches in some empirical investigations.

The general guidelines for these "explorations" are consistent with the orientations identified in the conclusion of the previous volume: specifically, an effort to steer away from subjectivism, to identify observable elements of culture suitable for investigation, to examine some of the patterns and relationships giving order to those components, and to look at culture in relation to social structure without engaging in sociological reductionism. In a very general way, these represent the distinguishing hallmarks of cultural analysis as the term is used here. Others obviously prefer to approach culture in different ways. The strengths and weaknesses of the present approach are presented toward the end of the volume in as candid a manner as possible.

Beyond these general guidelines, no attempt has been made to impose a single theoretical or methodological framework on the analyses. The term "explorations" is used quite explicitly. Different concepts and different levels of analysis have been deliberately explored in an effort to see how far they can be taken. Their strengths and weaknesses have become evident mainly in attempting to utilize them.

Pursuing these explorations has necessitated critical examination of some of the "sacred cows" of the study of culture. In Chapter 2, for example, an argument is presented that cultural analysis might be better served if its historic interest in the problem of meaning were simply abandoned; in Chapter 4, a concept of ritual is developed that denies that ritual is decidedly different from many other types of social behavior; in Chapters 5 and 6, an approach to ideology is outlined that to many may seem overly formalistic or even reductionistic. These ideas are not expected to be received without controversy. They derive from my having experienced frustration with commonly accepted formulations. They are also presented with full awareness of the theoretical and methodological divisions that currently characterize the study of culture.

This volume is directed primarily to sociologists who share an interest in rigorously pursuing the study of culture. Many of the concepts to which attention is given—meaning, ritual, moral order, ideology, culture—are of importance to practitioners in other disciplines as well (e.g., anthropology, political science, religious studies, history). Some benefit may accrue to these practitioners. It seemed better, however, to target the discussion toward the narrower body of sociological scholarship that is more familiar to the author. Even here, sufficiently different interests and orientations are evident that some attention has had to be given to specifying alternative approaches and levels of analysis.

Within sociology, one of the subfields in which considerable attention has been devoted to questions of meaning and moral order is the sociology of religion. The present volume is not especially oriented toward the study of religion as such, although some of the empirical material does deal with religion. It is well to recognize, nevertheless, that many of the issues and debates taken up here have been especially prominent in the sociology of religion, and the manner in which they are addressed here is undoubtedly in some ways a product of the author's having worked in that field. A degree of forbearance may at times be required of readers unfamiliar with some of the more general issues in this field.

One of the more amusing features of academic publishing that no student of culture is likely to miss is the importance of legitimating myths. Books, like people, have their histories, and these histories must conform to certain norms. As someone has pointed out, an academic book is scarcely a book unless it was written over a lengthy period of time and was in some manner inspired while the author was still in graduate school. It may be trite to say so, therefore, but in the present case both are true.

The chapters of this volume were researched and written over a ten-year period. Approximately the first third of that period was spent grappling somewhat unsuccessfully with some of the ambiguities that seemed to be frustrating work in the area of culture. Pursuit of both theoretical and empirical investigations during this period began to clarify some of the broad guidelines already mentioned. Subsequent efforts were devoted to exploring these ideas down different paths and then to evaluating and integrating the results. Several chapters contain material that has been published in some version before, but all of the chapters contain new material and new efforts at synthesis and evaluation. Collectively, the product of course is neither a single monograph nor an integrated treatise, but a series of explorations.

The initial inspiration for embarking on this venture came, in some respects unwittingly, from having focused primarily on cultural topics, such as religion, ideology, and prejudice, in graduate school. Charles Y. Glock and Robert N. Bellah, each in quite different ways, contributed much to this experience. As much as anything else, the fact of their offering two very distinct, yet to a degree complementary, perspectives on culture probably resulted in my having to think about the issues addressed here. Neither would likely feel comfortable with the specific direction in which many of these explorations have gone; yet there is clearly an indebtedness here that requires acknowledgment. Dedicating this volume to them expresses a token of this indebtedness.

Some of the reading, reflection, and research for this volume was made possible by funding from the William Paterson Foundation to Princeton University in the form of an honorific preceptorship that the author held from 1976 to 1979. This preceptorship provided a small research stipend as well as a full year's leave from teaching responsibilities. Grants and other funds were also received at various times from the National Endowment for the Humanities, the Anti-Defamation League, the Committee on Problems of the Discipline of the American Sociological Association, and the Committee on Research in the Humanities and Social Sciences of Princeton University.

Many students and colleagues have suffered through my attempts to formulate ideas about culture in seminars, colloquia, and informal discussions. A few who have undoubtedly experienced these trials to a greater extent than others are Albert Bergesen, Kevin Christiano, Robert Cox, James Davison Hunter, and Robert C. Liebman, all of whom also read and commented on sections of the manuscript. Meng Chee Lee, Andrew Flood, and Tim Miller worked at various points as research assistants, and much of the typing of initial drafts was done by Blanche Anderson. I am also grateful to Jay Demerath, Lester Kurtz, Wendy Griswold, and Robert Scott for comments on the entire manuscript and to Ron Aminzade, Barbara Laslett, John Meyer, and Theda Skocpol for comments on several of the chapters.

My deepest gratitude, as always, is to my wife and children, who, despite busy lives of their own, find the serenity to put up with me. Although an inveterate skeptic of psychology, I have over the years come to a greater appreciation of the idea that the fulfillment of basic needs for love and security takes precedence over many of the other needs that seem to drive academics.

CHAPTER ONE

Cultural Analysis

The founders of sociology all recognized the importance of culture in social life. Emile Durkheim spent nearly fifteen years at the peak of his career investigating the beliefs and rituals of primitive religion in an effort to grasp the symbolic bases of moral community. Max Weber was concerned with problems of culture to an even greater extent. From the Protestant ethic thesis to contributions on rationalization and comparative religions, his work was prominently oriented toward the values and norms that regulate and legitimate social institutions. From a quite different perspective, Karl Marx dealt extensively with ideology and class consciousness, with religion and legitimation, and with the bases of social knowledge. Other contributors—Toennies, Troeltsch, Tocqueville, Spencer, to name a few—were also deeply concerned with the role of culture in society.

The legacy of the classical period has been carried forward in the work of more recent sociologists and social scientists whose interests have also given special consideration to the patterning and functioning of culture. In Talcott Parsons one finds a clear emphasis, deriving particularly from Durkheim and Weber, on the importance of values and norms. Similar interests are prominent in the work of sociologists who came under Parsons's influence: for example, in Neil Smelser's work on collective behavior, in Robert Bellah's sociology of religion, and in Clifford Geertz's essays on the interpretation of cultures. Durkheim's legacy is evident in Kai Erikson's studies of ritual and deviance, in Guy E. Swanson's investigations of the social bases of belief, and in Mary Douglas's work on symbolic boundaries and moral order. All these examples demonstrate the importance of culture as an object of sociological inquiry. Weber's legacy has included a number of significant extensions of the Protestant ethic thesis, such as Robert Merton's work on Puritanism and science, Bellah's monograph on Tokugawa religion, and studies of English history such as those of David Little and Michael Walzer, as well as broader applications such as Ernst Troeltsch's work on the varieties of religion and Benjamin Nelson's study of usury. Marx's considerations on culture have been greatly expanded in the work of writers such as Georg Lukács, Antonio Gramsci, Louis Althusser, and Jürgen Habermas. In each instance the fundamental role of culture in society has been recognized. To say this without qualification, however, is clearly to misrepresent the field.

Although it is possible to point out specific studies in sociology that have contributed greatly to the understanding of culture, the discipline as a whole has not given particular prominence to the importance of culture. In fact, culture often appears in empirical studies as a vague concept to which relatively superficial attention is given or as an outmoded form of explanation that must be superseded by factors of greater objectivity and significance. Other studies ignore it entirely. These tendencies, of course, are not nearly as pronounced in European sociology, where the linkages between philosophy, social theory, and sociology remain stronger. In American sociology, though, the general tendency toward de-emphasizing culture is well in evidence. Several indications of this tendency are particularly apparent. For example, the once flourishing subfield known as culture and personality has largely receded as a legitimate area of concentration. The personality component has shifted increasingly into the discipline of psychology, while the idea of culture, especially national culture, having a decisive impact on personality has become widely regarded as an arcane concept. Or to take a different example, the sociology of religion—one area in which cultural factors are given much attention—appears to have become increasingly removed from the rest of the discipline. This separation is evident not only in the existence of separate journals and scholarly organizations but also in an obvious dissimilarity between the major concepts and theories that guide research. Major contributions in the sociology of religion dealing with dimensions of belief, sources of conversion, the functioning of rituals and symbols, and modes of religious organization appear to have had virtually no impact on the discipline at large. Other examples could also be mentioned, from the shifting of many of the more cultural aspects of social psychology such as cognition and attitude formation into psychology and away from sociology, to the tendency evident in recent years in political sociology to de-emphasize the role of political culture.

It is perhaps arguable that political science as a discipline has continued to display greater interest in cultural phenomena than has the discipline of sociology. It is far more apparent that anthropology has retained culture as a more central concept than has sociology. History as well, perhaps as a result of the influence of anthropology, has demonstrated a continuing, if not increasing, interest in culture. Sociology, in contrast, appears to have moved decisively in other directions. Topics such as social stratification, social networks, labor markets, ecological models of organizations, and structural theories of the state have animated the discipline in recent years far more than issues of ritual and symbol, belief and ideology, or meaning and moral order.

To some extent, it has perhaps become an accepted tenet of the discipline that the study of culture should be relegated to that of a rather marginal subspecialty (perhaps called sociology of culture) while the core of the discipline should be concerned with topics that are more genuinely sociological, such as stratification and organizations. Nevertheless, it remains surprising that the study of culture is so little emphasized in American sociology, for in virtually every discipline to which sociology is related culture is regarded with considerable seriousness. Anthropology, in which the study of ritual, symbolism, and even cognition and language continue to have high priority, is again the most obvious example, but the same is true in other related disciplines as well. Work on organizations done outside of sociology has paid increasing attention to the importance of corporate cultures; political science has incorporated a number of new ideas about language and discourse as dramatizations of power; meanwhile, studies of language and discourse have moved in directions that make them much more relevant to the social sciences.

It is of course possible to accentuate general tendencies in the discipline to the point of overlooking major exceptions or underestimating significant countertendencies. The purpose of accentuating these tendencies is neither to disparage the discipline nor to devalue the contributions that have been made, but simply to permit raising the question of what may be needed to advance the sociological study of culture. If all that is acknowledged is that cultural analysis no longer occupies as prominent a place in sociology as it did in the work of Weber or Durkheim, or even of Marx, then the possible reasons for this state of affairs can be explored.

One such possibility is that the changing place of cultural analysis in sociology is simply a function of the growth and substantive specialization of the field into separate subdisciplines. Thus one can trace a variety of specialties from the classical theorists—stratification from Marx, complex organizations from Weber, deviance from Durkheim, and so forth—of which culture is only one. As the discipline has become more diverse, proportionately fewer of its members have been interested in culture, and rightly so. Culture may well continue to draw the attention of specialists in particular enclaves of the discipline but need not penetrate into many other areas of inquiry.

The reason for pointing out this possibility—which by all indications seems an accurate appraisal of events—is, on the one hand, to sharpen the issue on which attention needs to be focused and, on the other hand, to raise a broader question about the study of culture. The sharpening of focus comes from recognizing that the problem raised by many social scientists with interests in culture is not why the topic fails to dominate the field but why relative to other topics it seems to have made frustratingly little advancement. For example, the editors of a well-known collection of essays on the sociology of religion concluded that, after more than a half-century of research and thinking, little had been done to advance significantly beyond the classics (Glock and Hammond, 1973). That assessment may have been overly pessimistic, but few would likely have been willing to draw the same conclusion for fields such as social networks, statistical methods, or complex organizations.[1] The broader question that needs to be raised, however, in view of the increasing differentiation of the field, is whether the study of culture can be most effectively advanced by treating it as a subfield or whether a broader focus should be taken.

Here, clarity is required about a further distinction—that between specialization on the basis of analytic strategy and specialization on the basis of distinctive subject matter. As in scholarly inquiry generally, it appears productive to specialize on the basis of analytic strategy. That is, culture may be chosen as an aspect of social reality on which to focus certain analytic perspectives. For example, a definition that will be used repeatedly in this volume conceives of culture simply as *the symbolic-expressive aspect of social behavior.* However, culture does not appear usefully distinguished as an entirely discrete entity that can be examined in isolation from other social phenomena. To put the issue more clearly, culture cannot be identified as a distinct or well-bounded institution to the same extent that, say, family or religion can be. Rather, it penetrates all aspects of social life and must, for this reason, be isolated strictly for analytic purposes. This means of course that the study of culture may reasonably be identified as a subfield of sociology, but it is likely to be one whose boundaries spill over into a variety of other subfields, a fact that may in itself be responsible for some of the problems that seem to hinder the development of this area.

Another possibility that needs to be raised in considering the seemingly neglected place of culture relative to other topics in sociology is whether or not significant contributions have in fact been made in this area in recent years. Assessments of this kind are exceedingly difficult to make, but, based on criteria such as awards and citations, contributions to the study of culture have by no means been absent. Geertz's *The Interpretation of Cultures*, Bellah's *The Broken Covenant*, Erikson's *Everything in Its Path*, and Paul Starr's *The Social Transformation of American Medicine* all treat aspects of culture in significant ways and have been the recipients of major awards. Much-cited books such as Berger and Luckmann's *The Social Construction of Reality* or Habermas's *Legitimation Crisis* also deal primarily with culture. These examples suggest that whatever frustrations the study of culture may have experienced in the larger discipline cannot be attributed strictly to more numerous or significant contributions in other areas. More likely causes are two related problems that can only be mentioned in passing at this point: the problem of institutionalizing major contributions so that they become less "works of art" than guidebooks for more ordinary sorts of investigation and the problem of orientations toward the study of culture that continue to separate it from orientations more prevalent in the discipline at large. Both of these problems merit closer attention later in the discussion here.

Related to these issues are also the discipline's quest to be more "scientific" and its dependence on funding agencies. The directions in which sociology has moved in recent years have partly been determined by both these factors. Funding has been readily available from government agencies for research in such areas as stratification, demography, and labor markets; it has been less readily available for studies of culture, except on occasion from private foundations for studies having practical applications. Related to this problem is the fact that, for historic reasons, culture has been more closely identified with the branch of sociology that emphasizes its humanistic elements rather than its scientific aspirations. Culture remains, by many indications, vaguely conceptualized, vaguely approached methodologically, and vaguely associated with value judgments and other sorts of observer bias. As a result, it is often tolerated as a kind of luxury, or perhaps even as a welcome balance of perspective, but is excluded from the more hard-nosed approaches that run closer to the centers of power and funding for the discipline.

These are all matters of considerable dispute, both as to their propriety and as to how consequential they may be for the study of culture. Scholars with different interests and different conceptions of what the discipline should be necessarily differ over their assessments of the role that cultural analysis should play. These disputes are not likely to be resolved, but making explicit some of the problems that currently face the study of culture is a necessary starting point for the considerations that follow. What seems undeniable is that the study of culture has in recent years, despite notable contributions, been neither a highly valued enterprise in the discipline at large nor a field that has been free of internal problems.

At present, some signs are evident that culture is again coming to be recognized as a topic worthy of serious sociological attention. An enormous amount of interest has emerged in the work of European theorists such as Foucault, Habermas, Althusser, Barthes, Lacan, and Luhmann, all of whom have written extensively on ideology, meaning, discourse, and other aspects of culture. Although much of this interest has focused on topics other than culture, the significance of these writers' contributions to the study of culture has not gone unrecognized. The impact of the Durkheimian tradition has been significantly extended into new areas of cultural investigation by studies examining the ritual aspects of organizations, political events, and deviance, as well as inquiries dealing with symbols of civic culture and societal integration. Much ferment has been evident in the sociology of religion, especially in areas that bridge out of institutional religion and make connections with broader dimensions of culture. A number of participant-observer and depth-interview studies have probed issues of meaning and personal worldviews, and some attention has been given to the study of discourse and language. All of these represent promising developments.

CONCEPTUAL AND THEORETICAL PROBLEMS

The problems one encounters in investigating culture nevertheless remain immense. One of the most fundamental of these problems arises from the fact that culture continues to have widely different connotations. For some, it consists chiefly of beliefs and attitudes; for others, it represents an objectified ontological system; others take any of a number of positions in between these extremes. The most apparent result of this ambiguity is that scholarly debates often fail to connect with one another. Replications fail to replicate; refutations fail to refute; replies fail to convince; and dismissals typically dismiss too much or too little. More serious, however, is that different conceptions of culture affect how culture is dealt with sociologically, particularly the ways in which investigators go about relating it to social structure. Some define it so narrowly that only social structure seems to matter; others see it as such a constitutive element of social structure that little opportunity is left to investigate systematic relations.

A second set of problems derives from ambiguities surrounding the objectivity or subjectivity of culture and, correlatively, the degree to which culture can or should be approached "scientifically." On the one hand are arguments that stress the essentially *interpretive* character of cultural analysis; on the other hand are perspectives that attempt to place the study of culture on a more solid empirical footing as a research enterprise. The two positions are by no means entirely incompatible with each other. Nevertheless, they greatly exacerbate the difficulties faced in attempting to reach agreement on the nature and purposes of cultural investigations. Adherents of the interpretive model often wish to draw a sharp distinction between cultural analysis and other sociological inquiries. In their view, cultural analysis should give the investigator ample latitude in mixing his or her own values with those of the phenomena observed, should disavow such canons of positivist science as replicability, and should not worry about contributing generalizable or cumulative knowledge. At the other extreme, scholars who may subscribe in principle to some of these ideas nevertheless argue that cultural analysis is all too often impeded by subjectivism, by a failure to employ rigorous methods of data collection and validation, and by a lack of attention to formalization of theories and concepts. Given these differences of orientation, substantive inquiries are frequently judged by widely discrepant standards, and programmatic treatises fail to generate agreement about what constitutes legitimate contributions to the field.[2]

A third, closely related problem is that much of the presumably sociological literature on dimensions of culture in fact consists largely of philosophical debate. Probably more so than in any other subfield in sociology (with the possible exception of theory itself), cultural analysis tends to be dominated by abstract discussions of the nature of culture, of the sources of knowledge, and of the humanistic purposes to which cultural knowledge might be put. These debates stem of course from the ambiguities already mentioned concerning basic definitions and boundaries of the field. In a favorable sense these debates constitute serious efforts to arrive at some resolution of fundamental questions in the field.[3] More often, though, the literature appears to be dominated by second-order and third-order disputes over the meaning of original texts—debates over Marx's concept of ideology, or Gramsci's interpretation of Marx's concept of ideology, or Althusser's interpretation of Gramsci's interpretation, and so on. For good reasons, it appears, many sociologists have learned to steer clear of books and articles about ideology and related concepts.

Also closely related to the foregoing is a fourth problem, namely, the question of reductionism. Largely as a function of sociology's historical evolution from philosophy and other forms of inquiry, the status of ideas, values, and other cultural concepts remains in doubt. Are they to be regarded as realities *sui generis,* should they be understood as properties of the individual, or should an effort be made to explain them with reference to social factors? The ontological status of most other phenomena in sociology has been, in practice although not in principle, resolved to a much greater extent. It now seems ludicrous, for example, to question the reality of suicide rates or state structures as objects worthy of sociological investigation. The same certainty has not yet emerged with reference to culture. As a result, investigators are typically beset with questions concerning the degree of reduction appropriate in dealing with cultural variables and with criticisms for either explaining away these variables too readily or attributing too much significance to them.

A fifth set of problems stems from the interrelations present in cultural studies between methodological styles and theoretical or metatheoretical assumptions. The use of survey research methods, for example, characteristically implies different assumptions about the nature of culture than does the use of participant-observation or archival methods. Nearly all the methods available to sociologists generally have been employed in cultural inquiries. Few efforts have been made, however, to determine whether the assumptions implicit in one method are appropriate for different methods or levels of investigation. This shortcoming is particularly problematic in the case of cultural variables because assumptions are generally made about the psychological or social psychological status of these variables. Considerable confusion may arise, for instance, in applying models of cultural change suitable to studies of individual conversion to questions of major cultural change in history. When different methods are employed, debates over the nature of the methods themselves often obscure deeper assumptions that need to be examined.

Finally, problems are also evident, as alluded to earlier, in the tendency to encapsulate cultural inquiries in different substantive areas, such as sociology of religion or sociology of science, rather than including efforts to draw generalizations applicable to a number of different substantive areas. At present, ideas about culture in the sociology of religion, for example, are largely separate from those in sociology of science or in studies of the state. Whatever cross-fertilization that might derive from thinking about ritual or symbolism in a more general sense has been extremely limited. Some progress has been made because of general perspectival formulations, such as those of Berger and Luckmann (1966) or Geertz (1973), but much remains to be done on this front in order to begin developing empirically grounded ideas about culture. This task is of course made all the more difficult by the other ambiguities that continue to prevail in cultural analysis.

Not only are there disagreements about the scope and purposes of cultural analysis; more general issues about how best to advance scholarship in a particular area are always present as well. Possibly the most promising prospect for advancement lies in the contribution of seminal and innovative studies themselves (cf. Mullins, 1973). Such studies not only add substantively to knowledge but also illustrate methods of analysis and encourage others who may aspire to make similar contributions. The problem is that such seminal works are likely to be rare in any field and may in fact be difficult to emulate. As already noted, cultural analysis has been the focus of a number of such works even in recent years, and yet many of these studies have been less than successful in inspiring second and third generations of quality research.

Another option for advancing work in a scholarly field is what Mullins (1973) has called a "program statement," that is, a secondary compilation or theoretical synthesis of the field that serves as a text and guidebook for future research. What program statements sometimes lack in innovativeness or in empirical content they make up for in clarity and integration. These treatises, however, require that a considerable degree of consensus has already been achieved in a field. Otherwise they are likely to represent a single perspective within the field but go only part way toward reconciling internal differences. Berger and Luckmann's *The Social Construction of Reality* has in some ways served as a program statement for the study of culture. Its value has been considerable in terms of identifying central problems and providing an orienting framework. Its limitations lie in the fact that it is an *orientation* representing only one of several possible ways of approaching the study of culture. A third alternative is to bring together empirical and conceptual essays that combine substantive and programmatic concerns. The weakness of this strategy is that it generally fails to provide the integration of a program statement or the luster of a seminal study. Its strength is that multiple concepts and methods can be explicitly compared. It can serve usefully in fields that are genuinely divided over basic concepts and assumptions.

SCOPE OF THE BOOK

The present volume is conceived of as an example of this third approach. It consists of a series of *explorations* that address some of the core issues in cultural analysis: the problem of meaning, the nature of moral order, the character and role of ritual in dramatizing moral order, the origins of ideology, its relations to resource environments and moral order, and the role of the state as a source of ideological production and institutionalization. These issues are explored in several ways: by looking at how they have been dealt with in the theoretical literature, by drawing together bits and pieces of inferential evidence, by borrowing approaches from other fields and attempting to determine how much mileage can be gotten from them in the area of culture, and by developing in greater depth several empirical investigations. There is in these explorations a deliberately self-reflective orientation because their intended purpose is not simply that of probing a set of empirical topics but also one of considering alternative approaches to the analysis of culture. There is no attempt here to work these explorations into a single methodological or theoretical perspective. The strategy is instead one of intentionally experimenting with several partially overlapping frameworks in order to assess their strengths, weaknesses, similarities, and differences at the end.

The explorations presented in this volume reflect four primary approaches that, although overlapping, nevertheless seem usefully identified as distinct alternatives. For brevity's sake they can be given the following labels: *subjective, structural, dramaturgic,* and *institutional.* They are distinguished mainly by the manner in which culture is conceptualized, which in turn has an important bearing on the kinds of variables and relationships selected for analysis. The descriptions of each of these approaches will immediately show that they are not mutually exclusive; indeed, one may argue that they should be regarded as complementary rather than as competing perspectives. Nevertheless, working with these approaches also shows that particular writers have tended to emphasize one approach or another to the exclusion of the others. Bringing the various approaches together as explicit alternatives, therefore, forces recognition of the similarities and differences.

The *subjective* approach focuses on beliefs and attitudes, opinions and values. Culture is conceived of from the standpoint of the individual. Ideas, moods, motivations, and goals form its components. It is subjective in a dual sense: the fundamental elements of culture are mental constructions, made up or adopted by individuals; they also represent, grow out of, express, or point to the individual's subjective states, such as outlooks or anxieties. The problem of meaning is central in this approach: culture consists of meanings; it represents the individual's interpretations of reality; and it supplies meaning to the individual in the sense of an integrative or affirming worldview.

The subjective view of culture runs through a variety of commonly employed methodological and theoretical perspectives. It is most obvious of course in social psychological studies dealing with attitude formation or with the relations among beliefs, cognition, deprivation, alienation, and so on. Culture is typically conceptualized in subjective terms in survey research studies of public opinion. Studies utilizing participant observation and depth interviews, although differing markedly in theoretical assumptions from many survey research investigations, frequently manifest an equally subjective view of culture. In these contexts culture consists less of an independent layer of reality than of one that has been internalized as part of the individual's worldview. Subjective approaches, however, are often evident in the assumptions underlying broader historical, comparative, or macrosocial investigations as well. In these studies culture may be conceived of as a belief system that is mediated by individuals' experiences. The mechanism by which social structure affects culture, therefore, is the experience of the individual and his or her subjective states.

The subjective approach, as manifested in several different theoretical traditions, appears to be one of the most commonly employed perspectives on culture in sociology, if not in the social sciences generally. Its assumptions and historical roots are examined in some detail in the next chapter. The manner in which this view of culture has been derived in American sociology from the classical theoretical tradition will be traced, as well as its roots in more recent "neoclassical" theories that have emphasized hermeneutic and phenomenological interpretations. Occasion will also arise to discuss it in Chapters 8 and 9 in the context of considering approaches to the relations between state structures and ideology. Because of its familiarity in sociology, the subjective approach provides a natural starting point. For the same reason, however, it also requires less attention than some of the other approaches that have been less commonly employed. In the context of examining it in the next chapter, we will also consider some of its limitations. These will again be addressed in the concluding chapter in comparing the strengths and weaknesses of all the approaches.

The *structural* approach focuses on patterns and relationships among cultural elements themselves. Its task is conceived of as identifying orderly relations and rules—structures—that give culture coherence and identity. This approach, as the name suggests, is evident primarily in the work of structuralists and poststructuralists. It is, in this sense, a relatively recent addition to sociology, although strong precedent for it can be found among the classical theorists. Its emphasis is on the symbolic boundaries or distinctions evident among cultural elements, the categories of discourse defined by these boundaries, the mechanisms by which these boundaries are maintained or modified, and the underlying rules evident in their construction.

The structural approach differs from the subjective approach in several significant respects. Culture is treated as a more objectified entity. This does not mean that culture is simply "out there," like an object that can be approached positivistically without any need for interpretation. It does mean, however, that culture is separated analytically from the internal, subjective states of the individual believer. Rather than being associated with the individual, its elements are regarded as relatively autonomous entities. For this reason, different terms are generally employed when discussing culture. Rather than it consisting of attitudes, beliefs, and values, it is characterized by boundaries, categories, and elements. In the structural approach, culture is portrayed as an object amenable to observation. It consists of discourse that can be heard or read or other kinds of gestures, objects, acts, and events that can be seen, recorded, classified, and so forth. It does not consist of or ultimately reflect subjective states of the individual. If information is obtained from individuals, say, in interviews, this material is treated as evidence in its own right—as discourse—instead of being taken as an indicator of deeper feelings or predispositions. The structural approach is also distinguished by its relative lack of attention to the relations between culture and other factors, whether individual meanings and experiences or broader social conditions. Instead, culture is examined internally, as it were, to determine the nature of its own organization.

Some of the theoretical underpinnings of the structural approach are examined in the next chapter, where "poststructuralist" assumptions (using the term in a nontechnical sense) will be shown to be evident in the work of a variety of recent theorists of culture. Rejecting the strict assumptions of earlier "structuralist" contributions, these writers have laid much of the groundwork for an approach to culture that is distinct from the subjective approach. In Chapter 3 these underpinnings are then extended by applying them to an analysis of the structure of moral codes. The concern of this chapter is with the symbolic boundaries that maintain essential distinctions within moral codes generally and with some of the problems that may arise from ambiguities in these boundaries. Although some relationships with social conditions are implied, the primary focus of this chapter is on culture itself as manifested in the symbolic structure of moral codes. Some empirical examples are considered in this chapter as a basis from which to infer generalizations about moral codes. In the last part of the chapter, an extended example is developed by considering the moral code underlying commitment to behavior in the marketplace. The structural approach is also drawn on to a degree in Chapters 5 and 6 in order to suggest contrasts among ideological systems. Here, however, the structural approach provides only a starting point for broader considerations of the role of resource environments.

The *dramaturgic* approach focuses on the expressive or communicative properties of culture. Rather than being conceived of as a purely (or largely) autonomous entity, culture is now approached in interaction with social structure. Unlike in the subjective approach, culture is said to interact with social structure not as a feature of individual feelings and experience but as an expressive dimension of social relations. Ideology, for example, is pictured as a set of symbols that articulates how social relations should be arranged. More generally, culture becomes identifiable as the symbolic-expressive dimension of social structure. It communicates information about morally binding obligations and is in turn influenced by the structure of these obligations.

This approach is like the structural approach in that culture is defined in a way that makes it more observable than in the subjective approach. Rather than consisting of subjective beliefs and attitudes, it consists of utterances, acts, objects, and events—all of which are observable, even behavioral in a sense. The relations or patterns among these elements remain important, as in the structural approach. But these relations are no longer examined strictly by themselves; they are now examined in conjunction with ideas about the ordering of social life. Of particular importance is the idea that social life requires a dimension of moral order, that is, a set of definitions about what is proper to do and what is reasonable to expect.

The term "dramaturgic" is used to describe this approach because of its emphasis on the capacity of rituals, ideologies, and other symbolic acts to *dramatize* the nature of social relations. It is in these dramatizations that definitions of the situation are communicated.[4] In saying that culture is symbolic-expressive, therefore, this approach tends to focus less on information that is simply and straightforwardly transmitted than on messages that may be implicit in the ways in which social life is arranged, in rituals, and in the choice of words in discourse. Put simply, what is "given off" may be as important as what is "given."

The dramaturgic approach can be traced historically to Durkheim's work on primitive ritual. Various interpretations have of course been imposed on this work. In a sense, the presence of structuralist and poststructuralist theories has contributed to a revival of interest in the dramaturgic aspects of Durkheim. Some—Erving Goffman, most notably—have taken this approach in directions dealing more with social interaction itself, but the relevance of dramaturgy for an understanding of culture has also come to be recognized. The symbolic-expressive aspects of ritual in particular have attracted renewed interest among sociologists, as has the idea of moral order.

Some of the theoretical considerations in the next chapter provide a background for subsequent explorations that utilize the dramaturgic approach. In Chapter 4 explicit attention is directed toward the nature and functioning of ritual. The communicative aspects of ritual are emphasized, and an effort is made to demonstrate the "ritual" character of social arrangements more generally. This chapter, building on the discussion of moral codes in Chapter 3, also considers the relations between ritual and moral order and presents an empirical case study that illustrates some of the central aspects of these relations. The case study presented draws on surveys of television viewers' reactions to the program "Holocaust," which is examined as a kind of "morality play" with characteristics similar to those observed by Durkheim in his work on ritual. Although the relations between ritual and culture have been dealt with in other ways, the conclusions drawn in Chapter 4 suggest that ritual may in some ways serve as a prototype of other symbol systems, such as ideology, that also dramatize features of the moral order. In Chapter 5 this implication is carried through in considering the moral basis of ideology. The importance of moral order is again emphasized, and ideology is conceptualized as a set of symbols that communicate something about moral obligations. These considerations are then extended to suggest some of the ways in which uncertainties in moral order may lead to a growth of ideological movements. As an example of this process, special consideration is given to the growth of millenarian movements. Some of these ideas are also applied to the discussion of ideological themes and ideological movements in Chapters 6, 7, and 8. Themes such as folk piety, fundamentalism, individualism, and rationality are considered in relation to different kinds of moral order, as are the origins of revitalization movements, ideological reforms, sects, and other kinds of movements.

The *institutional* approach adds further elements beyond those emphasized in the dramaturgic approach. Here culture is regarded not only as a patterned set of elements (as in the structural approach) that expresses something about moral order (as in the dramaturgic approach), but also as consisting of actors and organizations that require resources and, in turn, influence the distribution of resources. Although culture in the dramaturgic approach is, as some writers are fond of asserting, "constitutive" of social life, it is much more so in the institutional approach. Greater attention is given to the fact that culture is not produced or sustained simply by dramatizing moral obligations; instead, it is produced by actors who have special competencies and is perpetuated by organizations that in a sense process resources for the purpose of ritualizing, codifying, and transmitting cultural products. These organizations in turn are likely to develop relations with the state and other sources of power and may also be challenged by movements with access to other pools of social resources.

The contrasts between the institutional and the other three approaches can be illustrated by considering the element of culture that we call science. Were our attention focused primarily on scientific values or on how individuals' worldviews are influenced by beliefs about science, our research would probably exemplify the subjective approach. Were we interested in the patterns of discourse among scientists that maintain disciplinary boundaries or that deal with anomalous findings, our research would probably exemplify the structural approach.[5] Or, if the ways in which academies of science dramatize rationality or modernity as a mode of organizing the moral order were of principal interest, it would likely fit most clearly the description given for the dramaturgic approach. In contrast, the institutional approach would conceive of science still as culture, but in terms including not only the ideas produced but also the fact that these ideas are intertwined inextricably with an entire constellation of scientists, scientific organizations, funding sources, and communication networks involved in producing these ideas.

The discussion in Chapter 5 of the moral basis of ideology serves as a transition from the dramaturgic to the institutional approach. Starting with the relations between moral order and ideology, the model developed there suggests, on the one hand, the importance of social resources as factors influencing the character of moral order and, on the other hand, the importance of the tendency for ideological movements to become institutionalized. Chapters 6 and 7 utilize this framework but focus chiefly on the first of these two effects. Chapters 8 and 9 then draw attention explicitly to the production of ideological institutions, in the first case by examining the early development of science and in the second case by examining the processes by which Protestantism became institutionalized. In both cases the institutional approach is contrasted with previous explanations that have relied heavily on the subjectivist approach, and in both cases the role of the state is emphasized.

As indicated by this brief overview, the four approaches—particularly the last three—are explicated in the chapters that follow not as abstract frameworks but by employing them in conceptual and empirical analyses. In the concluding chapter the results of these explorations will be assessed. Points of similarity, difference, overlap, and complementarity will be suggested. Some of the conceptual weaknesses that by then will have become evident will be discussed, and the advantages of the different approaches will be summarized.

A cautionary word about the general epistemological stance from which the following explorations are presented also needs to be added. In much of what follows, emphasis will be given to the problem of rendering culture amenable to empirical investigation. Theories that conceptualize culture in radically subjectivist terms will be criticized, and other perspectives will be explored because of their intent on conceiving of culture as observable behavior. Attention will also be devoted to questions of method, to the marshaling of systematic evidence, and to canons of disclosure and replicability. None of this, however, means that sociologists are being called to return to a naive form of empirical positivism in the study of culture. Nothing could be further from the intent of this volume.

Throughout, the epistemological stance taken in this volume is that of *interpretive sociology*. The very business of sociology is assumed to be one of interpretation, not one of discovering objective facts from some Procrustean bed of empirical reality or of adducing lawful generalizations about the causal ordering of these facts. The hermeneutic circle, and all that it implies about the limitations of positivistic knowledge, is taken for granted. Cultural analysis, like any other branch of sociological inquiry, not only *should* be but *inevitably is*, whether we like it or not, essentially an act of interpretation. Whether the subject of investigation is "culture," the "state," the "means of production," or anything else, that object is itself a cultural construction, subject to the meanings we give it and interpretable in different ways. It could not be otherwise.

The goal of the present volume, therefore, is not to challenge the interpretive perspective but to enhance it. To say that culture must be approached interpretively certainly should not preclude a call to conceive of it in ways that render it more observable or to ask that investigators be more candid in disclosing their methods and assumptions. Cultural analysis remains a matter of interpretation whether we conceive of culture as subjective beliefs or as symbolic acts. But there may be strategic advantages to thinking of it in one way rather than another. As a community of scholars, our goal must always be to promote discourse about our interpretations, not to advance them simply as authoritative pronouncements. Too often, however, interpretive sociology has served as a masquerade for shoddy research and pious opinions. If cultural analysis is to advance not as a departure but as a fulfillment of interpretive sociology at its best, greater attention must be paid to how concepts are conceptualized, operationalized, examined empirically, and interpreted. Advancing this process is the aim of the present discussion.

CHAPTER TWO

Beyond the Problem
of Meaning

Like any other academic discipline, sociology has its own distinctive traditions. Members of the discipline share certain experiences that come from having read the same books and discussed the same ideas. Everyone knows something about Max Weber or Talcott Parsons and has heard of *Street Corner Society* and path analysis. It is not that these traditions are necessarily important in any cosmic sense, only that they are part of the shared subculture of the discipline. In a field divided into numerous subspecialties, as sociology currently is, these common experiences may be relatively few. They may consist only of having read some of the more influential works of the discipline's founders, of having been exposed to some of its more influential theorists, and of having learned to differentiate among the discipline's major methodological approaches. Nevertheless, even these relatively few common experiences provide the basis of a shared vocabulary. It is this vocabulary that is ritually reenacted each year at the discipline's annual convention. This is also the vocabulary that is used to classify different kinds of work—to pigeonhole people as "symbolic interactionists" or as "population ecologists"—and to legitimate what one chooses to investigate as well as the approach one chooses to follow.

To an even greater extent than in the discipline at large, shared vocabularies provide an essential backdrop to the work that goes on in any specific subarea of the discipline. Understandings of classical figures, of major theoretical terms, and of methodological styles serve as guideposts for many of the discussions, including those characterized by intense disagreement, that preoccupy scholars who share these traditions. Often these guideposts remain implicit simply because they are readily taken for granted as acceptable elements of discourse.

Among sociologists who share an interest in culture, a general familiarity can probably be assumed with regard to the works of such classical figures as Max Weber, Emile Durkheim, and Karl Marx. The work of a few contemporary theorists—Peter Berger, for example—may also have achieved a kind of totemic significance for debates in the field. In addition, work is likely to be guided by and evaluated in relation to certain understandings of the main methods of data collection currently available (participant observation, survey research, etc.). Consensus on the exact significance of these theoretical and methodological orientations may be relatively low, but their very existence gives a field some established landmarks with which to orient itself.

At the present juncture, sociological work on culture appears to be not only divided over the significance of many of its more familiar landmarks but also frequently uncertain, in a genuine sense, of the position of these landmarks in relation to one another. It is therefore difficult to gain very much simply by referring to a piece of work as an example of, say, "Durkheimian sociology" or "structuralism." Furthermore, it is probably too much to expect that even general characterizations of the orientations of, say, Weber or Marx are likely to evoke much agreement. Theoretical traditions have apparently become the focus of esoteric disputes or, at worst, arcane one-upmanship, rather than providing a starting point for serious work.

Unless this diagnosis of the current situation is overly cynical, it may be more profitable simply to ignore the available landmarks of the field either by inventing new ones or by launching headfirst into empirical inquiries. Indeed, both of these strategies can be seen in prominent contributions to the field. Nevertheless, there does seem to be some merit in taking stock, at least in passing, of the received wisdom before attempting to push forward. Several distinct orientations appear evident in the study of culture at the present time. Outlining the differences among these orientations should at least clarify some of the present disputes in the field—and perhaps illuminate the assumptions underlying these disputes. Beyond this, the field also appears to have been moving away from some of these orientations and toward others. It may be naive to think that various investigators will agree on any simple depiction of these differences or of current problem shifts. But such an attempt will help establish some common landmarks within the terrain of the present volume for the more focused forays that are to follow in subsequent chapters.

In the previous chapter it was suggested that present work on culture in sociology could be classified into four general approaches: subjective, structural, dramaturgic, and institutional. That mode of classification, however, refers to present work, not to the historical development of the field. Indeed, it was suggested that the last three of these approaches are relatively recent, at least as clearly identifiable approaches, and that much of the discussion in later chapters would be concerned with explicating these approaches and examining their strengths and weaknesses. For tracing the historical development of the field, therefore, we must temporarily adopt a different scheme, one that identifies three main theoretical traditions. The three traditions are distinct in historical prominence, but each has contributed to the present state of cultural analysis. The first two of these traditions, it will be argued, have contributed mainly to the development of the subjective approach to culture, the third, most clearly to the structural approach and in turn to the dramaturgic and institutional approaches.

The first tradition is best illustrated by writers such as Marx, Weber, and Durkheim, who wrote during the latter half of the nineteenth century and early decades of the twentieth century and who established the initial framework that was to guide the development of sociological work on the topic of culture. This orientation might be termed "classical." Second is a body of literature, perhaps appropriately termed "neoclassical," that borrowed heavily from the classical writers but also rejected some of their assumptions, drew in ideas from other traditions, and significantly redirected the approach taken to culture. Writers exemplifying this tradition include Peter Berger and Thomas Luckmann, Clifford Geertz, and Robert Bellah. Finally, there is a body of work that has developed mainly in Europe and has only in the past decade or so become of interest to American scholars. Drawing more heavily on structuralism than most of the work indigenous to the American context, this literature has abandoned most of the more extreme assumptions of structuralism but has managed to retain some of the structuralists' emphasis on the internal patterning or structure of culture. Writers such as Mary Douglas, Michel Foucault, and Jürgen Habermas exemplify this approach. For want of a better term, it will be called the "poststructuralist" tradition.[1]

This way of dividing up the main orientations in the field obviously runs counter to more familiar ways of thinking. It has been more common, for example, to think of Marx, Weber, and Durkheim as each representing three quite distinct traditions and then to trace more recent work to one or another of these lineages. That perspective is particularly useful for comparing the founding fathers' specific arguments and for highlighting the continuities that characterize work in the discipline. This, of course, is what most overviews of the theoretical literature in sociology have attempted to do. But the very strengths of this approach also turn out to have implicit limitations. In particular, they obscure the common assumptions shared even by writers as different as Marx, Weber, and Durkheim, and they underestimate the extent to which the discipline has moved beyond these earlier assumptions.

The distinctions drawn here are clearly intended to emphasize the temporal development of major theoretical orientations toward culture. There is, indeed, a generational aspect that partially underlies these distinctions. The classical writers constitute a distinct generation, the work of which falls roughly into the same time period (at least if Engels is included with Marx). The main figures representing the neoclassical approach are at some remove historically from the classical tradition, but they to an even greater degree fall approximately into the same birth cohort and represent contributors whose work came to full fruition during the late 1960s and early 1970s. More generally, the neoclassical approach as an intellectual orientation appears to have been contingent on developments in American sociology immediately following World War II that saw the classical theorists becoming reinterpreted in the American context and that also witnessed an American assimilation of such figures in philosophy as Heidegger, Sartre, Cassirer, and Tillich. Finally, the poststructuralists are distinguished not so much in generational contrast with the neoclassical writers, because the leading figures of both fall into nearly the same birth cohorts, but more in terms of the generation of American sociologists who came to be influenced by these writers. Because the main intellectual antecedents of this orientation were European, little influence is evident in American work on culture until the early 1970s, and much of this influence has taken root only in the 1980s. As a broader intellectual tradition, the poststructuralist approach also apparently did not become fully developed until some of the basic assumptions of the structuralists themselves had come under attack, a development that did not happen on a large scale until the late 1960s and 1970s.

To characterize these orientations as three distinct traditions, each with its own representative set of writers, is, of course, an oversimplification in the sense that any specific writer will be found to borrow assumptions from, or presage, some of the other orientations. Habermas, for example, draws heavily from Weber and shares some assumptions with Berger and Luckmann. Bellah shows common concerns with Habermas and with Mary Douglas. Durkheim and Weber, by some interpretations, represent earlier manifestations of some of the perspectives emphasized in poststructuralism. In the discussion of these writers that follows, an effort will be made to point out some of these areas of overlap. At the same time, it will be argued that quite distinct sets of assumptions can be identified in the broader intellectual traditions that have shaped work in the sociology of culture.

The main reason for delineating the three orientations in this manner is to highlight the changing conceptions of what has, by many indications, been the central problem in studies of culture: the problem of meaning. An effort will be made to show how this problem became prominent in the classical tradition, how it took on even greater importance in the neoclassical approach, and how it has now been reformulated in the poststructuralist orientation. In the process of examining these shifts, opportunity will be taken to indicate some of the ways in which the study of culture may have been hindered by its concern with the problem of meaning. The recent attempt in poststructuralism to reformulate cultural analysis in a way that goes beyond the problem of meaning, therefore, suggests certain possibilities for future work that need to be explicated.

There are many Webers and many Durkheims, just as there are many different ways of understanding the more recent theorists. What follows is an attempt neither to summarize in the full complexity of detail any of these writers' ideas about culture nor to suggest new interpretations of what the writers themselves "really meant." Either of these tasks would require an extended treatment that would go far beyond the intended scope of the present discussion. The remarks that follow are instead conceived of as an attempt to draw out some of the assumptions in each approach that, for whatever reasons, appear to have penetrated broader discussions of culture in sociology. That is, the assumptions to which attention will be given do not in every case reflect what the writer explicitly emphasized, in most cases represent only a simplification of the writer's more complex approach, and in some cases even contradict caveats found in the writer's own work; but they are present to a sufficient degree that subsequent work has been guided by them. To further underscore this point, what follows is intended primarily as an explication of the assumptions in each of these traditions, *specifically about culture,* that have, for whatever reasons, been emphasized in American sociology, not an attempt to summarize what each theorist may have actually thought about culture.[2]

It is difficult, of course, to establish with any certainty *how much* subsequent work has been guided by different assumptions. To present a thorough critique of the recent literature on these grounds would again take the present discussion far afield of its intended goal. All that will be claimed is that the assumptions identified in each of the three main approaches to culture bear on sufficiently important questions, and provide sufficiently distinct answers to these questions, that they represent genuine choices confronting investigators attempting to advance the analysis of culture.

CLASSICAL APPROACHES

One of the assumptions that most influences the classical tradition's perspective on culture is a tendency to regard the human condition in terms of a basic split between subject and object. This tendency is in a sense a reflection of the Cartesian dualism that penetrated the thinking of all the classical writers and provided the distinctive epistemological outlook on which their work was based. At the heart of this dualistic conception of reality was the idea of a gulf between the self, as subject, and the external world, as object. The self, acting chiefly in the Cartesian view as a thinking entity, was aware of itself and of the surrounding environment but felt cut off from this environment. In other words, a fundamental division in the nature of reality was identified that was thought to correspond basically with the way in which people experienced their worlds. According to this view, the fundamental characteristic of the human condition was alienation—the knowing subject's awareness of being cut off from the object world. Though framed in different ways, the concern for the subject's sense of alienation from the objective world runs through the work of Marx, Weber, and Durkheim.

MANIFESTATIONS OF DUALISM

For Marx, alienation is the philosophical or psychological counterpart of capitalism. It plays an especially prominent role in his earlier work and in this sense may be seen as one of the reasons for his interest in capitalism. That is, the analysis of capitalism was in some ways de-

rived from Marx's early concern with identifying the causes of alienation.[3] But of what does alienation consist? It consists essentially of the
condition in which humans feel their own powers to be entities outside
of themselves, exerting influence as self-subsistent forces over human action. This conception is most vivid in Marx's discussion of what he calls
"alienation of labor." "In what," he asks, "does this alienation of labor
consist?"

> First, that the work is *external* to the worker, that it is not a part of his na-
> ture, that consequently he does not fulfill himself in his work but denies him-
> self, has a feeling of misery, not of well-being, does not develop freely a physi-
> cal and mental energy, but is physically exhausted and mentally debased.
> The worker therefore feels himself at home only during his leisure, whereas
> at work he feels homeless. His work is not voluntary but imposed, *forced la-
> bour*. It is not the satisfaction of a need, but only a *means for satisfying other
> needs*. (Bottomore, 1964:169)

The Cartesian split between subject and object is, of course, clearly evident in this passage. The subject reflects on its well-being but finds itself
confronting the world of labor not as a seamless extension of itself, but
as an external object from which it feels estranged.

Alienation of subject from object is also a prominent theme in
Marx's discussion of labor-product relations. He writes:

> The *alienation* of the worker in his product means not only that his labour be-
> comes an object, takes on its own existence, but that it exists outside him, in-
> dependently, and alien to him, and that it stands opposed to him as an au-
> tonomous power. The life which he has given to the object sets itself against
> him as an alien and hostile force. (Bottomore, 1964:170)

Similarly, worker-worker relations are characterized by the same split
between subject and object. Competition in the marketplace forces
each worker to treat others as objects, as means to an end, rather than
being able to recognize the essential oneness that should be present
among humanity.

In Weber, the forces shaping society are ultimately conceived of in
terms quite different from Marx's. Yet there is again evidence of the Cartesian dualism between subject and object. Like Marx, Weber's interest in
capitalism arises from a deep ambivalence about its effects on modern
life. On the one hand, he credits capitalism with having disenchanted the
world of beliefs in superstition and magic, with having led to greater mastery over the environment, and with contributing to material comfort and
affluence. On the other hand, he fears that something fundamental has

been lost in the process. In larger terms, this process was rationalization. It was the increasing tendency in modern societies, of which capitalism was but a single (if powerful) manifestation, toward planning, toward more effective calculation of means and ends, and toward greater systematization and standardization of means. Although these were the tendencies leading toward greater control over the physical environment, they were also the sources of a potential loss of meaning.

The counterpart to Marx's discussion of alienation is Weber's concern with the problem of meaning—or, more accurately, the problem of meaninglessness. As rationalization increased, life was gradually being stripped of meaning. This was the problem that Weber identified toward the end of his treatise on the Protestant ethic as an "iron cage." The process of rationalization that had been decisively set in motion by the rise of Protestantism was nevertheless leading increasingly to a world from which the individual felt estranged.

> The Puritan wanted to work in a calling; we are forced to do so. For when asceticism was carried out of monastic cells into everyday life, and began to dominate worldly morality, it did its part in building the tremendous cosmos of the modern economic order. This order is now bound to the technical and economic conditions of machine production which to-day determine the lives of all the individuals who are born into this mechanism, not only those directly concerned with economic acquisition, with irresistible force. Perhaps it will so determine them until the last ton of fossilized coal is burnt. In Baxter's view the care for external goods should only lie on the shoulders of the "saint like a light cloak, which can be thrown aside at any moment." But fate decreed that the cloak should become an iron cage. (Weber, 1958:181)

The essential feature of the iron cage was that reality no longer faced the individual as a product of choice or as an extension of the individual, but instead as an external force, a constraint limiting one's freedom. Rather than living in relation to ultimate values that provided meaning, even in the face of death, the individual was caught within a mechanical system of rationally calculated means.[4] Just as Marx had decried the triumph of a "spiritless" and "heartless" world, Weber lamented the kind of existence toward which rationalization was leading: "For of the last stage of this cultural development," he wrote, "it might truly be said: 'Specialists without spirit, sensualists without heart; this nullity imagines that it has attained a level of civilization never before achieved' " (Weber, 1958:182).

In a fundamental sense, Durkheim was also driven by the perception of a widening gulf between subjective experience and the objective world. Certainly his work on suicide can be interpreted as an effort to understand the processes by which individuals become cut off from the normative order that shields them from anomie (Durkheim, 1951). But in a deeper sense it is in Durkheim's extended quest to understand the bases of moral community that his awareness of the split between subject and object becomes most apparent. Indeed, it was the search for a workable balance between the free expression of individual needs, on the one hand, and social forces governing the individual, on the other hand, that animated much of Durkheim's work.

As several observers have recognized (e.g., Bellah, 1973; Marks, 1974), there is a progression in Durkheim's work toward ever more complex methods of understanding and reconciling the needs of the individual with the necessary constraints of society. In his work on division of labor, Durkheim (1933) imagined self-interest itself as a sufficient basis of moral cohesion. Yet the very triumph of specialization in modern societies led to such a decline of mutual interests that estrangement from the community was an inevitable result. In dealing with professionalization, education, and the state, Durkheim (1956, 1958, 1961, 1962) came increasingly to recognize the need, on the other side, of mechanisms capable of restraining arbitrary social control over the individual and of providing the individual with representative groups from which he was not estranged. Finally, in his study of primitive religion, he came to an even greater awareness of the interplay between subjective consciousness, perceptions of external constraint, and the balancing of these in rituals and collective representations (Durkheim, 1965).

With some form of alienation or estrangement being identified as the fundamental problem facing human existence, the highest calling of scholarship in the classical tradition became that of finding ways to reunite subject and object. Indeed, the humanistic endeavor giving scholarship during this period much of its motivating force was the task of reclaiming the object world for the knowing self. In this manner, the two could not only be reconciled, but the self could be reinstated to its natural position of mastery over the world of objects. To this end, the central purpose of humanistic scholarship became that of *demystification*, which was to be accomplished through what Ricoeur (1973) has aptly termed a "hermeneutics of suspicion." Demystification of the object world and of the forces in it impelling fear and estrangement in the knowing self was to be accomplished by adopting a skeptical attitude concerning the "objectivity" or reality of the object world. By questioning its nature, the world of objects was to be unmasked and shown to be no longer an immutable fact of the external nonhuman world but rather a product of human creation. Once the world of objects was thus unmasked, it could be re-created, controlled, and appropriated by the self for its own uses. In this way subject and object were to be reunited, and alienation was to be overthrown.

Although many of the nuances of these arguments can be passed over for present purposes, the common philosophical outlook on which the sociological study of culture came into being registered considerable agreement on essential points: that all of reality was fundamentally divided into two categories consisting of subject and object, that humanity was broken by this division, and that this brokenness could be healed by the strategic application of skeptical scholarly knowledge. The source and function of knowledge—the epistemological agenda of the Cartesian perspective—lay in recognizing that the self was the originator of knowledge, that the world of objects existed ultimately through and only through the subject's knowledge of this world, and that the self gained mastery over the world and thereby conquered self-estrangement primarily by extending its knowledge of the world.

EPISTEMOLOGICAL IMPLICATIONS

The implications of these assumptions for sociological investigations of culture can be seen in the ways in which religion—the dimension of culture to which all of the founding fathers paid attention—was conceptualized. Religion tended to be conceptualized as a set of subjective beliefs or outlooks associated with the individual. Its content consisted mainly of beliefs about external objects or forces that were felt to exercise constraint over the individual. These forces were worshiped instead of being recognized as mere projections over which the individual could regain mastery. So conceptualized, religion served as a prime example to the Cartesian mind of the individual's tendency to reify, and therefore to feel estranged from, the external world.

In Marx's work religion is conceived of as one of man's "alienated life elements." That is, it grows out of the subject-object split and is an attempt by the subject to heal this split. The individual's estrangement from his labor, products, and fellows is the source of religious sentiments. "Religious distress is at the same time the expression of real distress and the protest against real distress" (Marx and Engels, 1964:42). Recognizing the fundamental depth of the subject's estrangement, Marx at times speaks almost tenderly of religion: "Religion is the sigh of the oppressed creature, the heart of a heartless world, just as it is the spirit of a spiritless situation" (Marx and Engels, 1964: 42). Yet Marx's perception of religion, as ideology, is clearly contingent on his diagnosis of the nature of this estrangement. Religious beliefs are beliefs that falsely objectify the social forces that are the root cause of estrangement. They not only arise from, but also sustain, the subject's estrangement from the world of objects. Religion consists essentially of the "fantastic reflection in men's minds of those external forces which control their daily life, a reflection in which the terrestrial forces assume the form of supernatural forces" (Marx and Engels, 1964:147).

Following the humanistic agenda of emancipation in classical theory, the implication of Marx's discussion is that religious beliefs, as false consciousness, need to be subjected to criticism in order to overcome the subject's alienation from the objectified world. But an epistemological agenda for the sociology of culture is also implicit in Marx's statement. Two features of this agenda are particularly important. First, culture is associated with the subject and thus becomes subjective—located, as he says, "in men's minds." Second, it nevertheless reflects social influences; indeed, it symbolizes the external social forces that the individual experiences as constraints.

Weber's work on religion, although crediting it with a more active role in shaping events than Marx, also evokes similar assumptions about the characteristics of culture. In his work on the Protestant ethic, Weber runs through a familiar litany of factors that have contributed to the rise of capitalism: separation of business from households, wage labor systems, rational bookkeeping methods, technological innovations, property and contract laws, stable governing systems. What he finds lacking in these is a motivational factor, that is, a set of beliefs capable of giving meaning to the acquisitive pursuit of capital. This he finds, of course, in Protestantism. From the outset, therefore, religion is associated with the individual, functioning as a motivational element, as opposed to the conditions of social structure, such as states and wage systems, that supply the more objective resources for capitalist development. This perspective is epitomized in Weber's depiction of Protestantism as an "ethic."

As in Marx, Weber's characterization of the content of religion also reflects the influence of subject-object dualism. Beliefs again tend to be pictured as the subject's perceptions of forces in the external world. This influence is partly evident in the Protestant ethic thesis (e.g., Weber's em-

phasis on perceptions of predestination as a controlling force), but becomes more apparent in his work on comparative religion (Weber,
1963). Generally speaking, theodicies—explanations of evil—play a
prominent role in Weber's comparisons of world religions. In some respects these are simply beliefs about those events and experiences that
fail to have intrinsic meaning. Yet in substantive terms they turn out to
represent conceptions of external forces impinging on the subject: laws
of karma, diabolical spirits, divine predestination, stellar constellations,
cycles of rebirth, and so forth. These conceptions of governing forces
then give rise to alternative beliefs about what one must do to be saved
from them (soteriologies), and these in turn imply certain attitudes
about how one should behave.

Durkheim's work on religion is similarly preoccupied with the subject's subjective perceptions of external, constraining forces.[5] This preoccupation is evident in the two main facets of his analysis of primitive
religion: the functions of ritual and the nature of religious beliefs. In
his discussion of religious rituals, Durkheim stresses the changes in consciousness that overtake the individual participant. These changes are,
of course, linked to broader considerations of the qualities of group
life, particularly moral community, but the nature of ritual's functions
for group life cannot be understood apart from its effects on the individual. These deal primarily with the individual's confrontation with
the forces of society that actually govern him but that may be experienced chiefly as a confrontation with the gods. In a familiar passage
Durkheim writes (1973:189):

> The believer who has communicated with his god is not merely a man who
> sees new truths of which the unbeliever is ignorant; he is a man who is
> stronger. He feels within him more force, either to endure the trials of exis-
> tence, or to conquer them. It is as though he were raised above the miseries of
> the world, because he is raised above his condition as a mere man; he be-
> lieves that he is saved from evil, under whatever form he may conceive this
> evil.

In other words, the believer who participates in ritual is able to confront
the forces that he believes constrain him and, in the process, gains
strength himself. No longer are these forces from which he feels cut off;
instead, they become, once again, internal to himself. In this sense, ritual
becomes a way of healing the split between subject and object.

In his discussion of religious belief, Durkheim builds on a similar set
of premises. Religious beliefs represent the individual's attempt to ren-

der intelligible the forces he experiences as constraints on his activity both in social life generally and in ritual particularly. The substance of these beliefs focuses on divine personifications of these forces: "a god is not merely an authority upon whom we depend; it is a force upon whom our strength relies" (1973:172). The subjective attitude attached to religious beliefs is one of respect, or devotion, that also arises from the force or authority that appears to reside among the gods. As Durkheim (1973:170) explains:

> When we obey somebody because of the moral authority which we recognize in him, we follow out his opinions, not because they seem wise, but because a certain sort of physical energy is immanent in the idea that we form of this person, which conquers our will and inclines it in the indicated direction. Respect is the emotion which we experience when we feel this interior and wholly spiritual pressure operating upon us.

Finally, Durkheim is at pains in these passages to demonstrate that the believer in a way transcends the estrangement of subject from object because the forces "out there" become forces "in here." Both at the level of religious belief and at the level of intuitive beliefs about society, the individual internalizes the sense of power that resides in the object world so that subjectively he too becomes empowered:

> The collective force is not entirely outside of us; it does not act upon us wholly from without; but rather, since society cannot exist except in and through individual consciousness, this force must also penetrate us and organize itself within us; it thus becomes an integral part of our being and by that very fact is elevated and magnified. (Durkheim, 1973:172)

The ways in which Durkheim, Marx, and Weber conceptualize the relations between the individual and society, of course, raise issues that go well beyond the focus of the present discussion.[6] For present purposes, the important observation to be made has to do with the highly subjective terms in which beliefs are portrayed. In each of the classical theorists, an implicit assumption about the division between subject and object sets the stage for conceptualizing the nature of religion particularly. The subject feels estranged from and constrained by forces external to himself. These are, for various reasons, not regarded as objects that the individual has simply created or ones over which he can exercise control, but rather as gods or other supernatural forces that must be feared, believed in, or in some way taken account of. The essence of religion, therefore, is a set of beliefs about these forces that the individual holds in an effort to bridge the gap between them and himself.

SOCIOLOGY OF KNOWLEDGE

The main research agenda that emerged from this conception of religion was one that might best be described as a radical sociology of knowledge approach. The aim of this approach was to demonstrate through empirical investigation of the social world that the forces believed in as divine entities were merely reflections of social experience. By stripping these beliefs of their reified, supernaturalistic quality, human beings could once again gain control over the forces from which they felt estranged. The way to accomplish this emancipation was by showing that the forces experienced were really elements of the social world and, as such, were only human creations.

Various writers, of course, diagnosed the true nature of these forces in different ways. For Marx, the forces believed to be supernatural were a form of "false consciousness" because they were really the products of capitalism, specifically, of the conflict between classes, the appropriation of surplus value from labor, and the competition among workers engendered by capitalism. Durkheim shared the view that when people worshiped the gods, they were really worshiping society because society was the source of external constraint that individuals experienced.[7] Yet in his view a certain degree of inevitability seemed to be built into these experiences, for individuals were always constrained to sacrifice some of their own autonomy for the sake of collective harmony. At best, therefore, the arbitrary nature of social constraint could be curbed, society could come to resemble a "moral" community, and the individual could come to grips with society's power by internalizing it ritually and symbolically. Weber credited religious beliefs with a high degree of independent influence in social affairs but also saw in the process of rationalization, which was in turn linked to industrialization and bureaucratization, an inevitable tendency toward social constraint that even rational religion could not fully supply with meaning. Only the possibility of a charismatic "breakthrough" held forth hope for a reinvigoration of social life with intrinsic meaning.

In varying degrees, the classical approaches manifest an epistemological thread that is *reductionistic* as far as the sources of knowledge are concerned. Understanding religious phenomena, in particular, is related to the capacity to discover their "sources" in various aspects of economic, social, and political life—or in other writers, in biological processes or psychological projections (cf. Bellah, 1970:246–257). Other types of culture also tend to be understood in the same manner. Ideology in Marx's view, for example, arises as legitimation for class domination; even the basis of scientific knowledge needs to be sought in experiences of the social and physical world (Cornforth, 1955). This search in the classical tradition for the social correlates of culture was made possible in the first place by the fact that reality had been divided into two components—the subjective and the objective. Only this division made it possible to argue that the two should again bear some empirical relation to each other!

Without attempting to trace its historical development, one can at least suggest that some of the initial attraction of the radical sociology of knowledge approach to culture lay in the fact that it seemed, paradoxically perhaps, to meet the humanistic agenda of reclaiming the object world for the subject, while also providing a firm scientific basis for the investigation of knowledge, attitudes, and belief. On the one hand, being able to demonstrate that beliefs about the gods were really beliefs about society was a way of stripping the individual of false consciousness, of overthrowing the tendency to reify external objects, and of revealing the true nature of these objects as human constructions that could, if desired, be transformed. On the other hand, a basis for scientific investigation was provided because at last the murky realm of subjective ideas could be related to something more substantial, more observable. The sources of ideas could be traced to objective features of the social and physical world.

But this fortuitous union of humanism and science failed to achieve its desired objective. In the name of humanism, as Marx saw most clearly, science found it necessary to invert the original subject-object relationship, focusing increasingly on the subjective elements of culture (i.e., belief), while attempting to explain these elements in terms of the more objective facts of the social world. Though rooted in the initial humanistic conception of dualistic reality, the radical sociology of knowledge tradition evolved in a direction that ran counter to both the philosophical and epistemological agendas that had inspired it. It ran counter to the philosophical agenda in practice because it became necessary to identify culture as a subjective phenomenon, which it then proceeded to alienate from the human actor by attributing beliefs to the object world from which the actor was already cut off. Rather than reconcile the object world to the subject, it tended to demonstrate that even the subject's beliefs about the world were not truly his but were merely the product of social forces over which he had no control.

This approach also departed from the original epistemological agenda that had inspired it. To understand this deviation, it is necessary to assert (largely without proof) that the strategy that has seemed most to capture the fascination of scientific investigators has been that of explaining the *known* in terms of the *unknown* (cf. Kuhn, 1970). Put in a way that may seem less counterintuitive, science has attempted to advance by relating facts (the "known") to underlying processes that had previously been unknown. Having done that, scientists have also proceeded to make "discoveries" of the unknown by extending theories of what is known into new empirical areas. But a qualitative difference exists between the two types of investigation. Discovering an unknown process that explains known facts is, to borrow Kuhn's familiar terms, "revolutionary science"; extending a known perspective to the study of new facts is essentially the business of "normal science." The radical sociology of knowledge approach subverted the higher order epistemological goal of explaining the (apparently) known—namely, the functioning of ideas—in terms of the (previously) unknown—the wishes and needs of the knowing subject. It replaced this higher order aim with what has always been the more rudimentary and less satisfying strategy of normal science—namely, explaining the unknown in terms of the known (here, belief in terms of observable social variables).

The chief difficulty in sustaining this inversion, apart from the inherent tensions that evolved in relation to its humanistic origins, was that the radical sociology of knowledge approach could be regarded as scientifically satisfactory only as long as the humanly constructed, and therefore further reducible, character of the objective life world to which ideas were to be reduced was denied. There was, therefore, an inevitable tendency within the classical tradition toward (1) reification of the object world—a tendency that became fully pronounced with the triumph of empirical positivism; (2) exaggeration of the distinction between culture, which was presumed to be subjective, and social structure, which was presumed to be objective; and (3) an increasing bias in research on culture toward focusing on its purely subjective dimensions, making it possible for culture to be conceived of in ways that seemed explicable in relation to social structure, instead of focusing on ritualistic, behavioral, and institutional elements of culture that could not be as easily separated from social structure.

These were problems that, over time, led to increasing levels of dissatisfaction with the classical tradition, or at least with the radical sociology of knowledge approach that had been derived from it. Before considering the nature of this dissatisfaction, however, we must briefly mention two further derivations of the classical tradition: its affinity with sociological research methods and its emphasis on the problem of meaning.

METHODS AND MEANING

The classical tradition has had a powerful impact on sociological studies of culture because of its affinity with popular sociological research methods, particularly survey research. This affinity seems paradoxical because of the relatively grand, macroscopic, historical emphases usually associated with the classical theorists, as opposed to the highly microscopic, cross-sectional, social psychological orientation of modern survey research. Once the subjectivist conception of culture that can be envinced from the classical tradition is recognized, however, the basis for this affinity becomes immediately apparent. Survey research has appeared to provide precisely the kind of tools necessary for eliciting subjective beliefs and for relating them to objective features of social structure. A study like Gerhard Lenski's *The Religious Factor* (1963), for example, sought not only to test Weber's assertions about the ethical consequences of Protestant beliefs but also to relate these beliefs to various dimensions of social stratification, community variables, and religious practice. Studies of other kinds have employed survey research to examine Marxian arguments about the effects of social class on attitudes and values, to measure anomie and feelings of alienation, to assess beliefs in different images of God, and to relate experiences of social authority to other kinds of attitudinal dispositions.

The reason for emphasizing this affinity between the classical tradition and survey research is to indicate one of the areas in which classical theory, so interpreted, continues to exercise a powerful influence in analyses of culture. Through the wide availability of survey data, culture often continues to be conceptualized as a matter of subjective belief that needs to be related to objective dimensions of social structure in order to be properly explained. This emphasis in empirical research has also affected interpretations of classical approaches to culture. Other emphases can be found in the classical literature, as will be seen presently, but the prominence of contemporary survey research approaches to culture has probably reinforced those interpretations that emphasize the subjective qualities of culture.

In relation to the problem of meaning, the classical tradition not only stressed the importance of this problem in various formulations but also cast it in a specific light. In particular, the problem of meaning emerges as central for the sociology of culture at several levels. At the most general level, all the classical approaches implicitly assume a requirement for meaning as part of the human condition. This assumption is most evident in Weber but is also apparent in Marx and Durkheim. All three portray the individual as a thinking entity that attempts to make sense of the forces that are experienced. Substantively, "explanation" tends to be identified in all three as an especially important feature of the individual's attempt to make sense of reality: explanations of the forces that limit one's freedom, of meaningless events such as suffering and death, of evil, and of what one experiences in ritual. Again, the split between subject and object appears at a fundamental level to evoke many of these attempts to find meaning.

In more specific terms, the problem of meaning in the classical tradition focuses squarely on the individual. This may seem trivially obvious; yet meaning is dealt with in sufficiently different ways in other approaches that its focus here needs to be made clear. Meaning is taken primarily as a condition under which a person's life, or significant events in it, "make sense" (i.e., have worth and relate to the subject's feelings of integrity, wholeness, and self-mastery). Meaning is for the most part not associated in this tradition with other aspects of reality, such as the meaning of language, of symbols, or of institutions. Although these constitute the frameworks in which individuals seek meaning, they tend to be dealt with not as discrete entities, but as aspects of the individual's beliefs and feelings.

Above all, the problem of meaning takes on central importance in the classical tradition as the issue with which cultural studies should be concerned. The developments associated with the growth of modern social structure, though conceived of differently by Marx, Weber, and Durkheim, are regarded as contributors to the increasing difficulty that the modern individual has in attempting to find meaning. The point of cultural studies, then, becomes the subjective counterpart of investigations concerned with problems of capitalism, industrialism, bureaucratization, urbanization, and so forth. Cultural studies should be concerned with the problems of alienation, anomie, and meaninglessness that confront the modern individual and with understanding the beliefs that assist or hinder individuals in their quest for meaning. This, of course, is only to say once again that the concept of culture in the classical tradition is closely connected with the subjective concerns of the individual. From a practical standpoint, culture acquires interest primarily because of the problem of meaning.

NEOCLASSICAL APPROACHES

The problem with radical sociology of knowledge derivations from the classical tradition that seems to have contributed most to inspiring alternative approaches is the problem of reductionism. Especially those who were oriented toward the humanistic agenda found in the classical tradition, and who felt that its scientific promise either had not paid off or was misguided, expressed fears that culture was too easily being explained away. Why, they asked, should not culture itself be taken more seriously, rather than being related immediately to class conflicts, interest groups, or other aspects of social structure? This question was often raised in the context of religious discussions because the reductionistic approach implied an inherently skeptical view of the validity of religion. But it was also addressed to the study of ideology and to the analysis of culture more generally.

In the work of theorists like Berger, Bellah, and Geertz, who led the way in articulating an alternative perspective on culture, the problem of meaning became the essential element salvaged from the classical tradition. Some of the Cartesian dualism of subject and object was retained, but emphasis shifted toward meaning in a deeper sense rather than simply the estrangement of the knowing subject from its objective surroundings. Marx, perhaps because he of all the classical figures was most insistent on finding the sources of ideas in social structure, tended to be almost completely ignored, except in Berger's (1969) formalistic recasting of the concept of alienation, which largely ignored Marx's relating of it to the structure of capitalism. Weber gained a certain renewed emphasis because his concern for the problem of meaning came closest to the broader definition given this concept. But Weber's work on bureaucracy, on the state, and on social classes as originators of religious ideas was for the most part downplayed. It was his concept of *verstehen*—the idea of developing empathy with one's research subjects in order to understand more fully their subjective meanings—that gained greatest currency. Durkheim also underwent a significant revision. His idea of society as the real force implicit in men's worshiping of the gods was de-emphasized or reinterpreted, and his emphasis on moral order, collective representations, and ritual was elaborated upon, all being treated as symbolic elements contributing to the individual's quest for meaning.

MEANING TO THE FOREFRONT

Meaning, in a formulation that went well beyond that of the classical theorists, became the centerpiece of neoclassical approaches to culture. Still emphasizing the individual, meaning nevertheless came to be regarded as an attribute of symbolism and as a function of the context in which a symbol, or the individual himself, was located. Bellah (1970: 260–261), for example, in writing about the meanings associated with religious symbolism, argued that meaning "is location in a context, in a larger interrelated framework defined by values or norms or a more general order than the specific act or object." Similarly, Berger and Luckmann (1966) emphasized "symbolic universes" as the contexts in which specific acts and events acquired meaning, and Geertz (1973) stressed the importance of overarching worldviews.

Neoclassical theorists in a sense circumvented the dualistic distinction between subject and object by emphasizing the "symbolically constructed" character of all reality, both subjective and objective. This emphasis relativized the objectivity of the external world by demonstrating that it, no less than the subjective world, was created symbolically. In place of solid, unflinching social objects, like capitalist classes and bureaucracies, therefore, everything became relegated to the world of symbolism.

Berger and Luckmann (1966) provided perhaps the most elaborate explication of the symbolically constructed character of reality. In their view reality is not simply "there" as an external object but is constructed by the subject. The world in which people live is, in this sense, of their own making. It is made with symbols. What we experience is shaped by our symbols. Indeed, we experience only that for which we have symbols. As research on the eye has shown, humans have the physiological capacity to experience about 6 million hues of color; yet we usually perceive only about a dozen because these are the ones for which we have common words (Farb, 1973). Or as anthropological work has shown, people in various cultures experience reality somewhat differently simply because they have diverse words that sensitize them to differing features of the environment. Research on language development in children also points to the importance of symbolism. According to some interpretations, youngsters learn concepts quite early but only gradually become skilled at using these concepts, not because they lack mental capacity, but because they have to start actually experiencing the world in a new way—a way that conforms to these concepts (Bruner, Oliver, and Greenfield, 1966). Even our sense of time may be shaped by the discursiveness of language and by the kinds of verbs we use (Langer, 1951).

Carrying these observations a step further, Berger and Luckmann suggest that reality is generally constructed in a highly stylized way. Although each individual seems to experience the world slightly differently from every other individual because of variations in symbolic tools, we nevertheless construct a reality that permits us to interact efficiently with others. This construction Berger and Luckmann call "everyday reality." Everyday reality is the world of waking consciousness, as opposed to realities such as fantasy and dreams. It is oriented to the "here and now"; that is, what seems most apparently "real" are the objects immediately around us and the events closest in time to the present. Everyday reality is also a pragmatic world, organized in terms of actions necessary for "getting the job done." This means it is also divided into discrete "spheres of relevance" because the objects relevant to one set of tasks (say, cooking supper) are compartmentalized from those relevant to other tasks (say, commuting or playing tennis). Everyday reality is thus a relatively efficient world in which to live. We bracket out any doubts we might have concerning the reality of this world. We simply take it for granted, maintaining it by acting as if it were real. For this reason, Berger and Luckmann describe it as the "paramount" reality. It is the reality to which we always return after "excursions," as it were, to other realities, such as fantasy or dreaming.

Everyday reality provides a basic threshold of meaning for the individual. It is constructed in an orderly fashion, is sufficiently familiar that we take many of our cues from it, and is made plausible by the fact that most of our time, as well as that of our acquaintances, is spent within it. But higher orders of symbolism also come into play whenever the taken-for-grantedness of everyday life comes into question. Berger and Luckmann distinguish four such levels of symbolism, or as they say, "machineries of legitimation." At the most fundamental level are "explanations" that are simply built into common vocabularies. These are not explicitly spelled out but supply an implicit categorization that accounts for the ways in which objects, events, or people are related. For example, referring to someone as "cousin" or "thief" provides an immediate, if only intuitive, sense of who that person is. Second are "rudimentary theoretical propositions" such as proverbs, moral maxims, and wise sayings. These are somewhat more explicitly formalized than simple explanations but still refer to a relatively discrete type of activity (e.g., "a penny saved is a penny earned"). Third are "explicit theories" that refer to an institutional sector, such as family, economy, or government. For example, price levels in market societies are often explained by theories about the relations among supply, demand, and price. Finally, there are "symbolic universes" that overarch and integrate different institutional sectors. These might range from relatively simple ideas, such as ideas about luck or freedom, that penetrate any area of institutional activity to more elaborate theoretical traditions, philosophies, and religious beliefs that also deal with events at the margins of everyday life, such as suffering and death.

The idea of meaning being dependent on context is clearly evident in Berger and Luckmann's formulation. This notion derives from work in linguistics that attributes the meaning of words to the broader context (sentence or paragraph) in which they appear (e.g., Saussure, 1959; Langer, 1951). In Berger and Luckmann's formulation the contextual determination of meaning is specified by locating the individual in an ever-widening series of symbolic contexts. The individual is first situated within a specific here-and-now sphere of relevance in everyday reality. This context organizes and thereby gives meaning to a portion of the individual's activity. But it is too immediate, too compartmentalized to provide meaning in any broader sense. Different spheres of relevance need to be integrated, near-term activities need to be organized around longer-term goals, personal integration of the self is required, sense must be made of other realities such as daydreams and of extraordinary experiences such as tragedies and moments of ecstasy, and coherence needs to be imposed on reality as a whole. The individual, therefore, also locates himself in terms of proverbs and maxims, theoretical traditions, and symbolic universes that attempt to capture meaning at a wholistic level.

A WHOLISTIC PERSPECTIVE

Meaning, so defined in terms of nested categories that encompass the individual ever more comprehensively, has been a particularly attractive concept in sociological studies of religion. For Berger and Luckmann, religion becomes a type of symbolic universe that transcends and orders reality wholistically, giving it a sense of sacredness.[8] For Bellah (1970), religion also constitutes an encompassing type of symbolism that transcends the pragmatism of everyday reality, differs from conceptual or denotative terminology, and embraces the individual in a transcendent framework that supplies meaning and motivation. Geertz (1973), too, stresses the transcendent meaning-supplying character of religious symbolism.

The contrast between neoclassical and classical approaches is especially evident in the two traditions' formulations of religion. The classical tendency toward reductionism, in which religion is often depicted as a kind of false or naive understanding of the forces impinging on the individual, is largely absent in neoclassical approaches. The contextual idea of meaning in a sense creates for religion a niche that is largely immune from reductionistic or positivistic attacks. The argument on which this conception of religion rests is essentially one that suggests a human requirement for wholistic meaning. As one moves toward larger and more encompassing contexts of meaning, a limiting point is finally reached where questions about the meaning of the whole of reality must be addressed. These include questions such as: What is the meaning of life? What are the ultimate conditions of existence? How did reality begin and how will it end? What absolutes can be identified within the whole of reality? Such questions occur either at a kind of vague, intuitive level in the midst of everyday life itself or as full-blown queries in more reflective moments. These questions, addressed tacitly or explicitly, have been the focus of the world's religions. In the neoclassical tradition, therefore, the distinctive feature of religious systems came to be identified as symbolism that attempts to evoke meanings embracing the whole of reality.

Equating religion with wholistic symbolism proved to be an effective way of protecting religion from the reductionistic tendencies inherent in the classical tradition. Wittgenstein (1974) inadvertently articulated most clearly the reason why. Defining the "world" in his familiar first proposition as "all that is the case," Wittgenstein went on to assert that "the meaning of the world must lie outside of the world," or in a more poetic assertion, "the solution of the riddle of life in space and time lies *outside* space and time." Put differently, the meaning of the whole of reality is itself not a part of the world of facts. Symbols that point to the meaning of the whole occupy a different plane than do those pertaining to the empirical world. The realm with which religion is concerned, therefore, is not reducible to the empirical world, nor can the meanings it conveys be investigated with the same tools used for other empirical inquiries (i.e., positivism). As Bellah (1970:242) plainly asserts, "Science can never wholly take over the job of making sense of the world."

Wittgenstein himself failed to grasp the full significance of his formulation as an alternative to the subject-object conception of reality and reverted in his own life to a form of private mysticism that protected his religious convictions from objective reductionism by making them purely subjective. Nonetheless, his formulation provided a simple statement of a new epistemological view that was to have a profound impact on the study of culture, albeit only remotely attributable to Wittgenstein's own influence.

As in the classical approaches, the neoclassical perspectives contain a distinct image of human nature and an epistemological agenda that reflects this image. The fundamental problem facing humanity is no longer identified as one of reconciling subject and object, but is defined as a search for wholistic meaning. The quest for meaning is of ultimate concern because reality is conceived to be fundamentally divided, just as it had been in the subject-object split, but now divided between part and whole (in this sense, it is appropriate to say that a basic dualism also lies at the core of the neoclassical tradition). The gap between part and whole leaves the events of life that the individual inevitably experiences as parts of a larger drama of existence fragmented and lacking in meaning because the meaning of the whole context of which they are a part cannot be grasped either cognitively or empirically. Yet, with the exception of treatments attempting to resolve this problem simply by denying the possibility of finding ultimate meaning, the prospect that the gap between part and whole can be mediated is held open. Symbols are the key. Rituals, transcendent experiences, art, and religious liturgy and doctrine are recognized as means by which faith in the existence of wholistic meanings can be inspired and communicated. These symbols operate at a variety of levels, some raising appreciation of art or nature, some linking the individual with a tradition or cultural heritage, some helping only to express a "signal of transcendence" in play or fantasy, others evoking commitment to public roles, and still others expressing deeper meanings about life and its purposes. The role of scholarship, therefore, is not so much to arrive at a cognitive understanding of the meaning of existence, because this is thought to be impossible, but to clarify the meanings that are conveyed by symbols.

The neoclassical tradition de-emphasizes belief and cognition, focusing instead on symbols. The source of knowledge of greatest value to the resolution of the human dilemma within this tradition is no longer the knowing subject but the symbol, for within it lie meanings that may be grasped only intuitively. Bellah's book *Beyond Belief* (1970), the very title of which expresses the neoclassical attitude toward belief and cognition, represents a major effort to redirect the study of culture—and particularly the study of religion—toward a deeper appreciation of the realities of symbolism. Describing his perspective as "symbolic realism," Bellah (1970:252) argues against the reductionistic tendencies in the classical tradition, warns against the limitations of Cartesian dualism, and differentiates the study of symbolism from empirical positivism:

> The canons of empirical science apply primarily to symbols that attempt to express the nature of objects, but there are nonobjective symbols that express the feelings, values, and hopes of subjects, or that organize and regulate the flow of interaction between subjects and objects, or that attempt to sum up the whole subject-object complex or even point to the context or ground of that whole. These symbols, too, express reality and are not reducible to empirical propositions. This is the position of symbolic realism.

Emotion, will, and experience become as important to this approach as cognition. The meanings associated with symbols are as likely to be grasped intuitively as they are to be understood cognitively. Cognitive knowledge becomes important in this approach only insofar as this knowledge enhances the capacity to understand how symbols function.

PREFERRED METHODS

The major methodological approaches that emerged within the neoclassical tradition were phenomenology and hermeneutics. The former, particularly in Heidegger's work, preoccupied itself with the question of Being in an ultimate or wholistic sense, focusing on how symbols convey meanings about the nature of Being.[9] Phenomenology fit compatibly within the epistemology of the neoclassical tradition in that it stressed the in-depth exploration of the meanings associated with symbols. Berger and Luckmann, for example, trace their intellectual roots specifically to phenomenologists in the German tradition, particularly Alfred Schutz and Arnold Gehlen. Hermeneutics also provided a methodology that gave supreme importance to the study of symbolism, particularly in its quest to reconstruct the meanings intended in written texts by their original authors and for their original audiences.[10] Geertz, for example, argues that the analysis of culture should essentially be a hermeneutic or interpretive, rather than a scientific, enterprise. He writes: "Believing . . . that man is an animal suspended in webs of significance he himself has spun, I take culture to be those webs, and the analysis of it therefore not an experimental science in search of law but an interpretive one in search of meaning" (1973:5).

Both phenomenology and hermeneutics provided particularly attractive methodologies for the study of culture because each explicitly denied the possibility of reducing symbolism to any other aspect of reality. Unlike the classical tradition, phenomenology and hermeneutics treated symbols as objective realities (from whence Bellah's term "symbolic realism") and stressed the value of examining the meanings attached to these symbols. The importance of phenomenology and hermeneutics can be seen both in the works of neoclassical writers themselves and in the work of those who have been inspired by their ideas. Like Geertz, Berger has generally attempted to employ an interpretive model (cf. Hunter and Ainlay, 1986). In examining aspects of social life as diverse as religion and cities or marriage patterns and Third World development, he has emphasized symbolically constructed realities and has attempted to interpret the meanings of these symbols. As a theoretical starting point, his work credits the actor with an active role in interpreting, or giving meaning to, events. The subjective reality that the individual experiences, or the "intersubjective" meanings shared by collectivities, interest Berger most.

Geertz's scholarship has ranged in many fields, but he too has emphasized both the phenomenological and hermeneutic methods. The influence of phenomenology is clearly evident in his advocacy of what he has termed "thick description" as the preferred method of cultural investigation. Rather than striving for general laws or empirical regularities across cases, Geertz seeks to *describe* the rich meanings present in a given situation. He likens his method to "clinical inference" in which the investigator probes ever more deeply into the significance of symbolic meanings by examining them in all their complexity, by seeing how they relate to one another, and by participating as fully as possible in them himself so that the richness of their meaning can be grasped.

Similarly, Bellah has drawn consciously from phenomenologists like Schutz and Cassirer and from hermeneuticists like Ricoeur and Gadamer. In his empirical work he has attempted to combine both methods. His work on civil religion, for example, typically approaches historical speeches as "texts" that are to be analyzed hermeneutically to rediscover their original meanings and to interpret whatever lasting significance they may have for the contemporary period (e.g., Bellah, 1975). In *Habits of the Heart* (1985) Bellah and his associates also draw heavily from phenomenology. Generally shying away from imposing theoretical constructs on their subject matter, and drawing on verbatim quotes from several hundred unstructured interviews as well as participant observation in clubs and voluntary associations, they seek to discover the contemporary meanings of individualism and commitment in American culture.

Those who have drawn inspiration from the neoclassical tradition have generally adopted methods quite different from those employed in "mainstream" or "positivist" sociology. If survey research bore a certain affinity with the assumptions derived from the classical tradition, participant observation has shown a special affinity with the neoclassical tradition. Rejecting quantification as overly simplistic, researchers in this tradition have preferred to obtain data in less structured ways in order to discern more fully how their research subjects construct meaning. Tipton's (1982) research on the cultural meanings of the 1960s and their aftermath, for example, draws heavily on Bellah's theoretical framework and utilizes data primarily from depth interviews and participation in social movements. Following more closely in Berger's theoretical tradition, McGuire (1982) and Ammerman (1983) have employed participant observation to examine, respectively, the culture of pentecostal Catholics and Protestant fundamentalists.

CONTRASTING MODES

It would be inaccurate, however, to depict work in the neoclassical tradition as being entirely separate or distinct from studies more closely allied with the classical tradition. Not only have the leading contributors to the neoclassical tradition borrowed from writers such as Weber and Durkheim, but the two perspectives also intermingle in studies of particular cultural phenomena. There are "Bergerian" versions of Weber, just as there are "Bellahist" interpretations of Durkheim. In substantive areas, considerable mixing of the assumptions of the various classical and neoclassical approaches is typically evident. In sociology of religion, for example, textbooks and monographs generally draw on definitions of religion from Geertz, or from Bellah or Berger, that emphasize symbolism, but then move on to empirical evidence that, rather than dealing with symbolism at all, focuses on beliefs and attitudes. Here, as in other cases, the failure to recognize clearly the different assumptions implicit in the two traditions often leads to conceptual confusion.

Studies of "meaning systems" represent perhaps the clearest area in which the conceptual problems that arise from indiscriminate mixing of assumptions from the classical and neoclassical traditions can be illustrated. Both traditions emphasize the problem of meaning. Research on this problem, however, has often combined elements of the two traditions in ways that are not entirely compatible. In the neoclassical tradition, for example, symbols are emphasized much more consciously than in the classical tradition. In either, meanings can be examined from the subjective perspective of the individual, but the neoclassical approaches also provide for investigations that focus more directly on symbols themselves. In short, meaning systems can be distinguished from worldviews.

A meaning system refers to the dominant meanings in a culture that are associated with a particular symbol or set of symbols. Its distinguishing feature is an identifiable set of symbols with which interpretations, feelings, and activities can be associated. A worldview or belief system, in contrast, consists of all the beliefs that an individual holds about the nature of reality. An individual's worldview can be comprised of beliefs about any number of different symbols. A meaning system, by comparison, pertains to one set of symbols, even though these symbols may be used in a number of different texts, settings, or collectivities. The two concepts are also differentiated in terms of the importance they attach to the role of cognition. Worldviews are creations of thinking individuals. The knowing subject of the classical tradition reflects on the world and holds beliefs about this world. The idea of a worldview implies that individuals function as amateur philosophers. This assumption is compatible with the Enlightenment image of man in the classical tradition, but clearly does not inspire as much assent now as it once did. The concept of meaning system necessitates no such assumption, only a willingness to treat symbols as objects in their own right. Meanings evoked by symbols occur at the emotional level and the volitional level as well as the cognitive level. A symbol provides a bridge between raw experience and some sense of a larger reality. But this sense may be as much felt, intuited, worshiped, held in awe, acted upon, hoped for, trusted in, or tacitly accepted as codified conceptually.

Studies of cultural phenomena in which survey research techniques have been employed have typically focused on worldviews instead of meaning systems. Among the properties of individual worldviews that are often examined in these studies is the property of *consistency*. That is, questions are asked to determine whether or not individuals respond in the same way to a variety of stimuli (e.g., about religion or about politics). A common expectation is that people should hold consistent beliefs, but empirical findings have generally disconfirmed this expectation. There is a strong capacity, it appears, to tolerate beliefs that to the outside observer seem highly inconsistent (cf. Converse, 1964). On the basis of this observation, however, some scholars have concluded that individuals do not have meaning systems.[11] This is the point at which the confusion between the two traditions becomes evident.

The concept of consistency reflects the subjective, individualistic view of culture implicit in the classical tradition as well as this tradition's historical emphasis on rationality. The fully functioning subject is expected to have a view of the world that is accurate and internally consistent. Inconsistency is tantamount to unsophistication, maladjustment, improper cognitive socialization, or, as in Freud, symptomatic of repressed drives. Even though the assumption that people strive to attain cognitive consistency has been challenged repeatedly by empirical findings (e.g., Westie, 1965), the emphasis placed on rationality in the classical tradition has made this assumption difficult to abandon.

The concept of coherence, in contrast, derives from the concern expressed in the neoclassical tradition with the meaning of reality. Whereas consistency is an attribute of an individual's belief set, coherence is an attribute ascribed to reality. Reality is said to have meaning if some sense of coherence can be attributed to it, that is, if it appears to hang together in such a way that its elements bear a relation to one another.[12] For example, when Berger (1969) describes religion as a *nomizing* mode, his reference is to order or coherence sensed as an aspect of reality, not to a pattern of consistency among individuals' beliefs. Wilfred Cantwell Smith's (1979:133) characterization of the modern skeptic "for whom life consists of a congeries of disparate items among which they find no coherence" clearly refers to an attribute ascribed to reality rather than a lack of consistency among beliefs. Moreover, such discussions have explicitly rejected the idea that a consistent cognitive worldview is a precondition for perceiving coherence and meaning in reality. Geertz (1968:97) describes religious traditions as "collections of notions" rather than well-formulated sets of beliefs. Dumont (1977:20) asserts that the coherence implicit in ideologies lies primarily in "unstated views." Smith's (1979) distinction between faith as a dimly felt perception of coherence and belief as an attempt to articulate faith also reflects this point of view.[13]

The point here is that different problems are likely to be emphasized in the two traditions. Although both emphasize the problem of meaning, one is concerned with rational consistency, the other, with wholistic coherence. In the one, consistency inheres in beliefs; in the other, meaning derives from symbolism but may actually be enriched by combining seemingly diverse or even inconsistent symbolic images.

LIMITATIONS

There are, however, internal ambiguities and limitations within the neoclassical tradition that also contribute to these problems. One is that the requirement for rational consistency, as an aspect of meaning, is sometimes implied by the neoclassical tradition just as it is in the classical tradition. In Berger and Luckmann's discussion of the machineries of legitimation referred to earlier, for example, two principles of differentiation, rather than one, are implicit. On the one hand, the difference between simple explanations and symbolic universes is a matter of scope (i.e., the latter encompasses reality *in toto*). On the other hand, there is also an implied movement from less elaborate to more elaborate theoretical systems. Explanations are part of ordinary speech; symbolic universes are elaborate theoretical traditions. If the latter interpretation is emphasized, then it does become implausible to suggest that people tend to be that rational, philosophical, or consistent in their outlooks on life. The other interpretation, though, appears to be more in keeping with both Berger and Luckmann's own work and that of other writers such as Bellah. Wholistic meaning may be evoked by a simple gesture, or by a rosary or mandala, as much as by an elaborate philosophical system.

It is primarily as a basis of *systematic inquiry*, however, that the neoclassical tradition runs into difficulties. Its strengths, compared with the classical tradition, are that it elevates culture (as symbolism) to a more prominent position, it resists reductionistic inclinations to explain away culture too readily by attributing it to other factors rather than grappling with its meanings, and it presents a more detailed formulation of the problem of meaning (as contextually contingent). This tradition has also clearly had appeal because of the broader humanistic or philosophical perspective it reflects. Individuals are credited with a more active role in shaping their own worlds, the complexity of human affairs is acknowledged, and the desire for meaning and understanding is emphasized. Yet the methodologies this tradition has inspired have proven frustrating, and certain elements of its perspective have seemed overly limiting.

The methodological frustrations derive from the fact that phenomenology and hermeneutics, as practiced in sociology, have defied systematization and have explicitly denied efforts to arrive at replicable knowledge.

Particularly when the observer is given a large interpretive role without having to make explicit the grounds for his or her interpretations, red flags go up on all sides about the kind of knowledge being produced. For example, in reviewing Geertz's book *Local Knowledge,* Lawrence Hirschfeld argues that serious danger is afoot when investigators take the extreme perspective that Geertz proposes: "In repudiating explanatory strategies for the understanding of cultural phenomena, Geertz . . . rejects . . . the very means for engaging the discourse in which the company of scientists communicate." In Hirschfeld's view, Geertz "has abandoned virtually all the strategic goals associated with scientific endeavors; not only strong ones like the ability to generalize across instances or to predict new outcomes, but also a weaker, but most basic one, the requirement to provide truthful descriptions" (1986:35). These, however, are familiar problems in methodological discussions that need not be gone over yet another time in the present context.[14] For the moment, it will suffice to suggest that approaches of a more systematic sort might be taken to the analysis of symbolism if the vision of interpretation were at least temporarily severed from the problem of analysis.

More limiting, it appears, are some of the particular problem foci that have been prominent in neoclassical approaches to culture. Among these, the continuing emphasis on subjective meanings appears to be especially important. Just as in the classical tradition, emphasis is attached to the problem of meaning as experienced by the individual. Although this problem has been significantly reformulated, it continues to animate the study of culture. This emphasis, it will be recognized, does not correspond in principle with the neoclassical tradition's orientation toward symbolism, particularly symbolic realism. That orientation suggests focusing on symbolism as objective elements worthy of investigation. Yet in practice, greater attention has been devoted to the meanings of symbols than to symbols themselves.

Both the phenomenological and hermeneutic approaches to meanings have limitations as far as developing empirical generalizations is concerned. Phenomenology stresses description of the rich meanings held by specific individuals or in specific situations; yet these meanings are not only complex but idiosyncratic and continuously in flux. Having discovered all the meanings a set of symbols conveys to an individual today, one cannot be certain that the same meanings will still be present tomorrow. Description of this kind, in short, becomes an endless task. What most investigators fall back on, of course, are certain generalizations that appear to be relatively enduring or common. But doing so violates the spirit of phenomenology and raises questions about how such generalizations are to be made. Hermeneutics has the same limitations. Discovering the meanings of a text is difficult enough if one knows a great deal about its author or intended audience; if the author is dead or unknown, of if the audience is capable of interpreting the text in different ways, then the search for meanings may be nearly impossible.[15]

An additional limitation that has been evident in many applications of the neoclassical tradition is a tendency to become preoccupied with the individual. Berger and Luckmann, for example, go to some trouble to suggest how their approach is applicable to collective levels of social organization as well as to the individual, but most of the appeal of their approach has been limited to investigations of individuals in relatively small collectivities. Their emphasis on the individual's requirement for meaning and personal integration seems compelling at the individual level; yet applying the same arguments to whole societies simply by analogy often fails to be compelling. Clearly, the symbolic dimension of flags and corporate boardrooms, of athletic events and acts of terrorism, requires a level of analysis that is not predominantly preoccupied with the individual's search for meaning.

Yet another limitation of neoclassical approaches, compared with classical approaches, has to do with reintroducing the relations between culture and social structure. Geertz (1973) has argued that the analysis of culture should proceed in two stages: first, examining the symbols and, second, relating them to social structure. But the second of these, for whatever reasons, has generally been ignored. Berger and Luckmann's (1966) concept of "plausibility structure" also suggests the importance of social structure. But the idea itself—simply conversation or other types of interaction that maintain a given reality concept—is relatively inspecific and again seems best suited to face-to-face contexts rather than social units at more macroscopic levels. What has seldom been successfully attained within the neoclassical framework are analyses that relate cultural systems to large-scale institutions, that deal with ideologies and interest groups, or that examine the resources used in the production and institutionalization of cultural systems.

Raising these issues is not meant to suggest that they are insuperable or that they are of sufficient magnitude to destroy the value of neoclassical approaches to culture. Major contributions have been made from within this framework toward generating greater sensitivity to the functions of religion and toward analyzing some of the problems of personal identity in modern culture. From a policy or practical standpoint, this may be all that can be asked. But from the standpoint of developing knowledge that meets standards of either empirical verifiability or theoretical generalization, many have expressed doubts about the value of neoclassical approaches. Whether or not these doubts have been entirely well founded, they have nevertheless prompted scholars to consider alternative approaches. Some have remained more convinced than ever of the value of the classical traditions; others have favored what has become increasingly identifiable as a third perspective.

POSTSTRUCTURAL APPROACHES

It is easy to overemphasize the differences between poststructuralist writers such as Douglas, Foucault, and Habermas and writers in the neoclassical tradition. The anthropological styles of Douglas and Geertz, for example, overlap considerably. Habermas's concern in recent work with the concept of "life world" stems from the same phenomenological tradition from which Berger and Luckmann have drawn. Foucault is more distinct but has by no means been insignificant as an influence on the work of such scholars as Geertz and Bellah. The three writers chosen here as representatives of the poststructuralist approach also differ sufficiently among themselves that clarity is required as to what they have in common. What they share, and what distinguishes them from the neoclassicists, is a significant encounter with structuralism.

BASIC ASSUMPTIONS

Structuralism and Lévi-Strauss are virtually synonymous as far as the social sciences are concerned. Both, however, mean many things. For present purposes, the intricacies of structuralist assumptions about binary qualities of the brain can be overlooked. The important features of structuralism are its emphasis on systematic patterns in cultural codes and its search for the underlying meaning of cultural codes through the process of identifying these patterns. For Lévi-Strauss the method of discovering the true meaning of a myth, for example, is to examine the relations among paired opposites in the story. By rearranging the story's elements in this manner, one can learn what the myth "really meant."[16] This strategy, of course, is not unique to Lévi-Strauss. The founder of semiology, Roland Barthes, for example, also distinguished between the signifiers that were readily observable in myth and the deeper meaning of myth that could be discovered by examining the relations among signifiers.[17]

Poststructuralists generally retain the structuralist emphasis on analyzing patterns or relations in cultural materials but reject the assumption that doing this will disclose the materials' "real meaning." In a close critique of Lévi-Strauss, Mary Douglas (1967), for example, demonstrates that a single myth may in fact have many meanings and that these meanings are contingent on time and place. She also rejects Lévi-Strauss's rigorous emphasis on relationships among paired opposites. Yet she retains his interest in the symbolic boundaries or categories that may be present in pairs or more complex configurations of symbols. Foucault's work was also deeply influenced by structuralism, so much so that some commentators on his work have described it as a type of structuralism—a description, however, that Foucault himself rejected. The imprint of structuralism on his work is again that of seeing symbols as dramatizations of conceptual categories or of boundaries between categories. As in Douglas's work, the idea of looking at opposites often carries over into his work as a concern with the boundaries between deviance and normality. In his work on madness, for example, Foucault (1965) considers insanity not in isolation but as a negation that clarifies the nature of reason. Habermas's indebtedness to structuralism stems less directly from Lévi-Strauss or Barthes, although one can be sure he has read them, but from structural linguists like Chomsky and Searle.[18] He also rejects much of the physiological binarism on which Chomsky's work, in particular, is based. But, as will become evident shortly, he shares with Douglas and Foucault an interest in the relationships among collections of symbols.

As with the classical and neoclassical traditions, the distinctive character of poststructuralism can be seen more clearly from examining its implicit assumptions about the human dilemma, the task of scholarship, and epistemology. The human dilemma is no longer the split between subject and object or the quest to transcend fragmentation and achieve wholeness, but the problem of communication. Humans are cut off from one another, but they need to communicate in order to decide on collective values. The importance of this problem is magnified by the fact that, in the absence of collectively chosen values, we may destroy ourselves by simply letting the taken for granted rule over us. Habermas has been most explicit about these assumptions. In his view we need to be able to communicate with complete openness about desirable collective goals; otherwise, our competitive interests will rule, and we will be guided only by the struggle to attain technical mastery over the physical environment and over one another. There is, as in all of Habermas's work, a strong element of eclecticism here. The basic dilemma that he perceives is in some ways reminiscent of Marx's sense that we had lost freedom and had become bond servants of our environment. It is also reminiscent of Weber's warning about rationality becoming a limiting perspective. In some ways it too is a rejection of the pragmatism of everyday reality and a quest for higher values. But there is also a new emphasis on the collective, or social, aspect of the present dilemma. The problem is no longer one of finding meaning in isolation or of symbolically grasping absolutes. In Habermas no absolutes remain, only those that are arrived at by consensus. Foucault, and Douglas to a lesser extent, register the same concerns. Communication can be blocked by vested interests and conceptions of power; it needs to become more open, more freeing, more sustaining of a consensually constructed moral order.

From this analysis, the task of scholarship becomes one of facilitating communication. The manner in which this is done stands somewhere between empirical positivism and hermeneutical interpretation. Communication and the factors influencing it need to be examined as objectively, as dispassionately, as possible. Insofar as the observer always functions as interpreter as well, the bases of these interpretations need to be made explicit. But the standards against which results are compared do not consist only of positivist canons, let alone criteria of technical mastery; instead, they should have practically assessable results as far as the promotion of communication is concerned.

The epistemological vision of poststructuralism is rooted, in the case of Habermas and Foucault, in an evolutionary framework that stresses the primacy of language for the current epoch and, in Douglas, in a more static conception of history that also emphasizes the importance of language. The principal barriers to communication, especially in the modern period, are assumed to be built into the character of language itself—broadly defined to include rituals and other physical gestures as well as verbal or written communication. What remains hidden (the unknown) that will presumably illuminate the problems that are known are the rules and patterns built into the structure of language. These are so commonly used that they are taken for granted; yet they determine the categories in which we think and maintain barriers and inequities among people.

AWAY FROM MEANING

Absent in all of this is the problem of meaning. At one level, the problem of meaning as a problem of the individual—estrangement or a lack of wholeness—is clearly missing. Indeed, the individual himself is missing. Everything becomes communication, speech, categories, even discourse about individuals, but the individual himself is de-emphasized. In this sense poststructuralism is, of the three traditions, the least subjective in its approach to culture.[19]

Symptomatic of the poststructuralists' de-emphasis of the problem of meaning is the fact that religion receives almost no attention—something that has aroused criticism from religionists and humanists alike. Foucault's work contains no references to religion, Habermas's references are limited to a few remarks on theologians who have stressed communication and to a brief reworking of Bellah's scheme of religious evolution, and Douglas has dealt with religion only as a secondary interest both in her work on primitive societies and in essays and books on modern culture. None of the three has been as concerned as the neoclassicists, especially Berger and Bellah, with the religious quest, and none has devoted as much systematic attention to the subject as Durkheim or Weber. In consequence, virtually nothing is considered about the kinds of symbolism that give meaning to life. Instead, the individual is largely conceived of as a cultural construction whose being, identity, and categories of discourse are reflected in the observable functions of culture rather than being dimensions of subjective integration.

At a somewhat broader level, the problem of meaning is also absent from the poststructuralists' discussion of symbolism. Again, this is largely a function of the fact that the idea of symbolism itself tends to be de-emphasized. Symbols in some ways remain the constitutive elements of culture. But they are treated in an importantly different way than in the neoclassical tradition. There, a symbol is symbolic because it conveys meaning. The nexus of investigation must, as a result, be that of the object or event in relation to the person or group for which it has meaning. In short, meaning always lurks in the shadows as the topic of genuine interest. In the poststructuralist approaches, in contrast, symbols are taken, as it were, more literally. Rather than their being objects or utterances that stand for something else, they are simply objects or utterances. Supposedly they communicate, because they exist, but the essential question has less to do with *what* they communicate than with *how* they communicate. The thrust of investigation, therefore, focuses on the arrangement of symbols and their relations to one another, not primarily their meanings.

The shift away from problems of meaning is clearly apparent in Douglas's work. Although she has never emphasized this shift as a matter of deliberate preference, it is evident in the major topics on which she has chosen to work. *Purity and Danger* (1966) is primarily concerned with concepts of pollution and taboo in primitive settings. It demonstrates how distinctions between and within communities are dramatized by the concepts, on the one hand, and how cultural classification schemes generate concepts of pollution and taboo, on the other hand. Many of these concerns are carried over into *Natural Symbols* (1970). Dealing with culture in a more general and theoretical sense, this book also focuses on classification schemes and their articulation in rituals and symbols. Among the arguments developed here is what has become the widely cited discussion of "group," consisting of external boundaries demarcating whole collectivities, and "grid," consisting of internal classifications within collectivities, from which Douglas constructs a fourfold typology of cultural styles. Many of these initial interests have continued to be evident in more recent works by Douglas on topics such as food (1984), material goods (1979), and concepts of risk (1982).

Foucault's historically oriented studies, covering topics as diverse as madness and criminality, medicine, the organization of work, the social sciences, and sexuality, also de-emphasize meaning and focus on cultural classifications and their dramatization in language and in ritual. So removed from these analyses is the individual or any concern for subjective meanings that Foucault sometimes appears to have been more enamored with speech than with the speaker. Running through all his work is an emphasis on authority—the authoritative discourse of doctors and other professionals, the speaker's authority as dramatized in common modes of discourse, and the state's authority as manifested in public rituals. Foucault's work seldom takes cultural categories for granted but instead examines them historically to discover their origins and shows how deviants illustrated them and how professionals legitimated them. His work on medicine, criminality, and sexuality reveals the importance of the human body as a locus of ritual dramatizations of cultural categories, an interest that also runs through Douglas's work. Ultimately, Foucault's expressed objective was to further human emancipation by unmasking the categories of thought typically taken for granted.

Habermas, in approaching sociology from a more explicitly articulated theoretical framework, provides perhaps the clearest discussion of why meaning has been de-emphasized in the poststructuralist tradition. The focal point of his work on communication has been the "speech act"—a significant reformulation itself because culture is now seen as a type of behavior instead of subjective beliefs and attitudes. The question Habermas raises about speech acts is what makes them *meaningful* enough to exist at all. He shows no interest in discovering what their meaning is. This interest, of course, stems from his concern with the conditions of communication. The problem is not one of determining how everything that is communicated will be interpreted, but of discovering the determinants of what can be said at all. In a general formulation Habermas suggests four such conditions: (1) the relation between the speech act and the speaker, a relation that must be characterized by sincerity or truthfulness; (2) a relation between the speech act and the physical world or, more generally, with actuality, that involves truth; (3) a relation between the speech act and language in which comprehensibility must be present; and (4) a relation between the speech act and social norms in which legitimacy is evident. All these relations, Habermas suggests, are to a degree dramatized in what is actually spoken. One can, then, by examining discourse and other symbolic gestures, discover significant patterns pertaining to the broader culture.

A version of the contextual idea of meaning has been retained in much of the poststructuralist work. Symbols—speech acts, objects, rituals, concepts—are never examined in isolation or simply as substantive themes (e.g., love, conservatism, etc.), but in relation to other symbols. This strategy is taken not simply to provide substantive contrasts (e.g., between love and hate), but to illuminate the relations between symbols and the rules employed in relating them. Douglas is frequently most interested in the symbolic boundaries that separate two or more symbols. These are, in her view, the bases of cultural order and are actively maintained by dramatic acts of violation, by blending and differentiation, and by specifying mechanisms of bridging and dissociation. Foucault's approach is in some ways broader and less systematic. Treating cultural systems simply as "dispersions of elements," his work endeavors to find no order of a tightly organized or systematic fashion but only a variety of rules that specify what can be said about what and by whom. For Habermas, the preferable strategy is to begin not with a dispersion of elements, but with a single speech act and then to work outward, finding other verbalizations to which it is related. Habermas's search for structure in culture is also influenced by an evolutionary scheme that depicts movement from simple to more complex forms of differentiation. Thus, his concern is not only with the relations among speech acts but with levels of differentiation between types of utterances. In all of this, the "meaning" that may be given by different contexts is, again, not the object of investigation; instead, the idea of context directs attention toward the patterns and relations of which contexts consist.[20]

COSTS AND BENEFITS

What the poststructuralists seem to have accomplished by taking an end run around the problem of meaning is an approach to culture that emphasizes its observable features. Rather than meanings that may be unconscious even to the subject himself, the "stuff" of the poststructuralists' investigations consists especially of verbal utterances but also of rituals, codified bodies of knowledge, and cultural artifacts such as ceremonial objects, bodies, and food. As a result of this emphasis, the study of culture is apparently placed on a more solid footing. This does not mean that cultural analysis somehow returns to the fold of positivistic social science; the poststructuralists work clearly within the interpretive framework, but the focus of cultural investigation changes. Its data are more readily observable kinds of behavior rather than being locked away in people's private ruminations. An additional consequence of this refocusing is that the idiosyncracies associated with individual meanings are circumvented. Instead of having to probe again and again into the fluid meanings that a person might attach to a symbol, the arrangements among symbols themselves are examined.

These gains are, of course, achieved only at a considerable price. What many find interesting about culture is precisely what poststructuralists ignore. How people perceive and interpret their worlds is not what the poststructuralist approaches attempt to discover. Nor do they promise to enrich one's capacity to "comprehend" the true significance of a text, of oneself, or of current events. Instead, they present simplifications that seem to have more to do with formalistic rules and abstract patterns than with what is really going on. The logic of their agenda, however, is to contribute results that can be compared in different settings and thus to illuminate the rules of which cultural patterns of various kinds are made up. Theirs, in short, is an appeal more to the longer-run aspirations of a cumulative interpretive science—aspirations that may or may not be well founded—than to the immediate problems of phenomenological description.

The poststructuralist approaches take a relatively broad approach to culture. Their definition of culture is generally not restricted either to beliefs and attitudes or to symbolic meanings of the kind emphasized in neoclassical work. Culture is sufficiently broad that it consists of not only verbal acts and written codes but also the symbolic-expressive aspects of the ways in which prisons are organized, clinics run, and meals partaken. There is, of course, a residual that seems to be implicitly excluded from this notion of culture. For example, Foucault treats the punishment of criminals as a form of culture that dramatizes the state's power, but the state itself seems to fall into another category; so also with his discussion of the factory or with Douglas's analysis of technology and the environment. Culture apparently includes far more than ideas, but is not simply equivalent to social organization in general. Although it is not spelled out explicitly, the definition of culture in this work seems to focus on communication. Thus, culture might be considered a communicative or symbolic-expressive aspect of social behavior. As such, it becomes constitutive of social life itself; yet the possibility of relating culture to other aspects of social structure also remains open.

REDISCOVERING THE CLASSICS

Before attempting any further evaluation of the implications of the poststructuralists' move away from the problem of meaning, some observations about the role of the classical theorists in light of these recent developments are in order. As noted previously, there are many Durkheims, Webers, and Marxes. If the neoclassical approaches drew out new interpretations that placed the classics in a different light, the poststructuralists do much the same. They provide some useful clues for reappropriating some of the classical contributions that may have formerly been de-emphasized or neglected.

In the case of Marx, a whole tradition of structuralist and poststructuralist Marxism has emerged that can in no way be done justice to here. Writers such as Althusser, Therborn, and Seliger, as well as Habermas, have contributed enormously in recent years to the revitalization of Marxist approaches to ideology. Suffice it to say that, although much of this work remains at a philosophical level with implications that are not yet apparent for empirical sociology, a significant reorientation away from the problem of subjective meaning is also evident in this work. As opposed to questions about alienation, emphasis has been placed to a considerably greater extent on discourse, communication, and the dramatization of power through the symbolic aspects of social institutions themselves. Therborn (1980:78), for example, states flatly that ideologies "do not constitute 'states of mind.' " Instead, he argues, ideologies need to be seen as ongoing social processes. As such, they tend to be identified closely with social movements, with political claims, and with demands on social resources. Pointing to Foucault as an example, he also suggests the importance of rituals as the embodiment of ideologies, again not as isolated ceremonies, but as the symbolic dimensions of states and interest groups. Above all, the study of ideology should, in this view, move away from "a subjectivist conception of history" and take greater account of the ideological aspects of "de-centered constraints and fissures, contradictions and reinforcements, such as are inscribed in the economic and political structure and process" (p. 102).

Reinterpretations of Durkheim are relatively easy to discern because Douglas has drawn extensively from the Durkheimian tradition. Downplayed are the sharper distinctions in Durkheim between ideas and social structure, the tendency to reduce the former to the latter, concerns about anomie, his assertions about the psychological transformations associated with ritual, and subjectivist interpretations of the nature of moral community. Even after all this is stripped away, a surprising amount is still left. A model of the ways in which symbolic boundaries are dramatized is found in Durkheim's discussion of the role of ritual and taboo in separating the sacred from the profane. Douglas, in fact, provides reason to infer that the boundary itself may often be regarded with greater "sacredness" than what is on either side. Moral order is reinterpreted to be a concept that is essentially about culture, consisting of implicit categories that define proper relations among individuals and groups. Rituals, in turn, serve as models of moral order and suggest analogous ways in which other types of symbols may clarify and communicate messages about the moral order. In much of this, the problem of meaning ceases to be a subjective attribute of the individual and becomes one of ambiguity or uncertainty in the ordering of social relations.

Weber also has been subject to reinterpretation. Habermas has continued to evidence interest in some aspects of Weber's work, but as a whole the problem of meaning in Weber has seemed so central that few in the poststructuralist tradition seem to have considered reappropriating his legacy. Perhaps the most promising direction in which such an endeavor might move is a reconsideration of Weber's comparative work on world religions. Although the problem of meaning looms large in this analysis, the more subjective features of religion need not necessarily provide hindrances to analysis, for religion is certainly objectified in cultural codes apart from its subjective meanings for individuals. As such, religious codes might usefully be examined to discover how categories are defined, separated, and related. Conceptions of evil and of salvation, ideas about the relations between ethical orientations and behavior, and about this-worldly conduct and otherworldly rewards all appear amenable to such investigations.

Rediscovering the classics may or may not be useful for specific investigations of culture. However, if advantages are to be gained in the analysis of culture by attempting to escape the subjectivism implied in the problem of meaning, then significant elements of the classical tradition that are not affected by this problem may still be applicable. This possibility again points toward the importance of not drawing too sharp a distinction between poststructuralism and some of its precursors.

For some, the major barrier to rediscovering the classical tradition is still likely to lie in its tendency toward reductionism. This may be a barrier approached from either side. That is, scholars oriented toward analyzing culture in its own right may be deterred due to a dislike of the reductionistic tendency; scholars on the other side who were in a sense convinced by the classics of the value of reductionism may be deterred from taking culture seriously because they tend to think of it only as subjective beliefs and attitudes.

The poststructuralist tradition has, it appears, solved the problem of reductionism—or at least minimized it. In fact, several options for escaping the reductionist problem are available. One is suggested by Habermas's fourfold set of conditions influencing the meaningfulness of symbols. Sociologists are likely to be most successful at examining the relations between symbols and social conditions—the relation that Habermas suggests is a contributor to the legitimacy of a symbol. In that sense, sociological work may be accused of reductionism. But the other three conditions should not be forgotten, particularly the possibility that a symbol may be meaningful because its relation to the real state of affairs is one of *truth*. Another option arises from the different epistemological orientation of the poststructuralist tradition. The fear of reductionism in the classical tradition grew mainly from the idea that falsely objectified beliefs, often religious, could be unmasked. The Cartesian dualism underlying that idea, however, is largely absent from the poststucturalist tradition. A third option derives from Douglas's approach, that is, simply to define culture in very broad terms (including rituals, food, etc.) and focus on the relations internal to it, rather than paying much attention to other types of social structure to which it might be reduced. Finally, Foucault's lead can be followed, seeing culture as in some ways a reflection of other features (the state, for example), but also recognizing the power of culture to act back on these other factors. In short, there seems little reason either to worry about explaining culture away or to think of it so narrowly as to be irrelevant to the study of social life.

BEYOND MEANING?

A shift away from the problem of meaning can be identified in the poststructuralist tradition, and some of the evidence for this shift has been suggested. It still remains, however, to consider whether or not this shift represents a useful direction for the analysis of culture to go.

The question is not one that is likely to result in ready answers or answers that will evoke consensus among sociologists interested in culture. But as an initial approximation to the problem, the question might be raised as to whether there are examples of major cultural events the meanings of which we might not be interested in knowing. At first glance, the answer would seem to be "no." Surely, if a revolution occurs, we would like to know what it meant to the people involved. If religious enthusiasm suddenly breaks out, we would want to know what meaning it contributed to people's lives. If racism flourishes in one period but not in another, we would want to understand the meanings of these cultural differences.

True enough. But what happens when we attempt to study these kinds of meanings? Suppose we decide to study the meaning of the French Revolution. Chances are, what we mean by "meaning" is not meaning at all, but "significance." What is the significance of the French Revolution, that is, its effects on other revolutions, its consequences for French society, or the importance we attribute to it today? But suppose we are serious historical sociologists and actually want to find out what the French Revolution meant to those who took part in it. Is not this a hopeless task? Most of the participants left no record of their thoughts and feelings. For sake of argument, though, suppose we are *good* historians, like Robert Darnton, and are able to track down a detailed autobiography from the period, like Darnton's (1984) discovery of the memoirs of Nicolas Contat, a printer's apprentice in *ancien régime* Paris.[21]

Unfortunately, Contat did not write about the Revolution; he wrote about killing the boss's cat. We decide to make the most of it anyway. After all, one good autobiography may be a valuable window into the underlife of the French proletariat. Drawing inspiration from Geertz's idea of thick description, Darnton sets out to unravel the meaning of the "great cat massacre." Contat's memoirs provide rich evidence of what the episode meant. Or do they? It turns out that Contat wrote about the episode more than three decades after it happened. His description tells more about the event's meaning in distant retrospect than at the time. Contat was also not particularly gifted as a writer. He struggled to express his thoughts and feelings but often failed. He was, too, a writer who knew he was leaving a legacy that might well become public. One suspects he is not always candid in expressing his feelings. Contat was also but one of the apprentices who perpetrated the incident. We know little of how the others interpreted it. Nor do we know anything about how typical or atypical Contat's views were in the Paris underclass at large.

Darnton is not unaware of these problems. Indeed, he rather quickly moves from Contat's own account to tell us other things about the life of apprentices, their rituals, the boss, cats, superstitions, and so forth. He greatly enriches the story by telling how common it was for cats and women to be associated in French culture, how the boss's cat was really his wife's, how cats and witchcraft were connected, and how animals in general were treated. In the end, we still know little of what the event meant to Contat (or anybody else), but we know a lot about the arrangement of symbols and rituals in French culture. Darnton's account turns out to resemble the kind of analysis characteristically produced by Foucault. It is a discussion of what was related to what. He demonstrates many different cultural and social conditions that made the cat massacre meaningful, even though its specific meaning remains in doubt— even more so by the time he is finished because his analysis suggests many possible layers of meaning that might have been present.

The story of the cat massacre, therefore, is interesting because it probes the relations among symbols. It reveals how cultural categories were dramatized in ritual acts and how these categories shaped the content of rituals. It would have been even more illuminating had Darnton taken the analysis one step further and discussed more self-consciously the rules evident in these constructions and in his own reconstruction. How was it, for example, that cats and women were associated? What showed this connection? Did the same mechanisms operate in other symbolic boundaries, say, between masters and apprentices, and so forth?

But getting back to the Revolution itself, suppose the question asked had been more typically sociological, such as what were the social conditions contributing to the Revolution? Would it be possible to ignore meanings and still provide a satisfactory answer? Theda Skocpol, in her book *States and Social Revolutions* (1979), responds affirmatively. Conceiving of "revolutionary ideologies" chiefly in subjectivist terms as the goals and intentions of revolutionary leaders, she argues that little explanatory significance can be attached to these factors. Revolutions, it seems, typically produce results quite different from those envisioned by their leaders. In her analysis, a "structural" approach to revolutions that emphasizes coalitions of peasants and urban workers against a weakened state is more promising.

Skocpol is probably correct in sensing that the subjective meanings of revolutionists do not explain the origins or outcomes of revolutionary movements. But, as so often happens in sociology, her dismissal of ideology on these grounds leads her to neglect cultural factors of any kind. If solidarity among peasants and workers is a decisive factor, how is this solidarity dramatized and maintained? How do revolutionists come to identify the state as a source of their grievances? It is the cultural, or symbolic-expressive, dimension of group life, of the moral economy of peasant communities, and of the state itself that needs to be investigated in order to address these questions.

Perhaps revolution is not the best example, however, for highlighting the importance of the problem of meaning. The example mentioned earlier of an eruption of a religious movement may be better. It is suddenly discovered, let us say, that a new religious movement, perhaps calling itself the Unification Church, has come into being and claims a world membership of several million young people, many of them from middle-class American families. Here, it would seem, is a case where the problem of meaning can hardly be ignored. Uppermost in our minds are questions about the search for meaning that has led these young people to join. We will want to talk with some "Moonies" to find out why they joined.

Before grabbing our tape recorders, though, we need to pause for a moment and consider what we hope to find out. First of all, we need at least to consider other options. The movement is itself a cultural phenomenon. If we are interested in studying culture, one of the things we might also explore, as sociologists, is the resources that have gone into producing this movement. Too often we apparently approach movements (especially religious ones) entirely from the "demand" side, as it were, hoping to account for them in terms of the subjective needs they seem to fulfill. This is a bit like trying to account for American capitalism by looking at consumer tastes. There is also a "supply" side in culture, just as in capitalism, that needs to be considered in looking at cultural movements. In our example, therefore, we should not regard matters of finance, organization, and mobilization as being unworthy of our attention.

Having examined those matters, however, our curiosity would probably still convince us that we should interview some members. If so, we should bear two things in mind. One is that the subjective stimuli for joining may not be obvious to the people we interview. Just as Durkheim was led to investigate suicide *rates* rather than suicide notes, so we may want to look at broader features of the society in order to *infer* some of the pressures creating potential members. This may seem a trivial point, because it is often made; yet it continues to be persistently ignored in cultural studies. The second consideration is that the product of our interviews will not be *meanings*, but *discourse about meanings*. We can either take it at face value (leaving aside questions of its validity and representativeness), or we can treat it as discourse. In the former situation, we accept it as evidence of an internal psychological state. In the latter, we admit our lack of knowledge about hidden states and examine the discourse itself, because that is all we have, to determine why it was meaningful for some things to be said and others not to be said. As with Darnton's cat massacre, we will probably conclude that more can be learned about the conditions under which a statement or act is meaningful than we can about its actual meaning.

Finally, the other case mentioned earlier—about the presence of racism in different periods—raises some different issues. Because racism is a fairly broad issue, we may want to relate it to larger features of the society. It is generally regarded as a social problem, so we will probably also want to do a hermeneutic interpretation of it that will not only describe, but also help eradicate, it from the culture. Even if that is our goal, we nevertheless need to begin with data as rigorous and systematic as we can collect. Just because we are planning a hermeneutic analysis does not permit us to get away with a subjective, idiosyncratic approach to the cultural materials that will be used in our interpretation. In studying racism, we will need to use the many opinion polls that have asked questions about racial attitudes. But we also need to steer a middle course between the two pitfalls that seem to be common in dealing with survey data: dismissing it too quickly or believing it too uncritically. If we assume survey data mean nothing because this information cannot possibly tell us what people really think, then we are naive about the role that surveys actually play. But if we assume that survey responses actually tap into underlying social psychological states, then we are also naive and are making a leap of blind faith that most scientifically oriented sociologists would not like to admit. Survey responses are again a kind of discourse, a text, or aggregation of texts. In examining relations among them, we may or may not be tapping attitudinal states, but we can examine the relations among elements of discourse, just as a structural linguist examines relations in language. What we can discover are the kinds of elements that can be associated with one another, those that are not, and perhaps some of the rules governing these associations.

As we turn from data on racism to the problem of interpreting its place in the culture, we must again be cautious about what we are really doing. We may use terminology that implies we are examining the cultural meaning of racism. But are we? Does not racism have nearly as many meanings as there are people (or social scientists)? We may be giving *our interpretation* of racism, saying what it means to us. But on what basis is this interpretation likely to be compelling? It can be compelling only if the bases of interpretation are made clear. We must build a compelling case by examining the relations that actually are observable in the culture between racial statements and other cultural elements. If we are asserting claims about biblical imagery and racism, for example, it does far more good to examine speeches in which these relations are actually present than to assert a general cultural affinity. Again, such speeches can be taken at face value, but they can also be taken apart to determine more precisely how configurations and categories are pieced together.

These examples seem to suggest that the problem of meaning may well be more of a curse than a blessing in cultural analysis. When we set out to study it, the available evidence generally makes it elusive. If we claim to have extracted something about it, we have probably claimed too much. When we think we have studied it, we have probably turned anyway to an examination of the relations among cultural elements. And if we have dismissed culture because of these problems, we have probably thrown out other facets of culture that are valuable to examine. This is not to say that the problem of meaning is a hopeless quagmire. In-depth analysis by psychologists or anthropologists with training at probing the subjective consciousness may be productive. But few sociologists have these skills, and the business of sociology as a discipline has generally run in other directions, specifically, toward analyzing observable data.

More generally, the brief reconnaissance of the classical and neoclassical traditions that has been undertaken here reveals some of the reasons why the problem of meaning has become so central to the study of culture. Many of these reasons were rooted in broader diagnoses of the human condition and in particular epistemological assumptions that no longer seem as compelling as they once did. At a minimum, the problem of meaning turns out to be contingent on cultural constructions rather than being an inherent feature of culture itself. Once this fact is seen clearly, culture certainly can be studied without making meaning the central concern. Whether it is *desirable* to displace meaning from cultural analysis is another matter. But the radical subjectivity with which this approach has traditionally been associated clearly leads to problems of evidence, method, and interpretation that would be desirable to avoid if possible.

Meaning, of course, as wags have been prone to point out, has many meanings. In addition to the radical subjectivity that has been discussed here, either as inner attitudes or as the deep subjective meanings individuals attach to symbols, are broader usages of the term "meaning." We may speak, as sociologists, about "shared meanings" or "collective meanings." Or, from the perspective of interpretive sociology, we may wish to assert the priority of interpreting the meaning of events as the main task of social inquiry. But both these usages really refer to something else and only obscure clear discussion by relying on the same term. The issue of shared meanings is really one of discourse and behavior; otherwise we have no basis for calling it "shared." As such, it falls squarely into the perspective, here associated with poststructuralism, that emphasizes the study of discourse. Or put differently, we focus on the messages that are communicated, but we do not become embroiled in the ultimate phenomenological quest to probe and describe subjective meanings in all their rich detail. As interpretative sociologists, we also focus on enhancing the *meaningfulness* of events, but in all humility must acknowledge that our interpretations are themselves subject to many interpretations. We do not in fact explicate "the meaning" of an event, therefore, but only try to render it meaningful by putting it in a clear interpretive framework. In a sense, then, we retain much of what has been seen to be of value in discussions of meaning, but we consciously try to move away from focusing cultural analysis itself on the radically subjective beliefs, attitudes, and meanings of the individual.

To suggest abandoning the problem of meaning is, of course, much like quitting the settlement and launching into the wilderness. Writers like the poststructuralists may be useful as guides. But there are no maps. It even remains uncertain whether the journey is a reasonable gamble. Only plodding efforts to deal with the problems that culture presents are likely to tell.

CHAPTER THREE

The Structure of Moral Codes

The problem of moral order, prominent in the classical tradition in the work of Durkheim, has in recent years also become a matter of broader interest. Questions about moral commitments to public responsibilities, changes in moral convictions, moral bases of self-worth, and the corrosive effects of modern culture on morality have arisen. These questions have obviously far-reaching ramifications in fields such as ethics, theology, education, and public policy. They also have an important cultural dimension and thus provide an opportunity to explore some of the ideas about culture that have just been outlined. This chapter draws primarily on Mary Douglas's idea of symbolic boundaries to develop a structural analysis of moral codes. A relatively broad, inductive concept of moral codes forms the basis of this analysis. A moral code will be defined as a set of cultural elements that define the nature of commitment to a particular course of behavior. These elements, it will be argued, have an identifiable symbolic structure. Examining this structure will thus provide an opportunity to illustrate some of the strengths and weaknesses of the structural approach to cultural analysis.

THE QUESTION OF MORAL AUTHORITY

Analysts of contemporary culture have persistently raised questions about the bases of moral authority in modern society. To many, problems evident at the level of moral obligations seem to have grown to crisis proportions. In his much discussed Harvard commencement address, Aleksandr Solzhenitsyn (1978:51), for example, summarized a prevailing view:

> The West has finally achieved the rights of man, and even to excess, but man's sense of responsibility to God and society has grown dimmer and dimmer. In the past decades, the legalistic selfishness of the Western approach to the world has reached its peak and the world has found itself in a harsh spiritual crisis and a political impasse. All the celebrated technological achievements of progress, including the conquest of outer space, do not redeem the twentieth century's moral poverty.

For Solzhenitsyn, the problem facing the West is at heart moral and spiritual. It consists of a diminishing sense of attachment or obligation to absolute values. The result is, on the one hand, an increasing substitution of technology and bureaucratic law for moral commitment and, on the other hand, symptoms of decadence and social disintegration.

From a quite different philosophical perspective, a similar analysis has been presented by Harvard sociologist Daniel Bell. In his view, religion has traditionally supplied the basis of social solidarity and moral responsibility. But the capacity of religion to fulfill this role has, for various reasons, been shrinking. Despite numerous indications of a fundamentalist revival, the larger prominence of religion in modern society has been eroded by the very institutions that fundamentalists have vainly sought to recapture—the modern bureaucratic state, an autonomous economic sphere, secular higher education, routinized legal procedures. The result has been hedonism, a thirst for novelty, a sense of rootlessness, a lack of moral responsibility. Bell (1976:84) concludes: "the social order lacks either a culture that is a symbolic expression of any vitality or a moral impulse that is a motivational or binding force. What, then, can hold the society together?"

From yet another quarter, deep concern has been voiced about a seeming increase in narcissistic individualism. Richard Sennett's *The Fall of Public Man* (1976), for example, portrays a decided erosion over the past century in moral obligations to public roles and participation. But for Sennett the problem is not simply a function of rising self-love at the expense of community involvement. Rather, a crisis also is evident at the individual level—a shattered sense of self-identity that leaves the individual desperately dependent on intimacy and shared feelings, but one that ultimately provides too little self-confidence to commit oneself to larger social causes. The social is, in short, inextricably linked to the personal. What appears publicly as a lack of moral responsibility is compounded privately as a problem in self-definition.

A somewhat similar diagnosis, again from quite different starting as-sumptions, has been advanced by Habermas (1976) in his discussion of the cultural problems present in advanced capitalism. Although Ha-bermas's concept of "legitimation crisis" has received the greatest attention, a parallel problem at the interpersonal level—termed a "moti-vation crisis"—comes closest to other writers' concern with moral au-thority. With Sennett, Habermas perceives a marked tendency in modern societies toward withdrawal from the public realm. The problem, how-ever, is not primarily a failure on the part of individuals, but a characteris-tic of the culture and, in turn, of political and economic institutions. Like Solzhenitsyn, Habermas recognizes a growing cultural tendency toward locating authority in technical and administrative performance. But this type of authority does not provide an independent base of legitimacy for the political system. Nor does it contain conceptions of intrinsically au-thoritative moral principles. The result again is an amoral dependence on purely rational legal codes, enforceable by coercion and utilitarian calcu-lations, and purely pragmatic considerations of market value and techni-cal performance.

Whether these diagnoses are correct or overstated has not been ex-amined rigorously, but public opinion polls and voting records docu-ment some of the more specific problems that have been discussed—de-clining voter participation, cynicism about public institutions, eroding commitment to traditional religious values.[1] Studies also demonstrate considerable change in standards of sexual morality and in gender roles, life-styles, and work values, all of which may have led to increas-ing uncertainties about moral choices and the bases for validating moral obligations. In public discourse, issues of ethics and morality have gained new visibility in the decade since Watergate, and research on self-identities supports the claim that personal meaning clearly de-pends on moral attachments and is adversely affected by ambiguities in these attachments (e.g., Wuthnow, 1976; Gallup Organization, 1983). Many of the more global assessments pointing to a crisis in moral au-thority, however, can be only partially verified by studies of this kind. Of more pressing importance, greater effort needs to be devoted to the task of trying to understand the nature of moral obligations in general.

Two distinct literatures have addressed this issue. One focuses on moral standards, the other, on moral development. The former has dealt mainly with substantive topics having a clear moral component, such as lying, sexuality, abortion, and cheating. Conceptually, this litera-ture deals with morality primarily in terms of norms or rules. The second body of literature, inspired to a great extent by the work of Lawrence Kohlberg (1981, 1984), has been concerned with stages in the development of moral reasoning. It has paid less attention to specific moral questions but has utilized moral dilemmas as a means of evoking evidence on how subjects arrive at—and legitimate—moral decisions.

Both of these literatures have considerable value, but neither is entirely satisfactory for present purposes. The moral standards literature seldom pays attention to the formal properties of moral codes, nor are these standards seen as cultural complexes with an internal structure or set of relations. Because virtually anything can qualify as a moral norm, the task of investigation also quickly proves unmanageable or else is limited arbitrarily to prosaic traditional moral rules. The moral development literature has given more recognition to the complex, formal patterns constituting moral reasoning, but this literature can be criticized for attempting to mold these patterns into a simplistic, heavily value-laden evolutionary scheme. Because this literature has been developed from examining subjects' reactions to contrived moral dilemmas, it also has doubtful applicability for answering the broader questions about moral obligations that Solzhenitsyn and others have raised. For these reasons, no effort will be made here to draw systematically from these literatures. A different approach will be offered, one that rests on relatively elementary assumptions about the structure of culture and that leads to some considerations not often addressed in the literature on moral order.

A STRUCTURAL APPROACH

To begin, let us imagine that some degree of order has to be present in people's behavior. In many cases the degree of orderliness required may be quite small, but some order can always be assumed to be present. If it were not, individuals would be unable to make sense of their behavior, and social interaction would be impossible. Let us also imagine, following Mary Douglas, that order has somehow to do with *boundaries*. That is, order consists mainly of being able to make distinctions—of having symbolic demarcations—so that we know the place of things and how they relate to one another.

From these assumptions we can also say that in analyzing moral codes we are going to be dealing with symbols—cultural elements that express boundaries—and we are going to be looking for some structure among these symbols. In other words, symbols have to be related to one another in some manner so that boundaries or distinctions are implicitly present. Structure, then, does not mean that any tightly organized or logically consistent system is present, only that some symbolic distinctions can be identified.[2] The payoff from this approach is that the boundaries identified may possibly be used to make sense of the areas in which problems in moral obligations may be likely to arise. What exactly one might look at can be discussed more clearly by introducing some examples. These will provide raw material from which some assertions about symbolic boundaries can be generated.

First, suppose one were to visit a fundamentalist church, talk with some of its members, listen to a sermon, and read some of its literature (this is a convenient example to begin with because many investigators have done just that; moreover, morality and fundamentalism are often thought to have a particularly straightforward relation).[3] In keeping with some of the methodological conclusions drawn in the previous chapter, it would be desirable if our information could be as readily observable as possible (i.e., not pretend to be about beliefs and subjective meanings but consist of utterances, objects, and events). Some of these events might be observed: baptisms, hymn singing, public prayers, sermons, Bible reading. One would also be likely to hear utterances about "God," "obeying God," "sin," "the devil," "Jesus," and being "born again," "saved," or "converted." Some behavior or utterances about behavior might also be worth noting: giving money to the church, attending church, abstaining from alcohol, and talking about marital fidelity, for example.

Next, suppose we visited some middle-class or working-class families chosen mostly at random (again because several investigators have done this and reported their observations and conversations in some depth).[4] Here we would probably observe people working, caring for children, engaging in neighborhood activities, doing volunteer work, and so on. We would expect to hear a lot of discourse about themselves and their children, their jobs, plans, goals, and successes. In keeping alert to discourse somehow bearing on morality and moral commitments, we might also hear utterances about "doing my best," "making things better for my kids," "helping people," "doing what's expected of me," and "not being a burden to other people."

Finally, to provide a contrast, suppose we made observations in a so-called "human potential movement," such as Scientology, Transcendental Meditation, est, or transpersonal psychology.[5] This location might be valuable for exploring some of Sennett et al.'s ideas about narcissism, but again, rather than prejudging the type of moral constructs involved, let us simply make note of the readily observable: people meditating, attending encounter sessions or T-groups, talking about "getting in touch with myself" and "learning to express myself," perhaps making somewhat more explicit reference to themselves or commenting on their behavior to a greater degree than in the other settings, and perhaps deviating (visibly or verbally) from prevailing types of dress, jobs, or marital patterns.

These materials require us to know relatively little about beliefs, inner states, reasoning processes, or moral dilemmas. As in any setting, they benefit from comparisons and from the observer's general familiarity with behavior patterns, but the observer need not make claims to understand in any detail the "meaning" of various acts and utterances. Nor is it necessary to assume that all the observations made in each setting constitute some "system" with an underlying set of assumptions or a consistent logic. Only the fact that these acts and utterances coexist in roughly the same time and place makes it possible to raise questions about their relations to one another and the kinds of symbolic distinctions that may be evident.

With enough materials, any number of symbolic distinctions and patterns among these distinctions might be identified in each example. For purposes of understanding the structure of moral obligations, three such distinctions seem to be particularly important and are evident in each of the examples. Sketching these distinctions will by no means provide a full picture of the structure of moral obligations but will suggest some of the ways in which this structure may be expressed symbolically.

MORAL OBJECTS AND REAL PROGRAMS

Some of the symbols in the examples clearly refer to an object of commitment. This object, as well as the idea of commitment to it, is evident in utterances such as "obeying God," "trying to do God's will," "making the world better," "making life better for my kids," and "getting in touch with myself." God, world, kids, and self represent objects of commitment. Other symbols in each of the examples refer more directly to what people do. These include activities such as reading the Bible, attending church, working hard at one's job, spending time on community activities, meditating, and talking about one's feelings. In many cases, the two sets of symbols are closely related. For example, talk of doing God's will may be especially common while people are participating in church activities; if asked why they work hard or meditate, people may answer that the reason is to make the world better or discover their true self. Yet the two sets are also clearly different. This is evident from the symbols themselves. The church is not God, one's job is not the world, and meditating is not the self. The two are related yet distinct.

It is in fact this subtle pattern of connected-but-separate that often requires special care to observe in investigating discourse. Two symbols are discursively connected, but one is emphasized rather than the other. In the television miniseries *Roots II,* for example, Alex Haley's father admonishes him, "Alex, you must get a college education, for your own good and for the good of your people." The connection in this familiar admonition is evident: an activity that Alex can perform (going to college) and an object to which one should be committed (his people). Performing one is a way of attaining the other. Alex's reply is also instructive: "Yes, father, I'll do my best." Best at what—going to college or doing good for his people? The two are distinct but sufficiently related that a more specific reply is not required.[6]

Many discussions of this type of moral logic would immediately identify a potential problem in this connection of objects and activities. To value one thing but then actually do something slightly different runs afoul of moral criticism. This may in fact be an area worthy of further consideration as a possible source of moral erosion. For the time being, however, it will suffice simply to identify this as one of the symbolic distinctions that make up the structure of a moral code. In order to identify it, we might refer to it as the distinction between the "moral object," on the one hand, and the "real program," on the other.

SELVES AND ACTORS

A second distinction emerges in the three examples in conjunction with symbolism about the person or the actor. When the fundamentalist is described as a person who has been "saved," a distinction is being made between two aspects or components of the self. One is the soul, the essence of the person, that is pure, forgiven, ultimately acceptable— indeed, imperishable, as suggested by the related idea of "eternal life." The other part is "flesh," mortal, subject to temptation and impurity. The middle-class breadwinner who says "I'm just doing my job" is in effect making the same distinction: there is a "real me" who is good, worthy, incorruptible; and this "real me" is different from the actor who works at a job that is often boring, beneath my dignity, and sometimes even compromises my integrity. Work may be fulfilling and provide a sense of worth; yet the real self is in some ways separate from the worker.[7] So it is, too, in the human potential example. What meditation does is to define the "true self" as an entity apart from the multiple roles one must play.[8]

In each instance the distinction between the real me and the roles I play permits, as it were, a degree of role distance. One can in effect say, "What you see me doing is really not who I am." This is the distinction that allows one to comment on—even criticize—one's own behavior. Woody Allen's title character in *Annie Hall* epitomizes this capacity. When she says, "Gee, Annie, that was a dumb thing to say," she communicates vividly that what she has just done or said should be distinguished from who she really is.[9]

The distinction between aspects of the self and the roles it plays is, of course, fundamental to modern social psychology. Two points nevertheless need to be emphasized. One is that this distinction is not simply the theoretical construction of social psychologists; it is also a cultural construction that can be seen in discourse itself. The other is that, contrary to some social psychological arguments, the self is not simply the sum of a person's roles. Symbols used in conversation at least suggest the idea of a true, real, or inner self that is different from any of these roles.

This distinction is again between symbols that are separate but also connected. Moral arguments in the conventional sense link character and action, self-worth and behavior. One's actions seemingly must derive from or reflect upon who one is. Yet the two must also not be confused. For present purposes this distinction can be named that between the "self" and the "actor."

INEVITABILITY AND INTENTIONALITY

In each of the examples some particularly powerful symbols are also evident. Some of these are personified (Christ, the devil, one's boss or guru); others are special events or concepts (sin, a pay raise, having an ESP experience). They have powerful symbolic value because they happen infrequently, are unusual or divine, and sometimes influence circumstances or represent changes in one's life. In some cases they also serve as objects that are pursued or venerated or are explicit sources of moral authority (e.g., Jesus' teachings). Their special quality or power, however, also suggests that they may symbolize important cultural boundaries. If, as Mary Douglas suggests, boundaries are essential to social order, then special significance is likely to be attached to these boundaries, and special power may be associated with beings or events that violate, transcend, modify, or uphold these boundaries.

Following this lead, many of these beings, events, and concepts appear to symbolize a distinction between what might be termed the "inevitable" and the "intentional." On one side of this boundary are forces that the individual cannot control; on the other side is a realm subject to the individual's control, a realm in which intentions govern, rather than obdurate conditions. Jesus struggles with the inevitable (death, evil, suffering) and wins; it temporarily violates him, but in the end he emerges triumphant. The devil, in contrast, is originally good, capable of controlling his actions, but then becomes a fallen angel who succumbs to evil and becomes its instrument. Whereas Jesus symbolizes the possibility of pushing back the inevitable, the devil symbolizes the intentional realm being intruded upon by the inevitable.

This pattern is in general one typified by heroes and villains. Heroes conquer that which was thought impossible; villains succumb to forces beyond their control and in so doing suggest the possibility that we too may be more vulnerable than we thought.[10] Contemporary heroes and villains follow this pattern. A villain such as the cult leader Jim Jones symbolizes the intrusion of the inevitable: the possibility that a cleverly administered bureaucratic organization can manipulate even our most cherished possession, the mind. We thought the mind was under our control, a landmark in the realm of intentionality, but Jones's seeming ability to "brainwash" his followers, even to the point of mass suicide, raises the spectre of external forces penetrating the will.[11] In opposite fashion, much of the same constitutes the basis of adulation for cultural heroes—the mystic guru who refuses to conform to bureaucratic rules, the fortune-teller who extends the mind's powers into new areas, the eccentric scientist who does the same.[12]

Nonpersonified entities, concepts, and acts may also symbolize boundaries between the intentional and the inevitable. Getting a promotion dramatizes one's efficacy; getting fired reveals the powerful forces one is up against. Deliberately not answering the telephone gives one a sense of seizing control of one's life; getting a headache excuses one from performing competently because it was beyond one's control. Concepts of free will permit persons to take credit for their accomplishments; concepts of determinism give them an "out" for their failures.

Although these distinctions do not exhaust the possibilities available in moral discourse, they nevertheless provide in combination a useful outline of the components involved in constructing moral codes. Each of these symbolic distinctions seems, on reflection, to serve a useful function in maintaining the authority of particular moral commitments. Cultural constructions that mandate certain courses of behavior as desirable, as "moral," can be viewed not simply as subjective commitments or attitudes, but also as codes that consist of many symbolic elements with an underlying structure involving boundaries between moral objects and real programs, selves and actors, and realms of intentionality and inevitability. Any erosion or blurring of each boundary, therefore, constitutes an area in which one might look to identify potential crises in moral authority.

AMBIGUITIES IN SYMBOLIC BOUNDARIES

The importance of a clear set of symbolic boundaries can be seen by considering the functions that each boundary may perform in sustaining commitment to a morally valued set of activities. The boundary between the moral object and the real program essentially removes the object of moral commitment from empirical observation. Only the real program of concrete activities lies in the empirical realm. Consequently, it becomes possible to fulfill one's real program (or to fail), but it remains impossible either to fulfill or to fail at fulfilling one's moral responsibilities. Who can say, for example, whether one is actually serving God by daily reciting one's prayers? The prayers are observable, and one can succeed or fail in diligently reciting them; God is not observable. This is true as well in other instances in which the object of moral commitment is not a supernatural being. Who can ultimately say whether or not working hard at one's job is making the world a better place? Who can say whether or not meditation practices actually reveal one's "true self"? Generally the moral object remains hidden; only the real program can be seen.[13]

The virtue of this distinction is simply that it maintains commitment to the moral object. Because effects on the moral object cannot be measured, thinking that one is fulfilling moral obligations, whether one in fact is or not, remains possible. Were it possible to actually measure these effects, one would either succeed, and therefore have to push on to something else, or fail to the point of becoming discouraged and abandoning the struggle. But the special connected-but-separate relation between the moral object and the real program allows one to discharge one's duties without fear of empirical disconfirmation.[14]

How might this special distinction become blurred? One possibility is from what might loosely be termed "rationalization" (i.e., substituting the real program for the moral object).[15] In an effort to make behavior more rational, efficient, or utilitarian, unobservable values may be replaced by observable activities. Attending church takes precedence over serving God; getting a good job, over serving humanity; obeying one's guru, over seeking inner knowledge. Another possibility is through philosophical criticism of the relation between object and activity. If philosophical criticism suggests that God, after all, is not served by attending church, then uncertainties arise about the moral worth of this activity.

In either case, an erosion of the boundary between moral object and real program is likely to result in cynicism, which is the opposite of moral commitment. Conflation of object with activity leaves activity without deeper justification. Dissociation of the two opens possibilities for doubts about which activities are most worthy. Thus, it is the delicate—and subtle—symbolic distinction that must be maintained.

The boundary between self and actor also plays a significant role in maintaining moral commitment. It assists in sustaining self-worth and minimizing guilt. On the one hand, the fact that one does act—or, more appropriately, that one is *the actor*—means that a sense of self-worth can be derived from engaging in activities deemed to have moral value. The fundamentalist can derive self-worth from attending church; the breadwinner, from providing for his or her family; the seeker, from meditating. Yet the fact that one is *not* the actor—that one has a "true self" different from the roles one plays—means that self-worth is partially independent from role performance. One can fail, or be lazy, and not suffer total demoralization. The erosion of this distinction can obviously lead to a loss of self-worth, insecurity, and perhaps a restless need to prove oneself.[16]

Among the ways in which this boundary might be eroded, two seem especially pertinent. One is through the loss of institutionalized roles for dramatizing that one is in fact a moral person. These consist mainly of highly symbolic roles that one can generally perform without great sacrifice and without risk of failure. Roles such as contributor to charities or volunteer for worthy causes serve as examples. Generally these are *voluntary* activities—a fact that helps demonstrate the relation between role and self ("I chose to do this"). The fact that such roles often occur in the private sphere, where the real self presumably resides, also reinforces this connection (thus, it is more worthy to give of one's free time than to say "I gave at the office"). These roles, despite their voluntary nature, are generally readily available through institutionalized sources, such as churches, fund drives, and community organizations. But they can become scarce as a result of professionalization and bureaucratization. Shifting social service activities to professionals, such as clergy and social workers, can diminish the value of volunteer activities. And bureaucratization—or the rise of complex institutions generally—can make it difficult to believe that one's voluntary activities really make enough of a difference to be considered a source of self-worth.[17]

The other way in which the self / actor distinction can become eroded is through a loss of what might be termed "purification rituals." These rituals are like a maintenance crew that sweeps out the self, rids it of failures or blame, and shores up the boundary between it and the roles it plays. Guilt that arises from a conflation of self and compromised or failed role performances can simply be denied if such rituals are not available—a technique that may not, however, be entirely satisfactory. Although some argue that this has been the modern tendency, the continuous invention of new purification rituals suggests their importance. In recent years the resurgence of charismatic religious movements, in which cleansing and healing play a prominent role, provides a notable example. Another example is provided by the continued, if not rising, quest for intimacy—having close friends who tell us we are really okay.

The symbolic boundary between inevitability and intentionality bears most directly on the question of moral responsibility. One can be held accountable only for those activities and outcomes over which one exercises control. Having a realm governed by intentionality is essential to the concept of moral responsibility. Having a realm of inevitability is equally important because it limits this responsibility to manageable proportions. It defines areas over which one has no control and, therefore, cannot be held accountable. Moral codes that survive for any length of time are likely to include some way of limiting responsibility. Otherwise guilt would rise to intolerable levels.[18]

When the boundary between the inevitable and the intentional is unclear, arriving at or instilling a workable concept of moral decision making becomes difficult. One becomes unsure whether a particular act can truly be considered a matter of moral choice or not. The likely result is apathy or frustration.

One of the cultural changes that can make this boundary unclear is secularization—or changes in religious concepts more generally. Changes in concepts that define the degree of individual accountability to God can have particularly important ramifications. Theological, as well as legal, controversies over the conditions under which a person may be held accountable for criminal acts provide an illustration. Another source of boundary uncertainty that is particularly prominent in contemporary culture is the role of science in pushing back the frontiers of the inevitable through new knowledge. On the one hand, science's success in this area has raised high expectations, often making heroes of leading researchers, and has thereby extended questions of moral responsibility into vast new areas, such as biotechnology, euthanasia, and space defense initiatives. On the other hand, these expectations can be exaggerated and lead to frustration and apathy over issues such as nuclear weapons and energy conservation. Science has also in some ways added to the ambiguities in determining moral responsibility by advancing a deterministic theory of causation that locates responsibility primarily outside the individual.[19] Yet another area in which uncertainties over inevitability and intentionality have been evident is in social and geopolitical conditions. At one level, social systems may be seen as collective attempts to assert control over the geopolitical environment. But as conditions change, the extent of any particular society's control is often left in doubt. Border skirmishes, summit meetings, and military showdowns all have symbolic significance as attempts to clarify these relations.

Considerations such as these obviously range well beyond conceptions of morality having to do primarily with standards of individual conduct or moral dilemmas. Morality in the present sense deals primarily with moral commitment—commitment to an object, ranging from an abstract value to a specific person, that involves behavior, that contributes to a sense of self-worth, and that takes place within broad definitions of what is inevitable or intentional. Moral commitment, although in some ways deeply personal and subjective, also involves symbolic constructions—codes—that define these various relations.[20] These codes include symbolic boundaries that can at times become ambiguous. As such, these boundaries provide strategic locations for seeking potential areas of moral crisis or erosions of moral authority.

Returning briefly then to the discussions of moral crisis summarized at the beginning of the chapter, it can now be seen that most of these crises pertain to one or another of the symbolic boundaries under consideration. The problem of narcissism, for example, concerns most directly the boundary between self and actor. Particularly in Sennett's description, narcissism arises from an inadequate separation of the self from the roles one plays.[21] Solzhenitsyn's diagnosis of law and technique substituting for commitment to absolute values concerns the boundary between moral object and real program. Possibly, the uncertainty of how law and technique serve ultimate values raises questions of whether moral commitment to these procedures is justified or not. Bell's discussion of secularization, hedonism, and declining moral responsibility raises questions about both the self/actor and the object/program distinctions. And Habermas's emphasis on withdrawal from public institutions, as well as his analysis of legitimate questions raised by new state/economy relations, highlights areas in which the inevitable/intentional distinction has become ambiguous.

In order to consider in greater detail how these various symbolic boundaries figure into the maintenance of moral commitment, an extended application of the model is developed in the next section with reference to the question of moral commitment to behavior in the marketplace. This application will also permit some further considerations to be raised about how symbolic boundaries can become ambiguous.

APPLICATION: MORAL COMMITMENT IN THE MARKET

The assumption on which the present discussion rests is that the market system is more than simply a means of exchanging goods and services. It is, to be sure, a mechanism for establishing prices, a means of creating profits, and a system that promotes productivity. This is the standard view presented in economics textbooks. But, whether we consciously acknowledge it or not, the market system is for most of us something to which we are morally committed. It needs to be understood more broadly than in narrow economic terms. It is an integral aspect of our basic values and our assumptions about reality.

The market is inextricably woven into the daily activities from which we derive a sense of self-worth. We invest market behavior with moral importance. We associate the market system with some of our most cherished values or moral objects. We also perceive the market in the context of symbolic boundaries defining realms of intentionality and inevitability. It follows that any change in the fundamental principles of the market system, however subtle, is likely to threaten more than merely our material standard of living. An erosion of the market system may threaten the very fabric of moral commitment and challenge some of the cultural sources from which self-worth is derived.

As already noted, some observers of contemporary culture argue that a deep moral crisis has begun to be evident, and many signs of this crisis relate in one way or another to the market system. Pollsters point to high levels of alienation from business and to skepticism about the value of work. Others speak of a disjuncture between the economic realm and the values that once gave it legitimacy. Still others link the rise of narcissism to changes in the market system.

These kinds of arguments point clearly to the fact that the market system is more than simply a supply-demand price mechanism—that it is an arena in which questions about moral commitments occupy an important place. But it is, again, difficult to assess these kinds of arguments without some model of how moral commitments are constructed and maintained in the marketplace. The foregoing considerations suggest the outline for such a model. Following this outline, arguing that the marketplace represents one area in which we often attempt to fulfill the moral responsibilities we have to the society in which we live seems reasonable. In pursuing activities of the marketplace, we derive a sense of personal worth. This sense of worth is, in turn, one of the gratifications that sustains our loyalty to the economic system. Moreover, the marketplace is closely associated with one of the nation's highest values—freedom. By engaging in market behavior, we do something that appears to advance the cause of freedom. Market behavior serves as a "real program" that is connected to the "moral object" of freedom. This also sustains commitment to the market system. Finally, we operate in the context of certain cultural categories that give us an "out" when we are unable to fulfill our moral responsibilities through the market system. Together, these cultural constructions serve as a kind of moral code that governs behavior in the marketplace and bestows legitimacy on the economic system. Understanding this code is therefore one approach to assessing the malaise—the problem of legitimacy—that some have identified in contemporary capitalism.

As a more general point, this consideration of moral codes as cultural constructions will suggest an alternative way of conceptualizing the problem of legitimacy. In classical terms, the problem of legitimacy focuses on the question of when, and under what conditions, a given institution or set of social practices is deemed to be "right" or "proper" by some significant aggregate of actors. If legitimacy is present, actors will presumably commit themselves to maintaining the institution in question. Identifying the structure of the cultural codes that define the nature of this commitment is therefore crucial to understanding the problem of legitimacy. The present discussion suggests that legitimacy is likely to be present when the symbolic structure defining moral-actor / real-program, self / actor, and inevitability / intentionality distinctions is intact. These distinctions maintain commitment by providing ritualized occasions for discharging moral obligations and thereby acquiring a sense of moral worth. Legitimacy, in this view, is not simply or primarily a matter of subjective belief but is an exchange relation consisting of expenditures of resources in return for moral rewards—a relation that has symbolic aspects containing an identifiable structure comprised of symbolic boundaries.

To say that the market system has associated with it a legitimating "moral code" is not to suggest that this code accurately portrays the character of market relations themselves. The kind of choice that dramatizes our freedom in the marketplace is clearly constrained by the nature of market demand, the institutions in which work is embedded, differences in the opportunities available to different social classes, and so on. The moral code underlying behavior in the capitalist marketplace is in fact an ideology—a set of common utterances and symbolic acts that communicates a pattern of assumptions about the nature of commitment to the marketplace. As such, it not only reinforces commitment but also plays an important role in maintaining the peculiar power relations on which the capitalist system is based. In what follows, the manifestations of this ideology will, however, be isolated from its broader institutional setting in order to examine the structure implicit in the ideology itself.

THE MORALITY OF THE MARKETPLACE

The marketplace is fraught with moral connotations. This is true not only in the sense of economic behavior being surrounded by moral injunctions to act honestly, ethically, and with integrity. The marketplace is one of the arenas in modern society in which persons have an opportunity to participate directly in public life. Market activities, and possibly voting, actually constitute the major forms of public participation. Buying and selling, working and consuming link individuals to one another and to the overall collective purposes of the society. The market, therefore, provides an important means of discharging moral responsibilities to the society in which we live.

The founders of modern economic theory clearly recognized the moral characteristics of the marketplace. Adam Smith, the great eighteenth-century spokesman for laissez-faire economics, was as interested in moral philosophy as in economic theory. In his analysis, the free functioning market was an instrument not only of exchange but also of human betterment. As each individual buyer and each individual seller pursued their private interests in the marketplace, the "invisible hand" guaranteed that prosperity would accrue to all. Happily, what was good for the proverbial pin maker was good for England too. The moral dimension of Smith's theory was that the pin maker contributed to the good of society by making pins. If he withdrew from the market or hoarded his pins, he not only damaged his own interests as a businessman but also failed to keep the public trust. For this reason, he was morally beholden to participate in the market.

In the eighteenth century the marketplace was also thought to serve as a buttress to moral virtues by placing a check on humanity's most dangerous passions. By rationally and reflectively pursuing one's economic self-interests in the marketplace, one channeled one's natural passions into socially desirable activities. Without the market, one was likely to fall prey to avarice, lust, fanaticism, and caprice. But with the market, one became disciplined and virtuous.

These arguments also had political connotations. A strong market economy was conceived to be the best protection against the unruly designs of the powerful. It was a means of promoting both domestic and international peace by making social relations more predictable. In the turbulent context of the eighteenth century, the prospect of peace was a powerful argument in favor of the market system. And again, there was a moral to the argument: the market was delicate, like a fine clock; it needed to be treated with respect and devotion. By acting responsibly in the marketplace, citizens performed a moral duty as far as the society was concerned.

How much these philosophical arguments may have actually filtered into the consciousness of eighteenth-century merchants and industrialists remains a matter of conjecture. At minimum, historical evidence suggests that these arguments were not limited to academicians alone. As Hirschman (1977) has shown, publications of the day were filled with claims and counterclaims about the moral qualities of the market. In these publications and in legislative actions of the period, the market system was not advanced strictly in the name of economic progress; it was legitimated in the name of individual and social well-being, for which participants in the marketplace were morally responsible.

During the nineteenth century the market system came to be such a pervasive feature of social life, not only in Europe and America but also on a worldwide scale, that it scarcely needed to be defended with moral arguments—it was simply a fact of life. Yet many of the earlier assumptions about the moral qualities of the marketplace lingered on and received new vitality. In the United States the market system was regarded as a source of freedom and dignity for the individual. The famous McGuffey readers, on which more than 150 million schoolchildren were reared, extolled the virtues of the marketplace as a means of building moral character. And in the popular "rags-to-riches" stories of the period, such as those of Horatio Alger and Russell Conwell, it was by struggling in the marketplace that one discovered one's talents, developed character, and contributed to the good of the society. Never in this literature was the market portrayed simply as an economic device.

These historical arguments probably do not carry the weight they once did. But they have contemporary counterparts. In subtle ways the market continues to be perceived in moral terms. Notions of character and simple moral virtues have been replaced by modern concepts of the self that stress social responsibility and the pursuit of self-esteem. But the need to think of ourselves as morally upstanding individuals has scarcely diminished. The market continues to be portrayed as one of the arenas in which we can, and must, demonstrate our moral responsibility.

The best-seller lists include moralistic treatises defending the market system, describing it as the only way of protecting the free world and the affluent life, and challenging us to be devoted to it. The news media and policy discussions also provide vivid dramatizations of the market's moral dimension. Consumers are called on to conserve energy in order to reduce dependence on foreign oil. In impassioned ethical pleas we are asked to buy American goods, to regulate our spending habits, to avoid hoarding and speculation. Presidents and their advisors characterize economic policies in moral terms, sometimes describing them as the moral equivalents of war, calling on breadwinners to sacrifice in order to conquer the enemy, and pitting the friends and foes of the free market against one another in a battle fraught with moral symbolism.

In these ways behavior in the marketplace is given moral significance. Consumer activity is defined in such a way that it cannot be considered purely a private matter; it affects the very well-being of the society. How one behaves is more than a matter of strict economic calculation; it is a way of acting responsibly toward the larger society.

The way in which moral commitments are symbolized in the culture is also demonstrated by the kinds of "moral crusades" in which we engage. In the past these crusades have included a mixed lot of move-

ments, ranging from Abolition, the Temperance movement, and various
nativistic movements against Jews and Catholics, to the more recent
struggle for civil rights. At present, the pro-family and anti-abortion
movements sponsored by such groups as the Moral Majority and the
Conservative Caucus provide visible examples of moral crusades. These
are movements that impute moral meaning to various dimensions of
public life.

In recent years America has witnessed a growing number of moral
crusades that have as their focus not the family or personal conduct, but
the marketplace. We have experienced the consumer protection movement, the environmental movement, and the antismoking campaign.
We have also witnessed the antinuclear movement, collective pressures
for equal employment and fair housing, and drives to control advertis-
ing and clean up television. Common to all these crusades has been the
assumption that the marketplace is an important focus for moral behavior. Whether to smoke cigarettes, to recycle beer cans, or to install solar
collectors become decisions of moral, as well as economic, significance.

What is the relevance of these moral claims to the legitimacy of the
market system? Let us assume that people prefer to think of themselves
as good and decent persons, as morally upright individuals, rather than
purely calculating utilitarians. If this is a reasonable assumption, then
the marketplace influences in fundamental ways how we think about
ourselves. We need ways to demonstrate that we are morally responsible in order to maintain our sense of self-worth. Activities that give us
these opportunities are likely to evoke commitment and sentiments of legitimacy because they give us this sense of well-being.

Economic actor is a role that individuals play in the marketplace. This
role is not synonymous with the self, but it is connected to the self. It also
has moral connotations. Performing this role responsibly becomes a way
of gaining a sense of moral worth for the self. The fact that market behavior has moral connotations means that marketplace activity is not simply
neutral with respect to the self. It potentially contributes self-worth, not
only from the satisfaction one might gain from performing any task competently, but also because these economic activities are linked symbolically to the public good.

In the past, military service, kinship obligations, religion, and philan-
thropy provided ways of demonstrating that one was a morally upright
individual. Although these activities continue to fulfill this function in
limited ways, the marketplace has come increasingly to play a major
role in our efforts to demonstrate to ourselves and to others that we are

moral persons. The great advantage of the market, compared with strictly voluntary activities, is that it conveniently combines activities that have to be performed to maintain one's standard of living with opportunities for moral display—being a responsible consumer, conserving energy, contributing to national prosperity, exercising one's "voice" in the marketplace.[22] As a result, commitment to the market system stems only in part from sheer economic necessity or from convictions about the market as a rational economic system. In addition, the legitimacy and stability of the market system rests on the fact that we obtain a sense of self-worth from fulfilling our moral responsibilities by participating in the market.

This assumes that the market actually provides opportunities to demonstrate convincingly that we are fulfilling our moral obligations. This is the catch. Such opportunities must, in fact, be present. It does little good, insofar as generating loyalty to the market is concerned, to set up moral obligations that cannot be fulfilled. We need ways to act out our moral obligations, if only in ritual forms, if we are to maintain our sense of worth as morally responsible individuals.

In any evaluation of the strength of the market system, an important question to be kept in mind, therefore, is whether the market actually does provide opportunities for fulfilling moral obligations or whether it somehow inhibits the performance of these duties. As suggested earlier, one of the ways in which the self / actor connection can become problematic is for the ritualized opportunities that permit actors to demonstrate their moral worth as persons to be institutionalized out of existence.

CAPITALISM AND FREEDOM

The relation between capitalism and freedom serves as an example of market activities, as a real program of observable activity, being linked with a highly valued moral object. Linking institutional arrangements of any kind with the highest values of a society is obviously a useful way to legitimate those arrangements. Apologists for the market system have often utilized the value of freedom in this manner. In the name of freedom, government intervention in the economy is opposed, private enterprise is extolled, and the open market is defended. Some go farther. In Milton Friedman's (1962) view, for example, the free market provides the only sure protection for freedom of speech, freedom of religion, and freedom of thought.

But it is of little value to assert a relation between capitalism and freedom unless that relation is carefully articulated and understood. The concept of freedom assists in the day-to-day legitimation of the market system, not so much by linking economic activity with abstract political philosophy as by providing further reinforcement to the sense of moral worth that individuals derive from the marketplace. This particular usage of the concept of freedom has come into prominence only in relatively recent times.

Among societies in which a fully developed market economy has not yet appeared, freedom has generally been understood as an attribute of *groups*. In traditional India, for example, individuals thought themselves "free" insofar as they occupied a clearly defined rank within the hierarchical structure of the caste system.[23] Studies of other traditional, archaic, and primitive societies suggest that even where trade was relatively well developed, as among the Polynesian islanders and in the Greek city-states, freedom was not associated with the individual merchant or trader but with the people collectively.

To the American colonists, freedom took on a distinctively collective cast rather than individualistic connotations. The freedom they valued most dearly was freedom from external domination by totalitarian monarchies. To the colonists this freedom was symbolized by opportunities to worship, to create standards of government, and to build new institutions deemed fitting for the New World. But these were collective enterprises. The Puritans and Calvinists of the seventeenth and eighteenth centuries were not the Protestant individualists of the nineteenth century. Freedom from external constraint meant close conformity to internal restraint, often on pain of expulsion or threat of divine punishment. The new land would remain free, the Puritan settlers often reminded themselves, only as long as the religious ideals on which their settlements were founded were strictly and collectively obeyed.

As the market economy grew to prominence during the nineteenth century, the earlier understanding of freedom underwent subtle modification. It ceased to be associated with the collective institutions of the American people and came increasingly to be associated with individuals. It was the rugged individualist on the American frontier, the heroic woodsman, the pioneer, the robust farmer who most symbolized freedom. Freedom came to mean self-sufficiency. One no longer needed to move in groups or cultivate close ties with neighbors and kin. To be sure, kinship and ethnic identities did not die easily, but now the market, rather than communal groups, provided an outlet for one's produce and a source of material necessities. As the market expanded, it symbolized the growth of individual autonomy, of freedom.

But self-sufficiency and autonomy, as definitions of freedom, could not survive without some revision against the growing social complexity that came to be felt with the rise of large-scale industry. Contrary to what some observers have argued, the growth of complex bureaucratic institutions did not erode the concept of freedom so much as give it a different meaning. No longer were free individuals able to think of themselves as purely separate creatures, like grains of sand on the seashore. Instead, freedom came to mean knowing one's place and knowing that one was functionally related to other individuals and groups.

The relations among individuals came increasingly, as Mary Douglas (1970) has suggested, to resemble those of a grid in which each cell was occupied by an individual. Each individual was unique as far as location in the grid was concerned, but these individuals were also related to one another in definite patterns. Often the idea of a grid was more than mere metaphor. The modern economy actually created cells—cubicles, offices, places on assembly lines—that shaped the modern image of the person (cf. Foucault, 1979). The identity of the person came to rest not so much on being self-sufficient but on having a unique function to fulfill in some larger organization or system.

In highly regimented settings such as these—assembly lines, military organizations, bureaucracies—the individual's functions are closely prescribed. But in an increasing number of contexts, such as professional and middle management positions, the individual exercises discretion in fulfilling his or her functions, and the individual's freedom is most clearly manifest in these acts of discretion. In setting priorities, in choosing among possible courses of action, in selecting jobs or career lines, and in making decisions as a consumer, the individual dramatizes his or her freedom. Freedom in the contemporary marketplace, in short, essentially means the *right to choose*. This is the immediate, tangible connection between capitalism and freedom.

Why is this type of freedom valued? In part, the right to choose represents freedom to explore personal talents and desires. It derives from fundamental considerations about the value and dignity of the individual. But this is only part of the story—and perhaps not even the most important part because many persons seem willing to give up much of their individuality in favor of conformity to collective norms.

What the right to choose dramatizes, even if that right is sometimes relinquished, is that one can be held responsible for one's own actions. Responsibility for an action can be imputed to an individual only if he or she could have chosen to do otherwise. If the sergeant calls out an order to march, for example, the soldier can take little credit for "deciding" to march. But if someone voluntarily decides to purchase and maintain a home, that person has shown responsibility. In exercising that responsibility, the person can take pride in knowing that he or she has acted as a moral self.

Freedom is important to moral obligations, then, because the idea of moral obligations implies, as noted before, voluntary action. If the market is to sustain a person's loyalty by nurturing that person's image as being good and decent, it must not only provide opportunities to discharge moral obligations; it must also demonstrate that the person is *free* and can therefore be held responsible for his or her actions. The legitimacy of the market system depends on its capacity to provide this sense of freedom.

It is probably fortunate that the concept of freedom, like other moral objects, remains somewhat vague. Generally it is poorly enough defined that we have considerable difficulty determining whether the market system actually reinforces personal and collective freedom or not. There are no standard, easily measurable criteria with which to assess freedom, unlike more specific economic concepts such as GNP or disposable income. Instead, there is simply the sense that making choices among the various products, services, and opportunities provided by the market constitutes freedom. As individuals experience discretion in their jobs or make choices as consumers, their freedom is likely to be dramatized to them far more vividly than if they thought about it as an abstract civic value. This is the "real," experienced freedom that pushes into the background more abstract questions about freedom, such as the issues of freedom for the poor, for those who cannot or who choose not to participate in the marketplace, or for those whose tastes are not represented by the market. The contemporary version of freedom is real enough that it is difficult to invalidate. This is why freedom remains such an important legitimating concept for contemporary capitalism.

Summarizing briefly, it has been suggested thus far that we have a fundamental desire to think of ourselves as good and decent, morally responsible individuals. Consequently, we seek out symbolic activities that allow us to demonstrate our goodness, decency, and moral responsibility—activities that contribute self-worth in these areas. These activities must occur in settings in which individuals feel themselves to be free, that is, capable of making choices, for only if there is choice can we take personal credit for our behavior. By acting responsibly in these settings, we obtain a sense of personal gratification. Our self-worth is affirmed. The gratification we receive, in turn, motivates us to continue participating in these activities and to regard them as legitimate forms of behavior. Our participation is maintained as a moral commitment. The marketplace is one of the chief sources of this type of gratification. The culture is constructed in such a way that we are able to fulfill moral obligations when we participate in the marketplace. As we go about our business, we think of ourselves neither as conniving utilitarians nor as evil capitalists, but as moral persons engaged in socially useful activities. We also are convinced that we are acting freely, voluntarily, because the marketplace permits us to make choices. This participation contributes to our sense of personal worth. And we, in turn, feel that the market system is worthy of our time and devotion.

ECONOMIC REALITIES

An additional set of assumptions also assists both in maintaining the connection between capitalism and freedom and in sustaining the conviction that we are acting as morally responsible individuals when we participate in the marketplace. This set of cultural constructions tells us, essentially, that there are certain economic forces over which we cannot be expected to have control. These forces are simply the laws of nature. Whenever our most conscientious choices lead to unexpected and undesired outcomes, we can blame these laws. The laws of nature define a realm of inevitability that limits the realm of intentionality, and they give us an excuse that limits self-blame. In this way we are able to maintain the fiction that we are morally responsible persons, even when evil results from our well-intentioned activities.

Like other moral codes, that of the marketplace limits guilt rather than simply creating sources of guilt. It holds individuals responsible for their choices but also absolves them of guilt by providing an explanation for failings in the system. This explanation consists largely of the concept of economic laws that are assumed to have their own objective reality, to operate according to their own principles, functioning in ways only partly comprehensible even to economists.

For us to be able to blame our failings in the marketplace on economic laws, it helps that these laws are objectified. They are understood as realities with an existence of their own, as forces or beings not subject to human control or manipulation. Just as the devil is objectified in other moral codes, so economic laws take on a reality of their own in the marketplace. In popular discourse, for example, the economy is often objectified in terms giving it the characteristics of an ominous, willful, living creature. The economy gets "sick," "recovers," falls into a "slump," "straightens itself out," "awakens," and "revives." Like earthly beings, interest rates "climb," inflation "soars," and productivity "staggers." More passively, the economy experiences "spurts," suffers "blows," and sustains "shocks." And finally, the caretakers of the economy, like wise physicians caring for an ailing patient, seek "remedies," attempt to "heal" the economy, and maintain its "health."

This kind of language livens up the newspapers. But it also plays an important role in sustaining moral commitment in the marketplace. These characterizations make the economy into something "out there" for which we cannot be held morally accountable. Propagandists know that the most effective way of legitimating an idea is to make it seem natural, inevitable. A mere idea is an extension of ourselves. It can be questioned: Is it right? Could it have been otherwise? A fact of the world, in contrast, simply exists. It stands outside the realm of choice. Therefore individuals need not blame themselves when something goes wrong. Such problems, after all, are simply built into the economy.

In contemporary culture the market system has largely been taken for granted as a feature of reality itself. It has been portrayed, as Polanyi (1977) has argued, in terms that can be characterized as an "economistic fallacy." This fallacy consists of assuming that the market system, as we know it, operates according to generic economic laws found in all societies. In other words, one manifestation of economic life is reified by equating it with economic life in general. Although all societies have had economies, the market system is but one form of economic organization. Due to its massiveness, complexity, and longevity, we may think it is simply a fact of nature. But it is a humanly constructed institution just as surely as democracy, communism, and the mass media are constructed institutions. There is, Polanyi suggests, nothing inevitable about it.

Yet we continue to think of the market economy as an inevitable fact of nature because this assumption limits the realm of moral responsibility. In a sense, we find restrictions on our freedom of action useful because we cannot then be held accountable for everything that may happen. Consumers can excuse themselves for not saving more of their income. Large corporations can excuse themselves for not making a profit. Even presidents are prone to point out their inability to perform economic "miracles" (although they are quick to take credit when seeming miracles do occur). Given the economic laws to which we are all subject, we need think no less of ourselves for not doing better.

THE QUESTION OF CRISIS

The implication of this kind of analysis is that the legitimacy of the market system rests on more than its productive capacity alone. The American system derives support from a number of cultural constructions that, in combination, sustain the convictions of those who participate in it that they are good and decent persons. These assumptions do not require formal adherence, as if to a creed, doctrine, or philosophical outlook. They are built into the fabric of the culture itself.

To recap, the marketplace provides an arena in which some of the moral obligations we incur as members of the society can be fulfilled. The capacity to make choices in the marketplace provides an object lesson in the relation between capitalism and freedom, however impoverished this concept of freedom may be. The notion of economic realities, in turn, limits this freedom, defining realistically attainable areas over which moral responsibility can be exercised. Together these assumptions provide security against doubt and cynicism—doubt that what we are doing is right and cynicism about the worth of commitment to the system as a whole.

Historians suggest that the market system gradually acquired these connotations during the eighteenth and nineteenth centuries. As the marketplace spread, incorporating more of the adult population in the production of goods and services for commercial exchange, it came to be an important source of moral meaning and self-worth. Indeed, some historians (Polanyi, for example) argue that by the end of the nineteenth century the market system had become the single most important institution, dominating both the broader organization of social life and the outlook of the average citizen. That the market has continued to play a significant role in the twentieth century goes without saying.

As indicated previously, however, some observers believe that the market system may be experiencing a crisis of moral commitment. Therefore, we must consider how the legitimating symbols—the moral code—of the marketplace figure in this crisis. The question at issue is whether larger events in the society or world are eroding these symbolic constructions in some significant fashion.

An affirmative answer—although different arguments can also be constructed—can be developed primarily by considering the effects that technology may be having on the moral code of the marketplace. In simple terms, it is arguable that the economy's growing dependence on technology threatens to undermine each of the basic symbolic boundaries comprising the moral code of the marketplace. With this development, the legitimacy of the market system and its capacity to generate moral commitment would also seem likely to be in danger. Several subsequent scenarios are conceivable: (1) technology could generate its own moral code and become a significant new basis of moral commitment; (2) technology and the market system could prove sufficiently compatible in the long run to reinvigorate moral commitment to both; (3) the two could exist in sufficient tension with each other that moral commitments would remain uncertain for some time to come. Which of these scenarios is most likely is not the matter at issue, however. Indeed, the relations between technology and the market system are probably sufficiently varied that no single scenario is likely to prove entirely accurate. What a consideration of the effects of technology provides is an occasion to examine in a specific context some of the ways in which symbolic structures may become eroded.

The moral worth traditionally obtained from participating in the marketplace has evidently already become precarious in some ways. The growing complexity of the marketplace makes it increasingly difficult for individuals to sustain the idea that their participation contributes in any significant way to the public good. Participation in the marketplace becomes less significant, in other words, as a ritualized means of discharging one's moral obligations to the society. As a result, the activities from which moral gratification is obtained tend increasingly to be relocated, as Habermas suggests, in the "private" realms—family, leisure, and voluntary associations. These are the realms in which participation still appears to make a discernible difference. To some extent, this tendency may have been slowed by the professionalization of the work force. That is, professionalization redefines work as "career," thereby suggesting that intrinsic fulfillment can be expected from work. But even among professionals, intrinsic commitment to working has declined precipitously (Blackwood, 1979).[24]

Although the meaning of these changes is not yet clear, there are indications that technology is coming to be imbued with the kind of moral force that used to be associated with the marketplace. Consider, for example, the accomplishments in which we take pride as a people: going to the moon, medical research, sophisticated defense systems, improvements in transportation and communication, breakthroughs in laser technology, the latest generation of supercomputers. Or consider what gives a sense of personal accomplishment: having made some small contribution at work to the development of these technological feats, being knowledgeable enough to discuss them intelligently, reaping the benefit from these accomplishments as consumers (of home computers, microwave ovens, videodiscs, and other gadgets), and taking satisfaction in educating our children to understand better the mysteries of science and technology.

The moral crusades that have been mobilized again indicate the nature of moral commitments. Although the marketplace continues to be the focus of some of these crusades, an increasing number have come to be oriented toward technology. Even as more people find moral satisfaction from contributing to the production of high technology, a smaller number attribute the highest moral importance to opposing the dangers of technology—nuclear annihilation, risks associated with nuclear energy, drugs making abortion and euthanasia easier. Moral Majority and similar groups have seized on these issues.

The idea of freedom has also been affected by the rising prominence of technology. The discussion of freedom increasingly centers around questions of technology rather than the marketplace as such. Although the marketplace dramatizes freedom of choice, awareness has increased that the production, consumption, and prices of goods represent more in most cases than autonomous individuals freely exercising personal preferences. The complexity and interdependence of the economy has in a sense eroded the connection between freedom as a moral object and behavior in the marketplace. In its place, technology seems to have become increasingly connected with freedom. We look to technology to expand our choices. Technology dramatizes both the highest capacity for expanding our freedom and one of the greatest potential threats to freedom. On one issue after another—birth control pills, abortion, genetic screening, gender selection, solar energy, fusion research, labor-saving consumer products, information-processing systems—technology symbolizes new freedoms and poses new threats to old freedoms. Insofar as freedom continues to be a cherished moral object, therefore, the real program that gains legitimacy from being associated with it is likely to be technology rather than the traditional marketplace.

Finally, the notion of economic realities that are simply there as "givens" in the world of nature and that serve as excuses when our best moral intentions go awry also appears to be undergoing a subtle redefinition. The growing importance of fiscal planning by government agencies and private firms alike renders it increasingly difficult to sustain the assumption that economic realities are simply "there," given in the nature of things, and that human decisions share no responsibility for their existence. As planning agencies assume responsibility for the economy, they also become susceptible to charges of culpability, ineptness, and moral failure. These agencies and their leaders are increasingly held accountable for failings in the economic system.

As the market system becomes fraught with ambiguities about the boundary between inevitability and intentionality, technology again acquires greater cultural significance in relation to this boundary. Technology comes to symbolize not only new freedoms but also areas that are beyond freedom and moral responsibility. Just as the idea of economic realities did at one time, so the notion of "technical capacity" now provides an excuse when our morally respectable intentions do not produce the desired effects. Because our technical capacity is limited, we pay what we do for oil and electricity, we must take risks in experimenting with nuclear power, and we cannot avoid the danger of nuclear war. Rather than having to take blame for moral indiscretions as managers, breadwinners, or consumers, we can attribute these problems to "the state of the art."

In defining an area of inevitability, technology has the added advantage of being regarded as a function of nature and scientific laws. We may no longer be as confident as in the past that the market system reflects the laws of nature, but we can believe that technology rests on proven evidence about the world itself. Hence, we can legitimate much of our dependence on technology by virtue of the argument that things are just "that way." With more knowledge and newer technologies, we may be able to expect more, but at present our limitations are excusable.

Technology, then, promises to become not only an institution of increasing economic importance, but also one having its own legitimating moral code. Our sense of moral worth, as we discharge moral obligations, as we conceive of ourselves as free individuals capable of acting responsibly, and as we recognize limitations on our freedom and responsibility, can become associated with the growing importance of technology. Technology, in turn, acquires legitimacy, not simply as a buttress of economic progress, but also because our sense of self-worth becomes attached to it.

In addition to the cultural consequences that the relations among technology, the market system, and moral commitments may have, this case also suggests an important feature of the symbolic boundaries that define the structure of moral codes. These boundaries are not only points of potential erosion and ambiguity; they are also potential points of decoupling and recoupling. In the present case, this is most evident in the connection between freedom and the marketplace. As the marketplace ceases to dramatize freedom, technology replaces it. A new program of observable activity acquires a connection with an established moral object. That this type of replacement can occur is again a function of symbolic distinctions. If the marketplace were synonymous with freedom, then an erosion of the former would lead automatically to an erosion of the latter as well. As long as the two are connected but separate, one can fall into doubt and be replaced by a different set of activities without radically disturbing the other.[25] The idea of symbolic boundaries therefore provides insight into some of the ways in which cultural systems maintain their flexibility.

CONCLUSION

Commitments to particular courses of action, whether to religious fundamentalism or to participation in the marketplace, are cultural constructions that have an identifiable structure consisting of symbolic boundaries. When properly articulated, these boundaries connect, but also keep separate, the concepts of moral object and real program, self and actor, intentionality and inevitability. In the example of moral commitment to the marketplace, market behavior is a real program that is closely connected, yet distinct from, the higher moral object of freedom; the role of economic actor is defined as a way of realizing the worth of one's "true self," even though this role is recognized as not entirely identical with the "true self"; and the notion of economic realities defines a realm of inevitability that limits the realm of intentionality and thereby restricts the scope of actors' moral responsibility. If social circumstances change sufficiently to make any of these symbolic distinctions ambiguous, as some indications suggest has happened in the marketplace, then a sense of uncertainty or "moral crisis" may come to be associated with the commitments at issue.

As an illustration of the structural approach to culture, this discussion has tried to demonstrate that even something as seemingly subjective as moral commitment can be examined, not as a set of beliefs locked away in someone's head, but as a relatively observable set of cultural constructions. The advantage of viewing moral commitments as cultural codes, it has been argued, is that materials can be taken from readily available sources, such as discourse and ritualistic behavior, without having to assume that one is tapping into the inner meaning of these materials. This example also illustrates the structural approach's quest for generalizable knowledge. Just as one might try to identify recurrent patterns in the exchange relations among social classes, so one attempts to specify orderly relations among the elements composing a cultural code. Here, the notion of symbolic boundaries has supplied a rudimentary model of "structure" that seems to have some generality for analyzing moral codes of quite different substantive content.

The present example also illustrates some of the limitations of the structural approach. Even though the approach strives for observable data, it in no way succeeds in generating positivistic knowledge. The analyst exercises discretion both in selecting the cultural elements on which to focus and in imposing categories on these elements. The kinds of symbolic boundaries on which attention has focused are clearly theoretical constructs rather than intrinsic attributes of the data. In short, structural analysis is inevitably interpretive. A further limitation of this approach is that it ostensibly tries to deal with culture in a social vacuum; it purports to focus only on the internal structure of cultural codes. Yet ideas about the broader social context—here, about capitalism, American history, technology, and so forth—constantly have to be brought into the analysis in order to make any theoretical sense of the data. The structural approach, it appears, begs to be related more systematically to the social context in which culture operates. The next chapter, taking the relations between ritual and moral order as a model, suggests a way of bringing social contexts back in.

CHAPTER FOUR

Ritual and Moral Order

Mary Douglas has written that the term "ritual" has become "a bad word signifying empty conformity" (1970:19). In her view this is not only a mistaken but also an unfortunate understanding of the term. Modern society cries out for a sense of community, for an enlivened spirit of commitment to moral obligations. All around are signs of fragmentation into purely self-interested competing social units, from the selfish individual to the self-serving nation-state. Yet the role of ritual, both actual and potential, in maintaining moral order has gone largely unrecognized. Although ritual is profoundly important in all the world's great religions and is found in every society and in virtually every aspect of social life, its character and functioning remain poorly understood. To the enlightened Westerner, ritual is simply a bad word, a troublesome vestige of some other time and place, or a symptom of personal maladjustment. It remains shrouded in stereotyped imagery even among otherwise educated people. Indeed, the stereotypic quality of the word itself is evident in the contradictory usages to which it is generally put.

On the one hand, the idea of ritual conjures up stereotyped conceptions of wildly emotional, frenetic activity. Half-naked primitive tribesmen dance before our eyes, mutilating their flesh in hopes of appeasing the demonic requests of animistic spirit-gods. Navaho Indians rise up in our imaginations ready to perform frenzied rites under the mind-numbing influence of peyote, hoping to revitalize some long lost civilization. Perhaps the anthropologist is to blame for these conceptions. Most of the best research on rituals has, of course, been done by anthropologists, often in primitive or emotionally charged settings.[1] But modern rituals are also tainted by these impressions of emotion-laden irrationality. The mass media graphically capitalizes on the collective hysteria of a ritual like the Super Bowl; introductory social science texts show pictures of saffron-robed Hare Krishnas dancing themselves into blind oblivion; educational films recount adventures in snake-handling cults in order to tell freshmen what ritual is all about.

On the other hand, mention of the word "ritual"—and especially the adjective "ritualistic"—evokes the image of perfunctory, meaningless routine. This connotation is almost exactly the opposite of the first. White-collar Christians sit impassively in Sunday morning worship services performing their duties to God "ritualistically." Daily life becomes habitual and unthinking, a matter of performing "rituals"—brushing one's teeth, driving to work, going through the motions without knowing or caring why. Robert Merton's (1968) discussion of ritual (in his much-cited essay on anomie) exemplifies this perspective. For Merton, ritual consists of blind conformity to standard social practices without really believing in the values and principles underlying them.

Both these popular conceptions of ritual, contradictory as they are, cannot possibly be correct. The essence of ritual cannot be captured by crazed emotionality if the same concept creates visions of impassive routine. Neither view tells very much about ritual or its role and importance in modern society. We would indeed be wise to reject ritual if these notions told the whole story.

THE NATURE OF RITUAL

What is needed is a concept of ritual that transcends these popular stereotypes—a concept that identifies an important dimension of social life even in the modern context. Let us begin, rejecting at least temporarily both of the stereotypic images of ritual, by simply listing some widely diverse kinds of activities:

tribal dances	jury trials
the Eucharist	revolutions
Muslim prayers	etiquette
brushing one's teeth	weddings
turn signals	holidays
political witch-hunts	protocol

By taking a list intentionally this diverse, we can begin to develop a concept of ritual that may have fairly broad applicability. Some of the activities listed here clearly seem to qualify, even on the surface, as examples of ritual. Others will take more careful consideration.

We can partially grasp the nature of ritual by contrasting some of the more obvious candidates on the list with some kinds of behavior that would in all likelihood not qualify as examples of ritual. Take, for example, the contrast between a wedding and repairing a flat tire. What is the essential difference? It is emphatically *not* a difference in the level of emotion involved. The anger and frustration associated with fixing a tire may be as intense as the joy or anxiety experienced at a wedding. Or both may elicit little more than mechanical activity. The difference between getting married and fixing a tire, as far as ritual is concerned, lies essentially in the fact that a wedding is structured to evoke and communicate meanings, whereas fixing a tire does not have this as one of its primary or alleged purposes. The music, physical arrangements, and preparation involved in a wedding ceremony are carefully structured to elicit and convey deep emotion, even if emotion is not naturally present. The same activities express beliefs about the nature and value of marriage and in most cases about religious values. These activities also communicate to the various parties involved that a redefinition of social relations has occurred, that consent has been obtained, and that good wishes are in order.

EXPRESSIVITY

This example illustrates the expressivity or communication involved in ritual. Ritual in this sense is a kind of symbol, or more specifically, a set of symbolic acts. Acts are symbolic if they stand for something else, if they communicate meanings rather than being performed for purely practical or instrumental purposes. Thus, in order to understand ritual, we must examine the nature of the communication process involved. The activities of which ritual consists cannot be understood on the surface alone. They communicate deeper meanings, often through subtle and implicit messages. Ritual is an aspect of culture.

The expressive quality of ritual has been acknowledged in much of the literature on this subject. This quality, however, has often been misconstrued. Noting that rituals involve expressive behavior, many observers have argued that the chief purpose of ritual is to express emotion and that the presence of deep anxieties, fears, or other feelings is likely to result in ritual activity.[2] The purpose of ritual has been depicted as one of coping with emotions, either by providing opportunities to vent them or by involving people in such routine details that their fears were forgotten. This was largely the position taken by Malinowski in his work on the rites and beliefs of the Trobriand Islanders.[3] Noting the hatred and anger, the frustrations of courtship and love, the anxieties and dangers involved in seeking subsistence and waging warfare in primitive societies, Malinowski (1925:30–31) concluded,

> Magical ritual, most of the principles of magic, most of its spells and substances, have been revealed to man in those passionate experiences which assail him in the impasses of his instinctive life and of his practical pursuits, in those gaps and breaches left in the ever-imperfect wall of culture which he erects between himself and the besetting temptations and dangers of his destiny.

As vivid evidence of the role of fear and frustration in generating ritual, Malinowski observed that the Trobrianders engaged in far more elaborate ceremonies when preparing to go fishing on the high seas, where the risks were severe, than they did when planning to fish in the shallow lagoons. Other observers who have taken essentially the same position include W. Lloyd Warner (1974) in his discussion of death anxieties as a stimulus to the celebration of Memorial Day services and Hugh Trevor-Roper (1967) in his discussion of frustration and scapegoating as an element in religious witch trials.

A more accurate rendition of the idea of expressivity is simply that communication is taking place.[4] The content of this communication may have to do with emotions, but it may also be strictly intellectual. Lectures in a Unitarian church on the concept of God qualify as rituals no less than do the emotional gatherings of Pentecostalists. A jury trial is clearly one of the central rites of the modern system of jurisprudence; yet the symbolic meanings it communicates may have very little to do with expressing emotions.

AN ANALYTIC DISTINCTION

Another common misconception is one that assumes ritual to be a distinct *category* of behavior. There are clearly some examples that qualify as distinctly ritualistic behavior. Weddings are one. National and religious holidays are another. In these cases the ritual activities are sharply demarcated from ordinary behavior. But consider etiquette. Although gestures such as exchanging "hello's" and "good-bye's" or opening doors for one another are merely stripped-down versions of the more elaborate ceremonies of public life, they blend in with other activities and, as Erving Goffman's work has shown, perform many instrumental functions in social interaction in addition to their expressive functions.[5] Or, to take a more extreme example, fixing a flat tire may involve symbolic communication in addition to whatever utilitarian motives may have necessitated it (e.g., the activity may communicate one's value to friends or family). By the same token, even an activity as clearly symbolic as a wedding may have utilitarian undertones (e.g., avoiding the embarrassment of pregnancy out of wedlock or ensuring the continuity of a dynasty).

Thus, the distinction between expressive and instrumental activity is not a hard-and-fast rule that can be used to divide the world into two categories. The distinction is, rather, an *analytic* distinction that allows activities to be arranged along a continuum, from those at one end that are primarily expressive to those at the other end that are primarily instrumental.[6] Most behavior falls somewhere in the middle, having aspects that are expressive and aspects that are instrumental. For example, meals are heavily imbued with both; exams may be largely instrumental but also communicate symbolic messages; holidays may be largely symbolic but also have instrumental dimensions.

The fact that expressivity and instrumentality represent an analytic continuum has important implications for the study of ritual. Ritual is not a *type* of social activity that can be set off from the rest of the world for special investigation. It is a *dimension* of all social activity. The study of ritual, therefore, is not distinguished by its concern with certain types of activity, but by the perspective it brings to bear on all activity, namely, emphasis on the symbolic or expressive dimension of behavior. For example, Meyer and Rowan (1977) examine the formal structure of complex organizations as ceremonial behavior. Their analysis differs from most investigations of organizations in that they do not regard formal structure merely as a way of getting work done, of allocating authority and responsibility, or of dividing tasks into manageable units. Instead, they argue that formal structure communicates important messages to other organizations in the same industry or environment. Having a department concerned with work safety, for instance, communicates to labor unions, the state, and other firms that an organization is respectable, law-abiding, and in compliance with industry norms. Here the distinction between purely instrumental and expressive dimensions of behavior is relatively sharp. A department of safety may perform instrumental activities, such as monitoring accidents or teaching workers about safety regulations. Whether it does any of these things, however, its very existence expresses something about the identity and social position of the firm. These messages may be as important for the organization's survival as the performance of its instrumental tasks. Ritual, then, is an aspect of complex organizations as much as it is of the primitive rites or religious ceremonies that have more typically been the focus of investigation.

This example also illustrates that ritual need not necessarily be a special or sacred event set off from everyday reality. This is a common misperception rooted in the fact that holidays, festivals, and religious rites have served as the prototypes for discussions of ritual. In his classic work on primitive ritual, Durkheim suggested that an integral feature of ritual was its capacity to separate the individual from everyday reality. "They are," he wrote in describing the participants in primitive ritual, "so far removed from their ordinary conditions of life, and they are so thoroughly conscious of it, that they must set themselves outside of and above their ordinary morals" (1973:179). For Durkheim, ritual set off a sacred realm and sharply delineated it from the defiling elements of the profane. But more systematic attention to the concept of ritual reveals that Durkheim's description holds only for certain kinds of rituals. It applies well to those ceremonial occasions that are designed especially for expressive purposes. On these occasions holding back the instrumental dimensions of behavior that ordinarily prevail in daily life becomes useful. Marking off the time as an unusual event allows participants to focus more attentively on the symbolic meanings conveyed in ritual activity. This is not to say, however, that ritual needs be removed from ordinary life to be effective. The regulation of daily life, as Goffman, Meyer and Rowan, and others have demonstrated, also depends on ritual and, for this reason, is imbued constantly with the ritual dramatization of symbolic meanings.

THE ROLE OF INTERACTION

Before going further, it is important to clear up another misconception about ritual that can be easily inferred from what has been said about the expressive quality of ritual. It is not necessary to have a gathering of people engaged in face-to-face interaction in order to speak of ritual. In the most common examples of ritual, such as tribal feasts, weddings, or church services, this condition is generally satisfied. But it need not be for ritual to exist in the sense of communicating symbolically. Meyer and Rowan's study of formal organizations provides one example of ritual occurring without face-to-face communication. The word about a firm having a department of safety can filter out to other organizations through a variety of means—letters, memoranda, reports, official documents, organization charts, government audits, informal networks—in addition to face-to-face interaction.

The case study presented at the end of this chapter provides an example of ritual linking persons through the mass media. Even though face-to-face discussions were involved, the main form of communication involved in the ritual was accomplished with television. Many of the rituals that play a vital role in the functioning of modern societies take this form. Although some of the ritual communication comes about on a firsthand basis, the larger share of participation occurs on an individual-by-individual basis with the media performing a critical function in providing feedback. Inaugurations provide a useful example because they have been examined as an important public ritual, especially in the literature on civil religion. The event itself involves direct communication among the various dignitaries of state. At least some of these dignitaries participate in the enactment of the ritual while others look on, applaud, and create an informal network of support for the occasion by their presence and interaction with one another. But the extent of participation in the inaugural ceremony is not limited to those present. Citizens participate in advance stages of the occasion by voting. The act of voting takes place largely in private as each citizen enters the voting booth alone and pulls the appropriate lever to register his or her choice. Yet the act is a highly stylized gesture by which the citizen interacts with the mechanism of state. The media, in turn, report back both the results of the election and the activities of inauguration day. In these ways a large segment of the public participates vicariously in the inaugural ceremony even though relatively few are physically present on the steps of the Capitol.

These examples illustrate possibilities of ritual occurring without benefit of direct interaction among persons in one another's immediate presence. A different question arises, however, in conjunction with rituals performed purely in private. It has been inferred from Mary Douglas's discussion of pollution rites, for example, that even a simple act of tidying up one's desk bears the marks of ritual activity. Horace Miner's (1956) tongue-in-cheek portrait of "Body Ritual Among the Nacirema" indicates that private acts of cleansing, such as brushing one's teeth, qualify as ritual. Other examples would include private acts of religious devotion, such as prayer and meditation. But can these private acts be considered ritual if ritual is an expressive dimension of behavior—if the essence of ritual lies in communication?

The answer, it seems, is strictly heuristic. There is value in distinguishing public from private ritual, especially in cases where the relation between ritual and broader processes of social integration is at issue. At the same time, ritual is generally regarded as playing a role in the moral tutelage of the individual as well, or as Durkheim described it, in disciplining the individual's interests. For these purposes it is valuable to recognize that ritual, even if performed in private, can communicate messages about the individual's position in a larger collectivity because the individual has internalized a conception of that collectivity. Hence, the act of tidying up one's desk may in fact be a symbolic gesture of one's relation to the boss, a particular role, or the organization for which one works. By the same token, brushing one's teeth may be an important rite of passage performed daily to mark the transition between one's role as a purely private individual and one's role as a representative of some larger collectivity. One has performed an act of communication, either consciously or unconsciously, in that one has expressed messages about one's relation to an internalized social entity. In these cases the individual acts as both performer and audience in the drama of ritual.

MOTIVES AND INTENTIONS

These considerations, then, bring us to a further problem—the extent to which ritual involves motives and intentions. If ritual is characterized by expressivity, a logical inference is that motives and intentions are what is primarily being expressed. In other words, ritual provides an occasion for making public what one thinks, feels, or intends to do. From this perspective, weddings are moments in which the bride and groom publicly announce their intentions to love and support each other, holidays provide opportunities to display sentiments of political loyalty, and religious worship is motivated by a desire to communicate with God. In each of these examples, the messages communicated in ritual reflect what the participants consciously intend to communicate.

The problem with this characterization is that ritual also communicates messages that may not be intended. Despite the obvious purposes of a wedding ceremony, one of the important messages that is likely to be communicated to the group assembled has to do with the social status and relative affluence of the families involved. The act of voting is *in-*

tended to register one's choice of candidates for political office; *unintentionally*, it also communicates one's status as a citizen and in this capacity one's support for the democratic system.

Ritual consists of both the messages intentionally given and those that are unintentionally given off. For this reason adequate understanding of ritual cannot be obtained merely by asking participants why they took part or what the ritual may have meant to them. A man driving down the highway is unlikely to be aware of any purpose of his behavior other than arriving at a particular destination; yet this activity contains an important ritualistic dimension—dramatizing, for example, that one is a law-abiding citizen—that is likely to have escaped the attention of the driver. The observer can examine the nature and functioning of these unintended or latent forms of communication, even though the participant in ritual may be unaware of their presence or importance.

This methodological issue has troubled anthropological research since its inception. The anthropologist is able to perceive certain patterns in the conduct of ritual that the primitive tribesman may not have recognized or thought important. The trouble has come from the anthropologist then concluding that ritual is nonrational and that the tribal group has merely deceived itself into thinking the ritual performs one function when in fact it performs another. An extensive literature debating the extent of rationality and nonrationality in primitive ritual has resulted.[7] On one side are those who have concluded that these rituals are inherently irrational. On the other side are those who claim this to be an ethnocentric point of view on the part of modern anthropologists. These critics argue that primitive ritual contains a great deal that is rational when understood within the framework of primitive culture itself.

The debate has been obfuscated by the fact of the rituals at issue being primitive. A better grasp of the problem comes from recognizing that the same issue crops up in the study of modern rituals as well. Here discrepancies are also likely to be present between the intended messages and those that are conveyed unintentionally. But this discrepancy says nothing about the rationality or nonrationality of the participant. The driver is scarcely irrational for assuming that his behavior is concerned with getting home rather than recognizing the messages about traffic laws that are implicit in this behavior. There are simply a number of different levels at which behavior can be understood.

In order to comprehend the various levels of interpretation involved in understanding ritual, one must recognize that ritual is subject to the same conditions as any other form of cultural communication. If it communicates in a language whose rules are known, it is likely (as discussed in Chapter 2) to communicate more meaningfully than if it conforms to no established rules. In the case of ritual, this condition may require activities to be performed according to highly stylized procedures or be accompanied by ample verbal explanation. Some portion of the communication involved in ritual therefore will probably be conducted simply to make the activities comprehensible in terms of known patterns of communication. This is one level at which ritual can be interpreted.

If the content of ritual conforms to realities that are generally believed to be true, the ritual's meaningfulness will also be enhanced. Ritual may, for this reason, be subjected to philosophical critique in order to investigate the truth value of its content. At this level it is entirely appropriate to question the degree to which the overt content of ritual subscribes to common notions of rationality, that is, is "rational" in conjunction with standard understandings of how the world operates. In this respect the issue of rationality in primitive ritual is a matter of philosophical critique entirely and can be judged only with reference to a cultural conception of reality, rather than being determined from the structure and intentions involved in ritual alone.

A third level of interpretation brings the question of intentionality to the forefront. Some portion of the overall content involved in ritual will convey its practitioners' intentions. These are likely to indicate both the practitioners' seriousness or conviction and their notion of the reasons for their participation. The latter is likely to require subjective information from each participant as well as the more public evidence displayed by their behavior. Such information will reveal whether the participants are sincere in their activities and whether or not they have in some way been deluded.

Finally, there are the social messages that rituals convey. These are of special importance in developing a concept of ritual that has value for understanding moral order. Weddings, bar mitzvahs, Fourth of July celebrations, even revolutions all communicate something about the passage of time. They mark the transition from one status to another in the lives of individuals or whole societies. In weddings it is the transition from single person to married spouse; in bar mitzvahs, the acquisition of adult status in the religious community; in Fourth of July celebrations, the maturing of a country and the memory of its transition to independence; in revolutions, where actual change may be relatively small, there is yet a significant symbolic transition in the identity of the society to its members and to other societies. Other rituals deal less with transitions than with the reaffirmation of collective values. Religious services reaffirm the common values of those who participate. Tribal dances remind participants of shared ancestry. Witch-hunts become occasions for discussing the implications of corporate loyalties. Still other examples reveal the importance of ritual for the alignment and regulation of routine social activity. The stylized remarks in which we engage upon winding up a visit at someone's house—leave-taking ceremonies, as Goffman has called them—signal the reasons for departing, sentiments of cordiality, and expressions of possibilities for renewed interaction in the future. Bureaucratic protocol regulates social relations in tense situations where personal feelings may be on edge and indeed helps define the situation as a moment of formality.

These examples reveal something very basic about ritual. Ritual regulates and defines social relations. It may do so by sharpening the boundary between two social statuses governed by different relations and expectations (rites of passage), or by reminding people of the relations they share and the principles underlying these relations (collective ceremonies), or by simply sending signals concerning the definition of positions and relations in ongoing social activities (etiquette, protocol, etc.). Metaphorically, ritual may be said to function as a social "thermostat," giving feedback about how to regulate behavior so as to better attain the collective goals of that behavior.

EMBELLISHMENT

Ritual has also been characterized as having *dramatic* or formal qualities. It tends to be more elaborate or embellished than purely instrumental behavior. Contrast the Eucharist with having a snack. Special garments, utensils, gestures, and words lend a dramatic quality to the former that does not characterize the latter. Or compare the act of tidying up one's desk with simply doing work. Tidying up takes time away from instrumental activity and may be done with a flair for orderliness—a degree of fastidiousness—that, if Mary Douglas is correct, dramatizes conceptions of purity and pollution. In both comparisons ritual is less dominated than its instrumental counterpart by considerations of efficiency.

The formal character of ritual has to do with its conformity to specified rules or patterns. The Eucharist is celebrated according to formalized guidelines and local traditions that shape expectations about how it is to be conducted. In this case each act is consciously performed with prescriptions and tradition in mind. A *coup d'état,* by comparison, may appear on the surface to be completely spontaneous and unpatterned. Insofar as it ritually demarcates a transition in government, however, it is likely to display greater patternedness and formality than originally meets the eye. Accounts of Bolshevik strategy between the February and October Revolutions in 1917, for example, give graphic testimony to the effort and planning that went into the Russian Revolution to lend an appearance that would resemble the events of 1789 in France. Comparisons of other instances of rebellion indicate that historians are likely to reconstruct successful rebellions to emphasize their compatibility with certain preconceived notions about the patterns that revolutions are expected to follow. This reconstruction assists contemporaries both domestically and abroad as well as future generations in identifying the event as a prototypical "revolution."

The dramatic, formalistic character of much that is known as ritualistic behavior aids communication. Embellishment in ritual serves the same function as redundancy in speech: it ensures that the message comes across. Consecrating the bread and wine each with a special prayer, though inefficient time-wise, enhances the likelihood of the communion service conveying its message of the crucified Lord. Embellishment also enhances communication by defining beforehand acts that are to follow. The use of turn signals is an elaboration beyond the act of actually turning because both convey messages about the status of one automobile in relation to another. But signaling gives advance warning of the acts that are to follow.

In much the same way, the formality of ritual also facilitates the task of communication. College graduation ceremonies mark the end of the college experience and entry to new rights and privileges because the activities involved conform to a familiar language of expectations surrounding such occasions. Patterns become recognizable so that common responses can be evoked in participants and observers. Additions of novel or improvised behavior will require verbal explanation if they are to communicate effectively. In short, what is regarded as "formality" is really a matter of behaving according to well-established rules, thereby enhancing the likelihood that familiar messages will be given off.

Although the elaborateness and formality of ritual enhance its communicative potential, these are dimensions on which ritual activity varies rather than defining characteristics of ritual itself. Fixing a flat tire, as seen already, can carry expressive elements that may qualify as ritual even though the activities involved are neither more embellished nor patterned than otherwise required for purely instrumental purposes. The variation in elaborateness and formality is particularly important to the analysis of ritual, however, because it allows a distinction to be made between those activities such as holidays and weddings that attract special attention and those less obvious rituals such as brushing one's teeth or fixing a tire that may merit attention only for certain purposes. The former are generally more elaborate and formalized than the latter.

By way of summary, we may briefly define ritual: *a symbolic-expressive aspect of behavior that communicates something about social relations, often in a relatively dramatic or formal manner.* This definition incorporates the idea that ritual must not be seen as a discrete category of behavior but as an analytic dimension that may be present to some degree in all behavior. It emphasizes the communicative properties of behavior and the fact that ritual often communicates more effectively because it conforms to certain stylized or embellished patterns of behavior. Also worth underscoring is the idea that ritual is essentially social: although it may express emotions or intentions, it clearly assists in articulating and regulating the nature of social relations. Thus ritual can legitimately be approached at the dramaturgic level, as outlined in Chapter 1, rather than treating it simply in terms of its subjective origins or meanings. To say that ritual dramatizes the moral order, however, obviously requires greater specification of the social contexts in which ritual typically functions.

THE SOCIAL CONTEXTS OF RITUAL

What causes ritual? Or, more precisely, under what social conditions does ritual become more important, more meaningful? Because ritual is a dimension of behavior common to all social activity, the question must be posed in relativistic terms. Some rituals require special effort beyond that expended on instrumental tasks. They may be characterized by greater embellishment, formality, intensity of participation, or interest and commitment. If the specific type of ritual at issue occurs spontaneously, rates of occurrence can also be compared. If its occurrence is institutionalized, as in the case of periodic celebrations or festivals, levels of intensity and involvement are likely to be the important measures of variation.

COMMON VIEWS

Several relationships between social circumstances and the incidence of ritual seem obvious enough at first blush. Groups heavily steeped in tradition are often thought of as having an especially acute interest in ritual—Russian Orthodoxy, for example, with its emphasis on ikons and liturgical practice. Religious groups in general tend to be thought of especially in connection with ritual. At a somewhat more sophisticated level, authoritarian societies or groups oriented toward hierarchy may be suspected of paying greater homage to ritual. Hitler's regime may appear to have made greater use of ritual than the United States during the same period, or the Roman Catholic hierarchy may seem more inclined toward ritual than the free church tradition in Protestantism. Other conditions that may appear on the surface to promote ritual would include smallness of social groups, such that community members can easily assemble and participate in ritual, and social cohesion or homogeneity, such that members would be encouraged to act out common values.

But all these notions reflect an inadequate understanding of ritual. They are rooted still in the traditional stereotyped conceptions of rituals that perceive it to be a trait characteristic of some other time and place but of little relevance to modern life. The connection between traditional cultures and ritual is rooted in the false conception that ritual has to be highly stylized and formal in order to communicate. The foregoing discussion has shown that embellishment and formality enhance communication, but neither of these characteristics has to be present in any pronounced degree for behavior to involve expressivity. Associating ritual with religious groups stems from the Durkheimian idea that ritual is set apart from everyday reality and is concerned with dramatizing and promoting worship of the sacred. This idea has to be stretched beyond recognition in order to accommodate rituals such as etiquette, protocol, or ceremonial display in formal organizations. The view that ritual is more common in authoritarian or hierarchical settings stems only from the fact that relatively more attention has been paid to these kinds of settings in the literature on modern rituals. Well-known studies have been done of purges and witch trials, coronations and inaugurations, and religious rites, but relatively little is known about the ceremonial aspects of, say, scientific conferences, communes, or traffic laws. The other notions—that ritual occurs more frequently in small or cohesive groups—reflect misconceptions about the necessity of face-to-face participation and common beliefs. As already shown, many of the rituals of modern life seem to require neither.

If these common notions are wrong, two other possibilities about the relations between ritual and social life can also be ruled out. One is the assertion that ritual does not vary and therefore cannot be expected to occur more frequently in some settings than in others. The argument here is much like the one heard frequently in theological circles, suggesting that the quest for ultimacy is a constant in human life. Ritual, like ultimacy, varies only in how it is expressed, according to these arguments. Whether or not this is true would be nearly impossible to establish. But adopting it as a working assumption necessitates overlooking what seems obvious and interesting about ritual, namely, that it does vary in its manifestations. Weddings happen more frequently at certain stages in the life cycle than at others. Religious services evoke more intensity of participation on some occasions than on others. To neglect these variations leads not only to an impoverished understanding of ritual but also to an inadequate grasp of its role in contemporary social life.

The second pitfall is to assume that ritual occurs entirely at random or that it depends so much on the whim of particular subcultures that no connections of a systematic sort with social conditions can be inferred. This view actually gains some support from the Durkheimian tradition because Durkheim believed the origin of ritual to lie in exogenous, unpredictable social shocks, such as floods, wars, and catastrophes. But Durkheim was also concerned with seeing patterns in these events. Although a flood may produce ritual spontaneously, the commemoration of this event is likely to occur in predictable ways. And the promise is also there that the careful observer can identify common dimensions of even seemingly spontaneous eruptions of ritual.

SOME EXAMPLES

The kinds of conditions that generate ritual, and in turn the role that ritual performs in social life, can be grasped most effectively by considering several examples. A few studies of ritual have been conducted in recent years with provocative results requiring only theoretical synthesis and interpretation. Other examples can be found amid the familiar texture of everyday life itself. Again there is value in starting with a diversity of cases in order to discover what patterns may have the broadest applicability.

The act of signaling for a turn while driving down the highway serves as a useful prototype of ritual because of its elementary nature. It contains in a highly abbreviated form all the ingredients of ritual—it is an expressive aspect of behavior distinguished, for example, from the more instrumental act of actually making a turn; it communicates something about the position of one driver in relation to others; it is an act rather than merely a belief; and it occurs in stylized or patterned ways that convey culturally comprehensible messages. The act of signaling is also familiar enough that the conditions under which it is most likely to occur can easily be examined in the absence of a full-blown study.

When is a driver most apt to signal? On a straight road or near an intersection? If all traffic is turning or only that particular driver? If turns can be made in only one direction or if turns are possible to both the right and left? If the driver is alone on the road or if the highway is filled with traffic? One complicating factor makes it difficult to answer these questions definitively. By law, signaling is required anytime one anticipates making a turn. If we assume for the moment, however, that our driver is less than scrupulous about obeying the law, we can make the following guesses about his behavior. He is more likely to signal when there is an intersection, when only some of the traffic is turning, when both right and left turns are possible, and when other cars are in view.

This example reveals something important about ritual. The common factor in these instances that distinguishes the high-likelihood situations from the low-likelihood situations is the element of choice and with it the degree of social uncertainty. The presence of intersections, varied traffic patterns, right- and left-turn options, and multiple vehicles increase the number of choices that can be made by the various drivers whose proximity to one another imposes a network of social relations upon them. With this increase in potential options, the overall level of uncertainty in the situation also increases. It therefore becomes imperative for drivers to signal—to communicate with one another through ritual—in order to maintain order and safety in their social relations with one another.

Something else about ritual is also illustrated by this example. The driver, not the passenger, signals. We shall see momentarily why this is important.

As a second example, rites of passage are worthy of consideration both because they qualify as ritual by any definition of the term and because they have been amply investigated. Among the most common of these rites are reproduction rituals (baby showers, baptisms, circumcision rites, christenings, dedication ceremonies), puberty rites (bar and bas mitzvahs, confirmations, commencement and baccalaureate services), rites of marriage and fertility (engagements, weddings, charivaris), and rites of death (extreme unction, funeral and memorial services, burial ceremonies, readings of last wills and testaments). By definition, these rites mark transitions in personal and collective lives.

The occasions on which rites of passage take place tend to be moments of ambiguity as far as social relations and identities are concerned. The presence of an infant imposes new demands on parents and may change the perceptions of peers or their own expectations about how they are to behave. Throughout most of history high infant mortality rates have also plagued the joys of childbirth with uncertainties about disappointment and death. Puberty rites come at times when it is unclear whether relations should be structured on the model of child-to-adult or adult-to-adult. In many societies children are indulged with special rights and privileges, but serious demands are imposed on all who are old enough to hunt, fight, tend crops, or bear children. However, maturation never occurs overnight, so a period exists when neither the maturing youth nor his or her guardians know for sure which expectations apply. Periods of courtship and marriage bring similar uncertainties. For the couple, uncertainty exists as to the extent of each other's affection and loyalty; those with whom the couple is acquainted have problems knowing whether to encourage the relation, to treat the couple as a unit, or to define the relation as ordinary friendship. Death likewise raises questions about the well-being of survivors, their immediate capacity to carry on with social obligations, and in many instances questions about inheritances and property rights. The community of bereaved family and friends not only experiences itself broken, as Durkheim argued, but also needs information in order to recreate damaged relations.

Like the situations evoking turn signals, those in which rites of passage occur tend to be fraught with higher than ordinary levels of uncertainty because the transitional period between two social statuses inevitably increases the number of options from which behavior can be selected. It is now possible to choose activities and relations specified both by the status one has occupied in the past and by the new position one is soon to acquire. Rules that formerly restricted options and channeled behavior into certain predictable patterns can no longer be enforced as effectively because new rights or exemptions from obligations can be claimed on the basis of the new position that has come to be partially occupied. For the larger set of social relations in which these statuses are embedded, the enhancement of choice brings uncertainty, and with uncertainty, potential for instability or collapse.

Rites of passage reduce uncertainty and latent sources of social instability by summarily redefining statuses, relations, and behavioral options. These rituals dichotomize the continuous progression of real time into two distinct periods as far as social time is concerned. They communicate to the parties involved that, upon completion of the ceremony, new relations are in order. Birth ceremonies confer legitimacy, religious or national citizenship, inheritance rights, and duties of parenthood on the various parties involved. Weddings, as dramatically revealed in recent years by their absence among cohabiting couples, clarify to all concerned what the status of the relation is, what subsequent relations with members of the opposite sex are expected to be, how greetings, invitations, and informal gatherings are to be structured, and so on. In each instance the performance of ritual may be a matter of custom or even be required by law. But it is the uncertainty of existing social relations and the need for communication in order to reduce uncertainty and clarify obligations that renders the performance a meaningful event.

A third set of examples is provided by material on witch-hunts. These have been carefully researched in a number of different settings and with particular attention paid to social correlates. The typical pattern of events in witch-hunts is that someone is accused of heresy, usually in the case of religious witch-hunts, or of subversion, as is more common in political witch-hunts. A hearing or trial follows in which charges are made, the accused is asked to confess or recant, and sentencing, acquittal, or punishment follows. Witch-hunts, therefore, are a type of ritual. They occur sporadically, unlike holiday celebrations. But they generally consist of public acts involving patterned events in which messages are communicated about values and norms that have allegedly been violated. Because witch-hunts occur sporadically, investigations have focused mainly on the timing and location of their occurrence and have looked primarily to larger crises or tensions in social arrangements for explanations. A perhaps simpler explanation would be to investigate the subversive activities of those accused. But this strategy has shown mostly that only a loose connection exists between objective offenses and witch trials. Similar activities evoke charges of heresy and subversion on some occasions but not on others. Moreover, the charges filed in many of the more familiar witch trials, such as those in Salem, Massachusetts, during the seventeenth century, seem to be largely without substance when viewed from an external perspective. Thus, the relation between witch trials and broader social conditions has proven to be a more fruitful avenue to explore.

The witch trials in colonial Massachusetts were examined from this perspective by Kai Erikson in his book *Wayward Puritans* (1966). Erikson showed that these trials had occurred not simply at random but in three distinct spurts. The first of these "crime waves" took place during the second half of the 1630s, the second occurred in the late 1650s, and the third broke out in 1692. The interesting feature of these outbursts was that they coincided perfectly with crises in the authority structure and values of the Massachusetts Bay Colony. The first followed closely on the heels of the so-called antinomian controversy involving Anne Hutchinson. The controversy poked at the heart of colonial authority because it challenged the worthiness of the Puritan clergy to legislate in spiritual matters. Hutchinson and her followers argued that the doctrine upholding the "priesthood of the believer" should be more strictly interpreted, giving residents greater freedom to decide on their own qualifications for religious and political participation or leadership. The second bout of witch-hunting came into being in 1656 and continued for nearly a decade. According to Erikson, it was instigated chiefly in response to the arrival in the Puritan colony of Quakers, who, though few in number, symbolized a departure from the Puritans' staunchly ascetic values. The Quakers' emphasis on inner spirituality challenged the theocratic discipline of the colony much in the same manner as Hutchinson's alleged antinomianism. Neither of these episodes involved accusations of witchcraft per se, only charges of heresy. The third outbreak did. It was the famed witch-hunt in the town of Salem. The crisis this time was more severe because it involved a genuine threat of serious potential consequences for the political leadership of the colony. This threat was from England, and it involved both the possibility of losing title to the entire colony at the hand of the king and a series of disputes with the Puritan hierarchy in England over theological points and questions of church discipline.

Erikson concluded from these three episodes that witch trials were collective rituals that emerged in response to "boundary crises" in the moral order of the Massachusetts colony. Following Durkheim, he argued that collectivities develop collective identities that define boundaries of membership and distinguish the collectivity from outsiders. When these boundaries change or become blurred, uncertainties about membership, authority, and shared values set in. Heretics and witches become figures symbolizing the boundaries; that is, they represent ways of violating or transgressing shared values. The ritual of trying, purging, and punishing these deviants serves as an occasion for clarifying collective boundaries and provides an object lesson to those who might be inclined to violate these boundaries.

Erikson's use of the term "boundary" is largely figurative. It subsumes a variety of collective values, definitions, and relations. Disputes over boundaries arise in a number of ways, including internal disagreements, ambiguities over the correct or effective application of cherished values, redefinition of boundaries by the physical inclusion of new members, and external threats. Hugh Trevor-Roper's (1967) discussion of witch-hunting in Europe during the same period provides instances where boundary disputes can be taken literally.

Trevor-Roper's account, as noted earlier, focuses heavily on psychological factors. But from a different perspective the study provides illuminating evidence on the social contexts of witch-hunting as well. Temporally, the main outbreaks of witch-hunting occurred during the early part of the seventeenth century. This was a time of reintegration and consolidation in the European state system.[8] The near hegemony of the Hapsburgs over the European system had been broken by the second half of the sixteenth century. France, England, and Holland had emerged as the new "core powers" politically and economically. Protestantism had become firmly established in England, Holland, Scandinavia, and parts of Germany; Catholicism had reasserted itself in France, southern Germany, and Poland and continued to be strong in Spain, Portugal, and Italy. The European states at the beginning of the seventeenth century were well on their way toward forming a new international system centered around mercantile trade and a balance of power among Holland, England, and France. The transition to this new world order was to occupy nearly the entire first half of the seventeenth century, however. On an international scale the relative strengths of England, France, and Holland continued to be negotiated through economic competition, shifting alliances, and intermittent wars. And domestically, each of the three core powers, as well as Germany, continued to be divided between representatives of different religions and political ideologies, interests, and relations to the state. One could conclude, following Erikson's line of reasoning, that uncertainties in collective values were also present as one of the preconditions of this episode of witch-hunting.

The spatial distribution of European witch-hunts, however, is more suggestive even than their temporal occurrence. It was primarily in border areas where Protestants and Catholics were caught up in controversies over geographical boundaries and political jurisdictions that witch-hunts broke out. Nor was it simply the presence of adherents to an alien faith that became the target of these rituals. Catholics did not round up Protestants and accuse them of heresy, nor Protestants, Catholics. Each group found subversives within its own camp, not traitors who were explicitly allied with the enemy, but weak souls endangering the solidarity of the total community by practicing sorcery.

Under threat of external attacks on the community's physical boundaries, greater certainty was needed about the statuses, loyalties, and values of members within the community. The presence of religious competition at the borders may have created uncertainties about the location of these borders themselves, but the more immediate source of ritual activity was the need for greater clarity about the social relations within the community. In order to mobilize its resources to the maximum, the community needed to know where its members stood and, more important, needed to shore up those loyalties to the community as a corporate entity that may have grown blurred with the passage of time and the pressures of individual or localistic demands. Witch trials became meaningful rituals under these circumstances. They dramatized the nature of collective loyalties and defined precisely the range of acceptable and unacceptable religious activity.

Several more recent studies have extended the discussion of witch-hunts to the political arena. A study of lynchings during the 1890s in Louisiana suggests that these events varied from parish to parish and from year to year in a manner closely corresponding with crises in the Populist party (Inverarity, 1976). The theoretical framework of the study, although drawn from Durkheim and Erikson, focuses on repressive justice rather than ritual. Yet the discussion can be subsumed under the more general perspective on ritual that has been presented in the preceding paragraphs. Lynchings were collective rituals in which traditional white Southern loyalties were dramatized. Participation in the ritual was an act of commitment to a particular reference group and set of values. For those who watched or heard about the event, the strength of these traditional relations among whites and against blacks was vividly demonstrated. The two conditions that made these events meaningful (i.e., meaningful enough to be performed) were a preexisting set of social relations and a disruption of these relations. The former inhered in the stability of uniform political orientations and was a function of religious homogeneity and ruralness. The latter manifested itself as an intrusion of Populist party organizing that promised to disrupt traditional relations.

The combination of these conditions made circumstances ripe for the appearance of lynchings. High levels of solidarity and cultural homogeneity are tantamount to extreme degrees of certainty or predictability in social relations. Not only is each actor sure of what the others think and plan to do, but also the relations among actors are "strong," in the sense of both frequent contact and multiple bases of interaction (economic, political, religious, familial). The stability of such relations requires a high degree of certainty about expectations and commitments. Few mechanisms exist to maintain stability in the absence of such certainty. For example, the market does not provide an intervening mechanism with which to aggregate the unpredictable activities of individual buyers and sellers into predictable patterns of overall supply and demand. Or at the cultural level, symbolic resources such as values of tolerance and diversity do not exist to decouple social relations from one another. Given potentially disruptive forces, such as the advent of a new political party, some measures are likely to be taken, therefore, to publicly articulate the fact that traditional expectations can still be counted on and that departures from these expectations will be rewarded with certain and severe punishment. In Louisiana, lynchings provided an economical means of communicating these messages.

Another study illustrating the ritualistic aspects of witch-hunting focuses on the Cultural Revolution in China (Bergesen, 1978). The American presence in Vietnam during the 1960s created a threatening situation for China's leaders. In response, the leaders sought subversives in their midst whom they publicly expunged and made symbols of potentially destructive forces against the Chinese people. The mechanisms used to reaffirm collective values included public accusations and legal charges, trials, large-scale ceremonies such as show trials and public rectification programs, and the formation of citizens' groups and government watchdog agencies. The implications of this study are much the same as those from Erikson's investigation and from the research on lynchings. Witch trials in China became meaningful in response to uncertainties in the dominant relations and obligations constituting the collective order of the society.

Perhaps the most extensive examination of political witch trials is Bergesen's (1984) quantitative investigation of more than five thousand witch-hunting incidents against political subversives in thirty-nine countries between 1950 and 1970. The focus of this research was not the temporal or spatial occurrence of witch-hunts but their distribution across institutional sectors (government, military, education, religion, etc.).

Bergesen's principal finding was that the degree of "corporateness" in a society—as measured by single-party versus two- or multiparty political systems—was associated both with higher overall rates of witch-hunting and a greater dispersion of these incidents across diverse institutional sectors.

Several interpretations of this finding are possible. One is that totalitarian regimes are simply better able than pluralistic regimes to hunt down subversives. But this explanation fails to account for other patterns in the data, such as the differences between two- and multiparty systems or differences in the distribution of incidents within various sectors of government. From the overall patterns, Bergesen concludes that corporateness involves an infusion of collective values within everyday life, and this interpenetration of the "sacred" into the mundane makes it more likely for rituals that dramatize collective values or forces opposing these values to occur.

> The more corporate reality that is present, the stronger, more clearly defined and more closely merged with everyday reality are those symbolic representations which mirror that corporate reality. Daily life becomes filled with transcendent political significance and, simultaneously, the enemies of the sacred purposes. The ritual creation of oppositions to representations of corporate social reality is one of the fundamental forms of the modern religious life. (Bergesen, 1977:230)

How does this conclusion fit in with the other studies of witch-hunts? The closest link is with the study of lynchings. There, solidarity and homogeneity, when they came under threat, contributed to the occurrence of witch-hunting. Here, the parallel concept is corporateness. Corporateness, like solidarity and homogeneity, makes certainty about social relations more important for the functioning of day-to-day social life. The infusion of collective purposes into daily life, if Bergesen's description is accurate, tends to unite these disparate activities into an integrated whole. No longer are the routine activities that go on within the university, church, or firm compartmentalized to a narrow "sphere of relevance," to borrow Berger and Luckmann's term. They are now coupled through a symbolic linkage with the overall destiny and purposes of the society. Under these conditions it becomes more important to have ways of expressing the projected activities of each institutional arena and the relation between these activities and those in other arenas. Any deviation from conventional expectations or any ambiguity in the face of novel circumstances creates uncertainties not only for the immediate actors in the situation but also for the larger society. Public rituals such as witch trials provide a means of coping with this uncertainty.

UNCERTAINTY AND RITUAL

At the most general level the conclusion that emerges from these otherwise diverse examples—turn signals, rites of passage, witch-hunts—is that ritual is most likely to occur in situations of social *uncertainty*. Other things being equal as far as the resources and freedom for engaging in ritual are concerned, the greater the uncertainty that exists about social positions, commitments to shared values, or behavioral options likely to influence other actors, the greater the likelihood that behavior will take on a ritual dimension of significance, that is, will involve important aspects of expressivity.

This conclusion can be stated more systematically within the framework developed in the preceding chapters. Uncertainty is an attribute of the structure that inherently exists within culture, where culture is understood to be the entire collection of shared meanings dramatized within a society or some other social unit. These meanings take on forms or patterns that vary in terms of predictability. The greater the degree to which component elements of these patterns or the patterns themselves can be predicted, the greater the level of certainty that can be said to exist. This characteristic of the symbolic environment provides the context in which the meaningfulness or legitimacy of any particular ritual (expressive aspect of behavior) can be understood. All else being constant, the meaningfulness of a particular ritual act is likely to be greater in situations where some uncertainty exists in the larger symbolic environment than where there is already a high degree of certainty. This formulation emphasizes the structural patterns or relations among cultural elements that influence the likelihood of any subset of these elements being meaningful. In the case of ritual, the sheer level of certainty or uncertainty that characterizes these relations appears to be one of the most crucial structural conditions.

Uncertainty is an umbrella concept that subsumes a variety of more specific observable variables. This is not the place to develop a complete inventory of these variables, but several of the more important types have already been illustrated in the foregoing examples and need only be summarized. In each case it must be assumed that other conditions do not change. One type of uncertainty is illustrated in both the turn signal and the rite of passage examples. In these cases, growing levels of uncertainty were indicated by increases in the sheer number of available options for behavior (e.g., being able to turn in more than one direction or being able to act according to the norms of more than one status). As long as other features of a cultural system remain constant, expanded options make predicting overall outcomes increasingly difficult. A second type of uncertainty, illustrated in the witch-hunting examples, involves external shocks to a cultural system. One way of interpreting the effect of these shocks is to say that they introduce new sets of contingencies into the system. Understandings communicated by external groups—the king, religious out-groups, Populists—now have to be related to existing understandings, whereas the two systems were formerly capable of functioning in isolation. The effect of solidary ties and corporatist symbolism is also to impose connections on symbols that otherwise might bear no relation to one another, thereby heightening the scope over which certainty or uncertainty prevails. Finally, uncertainty can be a function merely of equivocality with regard to particular symbols. The range of meanings evoked by some symbols, such as a turn signal, may be straightforward and unequivocal; the meanings associated with other symbols (a religious text, for example) may be diverse and therefore highly equivocal in any given situation. If the number of potential outcomes, intentions, or commitments that can be conveyed by any particular act or utterance is high, there is likely to be a high degree of uncertainty in the system. These are some of the varieties of uncertainty that are likely to influence the incidence of ritual.

One of the loose ends to which some attention must now be given is the allegation that ritual represents not so much a response to preexisting uncertainties in social relations but a means of generating such uncertainties. This argument has been made especially in anthropological studies of rituals involving moments of seeming chaos—what Victor Turner (1974) terms episodes of "betwixt and between"—but is evidenced in modern rituals as well. Encounter groups, for example, include rituals of face-to-face interaction, such as touching, pairing and staring, and verbal harangues. Despite temporary discomfort, these rituals have been popular in recent years because of the increasingly uncertain nature of face-to-face interaction in everyday life. Intimacy frequently goes unlearned and unexperienced even in the family. Interaction increasingly consists of fleeting contact with strangers and of necessity takes place in diverse contexts. Changing standards of dress, sex role behavior, and morality also promote uncertainty. Furthermore, popular psychology has taught us how fragile the self-concept is and how easily it may be damaged through bungled relationships. Encounter rituals take on meaning because of the precariousness of these contacts. But these rituals also generate uncertainty.

One might suppose from the argument thus far that encounter rituals would function mainly to reduce the ambiguities of face-to-face relations, perhaps by giving practice, teaching etiquette, or simply training people in the cues and expectations involved in close communication. To the contrary, these rituals demonstrate how poorly equipped most of us are to interact on a personal level. They illustrate the difficulty of establishing eye contact, of touching, of remembering names and faces; and they reveal starkly the defenses protecting us from truly empathizing and expressing our emotions. The rituals themselves serve only to heighten the fears associated with intimate contact.

Yet it is the nature of these rituals to arouse fear within a controlled setting. Encounter rituals take place in artificial settings removed from everyday life. Strangers unlikely to be seen in the real world provide guinea pigs for acting out one's fears and uncertainties. And these episodes are conducted, in most instances, under professional supervision and following careful guidelines. Although uncertainties are provoked, they are kept within limits, after which participants are gradually encouraged to face up to their fears and are eased back into everyday reality.

This is a pattern characteristic of many rituals, though by no means inherent in ritual in its broadest sense. Durkheim recognized it in Australian religion, where the primitive temporarily found himself confronted with the awesome uncertainty of communing with his gods. Van Gennep saw it as a common feature in rites of passage. The initiate is momentarily left without support, neither boy nor man, faced with the terrible responsibility of working through his own transition to adulthood. In witch-hunts, the spectre of chaos emerges in the accusation of subversion and pronouncements concerning the scope of incipient evil. In the Mass, Christ perishes under the weight of the world's sin before rising triumphantly on the third day.

These rituals are a special type. They do not *create* the uncertainty in broader terms that generates interest in what the ritual activities themselves portray. Rather, they *exaggerate* this uncertainty. Protected enclaves in which the latent uncertainties inherent in real life can be modeled at extreme levels are defined. This modeling allows the sources and implications of uncertainty to be objectified—to be imagined—and, once brought vividly into consciousness, to be transcended by confronting it and learning either to cure its devastation or to restructure relations in ways to avoid it.

In these rituals of uncertainty, the individual must act in order to overcome the ambiguities of his or her own fears. Ritual invokes moral responsibility to act. This is no less true in less extreme cases. It is, again, the driver, not the passenger, who must signal. Through ritual the actors' roles and obligations in each setting are dramatized to their confederates. This is why we feel compelled to participate in ritual. Voting constitutes an act of affirming our sense of duty and participation in civil society. Going to church bears witness to our faith. In ritual a bond is established between the person and the moral community on which he or she depends. It is in this sense that ritual reinforces the moral order. Modern society, no less than the tribal group, depends continually on this source of reinforcement.

AN EMPIRICAL CASE: "HOLOCAUST" AS MORAL RITUAL

Investigating ritual empirically is not a simple task. One can, for example, approach the subject as if ritual were a kind of text to decipher. This is essentially the approach taken by Shils and Young (1953) in their classic essay, "The Meaning of the Coronation." In this case the ritual performed was conducted basically the same each time and was not performed very often. Thus Shils and Young could concern themselves with the various phases of the ritual, the symbols in each, and the meanings of these symbols—the robe, crown, scepter, and so on. They argued that the meaning of the coronation lay in the social relations that were dramatized between crown and people, crown and estates, and crown and God. Yet the study ultimately fails because it claims too much. We have no way of determining whether this interpretation is correct or not. Chances are the ceremony elicits a variety of meanings at a number of different levels. When the queen-to-be stands momentarily before the audience in ordinary garb before receiving the robe, it may be, as the authors suggest, that a distinction is evoked between the queen's biological and social attributes. But it may just as well be that here is someone ordinary with whom the people can identify. To argue that *the meaning* of the ritual has been unearthed is clearly pretentious and unfounded.

Alternatively, one can take an ethnographic approach, as Clifford Geertz (1973) has done in his illuminating essays on the rituals of Bali.

Here one comes to the subject matter deeply immersed in the customs of the people whose participation is at issue. If these customs pertain to a relatively small and homogeneous population about which little else is known, the account is likely to come off as both credible and illuminating. Yet this approach can also be criticized. Too often the ethnographer purports to have found the true meaning that even the ritual's practitioners have been unable to recognize.[9] The ethnographer also has difficulty applying this method to the rituals of large, heterogeneous societies.

If one turns to the methods of sociology, some of these difficulties disappear. For example, Erikson and those in his tradition have shied away from saying what the true meaning of ritual witch-hunts is, claiming only to have identified some of the circumstances rendering these rituals meaningful. But new problems arise. Usually only a loose temporal or geographical connection is established between circumstances and ritual. Not much is known about the attitudes of those who actually participate. Furthermore, the analyst usually assumes that the ritual has some sort of function in restoring order to social life. But clear evidence of these effects is seldom given.

The need is evident, therefore, for fairly extensive information to understand even one ritual, let alone to fully develop a general theory about ritual. Without such information, the connections between moral order and ritual remain largely conjectural. What follows is an empirical case that affords a more detailed look at some of these connections.

A TELEVISED MORAL EVENT

On four successive evenings in mid April 1978, more than 120 million Americans looked on as the grisly horrors of violence, brutality, and mass extermination unfolded in graphic color on their television screens. The show was "Holocaust," a nine-and-a-half-hour adaptation of Gerald Green's best-selling novel by the same title. No program (except "Roots") had ever attracted so large a viewing audience. Nearly two-thirds of the adult population watched the program. In addition, the program stirred a great deal of public commentary. Newspapers editorialized about it, clergy discussed it in sermons, teachers assigned it to their students. In the days following the telecast NBC received more than twenty thousand letters about the series, expressing overwhelmingly favorable sentiments, and later the series became the winner of twelve Emmy awards.

"Holocaust" provides an example of public ritual by almost any indication. Whether in terms of Durkheim's specific view of ritual (as will be shown) or in terms of the broad definition of ritual that has just been considered, the program was a symbolic-expressive event that communicated something about social relations in a relatively dramatic way. In terms of minimal participation (viewing), it involved more of the public than virtually any other single event in recent times. More people watched than voted in either the 1976 or 1980 presidential elections. The series attracted about as many viewers as the Super Bowl, even though it took up four evenings and lasted nearly three times as long. Its audience was larger than that of all the nation's churches on any given Sunday. Moreover, the program dealt with a theme of grave moral importance and provoked interest ranging well beyond the series itself.

The program also became the focus of extensive research. A national telephone survey was conducted a few weeks after the series to assess viewers' reactions and to compare them with nonviewers' attitudes.[10] Some weeks later a nationwide survey was conducted among clergy in five major denominations to explore their reactions.[11] A parallel study was conducted in a national cross-section of high school social studies teachers.[12] Both studies included questions aimed at probing the connection between attitudes about the Holocaust and broader issues of moral order. A small survey of students in a midwestern high school provided some related information.[13] Several other studies were conducted in different parts of the country.[14] And at least two national samples were polled when the series was shown in Europe.[15] Thus "Holocaust" became one of the most extensively studied of any contemporary public ritual.

The evidence from these various sources provides strong support for treating "Holocaust" as a major public event. The telephone survey of U.S. adults showed that the number of viewers grew on each succeeding evening of the series.[16] Fewer than one in ten did not know the program was on. Almost all the clergy and teachers who had not watched said they had heard a lot about the program. The studies also documented the extent of activity and social interaction stimulated by the program—an important fact because the program might otherwise be dismissed as merely private entertainment. About two-thirds of the viewers in the telephone survey said they had watched with other members of their household, meaning that discussion of the program was likely at least within the family.[17] Newspapers, pastors, and teachers also played a role in making the event public. Twenty percent of the clergy had preached a sermon on the Holocaust, 80 percent had mentioned it in a sermon, 84 percent had discussed the program with people in their churches, and 55 percent had encouraged people to watch the program. Large numbers of teachers had also discussed the program—92 percent had talked about the Holocaust with students or colleagues, 56 percent had taught a class on it, and 69 percent had encouraged students to watch the program.

The evidence also showed how seriously viewers took the event. Television audiences are notoriously forgetful about what they watch. "Holocaust" viewers, however, were able to recall details of the program even several months after the series was shown. Among clergy (surveyed two months after the telecast) and teachers (seven months afterwards), three-quarters were able to recall the name of the Jewish family and the occupation of the father in this family.[18] Among those who had seen all of the program, better than 90 percent gave the right answers to these questions. Other measures also documented the program's cognitive impact on its viewers. In the telephone survey more than half the viewers said watching had helped them better understand "what Hitler's treatment of Jews was all about." Among the youngest viewers (ages 18 to 29), this figure was close to 75 percent. The clergy and teacher surveys included a battery of true-false questions about details of the Holocaust covered in the program. Levels of knowledge on these items were relatively high overall, but viewers who had seen the entire series were between 15 and 20 percentage points more likely to give correct answers than were those who had not watched and had not heard much about the program.[19]

"Holocaust" also evoked deep emotion among its viewers. About half the viewers surveyed by telephone said they had found some parts of the program "difficult or disturbing to watch." More than half the clergy and teachers indicated that the "violence and pain shown in the program" had bothered them a lot.[20] Another indication of how seriously viewers took the program is the extent to which they were bothered by interruptions for commercials. Mary Douglas (1966) has written that objects come to be defined as pollution when they somehow show that symbolic boundaries demarcating the sacred or pure have been violated. In the present case, the commercials appeared to be an intrusion of the profane into something very special. One-third of the clergy and teachers said they had been bothered a lot by "having the program interrupted by commercials"; another third said they had been bothered a little.[21]

The studies gave evidence as well on how viewers evaluated the series. In the telephone survey, 83 percent of the viewers said it was a "good idea" to show a program like "Holocaust" on television. About the same number among the teachers and clergy felt that TV specials dealing with atrocities such as the Holocaust "should be shown, no matter how shocking they may be."[22] Equally large proportions (about 85 percent) felt that the Holocaust "definitely raises some profound moral questions that we need to ponder very carefully."[23]

Finally, the studies showed that the Holocaust program took place within an atmosphere of more extended interest in the Holocaust and knowledge about it. In the telephone survey nearly half of those who watched all of the series said they were already very well informed about the Holocaust, as did about a third of those who watched parts of the series. Better than two-thirds of the clergy and teachers gave correct answers to the true-false questions. And books, classes, and professional publications had apparently contributed significantly to the level of knowledge among these groups. For example, fewer than one in five had not learned at least a little about the Holocaust during the past few years from books; better than half had learned things about the Holocaust from classes or lectures; and more than half had gained information about it from professional publications.[24]

In sum, the showing of "Holocaust" was an event that fits well the description of a major public ritual. Not only did it attract the attention of millions of Americans, but it also moved them emotionally, influenced their attitudes, and involved them in discussions about the Holocaust with friends and family and in classrooms and churches. In these respects, the program took on importance well beyond that of an ordinary television series. It dealt with a moral issue of profound significance that had already been the focus of much interest and debate in American culture. The program therefore provides an occasion to examine the social circumstances in the moral order that may arouse interest in particular kinds of rituals and symbols that help to reaffirm collective values. In examining these circumstances it is again important to emphasize that these are only some of the conditions that contribute to the meaningfulness of a symbolic event. In the case of the Holocaust, both its gravity as a historical episode and the skills involved in producing the television portrayal contributed immensely to the meaningfulness it apparently had for the American public. Even taking these factors into account, however, still leaves much to be explained, especially in light of the fact that some persons found the Holocaust considerably more interesting or meaningful than did others. It is to these differences that the issue of perceptions about the broader moral order becomes relevant.

THE EFFECTS OF MORAL UNCERTAINTY

The period in which "Holocaust" was shown was a time of widespread concern about the quality of American values and the strength of America's institutions. A survey taken in 1978 by Chicago's National Opinion Research Center found that 84 percent of the public had "only some" or "hardly any" confidence in the leaders running the executive branch of the federal government.[25] Congress fared about as badly, and the Supreme Court came out only a little better.[26] As with government, attitudes toward business also registered deep misgivings. Writing in August 1978, Seymour Martin Lipset and William Schneider concluded that "all the opinion polls agree that the reputation of business generally, and of every industry and company examined in particular, has declined, often precipitously." The polling firm Yankelovich, Skelly and White had documented a decline in agreement with the statement "Business tries to strike a fair balance between profits and the interests of the public" from 70 percent in 1968 to only 15 percent in 1977.[27] Other surveys showed a growing mood of pessimism about the future, widespread fears that America's power in the world was declining, and deep concern about the erosion of traditional morality.[28] According to polls conducted by the Roper organization, the proportion of Americans who felt the country had "pretty seriously gotten on the wrong track" rose from 44 percent in 1977 to 65 percent in 1979 (Lipset and Wattenberg, 1979). Indeed, enough evidence of this kind had accumulated by midsummer 1979 that President Carter was prompted to describe the declining national morale as a "crisis that strikes at the very heart and soul and spirit of our national will," a crisis that threatened "to destroy the social and political fabric in America."[29]

The clergy and teacher studies found that the concerns held by the general public were also pronounced among pastors and teachers. Upwards of 80 percent in these surveys indicated that dishonesty in the government, corruption in business, and a sense of powerlessness in the public were currently serious problems in the United States, and more than a third thought these problems were *extremely* serious.[30] Well over half felt that racial inequality and prejudice continued to represent serious problems.[31] Many could also envision future outbreaks of social disorder. For example, about half were convinced that racial violence could break out again, and almost this many thought unrest like that of the 1960s could happen again.[32]

If the argument developed in the previous section of this chapter is correct, uncertainties and fears of these kinds should help explain the tremendous reception that the Holocaust program evoked. "Holocaust" was a ritual event dramatizing the evils of social and moral chaos. These themes should have been especially meaningful to persons who perceived disorder cropping up in their own society. The Holocaust, in short, was a symbol of contemporary chaos, as well as a reminder of historic evil. Some evidence to this effect is present in the explanations that people gave for their interest in the Holocaust.

Several scenarios were advanced in the late 1970s to explain the public's interest in the Holocaust. One held that this interest had largely been manufactured by the media in conjunction with well-advertised productions such as "Holocaust," "The Diary of Anne Frank," and "The World at War." A second had it that events in Israel since the 1967 war were the reason. A third argued that people were actually acquainted with survivors of the Holocaust. And a fourth—proposed mostly because of the high interest evident among young people—suggested that the interest was a function of historical curiosity. None of these explanations gained more than limited support from the research, however. Fewer than a sixth of the clergy and teachers attributed their interest mainly to the media. Fewer than one in eight said the events in Israel were a major reason for their interest. Only a quarter indicated that personal acquaintance with Holocaust survivors was a major reason. And only a fourth of the clergy attributed their interest to historical curiosity (almost half of the teachers, however, did so).[33]

The explanation that seemed to account for most of the interest was the fear that something like the Holocaust could happen again. Newspapers had been quick to make this point. William Safire wrote in the *New York Times*, "Ask not how a previous generation could tolerate the murder of six million Jews; on a smaller scale, this generation is doing just dandy along those lines." In a similar vein the Nashville *Tennessean* editorialized, "The important thing to be learned is that it could happen again."[34] Teachers and clergy were prone to agree. More than half of the teachers and almost three-quarters of the pastors said the fear that something like it could happen again was a major reason for their interest.[35] This view was also shared by the general public. Of the two-thirds who thought the program was a good idea, 83 percent listed their reason for thinking so as the necessity of being aware of what could happen again.

More direct evidence of the connection between perceptions of danger in the contemporary moral order and interest in the Holocaust comes from examining the differences in interest between those who perceived danger and those who did not. Interest was significantly higher among those who perceived serious moral and social problems in American culture than among those who did not. For someone who thought dishonesty, corruption, alienation, prejudice, or inequality was an extremely serious problem in the country, the odds of that person having a lot of interest in the Holocaust were between 20 and 50 percent higher than for someone who did not think these problems were serious.[36] In other words, perceiving some threat or ambiguity in the moral order of American society, for whatever reason, appeared to enhance the likelihood that the Holocaust would be regarded as a meaningful symbolic event.

This connection did not result simply from differences in political views. Politically liberal clergy and teachers, as it turned out, *were* more likely both to perceive serious social problems in the United States and to be interested in the Holocaust than were their conservative counterparts. But liberalism was not the reason for the connection between perceptions of contemporary problems and expressions of interest in the Holocaust. Whether someone was politically liberal, moderate, or conservative, that person was more likely to be interested in the Holocaust if he or she perceived serious problems in the moral order than if no such problems were thought to exist.[37]

Political orientations did have one important effect on the findings, however. They revealed that some kinds of danger in the moral order can generate interest in ritual for some groups but not for others. Specifically, the effects of perceiving a decline in traditional morality varied, depending on whether this decline was perceived by conservatives or by liberals. The expectation was that conservatives would find declining morality more disturbing than liberals and therefore would be more likely to be interested in the Holocaust if they perceived such a decline than would liberals. The data confirmed this expectation. Among both clergy and teachers there was a sizable relation between the seriousness with which one regarded "declining moral standards" and interest in the Holocaust among conservatives. But among liberals there was no relation for clergy and only a weak relation for teachers.[38]

The data permitted another argument to be examined: the idea that the Holocaust was especially meaningful to those who perceived problems in the moral fabric of American society *because* the Holocaust symbolized an ongoing danger. In other words, it was the Holocaust as symbol of everpresent evil rather than the Holocaust as historical event that was of interest to persons troubled about the moral fabric. This connection became evident in comparing those who said they were interested in the Holocaust because it could happen again with those who did not select this as one of their reasons. Among both clergy and teachers there was a significant relation between perceptions of corruption and interest in the Holocaust for those who indicated that the fear of another Holocaust was a major reason for their interest. But among those who said this was not a reason for their interest, no such relation was evident between perceptions of corruption and levels of interest.[39]

This finding helps to interpret the relations between ritual and moral order. The connection is not simply that problems in the moral order of a society create personal insecurities that need to be vented, structured, or expressed in some form of ritual activity. That may be the case in certain instances, but it assumes a great deal more about the psychological basis of ritual than has yet been verified empirically. For example, watching the Super Bowl may be a way of venting the anxieties one feels because of corruption in business. But the connection seems unlikely or at best remote. Instead, strains in the moral order contribute to the meaningfulness of those rituals and symbols that directly and vividly dramatize moral decay itself. Witch-hunts occur in times of crisis not because they provide an emotional outlet, but because people genuinely believe that witches and subversives are selling out the country. By the same token, the Holocaust sparks interest not as catharsis alone, but because it symbolizes something that could happen again if present trends are not corrected.

The data also provided evidence that strains in one's personal situation, like perceptions of strain in the broader society, could generate interest in the Holocaust. Interest varied not only with intellectual concerns about the future of America but also with problems of more immediate, existential significance. For example, clergy in theologically dissonant contexts differed from those in consonant contexts. More specifically, liberal clergy in conservative denominations and conservative clergy in liberal denominations showed higher levels of interest in the Holocaust than their counterparts who were able to see their own values more fully realized in the denominations of which they were a part.[40] The study conducted among high school students in a midwestern community provided some further evidence of the link between personal strains and interest in the Holocaust. Students who said they were troubled by problems in their personal lives, such as loneliness, problems with school, or wondering what to do in life, registered higher levels of interest in the Holocaust than did students who were not bothered by these problems.[41]

The Holocaust was apparently more meaningful, or meaningful in a more immediate sense, to those who were troubled about threats to the contemporary moral order than it was to those who were not troubled in this manner. This finding is consistent with the arguments put forth by Erikson and others working in the Durkheimian tradition, namely, that ritual appears to be a response to crises or uncertainties in the moral order of a society. The present evidence extends this argument to the individual level, suggesting that within a single society individuals with greater concern about problems in the moral order or with greater ambiguity in their own lives are more likely to be interested in ritual or symbolism that dramatizes these concerns. The explanatory power of this argument should not be overstated. In many of the comparisons, percentage differences were relatively small, pointing to the fact that other conditions also enter into the picture. The fact that the differences were for the most part statistically significant and in the expected direction nevertheless supports the contention that uncertainty about the moral order constitutes part of what makes ritual meaningful.

DRAMATIZING COLLECTIVE VALUES

From a functionalist perspective, rituals not only become more meaningful in the face of moral uncertainties; they reinforce collective values—reaffirm the moral order—as well. By dramatizing and provoking discussion about the cherished values of a people, rituals help to restore moral order. But there have been two problems with this argument. The first is that rituals can just as well heighten value conflicts as promote consensus over common values. Particularly in modern complex societies there seems to be no reason to assume that rituals dramatize the same values for everyone.[42] The most prominent rituals may, in fact, be the ones that convey different messages to different groups. The second problem is that this argument has usually been made in the context of purely official rituals—those sanctioned by the state, such as inaugural addresses, Memorial Day ceremonies, and so on. The question is left open as to the effectiveness of nonofficial rituals for promoting moral order.

The Holocaust program was a nonofficial ritual, bearing no connection with the government and conveying no explicit messages about the legitimacy of the state apparatus. Indeed, it sparked special interest (as we have seen) from people who were concerned about corruption in the government. The program appealed to a higher-order set of concerns, rather than ones organized purely around the nation-state. In this important respect it illustrated a way around the traditional dilemma that has faced discussions of "civil religion," from Durkheim to Bellah.[43] It illustrated that moral concerns can be mobilized on a broad scale without reinforcing a kind of parochial nationalism. The Holocaust serves as a symbol of evil for humanity without respect to national boundaries.

At the same time, reactions to the Holocaust program also demonstrate that ritual can have a broad appeal without violating the spirit of cultural pluralism; that is, it can reinforce the diverse values of a pluralistic society, rather than merely promoting conformity to a least-common-denominator mode of consensus. This fact is evident both in the diversity of interpretations that viewers made of the program and in the correlates between these interpretations and other values.

Although the telephone survey obtained no evidence on the kinds of lessons viewers drew from the program, the clergy and teacher studies explored this issue in some detail. One indication of the diversity of meanings that the program conveyed is the variety of responses concerning how best to prevent something like the Holocaust from happening again. About a third of the clergy felt that "teaching people to be better Christians" would help most, but the remaining two-thirds were divided almost equally between an economic solution ("making sure that everyone has a good job and a decent living"), a political solution ("teaching people about democracy"), and an educational solution ("having students learn about it in school"). A few opted for solutions based on "limiting the power of big business and big government," having "strict laws against political extremists," and "showing stories about [the Holocaust] on TV." A number also offered solutions of their own. The responses from teachers were equally diverse, dividing almost equally among economic, political, and educational solutions, with a fair number opting for several of the other responses as well.[44] Had the program been reducible to any single meaning or interpretation, as analysts of ritual have often alleged in the absence of attitudinal data, some degree of consensus on these items would have been expected among viewers, at least more consensus than among nonviewers. A comparison of viewers and nonviewers, however, showed virtually no differences in responses to these questions.[45]

Considerable diversity was also evident in the responses of pastors and teachers when asked to say what they thought the main reason was for the Nazis' attack on Jews. Both groups distributed their responses across a variety of explanations, including Germans being taught to obey orders, Hitler's bureaucracy, economic conditions, the absence of democracy in Germany, and mentally disturbed leaders.[46] Again, viewers were as diverse as nonviewers in their interpretations.[47]

These responses are entirely consistent with the thrust of the program itself. Although it aimed to convey the moral atrocity of the Holocaust (a message that viewers did largely agree on), it did not attempt to communicate any single interpretation of the forces leading to the Holocaust or of how the Holocaust might be prevented from happening again. Instead, it relied on narrative to focus interest in the event and allowed viewers to draw their own conclusions. This approach, utilizing pictographic, ikonic, and expressive symbolism is in fact characteristic of a wide variety of rituals, from church services to patriotic festivals. It is common not only in primitive societies but also in modern societies, where the diversity of values reduces the effectiveness of structuring ritual around tightly defined cognitive themes.

The correlates between interpretations of the Holocaust and broader values suggest that people "read into" the program their own values. It was conceivable that clergy and teachers, when asked to say how something like the Holocaust could be prevented in the future, would suggest solutions that essentially placed the burden on some group other than their own. Instead, they used the occasion to indicate that their own activities could make a significant difference. Clergy opted heavily for the idea that the best solution was to make people better Christians. More than half said this would help a lot, and more than a third said it would help most of all. By comparison, only a quarter of the teachers thought this would help a lot, and only an eighth said it would help most of all. The teachers preferred solutions reflecting their interests in teaching and in social studies. Four in ten indicated that students learning about the Holocaust in school would help a lot (two in ten said it would help most); about equal numbers said they preferred giving people good jobs and a decent living as the best solution. Pastors were significantly less likely than teachers to select either of these responses. In short, these differences suggest that thinking about the Holocaust became an occasion for reaffirming values already held dear by the clergy and teachers.

Further support for this conclusion comes from comparing the solutions given by clergy holding different values and by teachers holding different values. Among both groups, those who selected the idea of making people better Christians as the best solution were also the most religiously oriented in their own values. They were likely to identify themselves as religious conservatives, likely to belong to a conservative denomination, and likely to value the importance of following God's will in their own lives.[48] For these people the Holocaust was an object lesson revealing the importance of adhering to traditional Christian values. Political values were also closely associated with the kinds of moral lessons that clergy and teachers drew from the Holocaust. Those who felt that good jobs and a decent living for all would do most to prevent a Holocaust from happening again were also the most likely to say they held radical or liberal political values.[49] In other words, the Holocaust dramatized the relevance of their political orientations to, among other things, the prevention of a major social catastrophe.

The important point illustrated by these relations is that a single symbol or ritual event can reinforce a variety of different values. Having people focus on a common stimulus, whether that be the Holocaust, the story of Christ's resurrection, or the American flag, need not promote uniformity of belief. Indeed, symbols and rituals of this variety are highly compatible with the concept of cultural pluralism. They afford a basis for communication across a variety of subcultures by providing a shared referent for discussion. But they allow different values to be expressed as well. As W. Lloyd Warner (1961:155–260) observed in his study of Memorial Day services, ritual itself can convey the idea of plurality. In classic Memorial Day services the concept of religious plurality is dramatized by the inclusion of Protestants, Catholics, and Jews in the same commemorative ceremony. In this instance pluralistic values are built explicitly into the performance of the ritual. The Holocaust dramatizes two additional and perhaps more subtle ways in which plurality can be dramatized. For one, the Holocaust itself stands as a vivid reminder of the dangers of totalitarianism (as evidenced in the number of responses stressing the need to teach democracy), and it symbolizes the chaos associated with an absence of pluralism. The massive destruction it represents also communicates by its very severity the necessity of ruling out no solution, no set of activities or values, that may contribute to the prevention of utter destruction.

The narrative structure of ritual also plays a critical role in the capacity of ritual to reaffirm pluralistic values. Ritual tells a story, a message of intentions and values dependent (as Durkheim recognized) on a larger mythology of shared experience, but communicated in graphic, ikonic imagery rich in connotative potential, thus amenable to highly variable interpretations, unlike strict conceptual terminology.[50] The expressive character of ritual permits persons or groups with different claims on the larger collective order to articulate their own position in relation to the moral order. Trevor-Roper (1967:90–192) observes in his discussion of European witch trials during the seventeenth century that the stories told and the images used as well as the punishments meted out were often remarkably similar in Protestant and Catholic regions; yet in one region the lessons derived had to do with clerical excess and in the other with incipient heresy. Each side learned the significance of its own values by observing the ritual of witch interrogation. Narrative also permits multiple layers of meaning to be communicated to the same person or group, thereby enriching the significance of the ritual itself and ensuring a more dramatic and sustained impact on its participants.

The capacity of stories about the Holocaust to elicit different meanings by virtue of their narrative structure has already been suggested by the variety of different explanations viewers gave to account for the occurrence of the Holocaust. These explanations, like the lessons about prevention, were also subject to influence from broader value predispositions. The few who saw the event as a part of God's plan were strongly oriented toward religious values more generally.[51] Those who focused on the role of economic conditions in Germany were likely to be politically liberal in their own views, whereas those who stressed the totalitarian nature of Hitler's regime were relatively more inclined toward political conservatism.[52] These relations suggest that the narrative structure of the Holocaust program allowed people with different values not only to draw different lessons about prevention but also to experience the event itself in different ways. That is, their more general value orientations led them to perceive different forces at work in the unfolding of the Nazi attack itself.

The danger of narrative in loosely structured rituals, like the dangers inherent in cultural pluralism itself, is that some chance necessarily exists for the reaffirmation of values that run contrary to the very nature of pluralism itself. This possibility was illustrated in the high school study. Students in this study were more willing to countenance repression as a means of preventing something like the Holocaust from happening again than were either the clergy or teacher samples. Twenty percent thought "strict laws against political extremism" would help a lot, another 20 percent thought this would help a fair amount, and 7 percent thought it was the best solution of all. Those who favored this solution were no less likely to have watched the program or to say the Holocaust interested them a lot than were other students.[53] They were also just as likely to give correct answers to factual questions about the Holocaust and to say they had learned a lot about the Holocaust in school.[54] The main characteristics that distinguished these students from others were (1) lower grades, (2) spending less time on homework, (3) being less informed about current events, (4) less interest in social problems, (5) less interest in helping the needy, and (6) less concern about social injustices and inequities.[55] In short, this group illustrates the importance of broader understandings to the interpretation of ritual. Although these students were as informed about the Holocaust itself as were other students, they did not have the broader cognitive sophistication about social issues to prevent them from favoring a preventive measure that actually resembled the repressive thinking that contributed to the Holocaust itself.

Finally, the diversity of values dramatized by the Holocaust also illustrates the fact that different types of uncertainty in the moral order are likely to produce different interpretations of the same ritual. In other words, ritual organized loosely around a set of narrative symbols can take on different meanings depending on the kinds of threat perceived to exist in the broader moral order. Any number of perceived threats to the moral order may enhance the meaningfulness of a ritual event, as we have already seen. But the specific meanings evoked will depend to some degree on the nature of the threats perceived. In the Holocaust case, the various interpretations that clergy and teachers derived for preventing another Holocaust bore a close relation to the kinds of threats they perceived currently endangering the future of American society. Those who thought the best prevention was to provide good jobs and a decent living were especially prone to perceive racial violence, social unrest, and police harassment as serious threats in American culture. This was true among both clergy and teachers.[56] Among clergy, those who favored teaching democratic values as the best solution were also somewhat inclined toward the fear of police harassment.[57] The fear of totalitarian repression in this case seemed to go along with wanting greater emphasis on democratic freedoms. In contrast, teachers and clergy who favored teaching Christianity as a solution to future Holocausts were likely to be especially concerned about declining moral standards.[58]

Summarizing briefly, the evidence suggests that the Holocaust was meaningful to the clergy and teachers surveyed for a variety of different reasons and that its specific meanings varied according to different values and different concerns about the moral order. The Holocaust, like many other symbols revealing the evils of which humanity is capable, reinforced the deeper religious and political convictions of those who watched or who thought about the Holocaust's enduring significance. Viewing the television series may not have shaped in any decisive way the lessons that people derived. But thinking about the Holocaust provided an occasion for reflecting on deeper values. The Holocaust served to dramatize the social and moral significance of these values.

VULNERABILITY AND POWER

There remains the question of mobilization. For Durkheim, the person who participated in collective ritual was a person empowered.[59] Confrontation with the gods left one with strength and encouragement for pursuing what was decent and good. Did the Holocaust program have these effects on its viewers? Or did it leave them with a sense of personal inefficacy, indeed, of vulnerability, in the face of such overwhelming evil?

The clergy and teacher studies asked people if they felt they might have gone along with the Nazis had they lived in Germany during World War II. The reason for asking this was to see if vicarious participation in the Holocaust program, like personal participation in a collective ritual, would leave participants with a sense of powerlessness before the collective events portrayed, or whether participants would in some way be fortified to resist these evils. Relatively few of the clergy and teachers (only one in twenty) admitted that they would have probably gone along with the Nazis. About a third, however, indicated they might have gone along with the Nazis. Fewer than a fourth felt they would have had the courage to actively resist.[60] More important, those who had watched all of the television series were most likely to say they might have gone along with the Nazis, followed by those who had watched some of the program.[61] In other words, vicarious participation seemed to be associated with feelings of greater vulnerability rather than an increased sense of personal efficacy.

This sense of vulnerability was especially pronounced among those who perceived within America itself collective weaknesses of the kind that led up to the Holocaust in Europe. A majority of the pastors and teachers felt it was probably true that "many Americans would do exactly what they're told to do, even if it hurt someone else, just like the

Nazis."[62] Among this number, 43 percent said they might have gone along with the Nazis, compared with only a quarter of the remainder.[63]

Perceiving collective weaknesses of this kind was, however, associated as well with actually doing something to communicate about the horrors of the Holocaust. Clergy who thought Americans would blindly obey were more likely to have preached about the Holocaust.[64] And teachers who felt this way were more likely to support the idea of including instruction about the Holocaust in their school's curriculum.[65]

Activities of these kinds, in turn, were associated with feelings of greater personal efficacy. Clergy who had preached a sermon on the Holocaust were almost twice as likely to say they'd have resisted the Nazis than were clergy who had not preached such a sermon. Those who said they had mentioned the Holocaust in a sermon were also more likely to feel this way than were those who had not. And teachers who favored significant doses of classroom instruction on the Holocaust were three times more likely to say they would have resisted than were teachers who opposed all but minimal levels of instruction.[66]

The feeling that one could have resisted the Nazis was also associated with the belief that one could resist evil on the part of one's own government. Clergy who thought they could have resisted the Nazis were five times more likely to say they would do what they felt was right no matter how much the government tried to stop them than were clergy who felt they might have gone along with the Nazis. The ratio among teachers was about six to one.[67]

The overall pattern, then, appears to be this: Confronted by the massive brutality of the Holocaust, the typical observer is likely to experience a sense of personal vulnerability in the face of such overwhelming evil. This is especially true if that person participates vicariously in the destruction portrayed, that is, if he or she thinks of the Holocaust's authoritarian mentality as an immanent propensity to which ordinary people may succumb. In this sense Durkheim was correct in suggesting that ritual participants find themselves temporarily weak before the collective power of the ritual drama. Ritual proclaims an objectified collective force that the individual cannot escape, whether that be the innocent frivolity of the charivari or the horrifying inhumanity of the Holocaust.

But the end result is somewhat more complicated than Durkheim recognized. When the ritual ends, its participants do not emerge emboldened and empowered simply from the experience of having been swept away in collective activity. The ritual must explicitly mandate a moral obligation for the individual participant, one that he or she can fulfill in service to the moral order that has been dramatized. This act of service demonstrates that the individual, too, can make a difference and has a moral responsibility to exercise choice. Every country preacher knows it is insufficient merely to catch the listener up in a terrifying vision of divine judgment; the sinner must be commanded to act, to make a decision in order to receive salvation. Those who watched the Holocaust portrayal and did nothing were left only with a renewed awareness of their own weakness to resist evil. But those who took action, who did something even as a symbolic gesture, came away with greater conviction that they could resist evil, even if their own government asked them to do something wrong. *Moral* ritual not only dramatizes a connection between a symbolic event and collective values; it also creates an opportunity for the individual to exercise moral responsibility in relation to those values.

THE PROBLEM OF MEANING (AGAIN)

This discussion of the Holocaust is intended to illustrate the dramaturgic approach to cultural analysis. Ritual is a symbolic act, a gesture performed for expressive rather than purely instrumental purposes. Whether it is a meaningful gesture depends on its relationship with some set of objective truths, the sincerity of the speaker or speakers involved, the degree to which comprehensible language is used, and its legitimacy in relation to social norms and circumstances. The Holocaust series, or accounts of the Holocaust more generally, can be examined in relation to all these criteria. Indeed, commentators and critics of the program were quick to discuss many of these aspects, for example, pointing out that the program's effectiveness was enhanced by the fact that it dealt with real events, but that this effectiveness was marred by occasional lapses of credibility; that the show had been translated into a grammar of symbolism that middle-class Americans could easily comprehend (particularly in its portrayal of the Jewish family); and that its thesis would have been more forceful had the commercial intentions of its producers (sincerity) been somewhat less apparent. But the distinctive role of cultural analysis is to understand the connections between ritual and the social setting in which it occurs.

The present approach to this task focuses on connections between the observable aspects of ritual and the observable manifestations of other conditions in the society. It makes no claims about the hidden meanings or psychological functions of the ritual event. It examines, instead, patterns among observable symbols themselves that appear to lend legitimacy to the event in the specific social context in which it occurs. In considering the Holocaust as an object of public interest in the late 1970s, this perspective led to a consideration of various expressions of moral concern in American society. Some of these were naturally occurring, such as the president's speech in mid 1979; others were contrived situations generated by pollsters and questionnaires that gave people an opportunity to make public utterances about the moral order. To determine if the Holocaust was more meaningful in some contexts than in others, people who articulated such utterances were compared with people who did not.

The results supported the idea of a connection between characteristics of the contemporary moral order, as evidenced in utterances about it, and the degree to which the Holocaust served as a legitimate mode of symbolic communication. Sectors of the public in which there appeared to be high levels of uncertainty about the efficacy of cherished moral standards vis-à-vis actual practice—in business, government, race relations, and so forth—were also ones in which expressions of interest in the Holocaust were most common. Other delineations revealed that settings characterized by dissonant values or personal worries were also likely to bear evidence of interest in the Holocaust. Varied types of strain in the moral order were associated with different aspects of the Holocaust being emphasized. Furthermore, sectors characterized by diverse values found different elements of the overall Holocaust narrative to be most meaningful. All these findings suggested that interest in the Holocaust functioned as a multifaceted symbol of good and evil that became especially meaningful when the signals given off by the arrangements and activities in the society at large or in more personal contexts contained implicit signs of danger, erosion, ambiguity, or disarticulation between symbolically constructed standards of moral order and actual events. The late 1970s was a time when such signals were easy to identify. But some people were more exposed to them intellectually or existentially than were others. And these were the people who found the Holocaust narrative most meaningful. Additional data would have been desirable to pin down these arguments beyond a shadow of doubt. But the available evidence conformed largely to this interpretation. In short, the program dramatized the moral order; it conveyed symbolic messages that dramatized uncertainties and reaffirmed collective values.

This approach to cultural analysis does not require abandonment of conventional research methods, only a more modest appraisal of the data collected. The present analysis was based on standard survey research data. Such data are advantageous for comparing different population segments, for establishing the empirical presence or absence of relations among different sets of symbols, and for eliciting utterances about various aspects of collective and personal life that might otherwise go unspoken or unrecorded. These data do not, however, necessarily reflect deeper attitudes, emotions, or subjective states of the individual. They *may,* but the survey researcher is usually in no position to know for sure. It is preferable to treat such data as a purely external, observable set of symbolic utterances. The purpose of analysis, then, is to identify patterns among these utterances in relation to the broader social context. This is the approach illustrated here. Theoretical considerations about ritual and moral order suggest certain patterns existing between the symbolic representations of social conditions in the larger society and the specific set of symbols embodied in ritual. Questionnaire responses about social conditions provide an observable set of symbols, the relations of which to similar responses about the Holocaust can be examined. These relations can be compared for different kinds of symbolism (e.g., utterances about declining morality versus ones about racial inequality) and for different contexts (e.g., dissonant versus consonant theological contexts) to further specify theoretically relevant patterns. At no point does it become necessary to make assumptions about the connection between these utterances and deeper subjective states of the individual. Responses to the Holocaust program may have been conditioned by differences in cognitive learning capacities or psychological anxieties, but these become relevant to the analysis of the Holocaust as symbolism only insofar as objective utterances can be measured. These are treated as utterances because the deeper states they may reflect remain invisible to the observer. The links between verbal responses about the Holocaust and the speaker's subjective sincerity could be explored (e.g., through projective techniques, depth interviewing, or intensive testing). But that is clearly a different issue from the study of cultural patterns. The present perspective sets the analysis of culture on an empirical plane, giving it a set of observable materials—materials obtainable from standard data collection methods—with which to work.

The method employed here allowed patterns to be identified among symbols and, in turn, permitted conclusions to be drawn about the social circumstances that enhanced the meaningfulness of the Holocaust program as a ritual event. But this method does not warrant assertions about the "real" meaning of the Holocaust or its meaning to particular individuals. Indeed, the evidence illustrates the futility of such claims. Even within the limitations of the questions asked, it became clear that people interpreted the Holocaust in different ways—some as a religious lesson, others as a lesson in social justice, still others as a message about democracy, and so on—and these different interpretations were contingent upon personal values and experiences. According to the data, the Holocaust has many meanings rather than a single meaning. Nor was the study's inability to reveal the true meaning of the Holocaust merely a limitation of the data. Had the ethnographic methods preferred by phenomenologists been employed, the complexity of the meanings involved would have simply become more apparent. The meaning of the Holocaust would have been different for each individual viewer, and for many the richness of its meanings would not have been easily exhausted. To have assumed that the real meaning of the Holocaust could be ascertained by probing beneath the manifest content to find some universal undergirding interpretation would clearly have been futile. The Holocaust, to be sure, contained multiple layers of interpretation. But the meanings at each of these layers would have varied immensely from one individual to the next, from one time to the next, and from one situation to the next. All that was discovered from the present analysis (and all that has been discovered in analyses that have claimed considerably more) were some of the overt patterns or structures among symbols that made the Holocaust differentially meaningful to some persons and in some settings more than others.

As employed here, the dramaturgic approach was able to draw heavily on the Durkheimian tradition and to generate conclusions supportive of Durkheim's general discussion of ritual and moral order. Yet the present approach departs from Durkheim in one significant respect. Durkheim went most of the way down the road toward arguing that the special, sacred qualities evoked and worshiped in ritual represent nothing more than the power embodied in society itself. That was an easy position to take in looking at primitive religious rites from the "enlightened" vantage point of modern France. No one would dare make the same argument about the Holocaust. Though ritual reminders of the Holocaust bear all the marks of sacredness and taboo that Durkheim observed, to suggest that these were merely conjured up by the moral uncertainties of present-day life would be a ludicrous proposition. Yet, as the evidence has clearly shown, these uncertainties did contribute to the meaningfulness of the Holocaust as people reflected upon it. The analysis of ritual and other forms of symbolism permits these conditions to be understood. But it does not deny that symbolism can also be meaningful because it reminds us of great truth.

CHAPTER FIVE

Moral Order and Ideology

The idea of ritual being a symbolic-expressive aspect of social life suggests an analog for understanding the social role of ideology. If the moral order consists of definitions of the manner in which social relations should be constructed, then signals concerning these definitions need to be sent—signals that social relations are indeed patterned in the desired manner and that actors can be counted on to behave in expected ways. These signals are in part communicated by social arrangements and actions themselves, as in the case of a simple economic transaction expressing definitions of expectations among the parties involved. But special actions may also be engaged in to provide anticipatory signals of intended behavior or to provide additional emphasis or clarity concerning the nature of moral obligations, as in the example of turn signals in traffic. In this sense, ritual is said to dramatize the moral order. It is this relation on which the dramaturgic approach to culture focuses. Ideology may be conceived of in the same way. It consists of symbols that express or dramatize something about the moral order.

Generally, ideology can be conceived of as a set of utterances (verbal or written). These utterances have a high capacity for cognitive manipulation and for this reason serve particularly well as methods of defining and communicating the nature of moral obligations. But ideology may also include visual representations (objects such as flags or pictures), symbolic acts (salutes and genuflections), and events (sets of related acts such as a parade or religious service). In this sense ideology obviously blends with and subsumes much of what is usually referred to as ritual.

The distinction between verbal or written utterances and physical acts remains useful because physical acts often provide the means by which utterances become institutionalized. But this conception of ideology also emphasizes the behavioral aspects of even this narrower set of ideological components. Utterances are a kind of behavior. The contrast between the dramaturgic approach to ideology and the subjective approach, then, is between utterances and beliefs. Utterances, as behavior, are observable to the investigator and can be examined like other elements of social life. Beliefs are the subjective correlates of utterances. They probably cannot be observed directly but can only be inferred from the frequency and force with which utterances are made and the kinds of bodily or social behaviors that accompany them. From this perspective, ideology ceases to be the subjective residue left over after the objective dimensions of social sturcture have been examined; it too is objective, behavioral, observable.

The sociologist may, as seen in Chapter 3, be interested in investigating the symbolic categories and boundaries that constitute the internal structure of ideological systems (i.e., a structural approach). However, this task will usually need to be supplemented by also considering the social context in which an ideology appears. If it is assumed, as just suggested, that ideology expresses something about the moral order, then its relations to the moral order will be of interest. A dramaturgic approach for considering these relations can be set up in the following way.

An intuitive or commonsense consideration of ideology immediately points to the fact of a tremendous variety of ideologies. One thinks of fascism, populism, utopianism, communism, gnosticism, individualism, and a host of other "isms," as well as any number of subtypes and combinations. Yet, despite this enormous diversity, another fact about ideology is equally striking—namely, that an even broader variety of ideologies is easy to imagine. Given ten minutes, ten sophomores can usually come up with ten new ideologies with no trouble at all. Nor is it unrealistic to point out that, with recent advances in computer-simulated artificial intelligence programs, a nearly infinite number of new ideologies could be generated simply as permutations of existing words and statements. The conclusion is that far more varieties of ideology are possible than actually exist at the present or than have existed in the past. Why?

The question here is comparable to that mentioned in Chapter 2 in the context of discussing poststructuralist approaches to culture. Asking why some ideologies exist is similar to asking why some speech acts are meaningful (i.e., why they are used). Here again it is possible to argue that ideologies exist (have been meaningful) because of various circumstances. They may be meaningful in a trivial sense because they conform to conventional rules of language usage—a condition that our computer-driven permutations could probably satisfy. They may be meaningful because they contain certain true statements about reality—a condition that might also apply to ideas developed as part of one's private worldview or as statements about physics or biology that we would not ordinarily associate with the term "ideology." They might also be meaningful because they are uttered forcefully by someone who seems really to believe in what he or she was saying—a case that might, however, brand one as being insane rather than a great ideological leader. What is missing, of course, in these conditions is a consideration of the moral order—the social conditions leading ideological claims to be regarded as legitimate.

If ideology is understood in the first place as dramatizing something about the moral order, then it becomes probable that ideology should have some systematic or predictable relations to social conditions. In a limiting (perhaps trivial) sense, the plausibility of this assertion becomes evident in considering whether or not ideologies have been distributed uniformly in space and time and whether or not they seem to be distributed randomly in space and time. The answer to the first question is certainly negative, and, to the second, certainly more likely to be negative than positive. Thus, it seems likely that part of the variation in ideologies can be understood by looking at social conditions.

To restate the issue, the most abstract formulation of the research problem is that of explaining why only some ideologies, among the many that are conceivable, actually exist. Implicit in this formulation of the problem, of course, is the assumption that ideologies actually exist. The reason this is important may be obscure. It is important because it provides a way of distinguishing ideology from culture more generally. Ideologies are sets of statements that actually exist, now or in the past; culture, within this framework, is the broader set of statements that either exists or is conceivable. That is, ideology is like speech or discourse in that it represents a finite subset of all cultural possibilities; culture is more like language, in the technical sense of the term, in that language is generally understood now not only as a finite set of words (a vocabulary) but also as an infinite or nearly infinite set of statements made possible by the rules that govern its usage. To say that ideologies actually exist is again to emphasize their observable qualities and to delimit the study of ideology as being somewhat more manageable than the study of culture generally. In practical terms, the central research question concerning ideology becomes that of explaining why particular ideologies or ideological themes (patterns) exist in some situations and not in others—the problem that derives from assuming that ideologies are not distributed uniformly or entirely at random. Linguists, philosophers, psychologists, and sociologists may all have something to contribute to answering this question. The sociological contribution is likely to consist primarily of examining social conditions to determine how they affect the distribution of ideological patterns.

Now that the problem has been set up in this way, another important consideration can be introduced. The nature of this problem is formally similar to that faced by biologists interested in explaining why certain species exist in some environments and not in others. Without suggesting any closer parallels between species and ideologies, this analogy nevertheless suggests that some value may be present in considering "population ecology" models in relation to ideologies, just as has been done in other areas of sociology, such as the study of organizations. The chief contributions of adopting a loose population ecology framework are those of emphasizing the dynamics of ideological change, of emphasizing the importance of competition among ideologies, and of creating sensitivity to certain formal characteristics of social environments. In terms of our broader interests, ideas from population ecology theory may provide a useful way of specifying some of the relations between ideology and the social environment that are central to the dramaturgic approach.

The dynamic aspect of ideologies' relations to the social environment is stressed in the idea of a three-phase analytic model. In the first phase ideological variation is produced. That is, some change occurs in the social environment that evokes an increase in the kinds of ideologies present in that environment. This variability then makes possible a second phase in which some of the ideologies survive and others perish. In this phase the effect of environmental factors in limiting the choice of ideologies from a broader menu of ideological possibilities becomes most apparent. Finally, those ideologies that survive are said to undergo some process of internal change that facilitates the likelihood of their retention in the social environment, even against subsequent environmental changes that may augur against their viability. In terms of the schema set forth in Chapter 1, this last analytic phase moves beyond the dramaturgic approach and raises questions primarily about how ideologies become institutionalized.

Implicit in the assertion that some ideologies survive and others perish is the idea of competition. In many settings multiple ideologies do in fact coexist and appear to compete with one another. At times this competition is evident in the copresence of ideologies and counterideologies that are explicitly opposed to one another, for example, in ideologies such as Prohibition versus Repeal or "pro-choice" versus "pro-life." At other times the competition is less explicitly recognized but nevertheless is likely to exist among ideologies that share the same environment (e.g., feminism, Methodism, and Republicanism). The importance of acknowledging the likelihood of competition among ideologies lies in the fact that a change of perspective is indicated. Rather than focusing on single ideologies, ideological *fields*—that is, sets of simultaneously copresent ideologies—need to be considered. The ways in which ideologies influence one another are of obvious importance in understanding the specific content of any given ideology. More generally, a focus on ideological fields shifts attention toward the kinds of themes and formal patterns among otherwise substantively diverse ideologies that may be particularly suited to some environments but not to others. In addition, the fact of competition among ideologies points to a feature that is generally associated with ideology in the sociological literature, namely, its concern with power. In struggling with one another for survival, ideologies inevitably include claims about power. They include arguments about the authority of their own claims, counterarguments concerned with neutralizing the claims of ideological competitors, and statements about the nature of power in the environment at large.

Population ecology models generally conceive of the social environment as a pool of resources that populations must in some way manage to exploit in order to survive. Relatively simple differences in environments can be favorable or unfavorable to different types of populations. Some populations seem better suited to environments with an abundance of resources, others to resource-poor environments. Some adapt to niches in the environment that are relatively homogeneous, others to heterogeneous niches. Changes in an environment over time also appear to attract or encourage different kinds of populations. Some populations are relatively better suited to stable environments; others adapt well to changing situations.

The idea of environments as pools of resources makes obvious sense in dealing with living organisms that physically consume resources or in examining formal organizations that utilize economic resources in turning out material products. Ideologies may seem less obviously connected to the idea of resources; yet the connection is there. Ideologies do not emerge simply from the effortless fantasizing of individuals. It takes time, energy, and other resources to produce them. Usually new ideologies are formulated and disseminated in social movements. The success or failure of an ideology, therefore, depends on its carrier-movement's capacity to extract the necessary resources.

In a somewhat less direct sense ideologies also depend on social resources because these resources affect the character of the moral order, and the moral order is intertwined with the ideologies that dramatize it. Moral order serves as the mechanism relating social environments and ideologies. Changes in the environment may not affect ideologies directly, but if these changes alter the moral order, then ideologies will almost certainly be affected. What this conception provides is an alternative to purely subjective or social psychological conceptions of ideology. Rather than positing individual moods as the link between ideology and social structure, moral order is posited as the mediating connection. From this perspective ideologies do not arise primarily from anxieties or feelings of dislocation or other psychological needs attributed to the individual. They arise instead from changes in the moral order—in public definitions of moral obligations—that make room for or necessitate new efforts to dramatize the nature of social relations.

The relation between an ideology and its environment is an interactive one. In utilizing resources and in articulating moral obligations, an ideology obviously depends on its environment. But an ideology is also capable of influencing its environment. The moral order that it articulates is itself concerned with the distribution of resources. In strengthening the prevailing moral order, an ideology may well legitimate the manner in which resources are distributed. In providing models of alternative moral obligations, ideologies can also undermine existing social arrangements. This again is to say that ideology is concerned with power. It not only describes reality in the abstract; it also tells how reality should be related to in the here and now.

The distinction between ideologies and their environments is inevitably one of perspective. In the case of a specific, well-codified ideology (Pentecostalism, for example) the environment from which it draws resources may consist of religious competitors—other ideologies—as well as "material" resources such as incomes, leaders, and buildings. For a general discussion of ideologies such as capitalism or communism, it may be necessary to focus on a broader range of societal conditions. Clarity about the specific niche an ideology occupies is also important. An ideology that appeals to a single social class may be described as having a relatively homogeneous environment, for example, whereas an ideology with cross-class appeal may be said to have a more heterogeneous environment.

Summing up briefly, then, the model that has been outlined posits a dialectic framework in which to consider the relations between ideology and moral order. This framework specifies a three-phase dynamic sequence: a phase of *production* in which the existing variation in ideologies is amplified, typically by the emergence of new ideological movements and in conjunction with some disturbance in the moral order; a phase of *selection* in which competition among ideologies for scarce resources—competition to provide plausible models of moral obligations—results in some ideologies or ideological forms being "selected for" and others being "selected against," depending on the nature and distribution of social resources in the environment; and a phase of *institutionalization* in which successful ideologies develop or take on additional features that make them less vulnerable to competition and less subject to radical alterations in the environment. In all three phases an interactive relation exists between ideology and moral order. The character of social resources and the definition of moral obligations in the environment have an arguable effect on the kind of ideologies that are likely to emerge, but in no way does this effect allow explanations that reduce or explain away ideologies by attributing them to their environment.

THE SOCIAL PRODUCTION OF IDEOLOGY

The question of why, and under what circumstances, variations in ideological forms get produced is of considerable importance to broader questions about social order and social change. The production of ideological innovations represents an example of cultural adaptation that frequently has important ramifications for the shaping or reshaping of societal goals. In some instances these ramifications have been quite dramatic. One thinks, for example, of the ideological movements that constituted the Protestant Reformation or of the various socialist movements that emerged during the nineteenth century. In other instances, of course, the broader implications are much less obvious (for example, in the case of many of the small religious cults that have arisen in recent years).[1] Yet even in these cases the total effect of all the ideological movements produced in a given time period may add up to considerable proportions, and short of that, the very emergence of new ideologies raises questions about the current condition of the moral order.

As mentioned previously, the production of ideology in a collective sense (as opposed to the production of individual contributions to knowledge) can often be associated with the rise of ideological movements, that is, to social movements in which innovative sets of symbols and rituals play a prominent part, as in most religious movements and in many political protest movements. A dynamic ecological model seems particularly suited to the study of ideological movements. It emphasizes shifts in moral order that result in the appearance of ideological movements in the first place, a competitive process of environmental selection among movements, and subsequent aspects of the institutionalization of these movements. This approach, however, has been little explored in the context of established work on ideological movements. Instead, there has been a prominent tendency to rely on social psychological assumptions about the sources of movements or to ignore the role of ideology entirely.

ALTERNATIVE APPROACHES

One of the more familiar approaches to the study of ideological movements has emphasized relative deprivation as the primary causal factor. Numerous kinds of relative deprivation have been identified: economic distress, downward social mobility, frustrated upward social mobility, loneliness, alienation, anomie, anxiety, ethical questions, and even problems with physical health (e.g., Glock, 1973; Schwartz, 1970; Stark and Bainbridge, 1985). Common to all these types of deprivation is the assumption that necessity is the mother of invention. In other words, people have to have some reason for inventing new ideologies (or adopting newly invented ideologies); thus, the researcher must examine social and other conditions as potential sources of subjective deprivation in order to discover what motivates people to deviate from tradition. An additional assumption in this literature is that the content of resulting ideologies can often be understood in terms of the compensations provided for the deprived. Otherworldly expectations in religious movements, for example, compensate people for the more tangible this-worldly rewards that they would really like to have had instead. From this perspective, ideology is often portrayed as a somewhat irrational response to the world. It either grows from such extreme personal anxieties that wild and misleading perceptions of reality are contained in it, or else it functions (as Marx suggested) as a form of false consciousness that prevents people from coping adequately with their problems.

The relative deprivation approach—and related approaches that emphasize the psychological problems associated with severe social crises—have been subjected to much criticism in recent years. Some critics have objected simply because these approaches seem to be rooted in a reductionistic view of the world that puts ideology in a negative light. Religion especially seems to find defenders among these critics. Their objections generally take the form of arguing that religion itself is a basic need and should not be thought of simply as a compensation for needs of a more tangible sort (e.g., Bruce, 1983). Other criticisms dealing with ideology more generally suggest that it should not necessarily be regarded as an irrational or distorted perception of reality. Still other criticisms have been launched primarily from empirical grounds. According to these critics, relative deprivation is not always obvious among the advocates of new ideologies or among their followers. Often, it appears, ideological movements occur among the relatively advantaged, are "upbeat" in outlook, and are mainly concerned with maximizing new opportunities rather than restoring some traditional values that have become endangered. At other times, deprivation does in fact seem evident among the followers of new ideologies, but no more so than at other times or among other groups where ideological movements remain absent.

As a result of criticisms such as these, studies of social movements have come increasingly to emphasize the role of other factors: social networks as means of recruitment and aggregation, leadership and administrative arrangements, financial resources, coalitions among constituents and with other movements, and so forth (e.g., Gerlach and Hine, 1970; Beckford, 1975; Richardson, 1982; Zald, 1982). Many of these studies have explicitly taken issue with relative deprivation approaches, arguing that these approaches need to be replaced by a perspective that pays more attention to the mobilization of resources. In reality, though, the assumptions on which deprivational arguments have been based have not been challenged; only the importance of additional factors has been highlighted. Nor has much attention been given to the broader structuring of resources in the social environment. The resources specified as having been mobilized are generally ones closely controlled by movements themselves, which therefore figure into the strategies adopted by these movements.

A criticism that challenges the relative deprivation approach at a more fundamental level is one that emphasizes its essentially subjective character. In focusing on internal psychological states, such as anxiety and other felt needs, relative deprivation models are basically concerned with explanation at the individual or social psychological level of explanation. As with other subjective approaches, these factors may or may not be present; the problem is one of knowing how to find out. Deprivation is generally inferred from theoretical premises rather than being studied directly. It is not studied directly with much frequency because it is a subjective variable that is largely unobservable, especially in historical contexts but often in contemporary contexts as well. Deprivation is sometimes even conceptualized as a condition that can only be inferred theoretically because subjects themselves are supposedly deluded by their own ideologies into thinking that they are not deprived. In short, deprivation becomes a *deus ex machina* that accounts for its own consequences without requiring any evidence of its actual existence.

DISTURBANCES IN MORAL OBLIGATIONS

The alternative being proposed here is to retain some of the insights of relative deprivation theory but to reconceptualize them so that they are seen as features of the social order itself. Ideologies need to be understood as inherently social in nature, apart from whatever psychological functions they may perform for individual believers. Ideologies always contain propositions about moral obligations—obligations of patrons to clients, of clients to patrons, of members to communities, of citizens to states and of state representatives to citizens, of persons to one another in their basic dealings (e.g., honesty and integrity), and so on (see Scott, 1977; Eisenstadt and Roniger, 1980; and Tipton, 1982, for various examples). These propositions specify how social relations should be conducted and therefore affect how social resources may be distributed. Insofar as ideologies also require social resources in order to be maintained, any disturbance of social resources that results in uncertainties about the nature of moral obligations is likely to result in some modification at the level of ideology itself. In other words, disturbances in the moral order are likely to be a factor in the production of new ideological forms. Several important observations follow from this line of analysis.

One is that disturbances in social resources need not lead directly to the production of alterations in ideology, nor are the disturbances that *do* necessarily the kind that result in feelings of deprivation on the part of the individual. Rather, disturbances in moral obligations appear to be the most likely sources of alterations in ideology. Moral obligations themselves bear some relation to the nature of social resources, but this relation is not strictly determined by those resources. Indeed, the role of moral obligations in many cases is to anticipate disturbances in social resources and to provide for the maintenance of social order in the presence of such disturbances.

Research on peasant societies, for example, indicates that a "moral economy" is often present—a set of expectations about peasants' obligations to one another and about the reciprocal obligations between peasants and landlords (often dramatized ritually)—that buffers the community against recurrent subsistence crises (Scott, 1976). In these settings, the occurrence of a subsistence crisis would not necessarily be expected to result in new or unusual ideological patterns. If, however, conditions were to change in such a way as to render inoperable or uncertain the system of moral obligations, then some degree of ideological effort would undoubtedly be expended to reconstruct, as it were, the nature of those obligations. The intrusion of foreign powers into peasant economies, for example, has often been accompanied by an upsurge of novel religious activity because, from this perspective, local elites are drawn into external alliances that permanently alter their relations to the existing moral economy of peasant life (e.g., see Scott, 1977).

In this example, peasant clients who suffer a loss of patronage from local elites may well experience some degree of subjective deprivation. Still, clients and patrons alike may experience the new conditions as a kind of liberation or as a situation that poses a new potential. Whether this is the case or not, the change effected at the level of moral order may in fact present an opportunity in terms of its potential for ideological innovation. The disruption of established moral expectations creates a situation in which new symbols can be advanced as interpretations of what the moral order should include. The capacity to exploit these moments of opportunity will depend, of course, on the availability of symbolic leaders, their capacity to generate recruits, and the kind of cultural materials present from which to construct new interpretations. Disruptions of the moral economy in peasant societies, for example, have seemingly been more productive of millenarian religious movements than have disruptions of the moral order among the urban proletariat—one reason being that folk beliefs, community rituals, and potential leaders remain more readily available in the peasant than in the proletarian setting. Other things being equal, ideological movements are also more likely to emerge when whole collectivities are affected by changes in moral obligations than when individuals are subjected to uncertainties and risks solely as individuals or as family units.

An emphasis on moments of opportunity provided by uncertainties at the level of moral obligations requires no assumptions about individual anxieties or individual needs as the inspiration for ideological innovation. Rather, it posits a requirement strictly at the social level for communication about the nature of moral expectations. It also posits that ideological codes provide a means of dramatizing and clarifying such expectations. Ideology creates, as it were, models of moral order that can be visualized and experimented with symbolically, enacted in ritual or in idealized communities, and implemented as a way of reconstructing social relations. Accordingly, any ambiguity in moral obligations creates possibilities for innovative ideological interpretations to be presented.

VARIETIES OF UNCERTAINTY

"Uncertainty" in moral order can be of several varieties. *Risk* may be defined as a situation in which any given activity (X) may or may not achieve its desired goal (Y). *Ambiguity* is a situation in which a given activity (X) either has or has not achieved its desired goal (Y), but for various reasons it cannot be determined whether or not the goal has been achieved. *Unpredictability* is a situation in which a given activity (X) may achieve any of several different goals (Y or Z), but it cannot be determined ahead of time which of these goals will be achieved. All three of these situations represent kinds of uncertainty.

The first—risk—can be illustrated by the case of a hockey player taking a thirty-foot shot at the goal. For various reasons (coordination, vision, etc.), there is considerable risk that the goal will not be attained, even though hitting the puck in that direction is clearly the best means of doing so. In this example, uncertainty consists of the fact that for any given shot it cannot be determined accurately whether or not a goal is likely to be made. Under such circumstances the best that can be done is to estimate a probability of the shot being made based on the player's previous performances under similar conditions.

The second type of uncertainty—ambiguity—can also be illustrated with hockey as example. Here, a shot has been attempted and a goal has either been made or not been made; however, because of a pileup of players, it cannot be determined immediately which state of affairs exists. The function of referees, umpires, and scorekeepers in sports is, of course, to minimize the role of ambiguity so that other types of uncertainty can prevail.

The remaining type of uncertainty—unpredictability—can be illustrated best by considering the uncertainties facing a hockey player who is considering passing the puck to another player. These uncertainties take the form of unpredictability because this player cannot tell in advance whether the receiver will then attempt a goal, pass to another player, attempt to move the puck himself, or allow a defensive player to gain control of it. In making a pass, therefore, the first player must be prepared for any number of outcomes, some of which may be desirable and others of which may be undesirable.

Translated into more naturally occurring settings, these examples suggest some of the ways in which the moral order can become uncertain and, therefore, some of the ways in which ideology may function to reduce uncertainty. In the case of risk, moral order is likely to be involved in efforts to reduce risk—for example, by specifying conditions under which actions should and should not be taken. Ideology functions partly as a purely communicative device, that is, as information about probabilities and relevant conditions for computing probabilities. In addition, ideology is likely to be involved in dealing with residual risks that cannot be reduced. Contingency plans, for example, may be part of prevailing ideologies, thereby providing anticipatory patterns of conduct to be pursued if desired outcomes are not obtained. Ambiguity is also likely to be resolved by the communicative aspects of ideology. However, if a possibly ambiguous outcome has already been attained, then means need to be available for communicating what has actually happened to other actors less privileged with respect to the relevant information. Ideologies specifying that families gather during times of illness facilitate the transmission of accurate information about what has actually taken place. As evident in the hockey example, ideologies may also resolve ambiguities by specifying how ambiguous situations are to be resolved (e.g., by legitimating the office of a decision maker). And unpredictability can be minimized ideologically by systems of ideas that specify what is to be done under particular situations. In sports, formal rules as well as play books provide for the team an ideological subculture that enables it to function without unnecessary confusion. Ideologies that legitimate rituals in which various courses of action are practiced also play an obvious role in reducing unpredictability.

More precision could be added to these specifications of the varieties of uncertainty, of course. Generally speaking, however, uncertainty is usually minimized in social relations by carefully patterning them according to commonly understood prescriptions. This is the function of schooling, laws, and bureaucratic methods of institutionalization. Ideology is normally built into these methods of institutionalization in the form of symbols that communicate standard expectations. Periodically, however, new uncertainties are added, perhaps most often by the addition of "new players" who have not yet learned these expectations, by "new rules" that change expectations, or by "new games" that happen as a result of changed circumstances, changed resources, or some combination of new players and new rules. Whenever any of these uncertainties come about, opportunities arise for new definitions of the situation to be articulated.

Any of the foregoing kinds of uncertainty can become sources of individual anxiety. The role of ideology may also be to alleviate this anxiety. But this palliative role for the individual is not at the core of the present argument. What is being emphasized is not the subjective or psychological role of ideology but its social role. That is, uncertainty constitutes a social problem: collective goals become more difficult to achieve, resources cannot be allocated as effectively, actions cannot be coordinated as well, and any particular actor's performance cannot be planned or evaluated as clearly. Even if there were no subjective anxieties involved in social uncertainties, therefore, ideologies would likely be generated in order to solve these social requirements.

Again, the presence of uncertainty in the moral order cannot be assumed to lead automatically to the production of new ideologies (any more than individual deprivation can). An authoritarian state may prevent ideas from being discussed, economic conditions may force actors to concentrate on short-term survival rather than giving attention to longer-range problems, or difficulties may be faced because of shortages in leadership, communication devices, and so forth. All these possibilities need to be considered as part of what was identified in Chapter 1 as an institutional analysis of ideologies. At the dramaturgic level, however, it remains important to consider simply the opportunities that uncertainties give rise to, other things being equal. In other words, uncertainties in moral order provide possibilities for new ideologies to be produced. These possibilities are probably necessary but are undoubtedly insufficient in themselves for predicting the occurrence of specific ideological movements.

COMPETING IDEOLOGIES

A second observation is that disruptions of the moral order generally elicit not one, but multiple ideological responses. The religious responses to changes in economic and political circumstances in the sixteenth century, for example, included not only Lutheranism and Calvinism but also a myriad of Erasmian, Arminian, and Anabaptist formulations, as well as counterformulations within Roman Catholicism and scattered episodes of mysticism and witchcraft. The social changes accompanying industrialization during the nineteenth century in Europe resulted in numerous variants of utopian socialism, Marxism, democratic socialism, Blanquism, and anarchism, all of which—sometimes quite directly—competed with one another to define the interests of workers and to mold these interests into political loyalties. Similarly, the social disruption of the late 1960s in the United States was accompanied by "new religions" as varied as Zen and Synanon and by various syntheses and modifications in Christianity, Judaism, and quasi-religious disciplines such as Scientology.

Multiple ideological responses occur partly because a disruption of the moral order, by definition, involves uncertainty—and this uncertainty evokes debate as to which response may be most compelling. The presence of this uncertainty is especially likely to evoke multiple responses in situations characterized by a high degree of cultural, political, or economic diversity (e.g., central Europe in the sixteenth century and the United States in the 1960s). In addition, multiple responses often result from the fact that the various entities that have been tied together by moral obligations may now find themselves separated and having to respond to different circumstances. Part of the diversity of responses in the sixteenth century, for example, can be attributed to the fact that the rising commercialization of central Europe opened different types of opportunities for urban merchants, artisans, landlords, and peasants. Each in a way became the primary carrier of a different form of ideological response. Studies of other periods of religious innovation, such as the early nineteenth century in the United States, also point to the importance of rising differentiation among various economic and occupational strata (e.g., Johnson, 1978). Multiple responses are also generated by the fact that movements' initiatives often invite counter-initiatives. The moral order conceived by one set of actors is likely to structure resources in a way that is inequitable or threatening to other actors. The sheer opportunities provided by uncertainty in the moral order may lead individuals to consolidate forces in hopes of protecting these opportunities once an alternative vision begins to predominate. As a result, ideological movements and countermovements frequently emerge in roughly the same contexts.

Another observation is that the emergence of multiple ideological responses often invites direct competition among the various movements associated with these responses. Ideological movements, often from the beginning, are compelled to compete with one another for scarce resources (e.g., members, leaders, finances), and some effort must be made to carve out a suitable niche that ensures access to resources and perpetuates the movement's ideology. This competition often transforms previously diffuse sentiments into an articulated ideology. Tai's (1983) study of Vietnam, for example, demonstrates that Maitreyan millenarianism and communism emerged at about the same time, both responding to the opportunities provided by France's declining position as a colonial power in the years immediately prior to World War II and each attempting to define a vision of the future in competition with the other. This example also illustrates another reason why episodes of multiple ideologies are likely to emerge, namely, that competing movements themselves add to the environmental uncertainty that ideologies attempt to restructure. In other words, what to anticipate and how to behave become all the more problematic because resources will be distributed quite differently if millenarianism, say, rather than communism becomes the dominant ideology.

The presence of multiple, competing ideological movements means that efforts to typologize or categorize kinds of movements have an important dimension beyond that of pure scholarship. Such efforts have, in fact, resulted in a proliferation of typological schemes, differentiated partly by differing conceptual and theoretical purposes, but also differentiated by the focus on different periods of social unrest or sets of ideological responses, each of which is of course historically unique (e.g., Robbins and Anthony, 1981; Wallis, 1984; Beckford, 1986). But social movements are related to one another not only in observers' typologies but also in the competitive reality of the social world; thus, modes of differentiation must be a part of the strategic ideology of any social movement. Symbolic markers must be adopted that set each movement off from its competitors and that cause it to be identified with certain classes of ideology rather than others. These are the materials that observers have sometimes used in constructing their own typologies. But the markers and classification schemes evident in movements' ideologies themselves remain a rarely investigated subject. These markers probably do not emerge simply as orientations toward the world in general, as some typologies imply, but as orientations aimed specifically at setting one movement off from its competitors. Gager (1983), for example, suggests that anti-Semitism emerged in early Christianity at least partly because Judaism posed a strong competitor to Christianity. In other settings, Anabaptists have taken their very name from opposing confessional Protestants, as have Protestants from opposing conciliar theological settlements; Marxists set themselves apart from Blanquists; Black Muslims define themselves against black Christian churches; pro-life, against pro-choice; populists, against statists; ultrafundamentalists, against moderate evangelicals; and so on (e.g., Heinz, 1983; Luker, 1984).

Further, the role of disturbances in moral obligations need not be limited to the emergence of whole ideological movements as such. The same logic applies to minor variations in the content of doctrines, philosophies, teachings, and beliefs that modify rather than change fundamentally the nature of existing moral codes. For example, Carroll's (1983, 1986) detailed investigation of the elevation of the Virgin Mary to the status of a near-deity in the fourth-century Roman Empire demonstrates its relation to the political changes that took place under the rule of Constantine. The effect of Constantine's rule was to alter radically the existing moral order by giving Christianity official recognition. Including such tangible resources as government funding for the erection of churches, this recognition permitted Christianity to expand beyond the relatively narrow niche it had previously occupied among the urban merchant class. As Christianity diffused among the population at large, which consisted mainly of the rural poor, it encountered a different type of family structure—a structure that had supported local goddess cults for several centuries. This environment also provided a niche conductive to the development of a goddess cult around the Virgin Mary.

IDEOLOGIES AND SELECTIVE PROCESSES

Once generated, ideological movements then become engaged in a struggle, as it were, to develop a suitable mode of adaptation to their environment. Decisions may be made according to rational calculations about maximizing potential adherents, securing favorable access to the media, instilling recruits with zeal for the movement's ideology, and cultivating respect for movement leaders. The ways in which movements adapt are not always this rational, however. Immediate crises may call for short-term solutions, and these solutions may be arrived at within the context of various opportunities and constraints presented by the movement's environment. Movements are not passive in this process, but their strategies are likely to reflect the fact that they must secure resources from the social environment in order to survive. Some ideological forms may be relatively flexible and therefore capable of adapting to a changing environment. In this sense the ideology "innovates" in order to survive. The flexibility to innovate may itself be a trait that is environmentally selected, however. Some environments will encourage flexible ideologies; other environments will encourage more rigid ones. Moreover, the ideology that a movement succeeds in propagating is likely to be highly contingent not only on the movement's success as a movement but also on the matrix of culturally defined moral obligations in which the movement functions.

AN EMPHASIS ON FORMS

What may be "selected for" or "selected against" is not always an entire movement in all its complexity, but particular ideological styles or themes that become characteristic of a wide variety of movements or become diffused far beyond specific movements. For example, the present approach does not offer a theory that yields predictions about the survival rates among specific religious movements, such as those produced during the 1960s. Even in retrospect it is evident that many factors would have been necessary in order to predict why the Unification Church succeeded to so much greater an extent than the Meher Baba movement. What might have been predicted, however, is that otherwise diverse movements frequently drew on scientific arguments for legitimation and adopted highly rationalistic styles of ideological argumentation; it might also have been possible to suggest some of the reasons why these ideological forms were better suited for survival in the American context than those adopted by some other new religious movements. In other words, examining the relation between environments and ideological selection requires a significant change in how ideological movements are usually conceived. The conventional approach is to choose a particular ideological movement (say, Mormonism) and ask about the conditions facilitating its growth, or else to classify movements into types (such as "cults" or "revolutionary sects") and ask similar questions about a particular category of movement. In contrast, the present focus shifts to specific dimensions or ideological forms. That is, an analytic level of investigation is specified that crosscuts actual movements. This amounts to simply becoming more specific about the object of investigation. An entire movement is likely to combine a number of different ideological forms, some of which may work at cross-purposes with others. And most typologies of movements also represent ideal-typical aggregations along a number of different dimensions. Focusing on specific ideological dimensions or forms allows examination of a closer link between environments and ideological selection. For more substantive purposes these dimensions can then be aggregated to see how a specific movement may operate.

Any number of ideological forms might of course be identified: utopianism, millenarianism, mysticism, nostalgia, collectivism, thaumaturgical motifs, and so forth. In Chapter 6, three ideological patterns having quite far-reaching applications—folk piety (and fundamentalism), individualism, and rationality—are considered in order to illustrate the selective relationships between ideological forms and social environments in some detail. Here, a somewhat briefer example—millenarianism—is considered as a way of introducing some of the environmental conditions influencing ideological selection.

THE CASE OF MILLENARIANISM

Millenarianism is generally conceived of as a kind of revitalization movement (see Chapter 7). It appears to share certain characteristics with other varieties of revitalization movements, such as cargo cults, utopian sects, nativistic movements, and revivalist movements. What this means is that all these movements have been observed to emerge under somewhat similar social conditions. Each may be regarded, therefore, as a potential competitor of the others. In this competition, millenarianism shares some ideological characteristics with the others but is also relatively distinct.

A common view of millenarianism is that it is typified by specific social movements. That is, millenarianism becomes the dominant feature of a specific movement, earning it the designation of a "millenarian" movement. Although examples can be found where this has been the case, a better approach is to disaggregate millenarianism as an ideological form into component dimensions or themes. Doing so reveals that millenarianism essentially comprises two ideological themes that differentiate it from other kinds of revitalization movements: an optimistic future orientation, and a collectivist or particularist orientation.

The optimistic future orientation in millenarianism takes the form of anticipation of a better world to be established at some time in the future. This may be literally a millennium—a thousand-year reign—of peace and prosperity, as prophesied in biblical writings concerning the Second Coming of Christ, or it may be something much less dramatic, such as an expectation of blessings, material goods, or success. Generally these expectations are couched not merely in an optimistic attitude that things will somehow get better but in a strong eschatological or prophetic orientation that offers definite predictions concerning the future. These predictions, therefore, take on a rationalistic quality, a systematic determinism that conceives of history as moving along a definite path toward an inevitable destination.

The collectivist or particularistic orientation is evidenced in the fact that the expected millennium is generally associated with the entire group of faithful aspirants. This again may be a fairly broad collectivity but is usually limited to a specific sect, church, or local community. This is the feature that distinguishes millenarianism from more psychological or individualistic expectations about the future. Whatever blessing or prosperity eventuates will accrue to the entire group. Nonmembers will be deprived or punished; members will become a remnant that escapes tribulation, receives rewards for their faithfulness, and may even become leaders of the new age. Because rewards are contingent on collective participation, strict membership requirements are usually included, and public demonstrations of one's loyalty are often required.

The combination of these two orientations reveals the similarities and differences between millenarianism and various other ideological forms. Cargo cults have the same formal characteristics because the material goods anticipated in the future are expected to benefit the group as a whole. Utopian sects generally combine both elements as well but envision an optimistic future being created through the work of the community itself. Nativistic movements, though seen as having backward-looking or nostalgic ideologies, may in fact espouse the components of millenarianism insofar as the "golden age" of the past is expected to return again in the future. Revivalistic movements, in contrast, generally emphasize an optimistic future for the individual (e.g., through individual salvation), but this future often is not linked directly with the entire group as a collectivity. Only the expectation of individuals in the collectivity sharing a similar future life approximates the collectivist dimension of millenarian ideology. Millenarianism is also to be distinguished from most gnostic and mystical ideologies, which may become manifest in communal settings but nevertheless emphasize individual enlightenment.

Millenarianism conforms closely to what has already been said about ideological production. It appears to have emerged historically in settings in which moral obligations were fundamentally disrupted. In early modern Europe, the millenarian elements of Reformation ideology, as manifested in the Zwickau prophets, Munzerites, and some of the Anabaptist sects, emerged primarily in areas in which traditional patron-client relations between landlords and peasants were broken. Peasants and recent migrants to the towns, often lacking stable moral communities, became reintegrated into a new moral order as part of millenarian movements. In many parts of the Third World, similar processes appear to have been at work in the production of cargo cults, prophet cults, and other millenarian movements. In many of these cases, however, millenarian ideology is but one of a number of responses to moral dissolution. More established religions, political parties, and individualistic ideologies also compete to redefine moral obligations. To understand why millenarianism gets selected for, at least in some instances, it becomes necessary, therefore, to consider the kinds of environmental conditions that may favor its major dimensions.

CONDITIONS FAVORING OPTIMISM

Optimism appears to be an ideological dimension that extends well beyond millenarianism as such and one that generally seems useful in attracting members to new social movements. Even in the contemporary United States, optimistic assumptions about human nature have been shown to be an important factor contributing to experimentation with alternative life-styles. Unlike many traditionally religious conceptions of human nature that focus on the "depravity" of humankind, symbol systems rooted in the social sciences (ones that attribute blame to social conditions rather than to human nature) or in humanistic versions of contemporary psychology appear to encourage participation in alternative social movements (e.g., Wuthnow, 1976; Aidala, 1984). Bryan Wilson (1979) has observed that new religious movements in both Japan and the United States have generally offered a more optimistic view of salvation than have established religions. A similar claim has also been made concerning periods of religious reformation more generally (Shapiro, 1973). It has also been suggested that heterodox or minority ideologies are more likely to regard human nature optimistically (i.e., as perfectible), and therefore in less need of institutional restraints, than are orthodox or majority worldviews (Douglas, 1980).

The value of optimism to fledgling social movements can be understood in relation to the performance-payoff nexus that informs much of social behavior. Optimistic ideology affects the balance between investments and rewards. It objectifies expected rewards, as in cargo cults, so that required investments appear justified, or it suggests that smaller investments can be made, as in substituting faith for doctrine and ritual, with no loss on expected returns. A comparative advantage over more costly relationships is thereby attained, affording access to new environmental niches.

The environmental perspective also allows an explanation for variations in the distribution of optimism. Common sense to the contrary, neither the richness of environmental resources nor the direction of shifts in their availability seems to have much to do with these variations. The millennial dreams of impoverished Munzerites appear to have been no less hopeful than the optimism inspired by Luther's doctrine of *sola fide* among the rising German magistracy. The primary condition favorably affecting the selection of optimistic ideologies appears to be environmental instability. Under unstable conditions, a deep moral obligation established at one time is likely to become disadvantageous for maximizing access to resources at a later time. Should the duration between environmental changes be relatively long, or should each change be regarded as a purely idiosyncratic occurrence, moral obligations capable of stabilizing social exchange over the long run are likely to retain adaptive value. If, however, the duration between changes is relatively short and the total period over which change is expected is relatively long, then moral obligations that can be maintained with minimal investments, and therefore can be changed to meet new environmental conditions, are likely to provide a comparative advantage over deeper, more enduring commitments. To the extent that optimism, in fact, readjusts investment-reward calculations in the direction of less costly investments, it is likely to be selected in these situations.

In the case of millenarianism, social environments appear generally to have been not only unstable but also unstable with respect to a critical threshold (i.e., subsistence). Instability took the form of radical vacillations in broader political and religious policies, often as a result of conflict between dominant religious movements (as in the Reformation), which intermittently encouraged and then persecuted particular doctrines and life-styles. In addition, economic crises often lent uncertainty to the situation by periodically pushing incomes below subsistence levels. The optimism of millenarianism contributed stability to social relations under these circumstances. As long as future rewards could be expected, investments in family and community life were more likely to seem legitimate. The appeal of millenarianism cannot be understood entirely on the basis of optimism alone, however.

CONDITIONS FAVORING COLLECTIVISM

The collectivist orientation in millenarianism in some ways complements and in some ways conflicts with its optimistic future orientation. The kind of environment in which collectivism is likely to be selected for can be illustrated by imagining a lifeboat adrift at sea with a handful of survivors aboard. Under these conditions "each man for himself" is not likely to be an ideal ideology. A strong sense of *esprit de corps* is needed for the group to survive. Food and water must be rationed and tasks must be shared, or the venture will fail. So it is with other environments favoring collectivism. The lifeboat illustrates a resource-poor environment that is relatively homogeneous and stable. Supplies are scarce, each person's fate depends on the same circumstances as every other person's, and for the immediate future no radical change in conditions is expected. A sense of *esprit de corps* in this instance protects scarce resources. This orientation is easy to maintain because the stability of the environment does not alter the nature of moral obligations. Environmental homogeneity also means that resources can be exploited as effectively, if not better, by the group than by a more diverse or complex structure.

Although collectivism and individualism may sometimes combine in curious ways, the two are essentially opposites of each other and are selected by different environments. Individualism, as will be seen in Chapter 6, is selected for in relatively rich, heterogeneous, unstable environments. Richness provides resources that individual units can exploit, apart from the group; heterogeneity means that decoupled units can overall adapt to and exploit the resources in diverse niches; and instability encourages ideologies that decouple component units to the extent that, if environmental changes cause some to fail, others will nevertheless survive. Collectivism in general contrasts with all these characteristics. It encourages conformity so that scarce resources will be divided among the group and keeps outsiders from taking advantage of group resources, survives best in a homogeneous niche in which resources can be exploited by the group, and fares best when there are few changes to up-set moral obligations within the group. It is not surprising, therefore, that millenarianism has been common in poor societies such as peasant settings in early modern Europe and the Third World and that it has flourished in homogeneous environments such as rural villages. The ne-cessity for stability, however, conflicts with the role of instability in re-inforcing optimism. This conflict is, in fact, an important feature of millenarian movements.

The conflict between optimism, as an ideological form suited to un-stable environments, and collectivism, as an ideological form suited to stable environments, manifests itself in millenarian movements in sev-eral interesting ways. On the whole, this conflict may explain the rela-tive infrequency of millenarian movements. For example, in early mod-ern Europe, estimates of religious patterns indicate that only about 1 percent of the population in any country or region became involved in the "radical reformation" of which millenarianism was a part. Simi-larly, Third World millenarianism, though widely discussed, appears to be relatively limited in occurrence, especially in comparison with ide-ologies of revolution, spiritism, revivalism, and so forth. Part of the rea-son may be that the instability that encourages optimism contradicts the stability needed to sustain collectivism. This conflict may also ex-plain some of the more common features of millenarian ideology as it evolves over time. In highly unstable environments, millenarianism of-ten appears in conjunction with a strong authoritarian leader. This leader's function is to maintain collective loyalty in the face of environ-mental conditions that would otherwise militate against such orienta-tions and to make decisions that would be difficult for a collectivity to make in the absence of strong leadership. Lacking strong leadership, millenarianism in unstable environments often takes the form of a rela-tively individualized optimism. In a rapidly changing environment such as the American frontier, for example, millenarianism as such appears to have been less prominent than revivalism, and the millenarianism de-scribed by historians seems to have included little in the way of collec-tivism other than diffuse expectations about the destiny of the nation. In contrast, millenarian movements in environments that become sta-ble, because of either sustained persecution or a normalization of eco-nomic conditions, veer toward collectivist sects with strong in-group boundaries but with weakened expectations about the coming of the millennium. This has been the trajectory of many sects within the Anabaptist tradition.

This example, then, suggests some of the ways in which even relatively crude dimensions of the environment can generate predictions concerning the relative prominence of alternative ideological forms. In the case of millenarianism, some value is evidently gained by treating it as a combination of two ideological forms rather than as a single ideological category. Although these two forms often are found together in actual millenarian movements, theoretical considerations suggest that they may not be entirely compatible, and thus that millenarianism may be a relatively uncommon or unstable ideological complex. In Chapter 6, a somewhat more detailed argument concerning the structure of ideological forms and their relation to various environmental characteristics is developed.

THE INSTITUTIONALIZATION OF IDEOLOGY

Stressing the environment's selective influence over ideological forms may cause objections that ideology is accorded too passive a role. These objections can be set aside, however, by reintroducing the third element—institutionalization—of the dialectic framework set forth at the outset. The process of becoming an institution involves developing a relatively stable means of securing resources, an internal structure for processing these resources, some degree of legitimacy with respect to societal values and procedural norms, and sufficient autonomy from other institutions to be able to establish and pursue independent goals.[2] An ideology that has become fully institutionalized is therefore capable of not only withstanding considerable alterations in its environment but also producing some of these alterations itself. The dynamics of institutionalization can be illustrated with respect to rituals, organizations, and the relations between ideology and the state.

THE ROLE OF COLLECTIVE RITUALS

Much of the ambiguity that has surrounded the study of rituals can be resolved if it is recognized, as shown in Chapter 4, that their social function is chiefly one of communication. Like verbal utterances, rituals are behavioral acts that explicitly or implicitly express something about actors' relations to one another. Rituals may be consciously orchestrated at specified times according to preestablished norms to commemorate or initiate some important event in the life of a community—

in which case the term "ceremony" may be more appropriate. Other rituals consist of relatively simple acts that nevertheless convey meaning (a soldier's salute or an automobile driver's signal to turn). Even acts that are conducted primarily for purely instrumental purposes (e.g., digging a ditch) may have expressive roles, depending on how they are performed. Thus, ritual may be more appropriately described as an analytic dimension of behavior than as a totally discrete type of behavior. Ritual is symbolic-expressive, and in order to accomplish this communicative task, it often conforms to formalized norms and has a built-in degree of redundancy that gives it an elaborated or ceremonialized character.

Although it is possible to conceive of ritual apart from ideology and ideology apart from ritual, the two often go together. Both articulate the moral order. Ideology is likely to consist mainly of verbal and written utterances, ritual, of behavior enactments. Ritual is a way of enacting the ideas that are uttered verbally or in writing. In this sense ritual integrates ideology into the realm of social behavior. Ideology thus affects social behavior, and this behavior reinforces and affirms ideology.

As suggested already, rituals are generated in much the same manner as other ideological systems. Both are likely to appear in situations of uncertainty in the moral order and to help clarify the moral obligations constituting that order. The very conditions in the social environment that are most conducive to ideological movements, therefore, are likely also to be conducive to rituals. Some of the cases considered in the previous chapter involved rituals sponsored by the established religious or political structures (e.g., witch-hunts sponsored by the Puritan authorities or political show trials sponsored by corporatist regimes). In these cases rituals provided occasions for dramatically reaffirming established ideologies. Just as likely, however, is the possibility that uncertainty in the moral order will generate oppositional ideological movements that sponsor their own rituals. The dissenters in Puritan Massachusetts had their own worship services; Protestants in the Reformation not only burned heretics but also engaged in ritual violence against Catholic ikons and sponsored their own form of the sacraments; millenarian movements in the Third World withdraw from and oppose dominant regimes and also draw their adherents into collective rituals.

As ideological movements progress, rituals not only serve as a response to broader ambiguities but also become part of the normal functioning of the movement itself. This pattern is especially evident in religion. As religious movements become established and form religious organizations, one of the prominent functions of these organizations is that of maintaining a regular set of ritual offerings. That is, religious organizations produce rituals as a kind of service to their members, in return for which resources are contributed. Worship services, funerals, weddings, and christenings are all examples. A religious organization's effectiveness in conducting rituals is likely to be one of the ways in which its beliefs are perpetuated. Its rituals are also likely to be one of the means by which it shields itself from its environment. This becomes most evident in rituals that not only utilize resources but also manufacture them.

One of the obvious ways in which rituals manufacture resources is by generating enthusiasm (what Durkheim called "collective effervescence"). Research on rituals emphasizes the role of charismatic leaders in evoking such enthusiasm. Studies have also led to greater recognition that enthusiasm, once generated, has to be carefully controlled in order to channel it toward realization of the organization's goals (see especially McGuire, 1982). For this reason, a strong charismatic leader may again be necessary. Or in other settings, carefully prescribed rules appear to operate to limit what may otherwise seem to be purely spontaneous behavior (Bainbridge, 1978; Zablocki, 1980).

Rituals also manufacture resources by providing collective confirmation of promised rewards. Testimonials play a special function in this regard. They not only confirm to the believer a particular alteration of self-identity but also provide the collectivity with evidence that its beliefs are efficacious. Seemingly supernatural claims acquire pragmatic justification as members point to the fact that "lives are changed" (Ault, 1983). Testimonials also dramatize the collectivity's legitimacy by demonstrating the "acts of grace" that have befallen its members (anything from good fortune in locating parking places to miraculous healings). The ritual publicizes these happenings: believers are thus encouraged to selectively perceive such acts of grace in order to have something to "share." Otherwise infrequent or random occurrences seem to become more common by virtue of being communicated to the entire collectivity (Kroll-Smith, 1980; Downton, 1979).

Rituals also help stabilize ideologies by solving the so-called "free rider" problem (i.e., the tendency for members of organizations to reap collective rewards without contributing resources) (Olson, 1971; Hilke, 1980). This is a particular problem for ideologies that attach a high degree of importance to individual conscience. These ideologies often give the individual the right to make choices independent of any group and, thereby, the ability to secure rewards without contributing to group maintenance. For example, many variants of modern religion bestow on the individual the capacity to communicate directly with God and thus the expectation of receiving supernatural rewards directly. The tendency for such beliefs to reduce involvement in religious organizations is mitigated in part, as Weber recognized, by the radical uncertainty that besets the individual with regard to salvation and thus the need for confirmation through legitimate membership in a religious collectivity. In addition, most religious organizations orchestrate rituals in such a way as to prevent the full benefits of the organization from being distributed to persons who are not actively contributing members. Persons having contributed at specially high levels may be accorded recognition in leadership roles as part of the organization's rituals, access to privileged information may require participating in rituals, having individual needs met may require making these needs known in ritual settings, and the belief system may simply define as high rewards such benefits as "fellowship" or "the worship experience"—rewards that can be attained only through ritual participation.

Most established religions in the West continue to rely mainly on these kinds of collective processes to ensure that sufficient contributions of time and energy are received to maintain their organizations. However, the professionalization of many of the welfare and charity services that religious organizations have traditionally provided their members may have eroded some of this capacity. In response, a tendency has become evident in some religious organizations to offer programs on a fee-for-service basis (e.g., educational programs, youth activities, and counseling) or to simply establish membership dues. Another potential problem for religious organizations that has only recently become the focus of research is the impact of religious television programming (Hadden and Swan, 1981; Horsfield, 1984). The question raised by the rapid increase in such programming is whether its convenience and availability to "free riders" may detract from personal involvement in religious rituals and organizations. Preliminary results from the United States suggest that this has *not* been the case in the short run but leave open the question of longer term effects (Gallup Organization, 1984).

ORGANIZATIONS AND IDEOLOGY

In addition to serving as a source of rituals, organizations represent a higher level of institutionalization than rituals alone in that they constitute an ongoing application of resources to the advancement of specific ideologies. Organizations serve as mechanisms not only for the extraction of resources from the environment but also for the coordination of these resources around the accomplishment of specific objectives, some of which may effect transformations in the environment itself. Thus, the essential components of an ideological organization include a system of drawing in resources, a relatively stable system of processing these resources, and a set of goals or tasks to which processed resources are committed. Organizations of all kinds can be said to be engaged in the propagation of ideology in that their very institutional structure is, as Meyer and Rowan (1977) have argued, a kind of mythic statement about their purposes in relation to the larger environment. Beyond this general connection between organizations and ideology, however, some organizations are explicitly concerned with the production and maintenance of ideology. Political propaganda agencies, scientific organizations, and religious bodies constitute prime examples. Some of these organizations' relations with the social environment will be considered in later chapters. Here, some of the ways in which social environments influence the structure of ideological organizations can be illustrated by briefly considering the patterning of religious organizations.

Beginning with Troeltsch, a basic distinction has been drawn between two types of religious organizations: *churches* and *sects*. These terms have been used widely in the literature on sociology of religion, but the distinction between churches and sects has often been confusing because localized examples, rather than conceptions of a more formal nature, were used. In keeping with an emphasis on the extractive relations between religious organizations and their environments, churches may be defined as religious organizations that extract resources in a relatively nonintensive way from a large segment of the environment; sects may be defined as religious organizations that extract resources intensively from a smaller segment of the environment.[3]

This way of distinguishing churches and sects clearly rests on not one but two distinctions: the *size* of the environmental segment from which resources are drawn (large/small) and the *intensity* with which these resources are drawn (low/high). Other things being equal, churches are more likely to be relatively large but make shallow demands; sects are more likely to be smaller but make deeper demands. Another way of making the same point is to say that churches attempt to regulate or fulfill a few of the activities or needs of large numbers of people; sects attempt to regulate or fulfill many of the activities or needs of small numbers of people. An attractive feature of this distinction is that it corresponds well with common usage of the two terms. The term "church" is typified by various national churches that encompass an entire society but elicit minimal levels of commitment by fulfilling mainly such limited functions as administration of sacraments; sects are typified by denominations that (though sometimes quite large) are small in comparison with national churches but provide an all-encompassing set of activities for their members and obtain high levels of commitment in time and money in return. Also typical of many contemporary churches are organizations that supply a wide variety of services but that involve any given member in relatively few of these activities (e.g., choir for one, youth activities for another).

An important implication of this way of defining churches and sects is that both can be viable means of adapting to the modern social environment—and therefore of propagating their distinctive ideologies. Contrary to an assumption prevalent in the literature, sects need not follow some inevitable path toward becoming churches. Indeed, the persistence of sects should itself be sufficient to cast doubt on this notion. Sects can maintain themselves by adapting to relatively discrete niches in the environment and by giving much but also demanding much. Churches can adapt by demanding little but specializing in services that at least secure a little commitment from large numbers of people.

Increasingly, too, religious organizations have adapted by combining elements of both styles, resulting in what sometimes looks like an inverted pyramid, with many members having few commitments and a few members having many commitments. Not only established religious organizations but also new religious movements have incorporated this strategy, providing low-commitment services such as public meetings and open classes, but also providing more intensive training for the few willing to make a commitment (for some examples, see Popenoe and Popenoe, 1984).

Some of the problems characteristic of sects and churches also seem to be closely linked with their particular modes of competing for resources. Sects, for example, turn their "consumers" into "employees" by relying on intensive commitment from small numbers of people. But this strategy increases the likelihood of having "labor" problems; hence, one of the traits typical of sectarianism is a tendency toward internal disputes, often resulting in relatively high rates of schismatic factionalism. Churches, in contrast, tend to follow mass market strategies oriented toward the casual consumer with relatively low levels of product awareness. As a result, educational programs are often underemphasized, audiencelike behavior is cultivated, high levels of organizational switching (low product loyalty) are evident, withdrawal becomes more common than efforts at reform, and organizational initiatives tend to come less from lay members than from the more heavily involved bureaucratic staff.

Churches and sects, however, represent only two of the four types of organizations conceivable from the cross-classification of size and intensity. Also conceivable are large/intensive organizations and small/nonintensive organizations. The former appears to represent a nearly "empty cell" as far as modern societies are concerned.[4] Institutional differentiation, resulting in many functions and resources being dissipated among other organizations, appears to preclude large numbers of people giving total commitment to religious organizations. The other option (small/nonintensive) appears to be a nonempty but neglected category of religious organization. This category is represented by relatively small religious organizations that make specialized demands of their members and fulfill specialized functions. The most appropriate term to describe these organizations is perhaps "special purpose groups."

Special purpose groups are exemplified by religious movements oriented toward the reform of some larger religious body or the larger society, by interest groups and professional organizations among laity or among religious specialists, and by coalitions that integrate or bridge interest groups across the boundaries of established religious organizations. Rather than dealing inclusively with core religious concerns such as worship and instruction, they tend to be oriented toward more specialized aims (e.g., music, evangelism, or church policies on race). Their ideologies define social relations within only a limited sphere of the moral order. For this reason, many are characterized either by fleeting existences or by fleeting memberships. The intensity of commitment required may be quite high (as in other social movements) but in formal terms tends to be routinized either as a professional interest or as a focused commitment, in contrast with the model of religious communities that purports to encompass all of an individual's interests and activities. Special purpose groups have a long history alongside churches and sects, but their numbers and memberships have apparently risen dramatically over the past half-century or so (Wuthnow, 1985).

The rising importance of special purpose religious groups appears in part to represent a kind of isomorphism in religious organizations with secular organizations (e.g., feminist movements in churches as counterparts to the broader feminist movement). In addition, special purpose groups may be especially adaptable to the modern environment. In more narrowly focusing the goals of an organization, they may gain greater adaptability in relation to an environment that is not only heterogeneous but also rapidly changing. Special purpose groups may arise in relation to a specific social or political concern, but then disband once this concern has passed. By clearly differentiating themselves from established churches and sects, special purpose groups can channel their resources in more specific directions.

An implication of this typology for the study of ideology is that highly diverse ideologies are likely to be sustained within any heterogeneous environment. Heterogeneity is unlikely to lead inevitably toward any single ideological form (e.g., secularization in the case of religious ideology). Heterogeneity may, however, reinforce a kind of polarization in broader ideological patterns. Those that adapt to broad niches, on the one side, may become increasingly similar to one another in basic form and may incorporate orientations perceived as being liberal, tolerant, and flexible. On the other side, ideologies that fill in the gaps by settling into homogeneous niches may be rather diverse among themselves but formally take on characteristics that outsiders tend to regard as conservative, parochial, or rigid. Certainly this kind of polarization has been evident in the religious orientations of many industrialized societies in recent years. It may also be a factor in political and economic ideologies. Rather than modernity promoting consensus around strictly liberal ideologies, it may promote both liberal ideologies and conservative counterideologies. The liberal ideologies may be best suited for generating minimal commitments from loose coalitions among diverse groups, whereas the conservative ideologies may be better suited for creating deep commitments in more homogeneous settings.

Neither of these ideological forms is ideally suited to many of the organizations and tasks that make up modern societies. For example, libertarian orientations in the polity, although useful for defending basic human rights and broad civil liberties, offer little in the way of legitimation for concrete government proposals on defense policies or interest rates. The highly communal orientations of families, sectarian religious bodies, cults, survivalist collectives, and so forth also fail to inform many of the more utilitarian aspects of economic and political life in the wider society. Consequently, special purpose groups that pursue these more limited objectives are likely to create—consciously or inadvertently—their own distinctive ideological forms. The substantive content of these groups is likely to be quite diverse, but similarities in basic form may be evident as well. These similarities may consist of a relatively strong em-

phasis on pragmatic norms of evaluation, technical competence, specialization, and proper procedure. These groups are therefore likely to demonstrate a certain degree of isomorphism in such ideological and ritual
practices as professionalization, certification procedures, rational organizational styles, and technological legitimation.

THE STATE AND RELIGION

A remaining aspect of institutionalization that can be used to illustrate this aspect of the ideology-environment nexus is the relation between ideology and the state. This relation has often been examined
from a teleological perspective concerned with ideology as legitimation.
From this perspective, ideology comes into being in order to fulfill the
state's need for legitimation: necessity (again) is the mother of invention. This institutionalization of ideology therefore receives little more
than a simplistic treatment in terms of its justification of state interests.

An environmental perspective emphasizes the role of the state as an
environmental resource that influences the selection and institutionalization of ideologies. Often the state constitutes the most significant factor
of all ideological institutionalization because this process may in fact be
mainly a matter of securing official recognition from the state. In short,
the state sanctions an ideology as official doctrine.

The state influences the process of ideological institutionalization in
many other ways as well. In its law-setting and regulatory functions the
state defines the environments that may or may not be open to ideologies
and imposes requirements to which ideologies must conform. It is widely
argued, for example, that the growth of the modern national state was a
factor conducive to individualistic ideologies because the national state
brought diverse local groupings together into a single collectivity with a
heterogeneous structure to which individualism was especially adaptable. As a wielder of economic resources, the state also significantly affects the distribution of material resources that may be at the disposal of
different ideological movements. For example, the rapid influx of federal
money into higher education in the United States since World War II has
contributed significantly to the resources available to campus-based
movements, such as the antinuclear movement, divestiture campaigns,
and religious cults.

Attention to the state points to the fact that ideological movements
do not actually compete with one another in a strictly free market of
ideological appeals or as movements with relatively equal access to ba-

sic resources. The environment in which they compete is likely to be shaped fundamentally by the state. Having such vast resources at its disposal, the state can sometimes simply "swamp" all other competitors by declaring a particular ideology to be official. In other ways, ideologies are likely to be greatly influenced by the stance that different movements assume toward the state. Even where the state is officially neutral with respect to different ideologies, awareness of its presence is likely to shape the strategies taken by various movements.

Religion again provides ample illustrations of these dynamics. The relation between religion and the state was ignored for a considerable time in sociology because of theoretical perspectives that concentrated on the growth of institutional differentiation between religion and the state.[5] Insofar as any continuing interaction was seen, it tended to be portrayed in terms of religious organizations fighting a rearguard action against the intrusion of the state into areas formerly under ecclesiastical jurisdiction. From this perspective it seemed evident that even by the end of the nineteenth century the church had withdrawn into comfortable isolation from the public affairs now supervised by the state. Yet recent developments in a number of societies, particularly in Latin America and the Middle East (but not excluding Europe and the United States), have heightened awareness of the complexities of the relations between religion and the state. In the last decade alone a number of solid empirical studies have been produced.[6] Many of these studies have of necessity been preoccupied with the sheer task of developing a descriptive empirical base; others have been devoted to questions of practical, legal, and ecclesiastical concern.

The topic of civil religion is one area in which much thinking has been generated about the relations between religion and the state. Civil religion has been defined as "that religious dimension, found . . . in the life of every people, through which it interprets its historical experience in the light of transcendent reality" (Bellah, 1975:3). In practice, civil religion generally consists of god-language used in reference to the nation (e.g., biblical quotations in presidential addresses, religious jeremiads directed at government policies, etc.). A society's civil religion includes a "myth of origin" that relates (and often reconstructs) the nation's history, a conception of the nation's purpose or destiny in history and in the world, definitions of what constitutes legitimate membership in the nation, and various taboos that define the society's external boundaries and differentiate it from other societies. Like religion generally, civil religion performs a dual function for the society: it legitimates the social order, evoking commitment and consensus; and it permits specific social policies to be criticized in light of transcendent ideals.[7]

Civil religion can be conceived of as an example of incomplete differentiation between religion and the state. It represents an intermingling of religious and political symbolism at the cultural level. Despite formal separation of church and state, the presence of a civil religion allows religious values to influence the state, on the one hand, and gives the state a means of influencing religion, on the other. The fact that these influences remain possible in highly industrialized societies suggests that the relations between religion and the state may be more complex than a strict conception of institutional differentiation would imply. Two empirical questions follow: Do religious organizations tend to benefit by having this form of access to the state, or does civil religion generally force them to compromise? Does the state benefit from having access to religious arguments, or does it function more effectively in terms of purely secular norms? These questions remain open, but available evidence indicates that answers are likely to vary from society to society depending on the nature of the state and the strength of different religious traditions.

The key limitation of studies concerned with civil religion to date is that they have concentrated almost entirely on matters of symbolism rather than including considerations of the institutional structure of the state and of religion. Greater attention needs to be given to how organizational constraints, resources, interest groups, and social cleavages—on both sides—affect the relations between religion and the state. For analytic purposes, these factors can be investigated at one or both of two distinct levels. At the societal level, the state becomes a relevant consideration chiefly as an element of the resource environment. At the institutional level, specific alliances and other forms of interaction between religious organizations and political organizations can be conceptualized.

As a feature of the resource environment, the state influences religion in a number of indirect ways. Other things being equal, the presence of a centralized state with legitimate rule over a sizable territory defines an environment that encompasses local and regional niches of considerable heterogeneity. Indeed, the expansion of the nation-state typically takes place at the expense of local and regional autonomy. In this manner, state expansion is likely to create an environment that selects for the kinds of ideological systems that adapt most easily to broad heterogeneous niches. As the defender of uniform laws and regulations, the state also in a sense establishes "rules of the game" to which religious institutions must conform.

The state not only defines the environment but also monopolizes many of the resources in the environment. To the extent that its monopoly over the resources religious systems need—charters, educational facilities, public buildings, communications media—is complete, religious competition may be reduced to an inconsequential minimum (as in the case of theocratic states or states banning all forms of religious practice). But states whose own legitimacy is in doubt or whose capacity to elicit consensus is weak are likely by default to create niches in which religious opposition is able to flourish. That is, pockets of opposition to the state become recognizable social niches in which alternative religions can develop. In these niches, more established religions may be unable to succeed because of their identification with the norms and values of the state. A strong sense of internal solidarity may also give rise to collective symbolism and rituals that take on religious connotations. Examples include such diverse movements as Shi'ism among the technical intelligentsia in Iran, Protestant pentecostalism among ethnic minorities in Latin America, and Eastern mystical religions among American youth during the Vietnam War.

In its capacity to manipulate resources, the state also produces alterations in the social environment that affect the capacity of established religious communities to maintain themselves. Matters as seemingly remote as government expenditures on space exploration and military installations can have significant ramifications for religious communities. In a society characterized by a high degree of religious involvement, such as the United States, commitments to the educational upgrading involved in space exploration and other highly technological programs lead indirectly to serious cleavages within religious bodies by altering the educational and occupational statuses of the members of these bodies; similarly, decisions to locate military installations in previously localized cultures give the religions of these areas greater interest in and access to national agendas (Hunter, 1980; Sweet, 1984; Wacker, 1984).[8] These effects cannot be summarized simply in terms of a decline in religious influence but rather have to be examined in terms of the *restructuring* of religious resources, organizations, and commitments. If religious systems constitute moral communities with patterned relations to their environments, then cleavages and other changes in the social environment are likely to produce a significant restructuring of religious organizations, commitments, and ideologies.

The other—institutional—level of investigation focuses on formal and informal interactions between religious organizations and state agencies. These interactions take place within the context of considerable complexity on the sides of both the state and religion. For its part, the state cannot be viewed as a static or monolithic entity but must be conceived of as a set of interdependent organizations, with both representative and intrinsic interests, having to secure resources from a changing environment, and subject to internal cleavages as a result of differential relations to the environment. On the religious side, different religious organizations are likely to be in competition with one another (and with secular organizations), will be characterized by different levels of resources, and will adopt strategies aimed at protecting or enlarging their niche in the environment.

During much of the period extending from the beginning of the sixteenth century to the middle of the nineteenth century, the relations between states and religious organizations in the West were deeply influenced by the breakup of ecclesiastical universalism and by the internal conflict between representative estates and central administrative agencies that accompanied the transition from medieval *standestädten* to the modern bureaucratic state. Competition among religious organizations was typically resolved by different organizations forming alliances with estates or central administrative agencies, the outcome of which was greatly affected by changes in the broader economic base and by the various groups' access to these resources.

Mary Fulbrook's (1983) comparative study of Puritanism in seventeenth-century England and Pietism in eighteenth-century Prussia and Württemberg illustrates the dynamics of this process. In Württemberg, Pietism was absorbed relatively easily into the state church and, for this reason, did not engage in direct political agitation as a means of enlarging its resources. In Prussia, eighteenth-century economic and military expansion led to an enlarged cleavage between the landed aristocracy and the central bureaucracy, with Lutheranism maintaining its traditional alliance with the landed elite. As a result, the central bureaucracy threw its support behind the Pietist opposition, in return for which Prussian Pietism came to associate fairly closely with proabsolutist sentiments. In contrast, English Puritanism developed strong antiabsolutist sentiments despite a close resemblance between its purely religious style and that of Prussian Pietism. The difference, Fulbrook argues, was the

fact that Anglicanism had been closely allied with the central bureaucracy, thus heightening the chances of an alliance between the Puritan religious opposition and the parliamentary political opposition.

At an earlier stage of political development, some of these processes
are also evident in the religious conflicts surrounding the Reformation in
the sixteenth century. Parts of central Europe, Scandinavia, and England
underwent rapid commercial expansion, providing central administrators and urban magistrates with resources no longer associated with the
rural aristocracy. In these areas, Protestant reformers were able to gain
strong support from central administrators despite resistance from the
landowning classes. Other areas such as Poland, France, and Spain benefited less significantly from commercial expansion or acquired military
obligations that retained the state's fiscal and administrative dependence
on the landed elites. These areas experienced Protestant agitation in
many urban areas but ultimately remained Catholic in the face of strong
pressures from the landowning sector on the central bureaucracies.[9]

In the twentieth century, interactions between religious organizations
and states in industrialized societies have been marked chiefly by the am-
bivalent character of the modern welfare state. On the one hand, the
modern welfare state continues to function in accordance with classical
laissez-faire conceptions that define its role as a guarantor of open market competition. On the other hand, it has taken an increasingly active
role in providing for public welfare, making available public services,
regulating and promoting economic growth, and supervising a greatly
enlarged set of civil rights. Many observers have commented on the tendency of welfare functions and civil rights regulations to interfere with
the traditional activities of religious groups, thereby producing a seemingly endless series of litigations (e.g., Robbins, 1985). These conflicts
have been taken as ready evidence of the further erosion of religious institutions in modern societies. Yet closer examination indicates that the
state's own ambivalence has played a role in these relations with religion and that religious organizations have adopted a wide variety of
strategies in dealing with the state.

As a rule, religious organizations have supported the laissez-faire conception of the state, at least in matters where religion is concerned, perhaps largely because the long history of religiopolitical conflicts has generated norms favoring religious tolerance and some degree of separation
between church and state. Most religions, it appears, have adapted to
the modern situation by developing quasi-commercial strategies that allow them to compete in the marketplace rather than relying heavily on

the state for resources (e.g., see White, 1972). This, of course, has been more the case in religiously diverse societies than in societies where a single religion can overpower all the others. In return, religious organizations' support of free market conditions in religion has often provided proponents of minimalist state intervention in economic affairs with ideological ammunition, if not supportive constituencies (e.g., Novak, 1982, 1984).

Where the strategies of religious organizations have been more varied is with respect to the welfare, service, and regulatory functions of the state. In part, these strategies can be analyzed in relatively straightforward terms based on the kinds of interests involved. For example, religious organizations with large investments in private schools are more likely to support tax vouchers than organizations without such investments. Not all of the relations can be analyzed this simply, however. Both the issue under consideration and the broader social position of the religious organizations involved are likely to influence the nature of the interaction.

Animating many of the relations between religious organizations and the state is the fact that religion tends to be concerned not only with human-divine relations but also with moral or ethical questions. The expansion of the welfare state into a broader range of regulatory and service functions has made it a relevant resource for religious organizations to attempt to exploit in implementing their moral and ethical programs. Religious organizations of all theological orientations have attempted to forge coalitions with state agencies and have greatly expanded their use of the courts in order to promote particular moral crusades, whether these crusades consist of drives against racial segregation, lobbying for gender equality, antipornography campaigns, efforts to promote prayer in schools, or movements in favor of or against abortion. The difference in religious organizations' attitudes toward government involvement has typically depended more on the issue concerned than on general orientations toward church and state.

At the same time, religious organizations' relations to the state are also affected by their position in the larger society. Again, access to resources appears to be a decisive consideration. Minority religions with limited resources are likely to favor relatively strict separation between church and state because religious freedom allows them to retain control over the limited resources they have acquired. Claims to religious freedom by Amish groups and Jehovah's Witnesses provide cases in point. At the other extreme, religious organizations with such an ample supply of resources as to be able to dominate the religious market also tend to support policies of government noninterference (except in the extreme case of theocracies, of course). These establishments have sufficient resources to achieve many of their own programs without government assistance; in arguing for strict noninterference, they in effect pit their substantial resources against other religious organizations with fewer resources (cf. Lindblom, 1977, for a related economic argument). Therefore, the groups most likely to support government intervention, other things being equal, are those in the middle—groups having enough resources to entertain hopes of being successful in relations with the state, yet lacking the resources needed to win over their competitors in strictly open religious competition. Such groups are particularly likely to become involved in the political process when actions of the state or changes in political climate give them a sense of political entitlement (e.g., Wuthnow, 1983).

None of this implies that religious organizations act according to strictly rational resource maximization strategies or that these organizations are, after all, more concerned with pragmatic matters than with articulating worshipful responses to the sacred. But social environments characterized by rational, pragmatic, technical procedures necessarily impose certain constraints on the manner in which religious organizations can function. How religion adapts—whether it maintains a critical role in relation to its environment or whether it compromises in serious ways—bears importantly on the direction of culture itself.

These examples obviously could be multiplied in areas other than religion, such as scientific and political ideologies. The following chapters suggest additional factors involved in the state's influence over the process of ideological institutionalization. Whereas the selective phase of the dialectic relation between ideology and the social environment focuses on relatively broad differences in the kinds of ideologies that are selected for or selected against, the institutional phase brings into consideration factors such as the state that actually link up ideologies and their environments. In this linkage the institutionalization of ideologies in rituals and organizations is also of importance.

Emphasis on the relations between social systems and their environments has been increasingly evident in the discipline more generally, as have related perspectives such as those dealing with the network structure of social systems and the structural arrangement of social resources. Although there may well be characteristics of ideological systems that make them different from other social entities, many of the distinctive concepts of the field can clearly be translated in ways that make them more compatible with formulations having wider use in the discipline. Thus, to speak of various processes of social production, selection, and institutionalization in ideology is to speak in words that have become relevant in other parts of the discipline as well. This chapter has been concerned primarily with amplifying the dramaturgic approach to the study of ideology. In doing so, some attention has also had to be given to issues that become central in the institutional approach. Before turning to a discussion of that approach, however, the next two chapters will develop some additional applications of the dramaturgic approach.

CHAPTER SIX

Social Selection Among Ideological Forms

One purpose of examining ideologies in relation to the social environment is to account for part of the wide variation evident in ideological forms. As suggested in the previous chapter, ideologies are vastly diverse, but not as diverse in any given social setting as we might imagine them to be. Some ideologies seem to be better suited to particular environments than others. We can therefore make some headway toward understanding the culture in which we live by considering how different environments reinforce certain ideologies and hinder others.

An essential starting point for this kind of investigation is the assumption that a multitude of ideologies exist at some time, with some eventually perishing and others surviving. This assumption is usually satisfied by the fact that disruptions in the moral order, from which uncertainties about social relations arise, generally result in a number of new ideologies, all of which compete with one another to redefine the situation. This competition does not consist of mere philosophical debates but involves claims on social resources—moral claims articulated as part of an operative ideology. The manner in which social resources are distributed, therefore, should be consequential for the types of ideologies selected.

This formulation of the problem requires no assumptions about interests or legitimation. Questions about interests and legitimation can still be raised, but as potential *consequences* of ideology. Too often these questions have substituted for careful consideration of the conditions that lead ideologies to be in existence in the first place. These conditions may be quite different from the functions an ideology fulfills.

Because the present approach to the study of ideology is in many respects new, it probably makes sense to begin with some fairly simple distinctions. Environments can be distinguished along relatively simple dimensions, and these variations can be associated with some broad differences in ideological forms. If persuasive at this level, the models can always be expanded by introducing additional dimensions and more elaborate distinctions. This chapter examines three ideological forms that are not only of some interest themselves but also permit illustration of some simple propositions about the effects of social environments: folk piety, individualism, and rationality. Considering these ideological forms will also provide occasion to introduce some further ideas about the internal structure of ideological systems.

FOLK PIETY AND FUNDAMENTALISM

Studies of contemporary culture have come increasingly to recognize the importance of what has been termed "folk piety." Whereas formal religion is characterized by codified doctrines, ecclesiastical organizations, and a professional clergy, folk piety consists of relatively amorphous beliefs, is extraecclesiastical, and is located among the common people (Vrijhof and Waardenburg, 1979). Folk piety tends to be syncretistic, drawing simultaneously from indigenous folklore (the "little tradition," in Redfield's [1956] terms) and the more formalized symbols ("great tradition") associated with historical or world religions (cf. Scott, 1977). Symbols are drawn from a wide variety of common sources—nature, work, food, music—rather than systematic theology; yet these symbols are distinguished from ordinary folklore in that they incorporate beliefs about divine or supernatural intervention in the realm of everyday experience. Examples include beliefs about demons and witchcraft, spiritualism, astrology, magic, miracles, and superstitions.

In a valuable introduction to the study of folk piety, Williams (1980:65) identifies six subject headings under which the beliefs and practices of folk piety can be classified: food, health and sickness, major transitions in the life cycle, death and the dead, predictions of the future, and problems of evil and misfortune. These categories also provide a basis for discussing the relations between folk piety and the social environment. Folk piety has been most evident in relatively nonmodern situations. Studies of medieval and early modern Europe, of Third World countries, and of traditional settlements in North America, such as Amish and Hutterite communities, give ample testimony to the importance of popular superstitions, charms and amulets, stories of miraculous happenings, and so forth.[1] The implied conclusion is that folk piety fails to adapt well to the modern environment. Yet more recent research has begun to challenge this inference. Numerous studies now suggest that folk piety may be remarkably robust even in the most modernized settings. Beliefs in astrology and extrasensory communication, contact with the dead and out-of-body experiences, superstitions about lucky numbers, mystical experiences, and trances, not to mention the quasi-sacred character of many holidays, sports events, and emblems of nature, all seem to be relatively common in settings such as the United States and Western Europe.[2] The question of how beliefs and practices that, on the surface, seem incompatible with the secular, scientific norms of modern culture could have proven so adaptable has therefore arisen. Scattered research evidence permits us to construct at least a partial answer.

ADAPTATION TO THE MODERN ENVIRONMENT

First, it seems important that folk piety tends to be relatively unformalized. That is, tenets of folk piety are generally ill specified in relation to one another. Specialists, to be sure, may develop systematic treatments of these tenets (manuals for astrological interpretations and theological treatises on spiritualism being prime examples), but to the typical practitioner, folk piety appears to consist of relatively discrete sayings, dictums, and aphorisms. It also tends to be notably anecdotal (i.e., moral maxims are substantiated less by formal argument than by personal experience or by narratives of others' experiences, thus minimizing the degree to which different elements become formally connected with one another). This looseness of structure also characterizes the syncretism of folk piety: discrete elements can be attached readily to other belief systems in diverse combinations (cf. Firth, 1984; Van Baaren, 1984).

More formally, folk piety can be described as a symbol system comprised of a relatively large number of elements, but with a low number of definite relations among pairs of elements. Other things being equal, a disconnected system of this kind tends to withstand external shocks relatively well because an alteration in any specific element or subsystem of elements need not affect the entire system.[3] Belief in demon possession, for example, might decline; yet if this belief is not logically related to other elements of folk piety, this decline could occur without affecting, say, the tendency to believe in life after death or the credibility of astrology.

A second point is that folk piety tends to gravitate toward the interstices of modern society. Most of the beliefs and practices in Williams's sixfold typology deal with the marginal or unanticipated—illness, death, misfortune—or with those transitional states that Turner (1974, 1977) and others have associated with "liminality" (i.e., with a feeling of being "betwixt and between"). Even seemingly ordinary beliefs and practices in this schema, such as those dealing with food preparation, turn out to be most concerned with high feast days and festivals and, as Mary Douglas (1966, 1984) has shown, symbolize deeper boundaries in social relations and understandings. Much of the impetus for folk piety appears to come from what Berger (1969) has identified as experiences of "marginality," which fall at the edges of ordinarily constructed realities.

The location of folk piety within the interstices of ordinary reality means that it is concerned with experiences that happen to nearly everyone at some time or another (e.g., illness, bereavement, tragedy), even in modern societies, but that are generally not dealt with adequately by the dominant institutions in these societies. Death and bereavement notoriously fail to be handled satisfactorily, except to be insulated from the rest of society.[4] Illness and tragedy, although subject to risk reduction and insurance schemes, continue to raise problems of personal adjustment because of their unpredictability and undesirability. And life passages are often inadequately handled because they occur precisely at those points of exit and entry *between* major institutions. The result is that folk piety is able to occupy a relatively enduring and important niche in modern society, just as it does in traditional society. Less obviously, the nature of this niche also reinforces the disconnectedness among tenets of folk piety. The events to which it relates are themselves disconnected, separated in time from one another in the typical individual's biography, largely unanticipated, and in most cases relatively limited in frequency and duration.

A third feature of folk piety is that its association with crisis events means it is likely to be associated with informal gatherings of close relatives and friends. Whether at birthdays or weddings, hospital visits or wakes, a small community of intimates is likely to be present, at least more so than at other times. Despite the occurrence of folk piety within modern society, the immediate context in which it takes place is likely to resemble in some ways the solidary communities in which it occurs in traditional societies. The general association of folk piety with solidary groups allows a further explanation of the nature of its structure and of its persistence in modern societies.

Bernstein's (1975) research on linguistic codes indicates that solidary groups are more likely to generate "restricted" than "elaborated" codes. That is, the high degree of shared understandings in solidary groups means that fewer words actually have to be spoken for communication to take place.[5] Because it is evoked in the presence of solidary groups, folk piety is likely to share the characteristics of restricted codes: much is left unspoken, few of the relations among its various tenets are spelled out, and what is spoken tends to be intertwined with the anecdotes and experiences—the folklore—of a particular group. In addition, the relative isolation of these experiences and gatherings from institutional life increases the likelihood that the material used to construct folk religious discourse will be the events of one's childhood, ancestors, or immediate acquaintances. As a result, "discourse" is indeed likely to consist of *discourse*—an oral tradition—rather than becoming subject to greater systematization through written formalization.

Finally, another body of research permits us to interpret the frequency with which folk piety seems to manifest a belief in, or experience of, divine intervention. A substantial body of empirical literature contains the idea, on the one hand, that major "life events" tend to evince stress, including emotional and physical symptoms, and that these events, on the other hand, evoke a wide variety of religious responses, ranging from mere questioning of the purpose of life to experiences of divine contact or revelation (cf. Dohrenwend and Dohrenwend, 1974; Thoits, 1981; Stokes, 1982). The connection between stressful events and religious experiences is in some ways obvious because the questions these events elicit may have culturally specified answers that fall into the domain of religious interpretations. This line of reasoning, of course, leads directly to the observation that *formalized* religious beliefs frequently play a role during crisis events and less directly to the observation that folk piety may also be elicited (because it too is culturally available). But such a cultural interpretation does less well at accounting for events in which an extraordinary intervention of the supernatural is actually *experienced*.

Here, a combination of psychological, sociological, and cultural explanations seems necessary. At the psychological level, a well-established body of research indicates a connection between crisis-induced stress and propensities to hallucinate, including visual and auditory components (e.g., Bender, 1970; Jaffe, 1966). At the sociological level, research suggests that patterns of family socialization that require individuals to act on behalf of the family itself (as opposed to acting on behalf of one's individual interests) create a propensity for individuals to feel constrained by purposes other than their own and as a result to be susceptible to a particular kind of hallucinatory experience in which they feel the presence of, or possession by, an external power (Swanson, 1978a, 1978b). And at the cultural level, evidence from studies of religious experiences points to the importance of either preconceived frameworks with which to interpret one's experience or else of associates who suggest an interpretation for what is at first a seemingly ordinary or ambiguous event (Laski, 1961; Carroll, 1986).

Placing these arguments beside one another therefore suggests that the persistence of folk piety in modern societies can be understood in terms of a distinct relation between its ideological structure and the social environment. The niches in modern society to which folk piety adapts are relatively common (as common as illness and death). Yet in actuality, from the standpoint of the specific person or group most immediately involved, these niches are relatively narrow, unstable, and discrete: narrow in the sense of happening to only a few people at a time who have contact with one another, unstable in terms of unpredictability of occurrence and duration, and discrete as far as any particular individual's biography is concerned as well as falling into the interstices between social institutions. The tenets of folk piety that are preferentially selected by this kind of environment also tend to be relatively discrete elements with few systematic relations with one another, thus permitting them to adapt with relative flexibility to diverse and changing circumstances.

THE SOCIAL LOCATION OF FUNDAMENTALISM

In some respects, fundamentalism may appear to be the polar opposite of folk piety. Strict adherence to doctrinal orthodoxy, a rigid conception of faith, and a lack of tolerance for superstition and the occult—all seem to set fundamentalism apart from folk piety. Yet the two bear certain similarities to each other. Like folk piety, fundamentalism has been studied mainly as an anomaly of modern culture that is presumably better suited to more traditional settings. Its origins have been sought in social crises that breed hostile reactions to the modernization process. Its content is described as a totalistic worldview, organized around absolute values and representing a countertrend to the process of cultural differentiation (cf. Lechner, 1983). Implicitly, fundamentalism is generally assumed to be a short-term phenomenon that is unlikely to survive in the modern milieu. But (again like folk piety) fundamentalism has surprised many observers by its persistence and, in some cases, its growth.

Kelley's (1972) research on the growth of fundamentalist churches in the United States initiated a wave of renewed interest in the study of fundamentalism (cf. Hunter, 1983, 1985). This interest was further stimulated by American fundamentalists' move toward political activism and by an apparent resurgence of fundamentalism in the Islamic world and in Judaism (Antoun and Hegland, 1986). Although most of this research has been limited to the American case, some general lines of interpretation have emerged. One is the view (just mentioned) that fundamentalism is a reaction against certain modernizing tendencies, such as greater emphasis on higher education and the penetration of local communities by the national state. Another is that fundamentalism, although rooted in traditional communities, is rapidly accommodating to modernity itself, gaining resources in the process, but losing many of its distinctive qualities. Both of these interpretations predict a relatively limited future for fundamentalism. A third view is that fundamentalism has grown mainly by default as liberal denominations have abandoned ultimate concerns to engage in social activism (Kelley, 1972). Bibby and Brinkerhoff (1973, 1983) suggest that fundamentalism's growth reflects little more than high fertility rates among its members. All these interpretations have some empirical support, but each is somewhat limited in its conceptualization of fundamentalism.

Participant-observer studies of fundamentalist groups have begun to fault the idea that fundamentalism is a totalistic worldview, tightly integrating behavioral norms with central values and lacking in usual kinds of cognitive differentiation. These studies suggest that fundamentalist beliefs focus on several highly salient aspects of behavior (family, for example) but leave most others up to the individual's discretion (Ault, 1983; Ammerman, 1983). In addition, the relation between central values and prescribed norms often appears to rest more on custom than on clearly specified arguments. Survey studies of fundamentalists support these conclusions, revealing relatively low correlations between fundamentalist beliefs and many other attitudes and demonstrating that identification with local custom is the principal link binding attitudes with beliefs (e.g., Rothenberg and Newport, 1984; Roof, 1978).

In formal terms, fundamentalism appears to be an example of an ideological system comprised of relatively few elements that are strongly related to one another. The elements generally considered essential in

Christian fundamentalism in the United States—the so-called "funda-
mentals"—are limited to no more than five or six beliefs (concerning
biblical inerrancy, the divinity of Jesus, his resurrection, the individual's
need for salvation, and so forth). These, as well as the relations among
them, were codified in great detail in a series of volumes published between 1910 and 1915 (Marsden, 1980). Empirical studies generally reveal a high degree of consistency in believers' answers to these questions
(e.g., Glock and Stark, 1965). Other attitudes popularly associated with
fundamentalism (premillenarian views, attitudes toward tobacco and alcohol, political conservatism), however, tend to vary widely among different fundamentalist groups. Indeed, the division of fundamentalists
into numerous small denominations means that, from the standpoint of
formal ideology, the core tenets of fundamentalism are connected in
widely diverse ways with other beliefs and attitudes.[6]

In comparison with folk piety, therefore, fundamentalism consists of
fewer elements with stronger relations. As an ideological system, it is
somewhat less stable than folk piety because the strong relations among
its elements mean that a change in any one is likely to affect all the others.
But fundamentalism is more stable than a comparable ideological system
having large numbers of elements. It is, on the whole, a conceivable candidate on formal grounds to persist in an otherwise changing environment.
Fundamentalism has in fact demonstrated remarkable resilience in relation to processes such as urbanization and industrialization and shifts in
political and economic patterns. Its weakness has been mainly in relation
to cultural processes of rationalization that add to the number of interrelated elements and thus increase the likelihood of change occurring in the
system. Increasing levels of education, imposing a greater consistency on
diverse ideological elements, has been one such process (for an interesting
empirical study, see Hammond and Hunter, 1984). Political movements
and moral crusades, welding tighter relations between religious beliefs
and social attitudes, have been another. Of the two, education appears to
have the more serious consequences. The reason may not be, as often assumed, that education provides alternative values that make more sense.
Rather, the effect of education may be to encourage a more rational systematization among fundamental beliefs, transforming them from the
"more fragmented and less internally consistent" beliefs characteristic of
the less educated (Scott, 1977:6), but at the same time making them more
vulnerable to environmental disturbances.

For these reasons, fundamentalism appears to function best in relatively homogeneous niches within the larger environment in which the

connections between core tenets and life-style issues can remain implicit. The introduction of heterogeneity into such settings frequently proves disruptive to the ideology, causing either a sectarian schism that re-creates homogeneity within each splinter group or an attempt at rationalization that may produce further strain among the ideological elements. Under these circumstances, it is not uncommon to find ideological flexibility being increased by a shift toward greater emphasis on the individual.

INDIVIDUALISM

Individualism is another ideological form to which much attention has been given. Its importance was identified by nearly all the classical contributors to sociology, thus rendering it an issue that bears on a broad range of theoretical questions as well as substantive questions pertaining uniquely to the study of ideology. Certain developments in contemporary culture have also opened new lines of inquiry into its nature. Like folk piety and fundamentalism, it can be examined beneficially in relation to the kinds of social environments in which it tends to be selected.

SOCIAL STRUCTURE AND INDIVIDUATION

In the classical tradition, individualism gained prominence in the work of Marx and Weber and to a lesser extent in the work of Durkheim. Marx and Weber regarded it as a uniquely compatible ideology in relation to capitalism. According to Marx, the emergence of capitalism, particularly in England during the seventeenth century, necessitated an ideology that had a corrosive effect on traditional solidary groups standing in the way of market relations and that legitimated individual property rights. Although in some ways present in all the Reformation doctrines, this ideology became prominent in an especially powerful form in English Puritanism. Weber's interpretation differed from Marx's in terms of the priority accorded to ideology as an independent contributor to economic change, but it also emphasized a unique compatibility between capitalism and Puritanism. Durkheim differed from both Weber and Marx in the causal factors to which he assigned priority, but he also envisaged a general increase in "the cult of the individual," as he described it, during the course of modernization.

The characteristics of Puritanism that in the classical literature qualified it as an example of individualism include the high priority it attached to personal salvation and direct accountability to God, its delegitimation of sacraments and offices associated with the ecclesiastical community, and the considerable degree of ethical responsibility it assigned to individual behavior. In Puritanism the individual stood alone before God, faced with ultimate uncertainty about personal salvation, yet free to make ethical decisions from which evidence of his or her moral worth could be discerned. Such accountability obviously bore strong similarities to the conditions under which entrepreneurs functioned in the capitalist marketplace.

The more recent sociological literature has provided theoretical and empirical evidence bearing on these initial formulations and has extended the idea of individualism into other areas. Much of this work has consisted of relatively technical reconsiderations of the classical materials themselves, constituting a body of literature that falls largely outside the purview of the present discussion. However, a number of important contributions have focused directly on the conceptualization of individualism and its relation to features of the social environment.

Rather than viewing individualism as a coherent philosophical system in its own right, treating it as a formal characteristic that can infuse many types of ideology may be more productive. That is, individualism, in the same sense as folk piety and fundamentalism, can encompass a relatively wide variety of substantive tenets, but common to all these variants are certain formal properties that distinguish the structure of the ideology itself. In the case of individualism, the most general effect of a strong emphasis on the individual appears to be a tendency to "decouple" the substantive tenets of any formalized set of doctrines or creeds. The effect of this decoupling is somewhat similar to that accomplished in folk piety but at a different level of ideological organization. Whereas the tenets of folk piety tend to be disaggregated by virtue of their intrinsic aphoristic quality and lack of formal codification, individualistic orientations are disaggregated at the level of the individual. Accordingly, for any particular individual, a highly integrated worldview may exist, but its components may be quite dissimilar from those of any other person's worldview. The extreme manifestation of individualism, therefore, lies in the dual formulation "do your own thing" and "anything goes."

From this perspective, it becomes obvious that individualism seldom takes on its most extreme manifestation. Rather, some degree of ideological effort is devoted to restraining the total disaggregation of personal convictions by defining the nature of the relations among individuals (i.e., in terms of moral responsibilities). In other words, individualism emphasizes the individual as decision maker—as the unit around which personal convictions crystallize—and yet the fact that individuals never function entirely in social isolation means that some conception of moral responsibility must be defined. Several implications follow from this observation, around which a fairly diverse body of theoretical and empirical literature can be organized.

Above all, the existence of any ideology that can be characterized as being individualistic requires a number of markers or cues to be present at the level of discourse itself that individuate the structure of that ideology. These cues may be "given" explicitly as part of the propositional content of discourse or "given off" implicitly as part of the illocutionary force of that discourse (Searle, 1969; Brummer, 1982; Taylor, 1984). In either case, the result must be to heighten the importance of any utterance's connection with its speaker as an individual (or in some cases, with the hearer as an individual).

Foucault's (1965, 1970, 1972, 1975, 1979) studies into the cultural developments that took place during the eighteenth and nineteenth centuries in Europe provide a number of examples of how discourse became individuated. In the realm of criminality, individuation developed in conjunction with theories and sentences that emphasized the individual's body as a relevant object of discipline and punishment. Notions of insanity, he suggests, developed in tandem with heightened conceptions of the mind and with medical concepts that dramatized disturbances of the mind. Even the development of modern social sciences, he argues, required that the individual be invented so that it could be studied and related to other concepts. More generally, Foucault's framework for the analysis of knowledge emphasizes the importance of "formations" that make it appropriate for the individual to speak, for individuals to be objects of speech, and for them to be related to other objects of speech that are not individuals.

In the case of contemporary religious discourse, for example, illustrations that show the high degree to which individuation is generally present are readily available. Religious beliefs are usually referred to as beliefs, rather than as teachings or symbols, implying that they are to be associated chiefly with individuals rather than institutions or cultural systems. The Protestant reformers' emphasis on the "priesthood of the believer" clearly sought to reassociate what had been an institutional role with the common person. Believer's baptism further emphasized the choice-making capacity of the individual, as have more recent pastoral emphases on conversion, being "born again," personal "faith development," and so forth.

Several empirical studies have examined the nature of individuation in religious discourse. McGuire (1982), in a study of Catholic pentecostalism, has demonstrated the importance of conversion testimonials for associating religious teachings with individual biographies. Hunter (1983), in a systematic content analysis of evangelical literature, has found evidence of a strong tendency to associate subjective concerns, such as emotional problems, guilt, worry, and personal adjustment, with religious assertions. Cuddihy (1978) observes that religious discourse now frequently is prefaced with such personalizing phrases as "In my experience" or "My own view of it is," which, he suggests, make religion increasingly a matter of individual preference and serve to introduce an element of civility into pluralistic religious gatherings. Bellah et al. (1985) present evidence of a fairly radical individuation of religious commitments in America in both liberal and conservative churches. Other research shows statistically significant tendencies among respondents in survey studies for beliefs about the importance of the individual to be associated with beliefs about the importance of religion (e.g., Wuthnow, 1976; Apostle et al., 1983). In all these cases, the evidence suggests a relatively prevalent tendency toward individuation in modern religion, thus raising the question about how this tendency may be preferentially selected in modern social environments.

Marx's interpretation was that the market system, especially under capitalism, reinforced individuation by forcing buyers and sellers to compete with each other as individuals whose relations were defined strictly by the supply-demand-price mechanism. Along similar lines, Durkheim (1933) argued that a division of labor inevitably accompanied market exchange that led to greater and greater specialization, thus breaking down homogeneous groups and causing the individual to become more clearly differentiated from every other individual. Foucault's (1975, 1979) work has added flesh to these assertions, demonstrating that individuation was reinforced through the very physical manipulation of persons. Holding pens gave way to individual cells in prisons, *narrenschiffe* were replaced by the psychoanalyst's couch, military regiments placed soldiers into distinct positions and gave them clearly defined duties to fulfill, and assembly lines eventually broke down the group character of work itself.

What has often seemed anomalous is how individuation could be ad-

vanced at the same time that bureaucracies became bigger and social institutions in general became more complex. Foucault's examples illustrate
that individuation may go hand in hand with the means by which effort in
such large-scale entities is coordinated. Studies of the state point in the
same direction. As Bendix (1977) has suggested, individuation on a societal scale may serve usefully in the state-building process as a means of
achieving social control. Autonomous individuals, simply, are likely to be
easier to control than are tribes, ethnic groups, collectives, unions, or
other solidary entities. Thus, modern bureaucratic states have generally
advanced individuation through, on the one hand, standardization—especially through schooling and language uniformities—which makes persons relatively interchangeable with one another, and, on the other hand,
through personalization, which attaches rights and responsibilities—
such as voting and paying taxes—to the individual. In short, individuation at the level of ideology, including religious discourse, appears
to be reinforced, relatively nonproblematically, in social environments in
which the social structure also tends to be individuated. Both seem to be
fairly general features of modern societies, even in the midst of relatively
large-scale bureaucratic institutions such as the modern army, the bureaucratic state, and the assembly line.

INDIVIDUALISM AS MORAL IDEOLOGY

But individuation and individualism are not exactly the same things.
Following Turner's (1983:160–161) valuable discussion, individualism
may be defined as "a doctrine of individual rights, which may be expressed in a variety of religious, political, economic or legal forms," as
contrasted with individuation, which consists only of "marks, numbers,
signs and codes" that identify and separate "persons as differentiated
bodies." The key to distinguishing individualism from individuation,
therefore, lies in the idea of *rights,* which of course always connotes a
set of *responsibilities* as well.

The sense of rights and responsibilities that individualism implies
helps clarify the nature of Puritanism as an example of religious individualism. Puritanism not only contributed to the individuation of persons—as did religious doctrines as different as Anabaptism and mystical
contemplation; it also specified a clear sense of rights and responsibilities among religious persons. Puritans not only stood alone before God,
but they also felt a duty, as Weber recognized, to work for the improve-

ment of humanity and to abide by the discipline and norms of the religious community. Out of this conception of responsibility, the Lockean theory of property rights was formed. This sense of a moral relationship also permitted the American Puritans to mold strong communities and served as a moral basis for that distinctive brand of American individualism that Tocqueville was to describe in the phrase "self-interest rightly understood."

What individualism consists of, then, is an ideological form, based on a sharp sense of individuation of the person, that defines certain rights and responsibilities between the individual and other individuals. Several features of this ideological form are crucial to its coherence and also constitute the components to which cultural imagery usually bears a direct relation. First, the individual must be conceived of as capable of possessing rights; second, the individual must be free to act as a locus of choice; finally, the individual must be conceptualized as having certain moral obligations to other actors.

With respect to the idea of rights, the individual clearly cannot be regarded simply as a self or as a conjuncture of interests and instincts. Instead, the individual must be a possessor of something that gives him or her membership as a unit of some larger system. Property ownership and citizenship have been two of the most common such possessions. In religious conceptions, salvation, sanctification, or election have served similarly to define individuals as members in good standing with rights to certain privileges. Not surprisingly, therefore, "religious tests," if only as informal expectations, have often been closely associated with the right to enjoy other social privileges, to hold office, and so forth.

Freedom to act as a locus of choice is a considerably more complicated issue. Its presence as an ideological element performs a dual function. It adds ideological flexibility by crediting the individual with the opportunity of making decisions. This is particularly important in the context of religion because individual freedom connotes the ability to render doctrinal interpretations and thus to adapt universalistic ideas to particular situations. In addition, the concept of individual freedom seems to provide the essential link between individual rights and individual responsibilities in that freedom is necessary for the individual to be held morally accountable.[7] That is, any sense of moral obligation requires that the individual be free to do otherwise; if not, no sense of having fulfilled these moral obligations is possible. Consequently, it is not surprising to find individualism strongly associated in many instances with notions of personal morality.

Finally, the sense of moral obligation is primarily an "other-directed" concept, defining normative relations between the individual and specified others. The individual is not simply free but is free to exercise certain responsibilities. This concept, of course, necessarily implies some notion of a community or social system with which one shares contractual obligations. Mary Douglas's (1970) idea of "grid" and "group" captures this notion: as a cell in a grid, an individual is individuated but also knows clearly his or her place in relation to other cells in the system; in contrast, an individual who is simply an unspecified member of a group fails to know precisely what his or her obligations are, and a person who has neither group nor grid is in the worst situation of all with respect to having clearly defined roles.

Returning then to the question of how the social environment preferentially selects for individualism, it can be seen that individualism is unlikely to flourish in a situation characterized strictly by autonomous monads (desert hermits, for example). Rather, it is likely to flourish best where the environment demands some degree of coordinated but flexible relationships. Such conditions are likely to be present in an environment with heterogeneous resources (e.g., a diversity of natural resources or a high degree of occupational specialization) and where the environment is organized across these various heterogeneous resources—requiring coordination rather than the mere coexistence of largely separate, internally homogeneous entities. Obviously, this kind of environment becomes relevant whenever a market system spans a relatively large area and when it leads to a kind of internal division of labor such that independence ("organic solidarity," in Durkheim's terms) becomes present.

Historical studies generally support the idea that individualism became more prominent in areas characterized by market conditions. Indeed, the appearance of market conditions, rather than capitalism as such, seems most closely associated with the rise of individualism. As trade expanded in the thirteenth century, for example, a heightened sense of individualism seems to have developed in various areas of Europe, particularly in the trading areas of Italy and England. In the sixteenth century, towns engaged in commerce over long distances, as opposed to those oriented strictly toward local trade, seem to have been especially prominent in adopting the new ideas of the Reformation (Wuthnow, 1986b). Davis (1981) suggests that part of the appeal was precisely the fact that Protestantism conceived of social relations more as a network of responsibilities among individuals than as membership in predefined local collectivities. Later still, the globalization of markets during the nineteenth century seems to have been accompanied by another wave of individualism. Thomas (1979, 1986), for example, has provided statistical evidence for the United States between 1870 and 1890 that indicates a close relation between the spread of capitalist agriculture and the diffusion of individualistic religious beliefs (especially Methodism).

CONDITIONS FOSTERING INDIVIDUALITY

The topic of individualism has not, however, been of strictly historical interest. A different series of studies has been prompted by recent discussions of the relations between narcissism, privatism, and religion. Writers such as Sennett (1976), Lasch (1978), Habermas (1976:75–92), and Bellah et al. (1985) have identified a type of individualism, variously referred to as narcissism, civil privatism, or expressive individualism, that seems to be an increasingly prominent feature of modern culture. Because this form of individualism appears to differ from its historical counterpart, it has proven helpful to refer to it by another name. Turner (1983: 162), for example, suggests using the term "individuality" instead of individualism. By this he means "a romantic theory of the subjective interior of persons, which is concerned with the growth of sensibility, taste, consciousness and will." Perhaps the clearest way of drawing the contrast, therefore, is to say that individualism emphasizes a concern for the moral responsibility of individuals toward other individuals, whereas individuality focuses on the moral responsibility of the individual toward his or her own self.[8] In the one, relationships are specified among individuals; in the other, relationships are specified among the component parts of the self. Individuation is an important precondition of both, but the two differ sharply in the kinds of relationships given priority. Discussions of narcissism and civil privatism correspond well with this definition of individuality. According to Sennett, the main feature of narcissism is its inability to distinguish among parts of the self—as in the case of Narcissus, who confuses his image reflected in the spring with himself and thus eventually falls in and drowns. The result, Sennett suggests, is a tendency to become preoccupied with relations purely within the self and therefore to become withdrawn from public roles (i.e., from moral relationships with other individuals). Habermas's discussion of civil privatism flows along similar lines, suggesting that withdrawal from public roles is accompanied by an inner search for meaning and purpose.

Examples of heightened individuality are not hard to find. Troeltsch's

(1960:691–806) contrast between mysticism and sectarianism in some ways parallels the distinction between individuality and individualism. Whereas the sectarian may emphasize individualism (in the form of religious rights and duties) as a protest against more organized churchlike religions, the mystic is more likely to withdraw from public roles and engage in a life of contemplative introspection. Public roles, such as political and economic participation, are thought to require too many compromises of one's ideals; consequently, the mystic carves out an inner realm over which greater control can be exercised. It has also been suggested that many of the "new age" spiritual disciplines that have become attractive in the West may represent this kind of individuality. Certainly those who are attracted to mystical religious movements and the various human potential movements are more likely to focus on fantasy, new insights about themselves, and symbolism (Wuthnow, 1976). What these movements appear to accomplish in many cases is a clarification of the various components of the self. Specifically, an inner self is often identified as a kind of command center that then becomes capable of defining the relations among other component selves (Fingarette, 1963; Tipton, 1982; Westley, 1983).

The social conditions promoting such orientations remain inadequately examined, but several plausible hypotheses have been put forth. One is that life in modern bureaucratic institutions becomes so well organized—so regimented—that any sense of free choice, and thus of moral responsibility, becomes incomprehensible; consequently, persons who have been socialized to value freedom and moral responsibility shift increasingly to private or inner pursuits over which they have greater discretion (cf. Wilensky, 1964). An alternative hypothesis is that individuality stems not so much from overorganization but rather from the greater degree of flexibility required in role performances in areas such as the professions or, indeed, in any complex situation where the different components of the self may need to become operative at different times (cf. Bell, 1977; Swanson, 1980; Yankelovich, 1982). According to this hypothesis, multiple role requirements lead to multiple selves, which in the extreme can lead to problems in forming a stable self-identity and therefore to a preoccupation with self-exploration.

There is greater agreement that individuality, whatever the source, poses relatively serious implications as far as modern social life is concerned. Rather than providing an ethical system that attaches importance to strict moral obligations, individuality seems likely to be associated with a highly relativistic outlook that focuses on inward pursuits and leaves public or collective values to be informed primarily by pragmatic considerations (Luckmann, 1967). At this juncture, much debate has in fact begun to appear over the ramifications of such an orientation for the stability of modern societies (e.g., Bellah, 1982; Neuhaus, 1984; Bellah et al. 1985).

RATIONALITY

Another general theme that has been of considerable importance in the study of modern culture, particularly in light of Weber's (1963) work on the process of rationalization, has been the role of rationality. Some of the discussion of this topic has been cast simply in terms of an apparent conflict between traditionalism, as a presumably nonrational belief system, and rationality, as manifested in the secular culture of modern societies. Weber's principal contribution, however, was to create awareness of rationality as a characteristic even of modern religion. In his treatment of the Protestant ethic, for example, he envisioned a relatively high degree of rationality in the teachings of the Protestant reformers that would, in his opinion, eventually produce a tightly rationalized ethical system that would damage the mysteriousness of the religious impulse itself.

"Rationality" is unfortunately a word that has a number of different technical meanings as well as a relatively vague set of popular connotations. Even in Weber's usage it had different meanings. Most relevant to the present discussion, however, are his references to rationality as a systematization of means or norms in relation to an end or goal. Behavior therefore could be considered rational insofar as it conformed to the norms that were accepted as efficient and effective means of attaining one's designated goal. In purely formal terms, rational ideological systems are thus ones in which the various elements (i.e., designations of means and ends) bear relatively strong relationships to one another. In addition, these relationships are subjected to a kind of performance calculation such that failure to attain specified ends casts into question the nature of the elements that are identified as means. All of this obviously suggests a relatively high degree of reflection about the relationships among the elements of a rational ideological system: an application of "reason." Rational ideological systems are also likely to be characterized by a high degree of universalism; that is, a conviction that the underlying procedures used to arrive at specified relationships between means and ends can be generalized to a wide variety of situations.

In attempting to identify the kinds of social environments in which a preferential selectivity toward rational systems is evident, it has been important to heed the warnings of a number of anthropologists who have pointed out that a type of rationality that might to the observer seem governed only by magic and superstition also exists in primitive settings (cf. Wilson, 1970a; Geraets, 1979). Nevertheless, the thrust of this debate in the anthropological literature seems to be oriented toward recognizing that a certain logic exists within nonmodern belief systems, but not toward arguing that the specific kind of rationality identified in Weber's work is present.[9] If the application of reason to practical tasks seems to be evident in virtually all societies, the development of a systematized, means-end calculus oriented toward performance and conforming to universalistic norms appears to be limited to a much smaller set of social environments.

HETEROGENEITY AND RATIONALITY

Other things being equal, rationality (so defined) appears to bear an elective affinity with heterogeneous social environments. In particular, rationality is likely to characterize those ideological systems that occupy a relatively broad niche in a heterogeneous environment such that the resources on which they depend are characterized by a high degree of diversity. The reason why this relationship appears evident can be specified along several different lines. One is that a heterogeneous environment presents a sphere in which learning can take place. In contrast with an entirely homogeneous environment, the presence of diverse stimuli means that comparisons can be made, and as a result, learning about the kinds of means that produce different consequences can be acquired. The exception to this process is a heterogeneous environment in which resources are distributed simply at random (e.g., an island fishing economy in which schools of fish swim around the island in entirely random patterns). Under such conditions, learning is sufficiently unlikely that the most efficient means of maximizing results may be one that also randomizes behavior (e.g., certain types of magic). Thus the attempt to make achievement predictable through a rational systematization of means and ends appears likely to prove most successful in an environment with heterogeneous but nonrandomly distributed resources.

Another line of reasoning that relates heterogeneity and rationality points to the need for greater degrees of coordination in heterogeneous environments. If the niche occupied by a population is sufficiently broad that a diversity of resources has to be utilized, then a complex system of social exchange will have to be developed. However, the greater the degree of complexity in any system of exchange—that is, the larger the number of actors and the more diverse the tasks involved—the greater will be the potential for uncertainty as far as the entire system is concerned and for unpredictability as far as any specific outcome is concerned. For interaction to be effectively orchestrated under such conditions, therefore, a high degree of communication must take place (cf. Beniger, 1986). Any belief system that functions either to impose predictability on the actors in the system or to facilitate communication is likely to be favorably selected in this kind of environment.

Yet another line of reasoning is suggested by the last observation concerning the need for communication. As mentioned earlier, Bernstein's (1975) work on language codes suggests that "elaborated" codes are likely to be more effective than "restricted" codes in highly diverse settings where communication is needed among actors with few shared understandings. Rational belief systems represent a type of elaborated code in that they have explicitly articulated relationships among their various elements and are framed in such a way as to be presumably applicable to a wide variety of settings. Thus, rational belief systems should again be preferentially selected in heterogeneous environments.

Many of the more familiar examples dealing with the development of rational belief systems in the West give *prima facie* support to arguments about the importance of heterogeneous social environments. Weber's own treatment of innerworldly asceticism, as epitomized in Puritan Calvinism, stressed the high degree of systematization that this orientation imposed on ideas about ethical behavior as well as the predictability that accompanied this systematization as far as the individual's behavior was concerned (cf. Schluchter, 1981). Both of these characteristics were, in his view, deeply compatible with the kinds of complex calculations required by the expansion of capitalism in the seventeenth century. During the same period, as Merton's (1970) application of Weber has suggested, Puritanism and capitalism appear to have provided conducive environments for the growth of rational experimental procedures in the natural sciences. In the following century, the extension of rational procedures to moral and political philosophy—indeed, the triumph of these procedures in the Enlightenment—appears to have been reinforced not only by a further expansion of the mercantile economy but also by a tremendous expansion of the bureaucratic state that added greatly to the complexities and uncertainties involved in formulating public policies.

Research that deals with less obvious examples has also pointed strongly to the role of environmental heterogeneity in the development of rational belief systems. LeGoff's (1984) magisterial history of the idea of purgatory, particularly of its development in the twelfth century, argues that the acceptance of teachings about purgatory needs to be understood in the context of changes taking place in the medieval social system. Among these was the rapid spread of a particular type of feudalism marked by a dual hierarchy of lords versus peasants and high nobility versus *chevaliers*. In addition, a tripartite system of estates came into being distinguishing the ecclesiastical, military, and laboring orders (respectively, *oratores, bellatores,* and *laboratores*). Other changes included geographic expansion, both in trade and in military conquests, monastic reforms, and a more detailed system of contract law, penal codes, and bookkeeping procedures. The idea of purgatory, LeGoff argues, was both an adaptation to and an extension of this increasingly complex social and cultural milieu. It added an important intermediate category between heaven and hell just when intermediate categories were being recognized in the social structure; it corresponded to a whole set of ternary logical models evident in social, legal, and philosophical classifications; above all, it introduced into eschatological visions a new kind of calculation, similar to that being introduced in the courts, in which fixed terms or "sentences" served as a more realistic mode of reckoning between behavior, rewards, and punishments.

In a quite different setting, Geertz (1968) has provided an insightful illustration of the shift toward religious rationalization that frequently apears to accompany the integration of localized social systems into the broader context of world markets and export trade. Both in Morocco and in Indonesia, Geertz observes a period in which Islam placed increasing emphasis on "scripturalism," including greater demands for strict adherence to Islamic doctrine and greater interest in religious schools. In both cases these tendencies toward rationalization accompanied waves of commercial expansion that eroded the personalized moral bonds between cultivators and rural landlords and gave merchants a stronger hand in establishing economic links with the outside world. Much the same phenomenon, it appears, took place in Brazil at a time when merchant classes were concerned with restricting spirit worship and other local folk beliefs and were seeking greater legitimacy with the church outside of Brazil (Ribeiro de Oliveira, 1979).

In a number of cases, the process of ideological rationalization appears to be mediated by the state rather than simply being a diffuse, undirected instance of cultural adaptation. In the Reformation, for example, the relatively high degree of rationality evident in both Lutheranism and Calvinism (especially in matters of church government and in procedures for settling theological disputes) appears to have occurred as a direct result of church leaders seeking the involvement of secular princes, courts, and parliamentary assemblies in ecclesiastical controversies. One result of this involvement was the development of standardized procedures that permitted these faiths to operate in relatively broad, heterogeneous environments. Similarly, in the case of early scientific development, as will be seen in Chapter 8, the scientific academies not only received direct patronage from the state but also consciously borrowed parliamentary procedures from the state for the conduct of their meetings. In other cases, the vehicle of rationalization was not the state but direct borrowing from other highly rationalized bureaucracies (e.g., the adoption of corporate methods of organization by many denominations in the United States during the last quarter of the nineteenth century).

INSTABILITY AND BLOCKING

An aspect of the issue of rationality that has apparently remained relatively overlooked is that, notwithstanding its seeming adaptability to heterogeneous environments, it is highly vulnerable to instabilities in its environment. This is because its structure, in formal terms, consists of large numbers of elements that are systematically related to one another. Unlike folk religions or fundamentalism, therefore, rational belief systems can be easily subjected to internal strain by a significant change in any subset of their many elements. On the surface, this feature may appear counterintuitive; yet the relative frequency and suddenness with which highly rationalized systems such as scientific theories or theological perspectives change suggests that there may be some truth to the matter. Perhaps because of this susceptibility to instability, rationalized belief systems appear frequently to incorporate one or both of two other formal properties.

One of these is individualism, which, as already seen, serves as a decoupling mechanism in ideological systems, heightening their flexibility by giving individuals the right to combine ideological elements largely as they choose. A further advantage of combining individualism with rational belief systems is that assertions about the individual's responsibility may be sufficient to lend the kind of predictability that is required in complex social environments. It needs to be added, however, that the radical relativism that comes with certain types of individualism is in some ways incompatible with a rationalistic orientation in a strict sense (cf. Jarvie, 1983).

The other property is a kind of formal "blocking" of rational belief systems into discrete subsystems. The division of knowledge into specified disciplines, specialties, and theoretical perspectives accomplishes this task in science. As a result of this division, alterations in one subsystem become less likely to have ramifications for the entire system. In religion, a similar function is fulfilled by formal divisions along denominational lines. These divisions, occurring in the context of certain shared beliefs common to all denominations, create what is sometimes called a "federated" structure that is usually highly adaptable to complex and changing circumstances (cf. Hannan and Freeman, 1977). Both of these properties—individualism and denominational blocking—help, incidentally, to explain why religious commitment has remained at remarkably high levels in the otherwise deeply rationalized context of American culture.

Blocking of a distinct kind often takes the form of distinguishing core tenets of an ideology, ones that presumably need to remain constant, from their practical or ethical applications, that may be regarded as situationally variable. This distinction gives added flexibility to rationalized belief systems by allowing them to be adapted in diverse ways in different environments. Communist ideology in China, for example, formally incorporated a distinction between "theory" (Marxist-Leninist doctrine) and "thought" (Mao Zedong's more practical interpretations), enabling the Chinese to develop their own programs even to the extent of critically distancing themselves from the Soviet Union (Schurmann, 1968). U.S. leaders of the "new religious right" have found it expedient to separate "morality," which they claim is agreed on by a large majority of the public, from "religion," which they acknowledge is divided according to sectarian preferences (Wuthnow, 1983).

If other conditions are constant, extreme fluctuations in the official reception given a belief system appear to promote this kind of blocking. Gager's (1975) study of early Christianity, for instance, suggests a close relation between the variable reception given it by different governorships and the emergence of a sharp distinction between universal millenarian doctrines and the more temporal apostolic teachings concerned with establishing Christian communities.

At another level, rational ideological systems appear to be particularly susceptible to processes of internal differentiation in response to changes in their environment. Such internal differentiation represents a method of reintegrating elements that have become seemingly incompatible by identifying a higher order of generalization to which these elements can be related. Modern religious systems are often characterized, as Weber recognized, by a type of rational integration which differs from that evident in more traditional religions. Specifically, purely substantive modes of integration that relate religious elements in terms of logical content (e.g., scholasticism) tend to be replaced by types of integration that emphasize underlying procedures or techniques. Emphasis on conscience, methods of biblical criticism, rules of textual hermeneutics, and norms of tolerance, therefore, may provide the level at which otherwise conflicting religious beliefs become integrated.

How cultural systems become internally differentiated has, in fact, been the subject of much exploration. Several comprehensive schemes that summarize a complex evolutionary process marked by increasing differentiation have been put forth. These schemes need to be understood, first, as having particular, if not unique, relevance to rational ideological systems, as opposed to other varieties such as folk religions, which may be less vulnerable to environmental shocks. Second, the process of internal differentiation needs to be clearly recognized as a mode of adaptation to fundamental changes in the social and cultural environment.

One of the most systematic treatments of the process of religious differentiation within a broad evolutionary framework remains that of Bellah (1970:20–50). He distinguishes five stages of religious evolution, ranging from the relatively undifferentiated to the most highly differentiated: primitive, archaic, historic, early modern, and modern. In the primitive stage, mythical realities and the actual world remain undifferentiated, whereas in the archaic stage mythical beings begin to be objectified as distinct gods. This process continues in the historic stage, which begins to distinguish clearly between the present world and a supernatural or transcendent reality. The early modern stage (notably Protestantism) breaks out the individual from other realities, making salvation more contingent on personal choice. Finally, the modern stage generates a more "multiplex" version of reality in which multiple realities replace the dualistic worldview of previous stages. Other aspects of religion, such as religious action, religious organization, and ethical systems, show corresponding increases in differentiation. With each successive increase in differentiation, religious systems presumably gain greater capacities to adapt to complex environments.

Habermas (1979a, 1979b) has taken Bellah's scheme, modified it by collapsing the early modern into the modern stage, and attempted to specify some further theoretical distinctions. In Habermas's version, cultural evolution is even more clearly specified in terms of increasing differentiation. At the initial (neolithic) stage, motives and behavioral consequences remain undifferentiated, as do actions and worldviews, human and divine events, natural and social phenomena, and tradition and myth. In the next (archaic) stage, greater degrees of differentiation occur between all these categories, producing a clearer sense of the linearity of history, providing for calculated action oriented toward the control of nature, and giving rise to rational law and the state. The third (developed) stage replaces myth and tradition with unified cosmologies and religions oriented toward high (monotheistic) gods, includes better defined moral precepts, and posits universalistic norms and values. The final (modern) stage is typified by an erosion of confidence in the validity of these higher order principles, replaces absolute laws with reflective applications of reason to collective problems, and invokes a greater degree of self-consciousness about the procedures used to test the validity of statements concerning religion and morality. Habermas's scheme, therefore, closely links the process of internal differentiation with the rationalization of culture. Each successive stage introduces a higher order of abstraction, usually focusing increasingly on procedural modes of integration, that resolves problems at the previous stage. These problems occur principally as economic and political systems develop to the point of having to coordinate activities over larger and more diverse environments.

Bellah's and Habermas's schemes are presented at a sufficiently high level of generality that their connection with concrete historical events is not always evident. What they suggest, however, is that the process of ideological rationalization represents a response to the inherent instabilities of rational belief systems against changes in the social environment. Evolutionary differentiation appears to be the basic method of gaining greater stability in more complex environments. But this process is clearly more applicable to ideological systems characterized by a high degree of rationality than it is to other kinds of ideological systems.

The obverse of the relationship between rationality and heterogeneous social environments is, of course, that nonrational ideological systems are more likely to be evident in relatively narrow social niches in which resources are homogeneous rather than heterogeneous. What nonrationality does is to inhibit communication with other environments, thus in a way protecting local resources from becoming subject to exploitation in broader environments. It is not uncommon in such niches, therefore, to find religious expressions such as trance states, emotionalism, glossolalia, and snake handling that seem unintelligible to the outsider (see Scott, 1977, for examples). These cultural expressions serve as dramatizations of a particular ideological style, just as other expressions, such as philosophical discourse, bureaucratic structures, and formalized creeds, provide public dramatizations of a "rational" style (cf. Meyer and Rowan, 1977).

AN ANALOGY

Additional clarity on the foregoing can perhaps be gained by considering briefly the similarity between ideologies and organizations. Organizations are, as the term implies, patterns of behavior, usually around some specific task or with sufficiently distinct external boundaries that one can be distinguished from another. The same is true of ideologies, except we usually think of ideologies as consisting of patterns of ideas, even though they could also be seen as consisting of a special type of behavior, such as utterances. Ideologies are simply sets of symbolic or communicative elements that bear some relation to one another. As the foregoing has illustrated, these relations can be modeled in quite simple (formal) terms, just as one might the units of an organization.

Thinking of ideologies in this way is not likely to be appealing to those who wish to explore the complexity of any specific ideology. The same is true, again, of organizations. Looking at the broad forms that organizations could take represented a considerable departure from studies that focused on the internal dynamics of an organization, that described the life of its employees, and that examined its products and profitability. The shift of perspective nevertheless proved valuable. It highlighted the fact that no organization was unique, nor did any organization exist in total isolation. Certain commonalities could be identified among the organizations in specific societies or industries, and differences in social structure seemed to affect these commonalities. So it is with ideologies. What we lose in rich descriptive detail as far as any particular ideology is concerned is balanced by what we learn about the similarities and differences among ideological forms in given social environments. Seemingly different ideologies—different because of their substantive content—often turn out to have quite similar forms as a result of the social environments in which they are nurtured.

A focus on ideological forms does not require the internal structure of an ideology to be neglected. In fact, this perspective attaches considerably greater importance to this structure than do many of the approaches that emphasize the interests served or legitimated by an ideology. Rather than assuming immediately that an ideology is really about false assumptions, social class, and so forth, this approach suggests the importance of seeing how the elements of an ideology are put together. Even simple variations such as the number of elements and the strength of their relations with one another may be significant to consider.

Like organizations, ideologies are, finally, assumed in this approach to depend on social resources from their environments. It may not take as many resources to maintain an ideology as it does to operate General Motors or the government of France, but resources are nevertheless required. Again, this observation can lead to inquiries about how revolutionary leaders, media, cults, and so forth actually muster resources and translate them into ideologies. Or broader relations between how resources are distributed in different environments and the tendency for particular ideological forms to be associated with those environments can be examined. Both are ways of specifying the connections between ideology and the moral order.

CONCLUSION

It is well to be reminded of the kinds of connections between ideologies and their social environments that have been suggested. It has *emphatically not* been argued that the structure of ideology simply mirrors the structure of the social environment (e.g., that diverse environments produce diverse ideologies or that simple ideologies correspond to simple environments). Some confusion on this point may be understandable because some of the literature reviewed in this chapter does in fact suggest such a straightforward connection. The problem with simply positing a direct correspondence of some kind between ideology and social structure, however, is that no plausible mechanism is provided to explain why this correspondence should exist or how it comes into being. Generally, the only connection specified is one of subjective consistency between individual experience and individual attitudes. Somehow, we are asked to assume, individuals shape their beliefs so that these beliefs reflect the exact shape of the social world. Subjectivism, again, plays the role of a magical theory in the absence of any testable explanations. This kind of argument will be considered in greater detail from a critical standpoint in Chapter 9.

Population ecology models, such as the one employed here, are also notoriously deficient in being able to describe the actual intervening processes that link certain kinds of organisms to their environment. These models are better at suggesting broad connections between certain kinds of populations and certain kinds of environment than they are in specifying how a particular population functions in its environment. General properties of populations such as size and complexity can often be explained by these models more easily than the traits of a specific organism or organization. Population ecology models can also involve theoretical mystification, just as the subjective approaches that have been criticized, when vague notions of fitness become an invisible hand guiding the selection process. These limitations notwithstanding, ecology models nevertheless do contain some useful arguments that go well beyond simple notions of correspondence when applied to the relations between ideology and social environments.

The linkage between ideology and the environment that has been specified here suggests that social movements typically become the producers and disseminators of new ideologies and that ideological movements generally have to compete with one another for scarce resources. The mechanism by which ideology and social structure are related is clearly an observable, collective entity, rather than simply the disaggregated, subjective beliefs of individuals. The process of ideological production and selection, moreover, does not focus on single idiosyncratic cases, but requires attention to be directed to larger fields of competing ideologies and ideological forms. Over a period of time, those that survive will be the ones that manage successfully to secure resources. There are, of course, many determinants of success in this context, some of which clearly involve social institutions, whose role has thus far been treated only minimally. In addition to institutional factors, however, ideologies have also been claimed to serve a symbolic-expressive role; that is, ideologies dramatize (clarify, reinforce, communicate) the nature of social obligations. Part of what influences their success or failure, therefore, is their capacity to dramatize social obligations.

It was also suggested that the formal structure of ideologies, particularly the number of elements of which they are composed and the relatedness of these elements, makes it more or less likely that an ideology will be stable over time. Specifically, systems of any kind that have fewer elements and weaker connections among these elements are, other things being equal, less susceptible to change as a result of external shocks than are larger and more highly interconnected systems. The specific examples considered—folk piety, fundamentalism, individualism, rationality—were discussed within the framework of these formal variables in order to make some assertions about their propensities toward stability or instability. Relatively simple features of social environments were used to offer some suggestions about the conditions under which these different ideological structures would be most viable. It was suggested, for example, that folk piety could be perpetuated in quite rapidly changing environments, especially if the contexts in which it was articulated did not require tight formulations of the interconnections among its ideological elements. Rationality, in contrast, was seen as a more tightly integrated kind of discourse that was likely to be required in highly diverse environments but was subject to instabilities that often led its elements to become decoupled by being combined with individualism or various blocking techniques.

The connections drawn between ideologies and their environments, therefore, depend primarily on assumptions about the formal structure of ideological systems and the capacity of these systems to withstand changes in the environment, on the one hand, and to facilitate necessary kinds of communication about social relations, on the other. There is, of course, never a guarantee that the most effective ideologies will actually emerge. But because it is assumed both that ideologies have competitors and that they are relatively flexible, it seems safe to argue that some form of adaptation between environments and ideologies will emerge over time.

The next chapter will pursue the relation between environments and ideological movements somewhat further. Thus far, the relation has focused heavily on formal characteristics, which can easily become too abstract to be useful in concrete empirical studies. The approach developed in the next chapter is more contextually situated in relation to specific historical developments. It, too, depends primarily on the dramaturgic approach to culture and, as such, focuses more on the symbolic-expressive qualities of ideology than on the direct institutional mechanisms by which ideologies are produced.

CHAPTER SEVEN

The Moral Basis of Cultural Change

Theories of cultural change have emphasized broad evolutionary patterns. The two theories of cultural differentiation mentioned in Chapter 6, for example—those of Bellah and Habermas—are cast in terms of an explicit evolutionary framework. Others—Talcott Parsons and Niklas Luhmann, for example—have adopted similar models. Still others, although rejecting the strict periodization of these schemes, have nevertheless stressed the gradual, linear, and unidirectional character of cultural change. Most of these arguments are framed, explicitly or implicitly, in assumptions about modernization. Most deal with advanced industrial societies and assume that other societies will eventually follow the same patterns. Most emphasize increasing differentiation, both among institutions and within cultural systems, as the central dynamic of cultural change. This argument depicts the nature of cultural change largely as a product of preexisting capacities within the cultural system itself. In addition, evolutionary models have often suggested an increasing disjuncture between culture and social structure, as one manifestation of differentiation, that results in cultural change becoming independent of other aspects of the social environment.

Evolutionary theories of culture have a number of strong points. They highlight general differences between primitive, traditional, and modern societies. They provide a broad description of the directions in which modern culture may be headed, thereby suggesting some of the important problems with which social inquiries should be concerned. In separating culture from social structure, they avoid positing any kind of one-to-one correspondence between the two that might be taken as a basis for sociological reductionism. They nevertheless posit a loose relationship between social environments and cultural patterns; for example, traditional ideologies are said to be increasingly difficult to sustain in the modern environment. Indeed, these theories are not difficult to reconcile with some of the arguments about the connections among heterogeneous environments, individualism, and rationality in Chapter 6.

Yet there is a growing sense of dissatisfaction with evolutionary models of cultural change. One of their chief limitations is the fact that such large time periods are lumped together and seen operating according to a few linear tendencies. Most of these models consider the entire "modern" period—covering the half-millennium since the fifteenth century—as a single evolutionary epoch and portray cultural changes simply as shifts in the direction of greater modernization. They offer little assistance in dealing with shorter term changes or comparing one century with another. A second limitation is the lack of attention paid by these theories to concrete mechanisms of cultural change. They seem to assume in principle that change is incremental and relatively uniform within each cultural epoch, apparently resulting from the aggregate impact of numerous individual changes or minute adjustments in the culture at large. They do, however, posit profound changes occurring in the transition from one epoch to another. In practice, they also point to concrete events (e.g., the Reformation or the Enlightenment) as having special significance. But no effort is made to account for these events or to suggest what transpires in the shift from one epoch to the next. A third, closely related, limitation is the failure of these theories to focus on specific historical details that would validate or invalidate them. The models seem to be articles of faith—metatheoretical frameworks—rather than testable hypotheses. Seldom are detailed historical studies conducted with an eye toward testing or modifying these theories. Fourth, only progressive, unidirectional changes are emphasized. The progressivism of these theories is a value judgment that may or may not be warranted. Their unidirectionality is more simply an empirical weakness that causes them to concentrate on some kinds of change but to ignore the many ideological movements that fail and to neglect the importance of counterideologies that arise in opposition to presumably dominant cultural tendencies. Finally, these theories are limited by their tendency to be either intrasocietal or asocietal rather than inter- or transsocietal. That is, culture change is depicted in terms of specific national cultures, such as the United States or England, or is treated simply as "modern" culture—as if there were no important societal distinctions. Seldom has attention been paid to the differing positions of societies in the larger world order, to the ways in which their interaction affects the domestic moral order, or to transsocietal environments that may in themselves constitute a type of moral order.

The objective of this chapter is to outline an alternative approach to the study of cultural change. This alternative posits the importance of going back to the historical record in order to see how concrete events influenced the production, selection, and institutionalization of cultural developments. Instead of relying on broad deductive assumptions about modernization and cultural evolution, we develop a more inductive model based on comparisons of the social trends and ideological movements characterizing different periods in European history since the sixteenth century. Drawing on the general arguments put forth in Chapters 5 and 6 about moral order and social resources, the model represents an effort to extend these arguments by considering specific historical developments in the moral order and in ideological movements. To transcend the societal focus of the evolutionary literature, we borrow from some of the recent globalistic perspectives such as world-system theory. After considering the assumptions of these perspectives, we present a tentative typology of modern ideological movements. This typology affords an occasion for considering some of the changes in moral order that have resulted in various kinds of ideological movements.[1]

THEORETICAL CONSIDERATIONS

Globalistic perspectives in the social sciences cast a distinct shadow across the prevailing paradigm that has guided sociological theorizing about the dynamics of modern culture. That paradigm of course remains deeply indebted to the classical European trinity (Marx/Weber/Durkheim), as interpreted by the structural-functional tradition. Among the widely accepted tenets of this tradition are the ideas that cultural changes can be understood with reference to a linear evolutionary progression, that the sources of cultural evolution are located principally in the internal dynamics of individual societies (e.g., structural differentiation, industrialization, urbanization), and that the overall consequence of "modernization"—the term most frequently used to summarize these processes—is a gradual shift in the direction of secularization.

The most direct challenges posed by the globalistic viewpoints are, first, that societies may not be the only—or even the most natural—contexts in which to examine cultural developments and that it may be possible to identify social systems transcending societies. Second, the new perspectives challenge the temporal assumptions of the traditional paradigm, suggesting that social processes in the modern period may be understood better by focusing attention on cycles, phases, periods of expansion and contraction, and even relatively abrupt or cataclysmic transformations.

It seems important to consider seriously whether there is anything in the emerging global perspectives that can be of use in understanding patterns and changes in culture. This task requires, first of all, a candid assessment of the assumptions required in moving from societal to more global models of social structure. To make this task more manageable, attention can be concentrated on four questions: (1) What is the difference between global models and theories of history? (2) How is it possible to conceive of models that include cataclysmic social transformations? (3) Is it legitimate to look for social systems at the global level? (4) Can a general process of social transformation within such systems be identified?

MODELS AND HISTORY

The first question—the difference between global models and theories of history—arises in the present context because of the shift in spatial scope from single societies to modernity in general and because of the tendency in current global perspectives to entertain the possibility of recurrent social cycles. The latter, in particular, brings to mind shades of Spencerism, Spenglerism, and Toynbeeism and, not surprisingly, suggests that the same historical errors are being committed once again. It becomes necessary, therefore, to state much more explicitly than one generally finds in this literature the delimitations that circumscribe globalistic models. One of these, most apparent in the work of Immanuel Wallerstein (1974, 1979), but implicit in other discussions as well, is that the focus of analysis is uniquely the modern capitalist world-system since about the sixteenth century. Concepts such as *core* and *periphery, cycles,* and *interdependence,* though framed as theoretical abstractions, have empirical referents only within this context. Thus, although it is tempting to draw analogies between the modern capitalist system and other times or places (the Roman empire, Byzantium, the Ming dynasty, the Italian city-state system), such generalizations may not be warranted because the social forces associated with capitalism are lacking.

This delimitation greatly restricts the capacity to go beyond historical description to the development of general theory because there has been but one case of modern capitalism. Accordingly, we commonly find a new *rapprochement* in the world-system literature between social scientists and historians. Comparative societal analyses also remain of value because a dearth of larger units makes it imperative to compare units *within* the capitalist world-system itself in order to understand the structure of this system.

The second limiting factor differentiating present global models from theories of history is that these models, however encompassing spatially and temporally they may appear, are always restricted to a specific, and often thin, *analytic* slice of historical reality. One may differentiate the political dimension of world order—or, by the same token, the cultural dimension—from much else that goes on either within smaller social units (nation-states, interest groups, voting districts) or within other dimensions of world order (population, trade, migration). Thus, rather than being a theory of history, a global model is merely an analytic tool focusing attention on one set of phenomena so that it can be understood internally or related to other theoretically relevant conditions.

The confusion between global models and theories of history, such as those of Spencer, Spengler, or Toynbee, arises principally from failure to make explicit these delimitations, not from any inherent fallacy precluding analysis at a higher level than that of the society.

DISCONTINUITIES

The second issue—how it is possible to conceive of models that suggest cataclysmic social transformations—occurs in response to the fact that the emergence of global models has been associated with a strong renewal of interest in the idea of cycles, phases, and discontinuous social patterns of various sorts. These ideas contrast sharply with the linear evolutionary view that has dominated the social sciences.

The clearest exposition of why these tendencies—globalism and cycles—should have appeared simultaneously comes from Michel Foucault (1972). He observes that as long as scholars focused on the empirical events of history themselves, and as long as the objective of historical scholarship was to organize these events into a coherent framework, the dominant tendency was to seek to emphasize continuities because the important fact of history was its progression from point X to point Y. But once a clear separation of distinct analytic levels of historical reality had been made, and once attention shifted (as it has, for example, in Foucault's own work) toward seeking the rules that constitute a system within each analytic slice, then the important fact of history is that any such system exists only for a certain time, and over any given period of time, there are likely to appear at least several such systems having quite different regulative structures. Hence, the focus of scholarship becomes that of explaining how one system forms and is then replaced by another; in short, discontinuity supersedes continuity as a problem of epistemological importance.

Foucault's point can be illustrated with reference to the concept of world order. Once analytic distinctions among the concrete events of history have been put forth such as to make it possible to conceive of something called world order and to posit that world orders might be examined to discover the rules lending internal unity to each, the fact that there have been quite different world orders (empires, mercantilist state systems, free trade economies, detente) becomes paramount. Within this dimension of reality, a theory emphasizing discontinuity becomes entirely plausible.

LARGER SYSTEMS

If Foucault's argument is accepted as one justification for the current interest in global historical discontinuities, the question of whether it is legitimate to look for unities or systems, such as Foucault describes, on a level that transcends society nevertheless remains (the third question mentioned earlier). Foucault himself argues, much as Wallerstein has in the more immediate context, not only that it is legitimate to look for such systems, but also that a devoted effort *should* be made to identify the larger but less obvious unities within social reality, rather than relying on surface distinctions that social actors themselves may employ.

Still, there are sufficient pitfalls in applying systems analysis to the study of social life that it is imperative to tread carefully in pursuing this path. Above all, it must be clearly acknowledged that a system is not something discovered from examining reality. It is a construct imposed on reality by the observer. The appropriateness of the construct is not to be judged in terms of how obvious it may be from observing empirical events, but in terms of how useful it is for understanding certain aspects of these events. Again, we are in the realm of interpretive sociology, not positivistic science.

World order is a "system" not because there is integration at the world level of the same kind that may be expected within national societies, but because certain useful understandings emerge from taking a more totalistic view of world events (i.e., not as disparate, unrelated phenomena). It has proven useful, for example, even in empirical studies concerned with developments within individual societies (such as economic growth, income inequality, and educational development) to consider the *position* of these societies in a larger matrix of trade and diplomacy, rather than focusing only on properties internal to the societies themselves (e.g., Chase-Dunn, 1975; Rubinson, 1976).

The fallacy of equating consistency with systems must be avoided as well. In the strict sense of the term, a system implies only relationships, even relationships consisting of nothing more than spatial or temporal copresence. The term does not imply consistency or integration among these elements. To cite Foucault again, there is a "dispersion of elements" for which one wishes to discover the rules that allow their simultaneous presence. In treating widely scattered events within the world community, this is clearly the connotation that needs to be kept in mind.

TRANSITIONAL TYPES

Finally, the question arises: can a general process of social transformation within a global system be identified? The remarks thus far show that the transition from one system to another at the global level has high priority as a problem for investigation. For the study of cultural change, this is also the point at which analysis is likely to be most productive. Yet this task will prove elusive if it is assumed simply that crises and transformations are interstices—periods betwixt and between stable world orders. The key to examining the transition from one form of world order to another (such as empire to mercantilism) is to recognize that systems need not be limited to equilibrium states, but that *dynamic* systems can be conceptualized, having as their main characteristic the very presence of change, even crisis.

A variety of alternative models of social change meeting these general requirements might be put forth (e.g., models concerned with the rise and decline of hegemonic states, with the expansion and contraction of colonial powers, or with the cyclic character of economic upswings and downswings). For present purposes, considering the following as distinguishable types of dynamic world systems seems useful: first, *expansionary systems,* characterized by overall growth in population, territory, physical resources, or technology contained within an exchange network of the kind that Wallerstein has taken to be the defining element for membership in the capitalist world economy; second, *polarized systems,* in which overt conflict is present between periphery (dependent) areas and core (dominant) areas of the capitalist world economy; and third, systems in the process of *reintegration,* characterized by conflict among interest groups in core areas, particularly between interest groups whose fortunes have risen in conjunction with emerging patterns of new world order and interest groups whose fortunes have been tied closely to previous patterns of world order and are therefore declining. These systems are obviously distinguished in a way that again emphasizes the availability, distribution, and stability of social resources and, as will become evident, the structure of moral obligations.

Each type of system can be illustrated with reference to distinct historical periods, although there is much disagreement about the exact limits of these periods. Wallerstein's work on the sixteenth century is compatible with more standard historical treatments of the period (e.g., Wilson, 1976) in identifying the late fifteenth century and early decades of the sixteenth century as an expansionary system, principally because of the extension of the Hapsburg military domination over new territories, rising population, and growing regional interdependence in the grain, lumber, shipping, and woolens industries; the second half of the sixteenth century represents a period of polarization, marked by wars against the Hapsburg dynasty; and the early to middle seventeenth century serves as an example of reintegration with the emergence of mercantilist-centered interest groups in England, France, and the Netherlands. The transition from mercantilism in the seventeenth century to free-market capitalism in the nineteenth century also provides examples of these intermediate systems, although the concrete events constituting each period were quite variable. The first wave of colonial expansion provides the clearest instance of an expansionary system during these two centuries. Then a polarized system can be identified in the last quarter of the eighteenth century, during which the main colonial wars of independence occurred. And, as Michael Kammen's (1970) informative study of interest groups in Britain during the early part of the nineteenth century suggests, this period, fraught with conflict between free-trade and mercantilist interests, provides an instance of a system undergoing reintegration. Finally, the period encompassed by the free-market system, which existed largely under the tutelage of the *pax Britannica* from the second half of the nineteenth century to the middle of the twentieth century, also provides examples of each of these transitional systems. Polanyi (1944), Wallerstein (1979), Kuznets (1966), and others manifest close agreement in identifying trade and colonial patterns during the last quarter of the nineteenth century as an example of an expansionary world order, the period encompassed by the two world wars as an example of a polarized world order, and the period since 1945 as an example of a system undergoing reintegration. Students of post–World War II international relations differ in the extent to which they emphasize U.S. hegemony as a stabilized world order, but the instability in economic and diplomatic relations that has characterized much of this period argues for treating it as a system still in the throes of reintegration, marked by a juxtaposition of interests rooted principally in prewar free-trade patterns to a new set of interests oriented more toward a controlled balance of power.

SOME GENERAL PATTERNS: OVERVIEW

With this preliminary framework in place, and with the help of the brief historical examples just mentioned, attention can now be directed to sketching some of the broad cultural developments that can be identified as correlates of expansionary, polarized, and reintegrating patterns of world order within the capitalist world economy. In the following section the specific types of ideological movements associated with these various patterns will be discussed in greater detail. The present section will concentrate primarily on an overview sketch of the relevance of world-level factors for understanding cultural movements and on some of the consequences of these movements for the subsequent structuring of moral order at the world-system level.

THE ROLE OF EXPANSION

Rapidly expanding world-systems, such as the early sixteenth-century Hapsburg empire, the early eighteenth-century mercantile state system, and the late nineteenth-century British free-trade system, have been characterized by frequent and widespread ideological turmoil, especially in newly annexed peripheral areas. The intrusion of external social forces appears to be most disruptive of established moral communities in these areas. Particularly among affected subsistence-level communities, this turmoil takes the form of revitalization movements, and, although there are many local variants of these movements, their connection with the expansion of the larger world economy is sufficiently straightforward that most studies have acknowledged the importance of extrasocietal forces.

At the most general level, these movements appear to emerge in response to a disruption of traditional moral obligations between the lower strata and upper strata on whom they have depended for protection, either economically or militarily. With the expansion of core political and economic forces into peripheral areas, local elites acquire new economic opportunities or, alternatively, may be exposed to an imposition of new economic demands, either of which changes their interest in, or capacity to fulfill, traditional moral obligations to subject populations. As the local moral economy is disrupted, revitalization movements develop among the lower strata, taking different forms depending on how their members have been incorporated into larger economic and political structures. But these movements share beliefs that, among other things, help to restore a sense of moral economy (e.g., the communitarianism of millenarian movements, hopes in cargo cults for divine intervention, and so forth). Again, in keeping with the arguments developed in Chapter 5, the disruption of *social relations*, rather than subjective feelings of deprivation, provides moments of opportunity in which these movements, as ideological reconstructions of the moral order, can arise.

In addition to revitalization movements, the long-term fortunes of which are linked closely to the positions that the lower strata come to occupy in the world economy, there has been a tendency for expansionary world-systems to generate sweeping ideological reform movements having much wider social consequences (e.g., the Protestant Reformation in the sixteenth century, certain aspects of the Enlightenment in the eighteenth century, and Marxist socialism in the nineteenth century). These ideological revolutions find carriers among elites in peripheral areas and sometimes in core areas as well—the landed aristocracy, city magistrates, and merchants—who have gained greater opportunities to disavow traditional obligations to the lower strata and who can be united in their opposition to the expanding power of the ruling class in the core of the world-system. Although much depends on specific circumstances governing the relations among local elites, mass populations, and representatives of external forces, the success of ideological revolutions (in comparison with that of most revitalization movements) can be traced to the greater social resources of their carriers, especially access to the resources of central, territorial, or municipal regimes; to the rising influence of these elites within larger networks of regional or global trade, thereby giving them a resource base not controlled by segments of the elite with close ties to established modes of cultural production; to their exposure to cosmopolitan communication channels that provide means of developing common ideas and values; and to the unifying effect of their common opposition to the values and institutions that legitimate core domination.

Most of these assertions can be supported with evidence from conventional historical accounts of revitalization movements and ideological revolutions, and, though framed differently, the present account does not contradict the main observations of these studies. Still, the more global perspective appears to provide some additional mileage. Revitalization movements have flourished more widely in some periods than in others. Linking them to waves of expansion and contraction in the world economy helps account for these variations. This perspective also highlights the external forces disrupting moral obligations between local elites and mass populations, underscores the reciprocal relations existing between the kinds of movements that develop among each, and helps account for the transsocietal diffusion of ideological revolutions.

Arguments concerning the costs of taking a global perspective, as opposed to focusing on domestic societal structures, can also be put forth. Thus, some justification must be found for suggesting a leap to this broader level of analysis. The more provocative question this perspective raises concerns the relation between an expansionary infrastructure at the world level and the larger world culture that develops as a result of ideological movements during such periods. Addressing this question requires a conscious shift in perspective away from examining component parts of world order (such as the presence or absence of local movements) toward considering the structure of world order as a social unit in itself (i.e., in much the same manner as required when shifting from individual-level analysis to that of examining societies as social facts in their own right).

Making this shift in the present context generates an insight that directly contradicts an argument of the conventional modernization framework, namely, that the cultural effect of modernization, at least in the relative near term, is to act as a so-called universal solvent, producing cultural convergence. Rather, the expansion of core economic and political influence promotes cultural heterogeneity. Incorporating peripheral areas into the world-system does more than erode traditional cultures; it promotes new cultural forms (revitalization movements and ideological revolutions) that differ both from tradition and from the culture of core areas. We can, therefore, reconcile the fact of economic modernization with the obvious persistence of local and regional cultural differences, for they are elements of a common process.

Further, a more highly diverse cultural pattern at the global level may also be conducive to further material expansion. The relevant comparison here is between a monolithic but highly general cultural pattern, on the one hand, and a more pluralistic pattern, on the other hand, consisting of loose integrating assumptions (as present in the West since the Middle Ages) coupled with a much more diversified array of specialized, local cultural communities. The second pattern not only is more adaptable to a broad variety of local conditions than the first, but it also decreases the administrative burden required to maintain cultural cohesion (a burden, for example, that weighed heavily on the Hapsburg empire). The second pattern encourages the development of middle-range, semiautonomous power centers in peripheral regions and, in the case of ideological revolutions, provides a new basis for the integration of peripheral regions—or new centers of power in core areas—one with another. In other words, what may appear at one level as highly local, reactive ideological movements may at a more general level constitute a cultural pattern well suited to further expansion of the world-system. At the same time, this argument needs to be limited to the near term because the cultural patterns that form in conjunction with rapidly expanding world-systems also provide the groundwork for subsequent polarities in world order.[2]

EFFECTS OF POLARIZATION

World-systems characterized by polarization (such as the war between Spain and the Netherlands in the second half of the sixteenth century, the era of colonial wars of independence in the late eighteenth century, and the period of decolonization in the Third World that coincided roughly with World Wars I and II) also provide a climate conducive to ideological turmoil, but of a different variety. Although there is conflict between core areas and periphery areas seeking to gain greater autonomy, this conflict must be seen in the full context of economic stagnation at the world level and conflict among core countries (especially in the absence of clear hegemony by any single country)—conflict precipitated by declining economic growth and, in turn, consuming the resources of core areas sufficiently that they attempt to impose greater restrictions on peripheral areas at the very time when they are less capable of enforcing these controls. The net result is greater incentive and opportunity for periphery areas to seek political and economic independence. In each of the three periods that provide clear examples of this pattern of world order, the most striking ideological developments were, first, militant movements in the periphery that drew on and extended the ideas of earlier ideological reformers to legitimate the use of force against core powers and to promote solidarity among the groups involved and, second, a strong reactive or "counterreform" movement aimed at buttressing the corporate identity of core areas, especially with respect to their own populations. The simultaneous presence of Calvinist militancy and the Tridentine counterreformation, of Jacobin militants and Gallicanism, and of Bolshevism and nationalism can be cited as examples. What is obvious about these two kinds of movements, apart from the differences that can be accounted for by their differential locations in core and periphery areas, is that both are efforts to reintegrate institutions previously differentiated, particularly religious and political institutions. Moreover, both stress collective loyalties to a greater extent and on a more encompassing scale than is true of movements in less polarized settings.

The international political context of these movements provides insights into their character and development. Again, however, the world-system perspective is probably less useful for what it reveals about the origins of specific movements than for the questions it raises about the structure of world order itself. At this level, militant movements and countermovements constitute a highly corporate world order divided along deep ideological boundaries. Although there remain overarching rules governing the conflicts present, the main foci of loyalties are particular ideological blocks in the world-system. Considerable effort is expended to maintain these ideological divisions, which, in turn, have important consequences for the further development of the global system.

First, in the face of global economic contraction, sharp ideological boundaries assist in reducing economic interdependence, in checking the extension of an international economic division of labor, and in promoting the utilization of resources that had been marginal under conditions of full international competition. Second, collective ideological loyalties provide a basis for reinstituting the moral obligations between upper strata and lower strata that were disrupted by economic expansion and previous ideological movements. Among the results is a greater availability of resources for collective purposes despite economic contraction (i.e., extractive power). Finally, and perhaps most important, the division of world order into largely autonomous ideological zones promotes the full institutionalization of alternative social and political patterns within each of these zones, a process that appears to be crucial in determining the role that these different zones come to occupy in subsequent stages of world economic development.

To the extent that core areas are competitively weakened by the administrative costs of waging counterinsurgency wars, for example, or by fixed costs associated with maintaining the position of traditional interest groups, the presence of a strong counterreform ideology may ease the economic decline of these areas by legitimating the importance of traditional ways of life. By contrast, ideological divisions at the world level appear to be particularly conducive to the development of those periphery areas that gain independence from the core relatively early in comparison with other dependent regions (e.g., the United States early during the demise of the mercantilist system, and the Soviet Union as the free-trade system began to decline). These areas provide relatively protected pockets of social innovation and frequently play leading roles in the formation of new global patterns. This, then, brings us to systems undergoing reintegration.

REINTEGRATION

The term "reintegration" is used to characterize a world-system that has recently passed through a time of polarization and contraction, to the point that the rules on which world order was formerly based no longer function effectively, and in their place a new set of rules is beginning to emerge. The period since 1945 can be taken as an example of reintegration, especially in view of Karl Polanyi's (1944) useful discussion of the erosion prior to this period of the institutions on which the nineteenth-century system of free trade had been established and more recent analyses of the ad hoc economic policies that have been tried in the absence of these institutions (e.g., Block, 1977). The corresponding transition from mercantilism to free trade occurred primarily in the 1830s and 1840s and the transition from the Hapsburg empire to the mercantile system, in the period (roughly from 1618 to 1660) that has been termed "the general crisis" of the seventeenth century.

Because of the tremendous variation in social patterns in periphery areas during these periods—partly a function of different degrees of independence from the core and partly because of different rates of economic and political development—attention is perhaps best restricted to core areas during periods of reintegration, at least in this kind of initial formulation. The most striking aspect of these periods in core areas is the degree of domestic social tension between interest groups linked to previous institutions of world order and interest groups with power that has risen more recently because of the emergence of new institutions of world order (e.g., between "court" and "country" in the transition to mercantilism or currently between advocates of free trade and the so-called new class of technicians, state planners, and policy officials). This tension, coupled with international economic and political instability, generates a succession of political realignments within core countries, a reshuffling of the power and membership of interest groups, and not infrequently, civil wars or domestic violence on a smaller scale.

These instabilities are also felt at the level of ideology. Movements of accommodation (such as mergers), shifts in the direction of mainstream values, or movements aimed at improving public welfare develop among groups whose influence is rising as a result of emerging patterns of world order; sectarianism occurs among groups whose fortunes are declining, often taking the form of splinter groups that break away from other organizations undergoing accommodation. These developments, for example, have been described in the "church-sect" literature and have been illustrated by recent religious and political movements in the United States. The value of examining them in the context of world order is, first, that what may appear superficially as a bewildering array of interest groups and alliances can often be sorted into meaningful patterns once their structural position in relation to international political and economic forces is recognized.[3] Second, historical comparisons can be selected on a more systematic basis (e.g., strong similarities would be expected between the overall pattern of movements in the 1960s and the 1830s, but not between these patterns and those giving rise to the Reformation).

Once again, questions can also be raised about the relevance of these ideological patterns to the structuring of world order itself. If a metaphor can be used, it is as though ideological communities provide lubrication during the process of shifting gears—that is, the process of rearranging interest groups—to form a new world order. For some groups, ideological communities provide moral capital sustaining them in the face of declining influence; for others, ideology provides linkages with other groups and with larger national purposes; and for still others, ideology rescues them from being entirely displaced during the transition. The result (greatly simplified) is the construction of a stabilized world order in which dominant institutions (multinational corporations, cartels, international standards of human rights, technology transfer mechanisms, etc.) enjoy the support of legitimating moral communities, while less advantaged groups also retain a place in the moral universe.

This is a simplification because the social unrest associated with periods of reintegration also provides fertile ground for seeds of social criticism to be sown—certainly more fertile than that provided by a more stable world order. For example, the seeds of the Enlightenment began to germinate in the formative years of mercantilism, just as Marx began to formulate his vision of communist revolution in the era of nascent free trade.

VARIETIES OF IDEOLOGICAL MOVEMENTS

With these preliminary considerations in place, greater attention can now be devoted to describing the specific kinds of ideological movements that appear under different conditions in the broader world order. It has been suggested that movements are likely to differ, depending on whether the broader world order is primarily characterized by expansion, polarization, or reintegration. It has also been suggested that these periods correspond roughly to phases in the overall development of different patterns of world order, at least in the expanding capitalist world economy that has characterized first Western Europe and then increasing shares of the globe since the sixteenth century. Many different depictions of this process have been advanced, the differences depending mostly on which aspect of development and what time frames were being emphasized.[4] There is much agreement about general patterns, however, in discussions that have been concerned with shifts in the overall patterns of capitalist world order as evidenced not only in sheer growth or decline but also in the dominant kinds of institutions and institutional arrangements governing the distribution and exchange of resources on an international scale. These discussions emphasize mercantilism as one dominant period in the development of Western capitalism, free trade as another. Both are contrasted with the imperial, aristocratic, or feudal system that characterized the late Middle Ages and continued to subordinate much of Europe in the sixteenth century under the Hapsburgs. Both are also contrasted with the present form of world order in which a high degree of planned state intervention has come to alter the earlier terms of free trade. What must be understood in attempting to relate these forms of world order to the development of ideological movements is that none of these forms represented a stable system that characterized a long period of modern history. In purest form each was relatively short-lived (mercantilism reaching its fullest expression only during the latter half of the seventeenth century and free trade occupying a relatively brief period during the 1860s and 1870s). It is for this reason that attention has been devoted mainly to identifying major phases in the transition from one system to another (hence, the phases of rapid expansion, polarization, and reintegration). These phases, although in some ways analytic abstractions, may correspond roughly to actual historical periods in the development of the capitalist world-system.

During the long transition from the Hapsburg imperial system to the mercantilist system, the expansionary phase was most closely associated with the first half of the sixteenth century, the period of polarization with the second half of the sixteenth century, and the reintegration phase with the first half of the seventeenth century. After a period of relative stability under the mercantilist system in the second half of the seventeenth century, another long transition can be seen, culminating in the free-trade system of the nineteenth century. This transition was marked roughly by a period of expansion lasting during most of the first three-quarters of the eighteenth century, a period of polarization that dominated international relations from about 1776 until 1815, and then a reintegration phase that lasted until about 1860. In the development of the world-system from the beginning of the free-trade era until the present, the period from about 1870 until 1914 is characterized mainly by expansion; from 1914 to 1945, by polarization; and the period since 1945, by reintegration. This of course is an extremely general periodization that must be understood in the rather specific context for which it is intended and needs to be qualified in examining the development of any specific society because not all societies developed at the same rate or experienced each transitional phase to the same degree.[5] It nevertheless provides a framework that highlights some of the conditions in the broader resource environment that were likely to have influenced the pattern of ideological movements in each period.

The kinds of ideological activity generated in each period also differ, it appears, depending on whether that activity occurs among groups whose relation to power is rising or among groups whose relation to power is declining (cf. Tilly, 1969). In expansionary periods the main groups whose power increases include new political and economic cadres in periphery areas, and the main groups whose power decreases are members of the lower strata in periphery areas who lose traditional rights vis-à-vis these cadres.[6] In periods of polarization, representatives of the rising periphery areas that are struggling to secure independence from the dominant core have tended to gain power, whereas representatives of the core have typically lost power relative to these rising areas in the periphery. In periods of reintegration, strata associated with emergent patterns of international exchange within each society have been most likely to gain power, and strata associated with decaying patterns of international exchange have been likely to lose power. These periods, of course, are characterized by considerable back-and-forth movement in the position of interest groups, often over a period of several decades. It is therefore important to examine the power of specific groups in relation to their position in the broader world order, rather than allowing purely domestic or short-term considerations (e.g., profit margins or electoral counts) to be the decisive factor.

The perspective afforded by regarding the context of ideological movements as world order, rather than single societies, makes it possible to identify commonalities among movements that have sometimes been overlooked and to suggest some of the ways in which resources and moral obligations at the international level may affect these movements. A population's place in the larger world order is likely to influence how it defines its major problems—how it defines its moral obligations to other actors locally or internationally—and therefore to affect the form or content of its ideological movements. Some of these influences may be quite explicit and direct, such as those affecting the ideology of an anticommunist movement in the contemporary United States. Others may be mediated through more localized networks of moral obligation—for example, the ideology of a prayer group that responds most directly to decisions made by a religious hierarchy or to changes in the occupational status of its members, both of which are in turn subject to influences from the broader economic or political condition of the world-system. These movements, in turn, ultimately have some effect, directly or indirectly, on the development of the world-system. Again, their survival is likely to depend on the availability of resources to specific movements and on the degree to which specific ideological forms are selected for or selected against by the pattern of environmental resources. Thus, any specific sector of the core or periphery of the world-system will differ from others in its propensity to sponsor ideological movements. The wider perspective affords a context that sets broad parameters on these more immediate propensities. As the foregoing discussion has suggested, ideological movements of the following kinds seem distinguishable in terms of this framework: revitalization movements, ideological revolutions, militant ideologies, counterreform movements, ideological accommodation, and sectarianism. A brief consideration of each is now in order.

REVITALIZATION

The term "revitalization" is Anthony Wallace's (1956). Here, however, it seems better to give it a restricted meaning that is both more in keeping with the movements with which Wallace was most concerned and more useful for discriminating among kinds of movements. Revitalization movements are attempts involving some form of religious, quasi-religious, or political ideology to collectively restore or reconstruct patterns of moral order that have been radically disrupted or threatened. The main varieties of revitalization movements include (1) nativistic movements, which attempt to purify their members from the influences of alien persons or customs; (2) revivalistic movements, which attempt to rediscover simple or natural styles of life perceived as being threatened by modern culture; (3) cargo cults, which attempt to import advantages supposedly available from alien persons or ideologies; (4) millenarian movements, which attempt to prepare their members for the coming of an apocalyptic world transformation; and (5) messianic movements, which attempt to prepare for the coming of a divine savior. Periods of revitalization may combine a number of these kinds of movements.

Conventional accounts of revitalization movements have generally emphasized social disruption as their source. But not all sorts of disruption seem to produce revitalization movements. Natural disasters often displace entire communities but have seldom been the source of revitalization movements. Wars produce disruption, too, but usually without revitalization movements arising. During World War II, much of Europe fell victim to extreme devastation, but largely without such movements developing. The kind of disruption that has most often resulted in revitalization movements has come from contact between traditional populations and a dominant cultural system (cf. Worsley, 1968). This kind of contact also varies, both in the type of disruption produced and in its tendency to evoke ideological movements. Occasionally such contact is disruptive in a very radical or physical sense: forced migration, resettlement, violent conquest. These kinds of disruptions, despite their severity for the victims, usually have not resulted in revitalization movements, however. The reason seems to be that they either decimate the population or impose a totally new form of social organization on it (e.g., see Wolf, 1959:176–201). Thus, a special type of disruption is most conducive of revitalization movements. As argued in discussing the production of new ideology more generally, disruption has to create new uncertainties in the moral order. In the case of revitalization movements, this uncertainty seems to arise mostly from social changes that create cleavages between local elites and the broader mass of the population.

Cleavages of this sort have occurred on the widest scale during periods of rapid expansion in the capitalist world-system. As trade flourishes and new markets become integrated into the world-economy, local elites who have previously depended on local economies participate in the benefits of broader markets. Their new prosperity gives them greater power vis-à-vis subject populations, whose traditional rights can now be restricted or neglected entirely. In other instances, the process may be more complex. Rather than there being simply elites and subjects, lesser elites often provide the key in maintaining the balance between upper elites and subjects. But broader economic expansion may seriously undercut the position of these lesser elites. Upper elites gain the resources to "buy out" these elites, to pass laws that weaken their position, or simply cease to provide the higher sponsorship on which these elites depend. As a result, subject populations may come under increasing degrees of exploitation or find themselves in direct competition with lesser elites who have now entered their own ranks. In still other cases, cleavage between local elites and subject populations results from an increasing degree of specialization in the local economy, often as a result of the increased profitability of a single export commodity. Elites in this expanding sector of the economy are likely to gain political and economic power, even to the point of becoming absentee owners who pay little attention to their lower status dependents; elites in other sectors are likely to be driven into desperate economic circumstances, sometimes to the extent that they may become involved in the same type of movements that appeal to the lower strata. Cleavage between local elites and subject populations, whatever specific form it takes, is likely to be not only economically disadvantageous to the lower strata but also disorganizing as far as the moral order is concerned, for local elites in these settings have typically been the main source of social welfare and have enforced the customs and regulations that affect daily life. Revitalization movements provide symbols that transcend immediate deprivations and inspire new modes of structuring the moral order. As observed in discussing millenarianism, these movements generally attract relatively small proportions of the broader population that is faced with a disturbance of moral obligations. Other factors—available leadership, kin networks, the stability of local communities, the capacity of religious or political organizations to fill the gap—all influence the likelihood of revitalization movements occurring. But for those who become involved, these movements reconstruct some of the moral bonds that have been shattered, often by imposing tight communitarian discipline on the collectivity.

The conditions giving rise to revitalization movements are clearly illustrated in the origins of the Anabaptist movements of the early sixteenth century. These movements developed during a period of rapid expansion in trade, population, prices, political hegemony, and capitalist agriculture throughout Europe, but especially in central Europe, where Anabaptism had its origins and greatest successes. This expansion brought to the territorial landlords and city magistrates of the German states, Swiss cantons, and Hapsburg sections of Austria and Hungary new opportunities for production and exchange beyond the local market and permitted or encouraged the erosion of traditional seigneurial obligations. The sale or division of common lands, the replacement of land tenure with contractual obligations, and the centralization of judicial functions resulted from this growth. In the wake of these infringements of traditional peasant rights under the "old common law," the Anabaptist movements occurred first and most extensively among those peasants who had enjoyed the greatest prosperity and freedom under these customs and who therefore were most disinherited by their erosion (Williams, 1962).[7]

Similar effects are again apparent in the early eighteenth century during the commercial and colonial expansion of the mercantilist system (e.g., in the early Methodist movement among the miners at Bristol, in the religious awakening among the urban poor in Scotland, and in the various prophet cults among the Indians of North America). The same effects are also evident during the early years of the twentieth century in areas newly incorporated into the free-trade system (e.g., the Watchtower movement in South Africa, the widespread influence of Pentecostalism among the Toba Indians in northern Argentina, the spiritualist movement in Singapore, and the cargo cults in Melanesia [Wilson, 1973]). In all these cases the communal form of tribal, peasant, or village life provided the initial basis from which new movements could be mobilized. The hierarchical patronage system on which communal bonds had depended was disrupted by an intrusion of the broader—in many cases, actually foreign—world-system. This disruption generally took the form of a horizontal cleavage between a significant segment of the local elite strata and the lower strata of the community. What was left among the lower strata was then reorganized into a new moral community by the ideology of revitalization. In a few cases violent opposition to the alien culture erupted, but revitalization seldom took a militant form. Rather than launching political attacks or attempting to overthrow established cultural institutions, most of these movements focused on reorganizing the lives of their members. Far from representing a mere nostalgic or escapist form of ideology, they offered members tangible goals to strive for, reaffirmed individual discipline, created new moral obligations, and made provisions for personal care and social welfare.

The distinctive diversity of revitalization movements is a function, first, of the fact that these movements are aimed at restoring disparate local customs in the face of an expanding world economy and, second, of the different forms in which this expansion becomes manifest. For example, revivalistic movements that stress individual salvation and piety, such as early Methodism, have been more common where individuals have been displaced from traditional groups and incorporated separately into new economic contexts. In contrast, cargo cults and nativistic movements have been more likely where whole groups have been collectively displaced, as among the North American Indians.[8]

The evolution of revitalization movements has also varied with the kind of expansion experienced. Where commercial expansion has been accompanied by settlement colonies, revitalization movements have tended to be short-lived because of the reorganization or extinction of native populations. Where expansion has occurred through the incorporation of domestic lower classes into new occupational roles, these movements have generally evolved into established religious organizations, as in the evolution of Methodism in England. Revitalization movements have persisted as such on the widest scale among populations exposed to the dominant world order but not fully incorporated into its rights or style of life, as evidenced by the continued spread of these movements in the Third World.

One implication of these last considerations that bears comment in passing is that the usual trajectory from sect to church or from cult to church that has been inspired by the history of revitalization movements in Europe and North America may be misleading in many other contexts. The successful transformation of a small revitalization movement like early Methodism into an established church depended to a large extent on the high degree of economic expansion and social integration of the working class in the British context. In other cases this expansion and incorporation have been less successful. For example, the refeudalization of eastern Europe during the latter half of the sixteenth century and the seventeenth century left many of the smaller Anabaptist groups that had settled there in a state of permanent serfdom. Not until some of these groups migrated to the United States in the nineteenth century did their social position and religious outlook change significantly, and even then the die had been cast in many cases.[9]

IDEOLOGICAL REVOLUTIONS

Ideological revolutions occur under conditions broadly similar to those in which revitalization movements develop, but they differ in both their content and location relative to centers of power. In the modern period three such movements or clusters of movements appear unquestionably to qualify as ideological revolutions: the Protestant Reformation in the sixteenth century, the Enlightenment in the eighteenth century, and the growth of Marxist socialism in the nineteenth century. Each of these movements was "revolutionary" in the sense of successfully institutionalizing a whole set of assumptions that differed radically from previously accepted definitions of reality. Rather than simply restoring a conception of moral community, they radically challenged the prevailing cultural order, primarily with words, however, rather than with force, and succeeded in becoming the official ideologies of whole territories in the world-system. Of the various kinds of ideological movements, these are the most distinctively international in scope and clearly require a transsocietal perspective in order to understand their social origins.

Ideological revolutions have been carried out by elites with rising degrees of power and autonomy, often in areas that were previously peripheral to the core of the world order, during periods of rapid expansion in the world-system. Overall economic expansion incorporates these elites into wider markets and, as previously suggested, increases their freedom relative to subject populations. As rising elites, these groups often gain new access to the state as well, thereby securing a powerful resource for institutionalizing their ideologies. Other states that remain dependent on interest groups whose resources are not expanding or whose moral obligations draw legitimacy from established cultural institutions simply have fewer opportunities to take the vanguard role in pursuing new ideologies. In the extreme, economic and political expansion may also create greater administrative burdens for core areas than for periphery areas, significantly increasing the competitive advantages of rising elites in relation to the core. The correlative shift in the distribution of world power has afforded opportunities for the growth of new ideas, especially ones that challenge the hegemony of the core—or the hegemony of older status groups in the core—and legitimate the rising status of new elites whose resources are linked to the expanding world economy.

The Protestant Reformation occurred in the context of rapid population growth, a long-term rise in grain prices, great expansion in the volume and circulation of money because of the importation of American bullion, naval and military innovations, and an intensification and broadening of trade. This expansion greatly benefited the German and Swiss city magistrates, Dutch and English merchants, and many of the monarchs and territorial princes in northern Europe, all of whom prospered from the expanding trade between the Baltic and the Mediterranean, through the Rhineland corridor, along the Atlantic coast, and through the Danish Sound. It was among these previously peripheral cadres, long secondary to the economic powers of the Mediterranean princes and the political strength of the Spanish Hapsburgs, that the Reformation first became institutionalized. The reformers' attacks against the church implicitly desacralized the Hapsburg empire because its legitimacy rested heavily on the idea of a universal faith, whose defender was the Hapsburg monarch. The reformers' teachings also significantly broadened access to legitimate authority by encouraging preaching in the vernacular, by championing salvation by faith alone, and by substituting scriptural for ecclesiastical authority. In the German lands, Low Countries, Scandinavia, and England, the Reformation prompted the secularization and sale of church lands, giving elites revenues independent of church tithes and other taxes and encouraging land reform that was in the long run beneficial to the development of commercial agriculture. The net effect of these changes was to place the periphery of northern Europe in a more favorable trading position in the world economy. After the middle of the sixteenth century, significantly as a result of the financial burdens that Spain incurred in attempting to suppress the Protestant heresies, the core of the European economy shifted increasingly to the north, and with it, the Reformation became firmly established.

Like the Reformation, the Enlightenment and the institutionalization of Marxist socialism also took place during periods of demographic, economic, and territorial expansion, the first during the years in which the mercantilist system had spread to its farthest reaches through commercial, industrial, and colonial expansion, the second during the global explosion of trade and imperialism that occurred toward the end of the nineteenth century. The Enlightenment attracted the rising commercial and industrial classes in areas that had previously been peripheral to the dominant axis of the world economy—members of the new elite in areas such as Manchester, Edinburgh, Berlin, St. Petersburg, Boston, and Philadelphia. Unlike the Reformation, the Enlightenment also became institutionalized in core areas such as Paris and London (but scarcely at all in Amsterdam), partly because the growth of the state was a significant resource for Enlightenment scholarship, and partly because France and England (unlike Spain in the previous period) maintained their position in the core of the world economy despite its transition from one mode of organization to another. Marxism also eventually became most successfully institutionalized in areas other than the core of the world economy, namely in Russia and later in parts of the developing world, although socialism more generally experienced considerable success among the political leaders of the working classes in rapidly rising sectors of Europe itself, such as Germany, Austria, Sweden, and Belgium. Both of these ideological movements challenged the legitimacy of prevailing patterns of world order and encouraged successful economic reforms, respectively of labor and capital. In all three cases, these were revolutions "from above," gaining institutionalization before achieving mass popularity.

Like revitalization movements, ideological revolutions have been characterized by much internal diversity. Reformers, writers associated with the Enlightenment, and socialist parties all competed with one another for ascendancy. Yet there has been a coherence to these ideologies—a common set of assumptions—that has not been the case for many revitalization movements. Part of this coherence can be traced to the efforts of movement leaders themselves, many of whom (Luther, Marx, Engels) worked unceasingly to impose unity on movement ideology as it began to diffuse. Part of it can also be attributed to the greater supply of resources available to these movements for purposes of communication and formalization. In addition, a significant factor has been their opposition in each case to the sacred assumptions underlying the established world order. These assumptions were often made the explicit objects of profanation: church as harlot, mercantilist protectionism as inimical to national wealth, bourgeois culture as false consciousness. Each ideology also vigorously attacked the rituals binding people to their most sacred institutions: the sacraments (for which Luther was excommunicated), the laws and tariffs of the mercantilist state, the fetish-ism of commodities in the free market. At the same time, each ideologi-cal revolution posed a new definition of reality that liberalized access to the "sacred": salvation by faith, freedom in reason, justice through pro-letarian revolution. Each movement's success was determined by the conjunction of these ideas with the rising status of the elites that were at-tracted to the new definitions of reality.

MILITANCY

Relatively little attention has been paid to militant ideology as a type of social movement, although some of the more familiar of modern po-litical and religious movements have been of this kind. Calvinists, Jaco-bins, and Bolsheviks all provide cases in point. Ideological militancy can be defined as a diffuse social movement that actively attempts to over-throw an established social order through violent or forceful means and legitimates its efforts in terms of an ideology radically opposed to pre-vailing cultural institutions. The successors of ideological revolutions, these movements typically espouse an even more strident critique of the established order, believe (in the case of religious movements) in an avenging God, and champion the authority of the minority over that of the majority. The more radical departure from established definitions of reality can be seen in Calvin's rejection of Luther's hope of working for reform within the established church and in the increasingly radical turn of the Enlightenment after about 1750, especially in Febronianism and militant atheism. The emphasis on vengeance and judgment is evident in Calvinism, Jacobinism, and Leninism—all of which have an avenging and deterministic view of history. They have also generally been orga-nized into tightly knit, strictly disciplined struggle groups.

A militant stand has sometimes been associated with all the ideological movement types under consideration here, but ideological militancy as an extreme type has usually been most common and most successful among cadres in the periphery of the world-system during periods of deep polarization and conflict. The radical Calvinism of the Huguenots in Navarre or of the Sea Beggars in the Netherlands, the Reign of Terror fol-lowing the French Revolution, and the Union of the Godless in the Soviet Union during the 1920s all serve as examples. These have been periods in which widespread economic instability, including stagnation, has pro-duced divisive political strain within core areas, especially where these ar-eas have been politically decentralized (i.e., divided into competing core states). Instability and strain of this sort have typically resulted in efforts on the part of the core to tighten control over economically or politically strategic periphery areas. Often these efforts have taken the form of colonial and imperial ties; in more recent periods, neocolonialism, protectionism, trade partnerships, and military intervention have been the more common strategies. These restrictions on core-periphery relations have seldom been received lightly in the periphery, particularly among elites that have grown strong in autonomy during times of expansion and prosperity. The usual consequence has been conflict between periphery and core areas, as in the revolt of the Netherlands against Spain toward the end of the sixteenth century, the American Revolution against England in the eighteenth century, and the various anticolonial revolts of the twentieth century. As these examples suggest, militant revolts have had an episodic character, have included relatively few that resulted in an eventual triumph of the periphery over the core, and have generally been of great importance in the history of those areas that successfully resisted the core.

The emergence of ideologically militant groups has been a function, among other things, of the distinctive state of world order during periods of polarization. The weakened position of the core because of economic reversals and increasing military and bureaucratic expenditures has inhibited its ability to crush the formation of militant movements in the periphery. This has particularly been the case when the resources of the core were preoccupied with internal factionalism and war. Militant movements have been facilitated as well by the social disorganization accompanying war. A large number of the Dutch Calvinists who revolted against Spain in the late sixteenth century, for example, were exiles from earlier purges in the Netherlands and from elsewhere in Europe (Geyl, 1932). Beyond this, a decisive circumstance contributing to the rise and spread of ideological militancy has been the fact that periods of polarization in world order have usually followed on the heels of successful ideological revolutions that have left the world divided ideologically and politically.

The important consequences of previous ideological ferment for the formation of militant ideological movements have been primarily twofold. First, these movements have been able to gain strength through international alliances and, indeed, have typically espoused internationalistic orientations (a fact that Troeltsch [1960] emphasizes in his discussion of Calvinism, for example). Second, international political divisions have tended to promote competing domestic factions benefiting from, and therefore supporting, alternative foreign policies (the War of the Three Henrys being an extreme example). Internal rivalry of this sort has necessitated disciplined loyalty within the ranks of such factions. Militant ideological devotion has been of strategic value to political mobilization in such periods of polarization.

COUNTERREFORMS

Counterreforms may be characterized as movements among representatives of established cultural institutions to strengthen the moral obligations that bind individuals to the corporate order. The ideologies of these movements conceive of reality in corporatist terms and stress the immanence of ultimate reality in institutions representing the corporate order. Attainment of a relation with ultimate reality is made contingent upon participation in corporate sacraments and ceremonies. Examples include the renewal of Thomism in sixteenth-century Spain (the so-called Counterreformation), the Gallican revival in eighteenth-century France, and the religious and political nationalism of the interwar years in the present century. Again, these are manifestations of ideological tendencies that have been present in other movements as well, but they have been the most pronounced themes in a few highly corporatist movements.

Counterreform movements have been especially evident in core areas during periods of polarization in world order, usually at least partly in reaction to the challenge presented by ideological revolutions and militant ideological movements. It was in the context of the Protestant revolts, military setbacks, price inflation, and imperial bankruptcy that the Counterreformation experienced its greatest successes in the Hapsburg domains. It was in the period of colonial revolt against the mercantilist system, accompanied by growing disaffection among the lower classes and increasing rivalry and conflict among the core powers, that the romantic reaction against the Enlightenment, and (soon after) the Napoleonic corporatist state, emerged in France. Similarly, it was in the aftermath of World War I, followed by the collapse of the balance of power system and the international gold standard that had undergirded the free-market system, that fascist ideologies commanding quasi-religious devotion spread throughout much of Europe.

In each case, the geopolitical conditions were much the same. Increasing military and administrative expenditures on the part of the core, together with declining export markets and enlarged foreign debts, produced an unfavorable balance of trade for the core, weakening further

its domestic economy. To maintain the traditional system of stratification under these circumstances placed greater burdens, especially in the
form of taxation, on the lower strata. Declining economic opportunities
among the upper strata also produced pressures on the polity to absorb
excess members of these strata into the administrative bureaucracy, especially through the bestowal of honorific titles, military pensions, and—
wherever available—ecclesiastical offices.

The incentive for counterreform came most directly from the need to
reinforce the loyalties of the lower strata to the social order in the face
of declining material rewards. Thus, the activities of counterreforms,
although including proselytizing activities toward the periphery, have
been focused for the most part on the lower strata within the core, directed especially at undermining local, family, and ethnic ties providing
alternative sources of identification with the social order. Successful carrying out of such reforms has been enhanced by the influx into the central bureaucracies of new personnel representing the established order.

Although the emergence of counterreformist ideologies has been
most evident during such periods of crisis and polarization, these movements have generally appeared only in some segments of the core areas.
Other segments (England in the eighteenth century, for example) have
made the transition to core status under new rules of world order, thus
escaping some of the domestic retrenchment called for in other areas.
On a smaller scale, counterreform ideologies have sometimes also been
present under less severe economic conditions, occurring mainly in response to the threats perceived from militant ideologies that challenge
the established order.

ACCOMMODATION

The term "ideological accommodation" is used to indicate an adaptation of ideology to emerging forms of world order during periods of
reintegration in the world-system. Some of the varieties of ideological
accommodation include (1) liberal reform movements; (2) movements
concerned with alleviating social problems; (3) movements oriented toward the rights and the social incorporation of minority or sectarian
groups; and (4) defections from established cultural institutions that
serve the purpose of stripping these institutions of traditional moral obligations. Although the form these movements may take is likely to
vary, they all bear evidence of the influence of a broader transition toward a new world order—an attempt, at some times more conscious

than at others, to emphasize ideas and values that seem to be in keeping with the new rules around which world order is organized.

Movements of these kinds have been particularly evident in core countries of the world-system at times when new patterns of world order were becoming institutionalized. The emergence of the mercantilist system was accompanied by the Arminian movement in Holland, by the charitable movement initiated by Vincent de Paul in France, and by the incorporation of the Separatists and Independents in England. Similarly, the rise of the free-trade system coincided with the Liberal-Catholic movement in France and Belgium and the great theological reforms of Schleiermacher, Hegel, and Strauss, the French monastic renewal oriented toward ministering to the poor, the incorporation of Protestant dissenters in England through the repeal of the Test and Corporation Acts, and with what Eric Hobsbawm (1962) has aptly called "the secularization of the masses" in speaking of the widespread religious defection that took place among the middle and lower classes during this period—to list but a few of the more prominent examples.

The social contexts nurturing these movements are too complex to subsume under any simple typological scheme, but at the level of world order, the following conditions appear to have contributed significantly to the prominence of these movements: the declining status of formerly dominant core areas during periods of reintegration, the rising status of new core powers, new relations with periphery areas, and the temporary absence of a stable international monetary and diplomatic order. The major consequence of these conditions for ideological movements is an erosion of economic groups whose power has been protected by former patterns of international exchange and a strengthening of economic groups oriented to new patterns of international exchange.

This realignment of the power of interest groups, together with the overall economic instability that derives from the absence of an embracing international monetary order, generates civil conflict that often results in some degree of political reform. This process occurs within the limits imposed by the interests of other nations and is conditioned by the presence of similar conflicts elsewhere. The net result consists typically not only of a change in the position of domestic interest groups but also of a redefinition of government policy and of national roles in the world-system. The effect of these changes is often apparent among religious or ethnic groups that have created an ideological form closely linked to an established moral community. The transition in the broader social infrastructure cuts through these moral communities, as it were, creating new bases of moral cleavage, dividing solidary moral orders into competing interest groups, and giving the various factions a different place in the larger social order. For established religion, especially where it has been in some measure subordinated to the polity, the consequences have usually included rising legitimacy for minority religions formerly critical of existing social arrangements, defection by groups dissatisfied with the ossification of religious organizations, and efforts by others to reform religious organizations in keeping with new political and moral climates. These have often included social service activities functioning to alleviate hardships brought on the lower strata by the economic and political instability of the times.

As a brief example, the religious situation in England during the first half of the nineteenth century may be considered. England is a particularly obvious example because the degree of religious pluralism that had become institutionalized there made it possible for a greater degree of ideological maneuvering to surface in specific ecclesiastical and political reforms than might have been likely under less pluralistic conditions. By 1815, the mercantilist system of protective tariffs, colonial bilateralism, and state monopolies had been rendered obsolete by the successes of the American and French revolutions, the high costs of the Napoleonic Wars, and the popularity of Enlightenment ideology. A new system of world order organized along principles of free trade was emerging, creating pressures for changes in domestic social organization. Most urgently needed was reform of the protective tariff policies on shipping and grain that kept British food prices unnaturally high in view of cheaper sources from the United States and Prussia, thereby preventing wage levels from sinking to internationally competitive levels, creating unrest among the working classes, and maintaining undue privileges among the landed aristocracy (Knorr, 1944). Conflict between the landed aristocracy and the rising industrial, commercial, and financial interests came to a head in a series of parliamentary clashes between the Whigs and Tories, culminating in the repeal of the Corn Laws in 1846 (Kammen, 1970). In religion the changing climate of political power and opinion led to increasing legitimacy for those minority bodies (largely Evangelicals and Dissenters) that had been early advocates of political reform and that could be counted on for further support of the new government policies. It also led to the reforms of the 1830s, the purpose of which was to effect changes in the Anglican church, both in theology and organization, making it more compatible with the views and interests of the new commercial classes, many of whom had defected from the church over its support of aristocratic privileges. Finally, this period saw increasing efforts by the church—especially among its more evangelical elements—to minister to the needs of the urban poor.

SECTARIANISM

The remaining kind of ideological movement to be considered is what might be called, drawing mainly from religious examples, sectarianism. This variant, like ideological accommodation, has also been especially evident in periods of reintegration in the world-system but has occurred more commonly among groups whose relation to power was declining than among groups whose relation to power was increasing. Sectarianism includes movements in which a strong element of "backlash" is often evident, sometimes as a specific reaction against movements that have accommodated themselves to new social circumstances. These movements have been noted especially among groups with formerly high levels of status. Sectarianism also includes movements that arise among the lower classes, sometimes as a result of the pressures placed on these classes during times of major economic and political transition. And it includes various radical and utopian movements such as those that frequently arise among intellectuals and students during these periods.

The accomplishment of so-called liberal reforms in religious or political organizations often takes place against a backdrop of opposition from those whose interests were better protected by previous patterns of world order and by previously popular domestic policies. When this opposition contains moral as well as purely political dimensions, it frequently results in religious schisms—splinter groups that object to reforms being made by parent organizations. If not contained, these schisms often lead to the formation of new minority religious bodies. The *dévot* movement in France, arising in opposition to Richelieu's policy of cooperation with the German Protestants, is a clear example of this kind of movement during the early mercantilist period. The Oxford movement, which developed in reaction to the liberalization of the Church of England in the 1830s, provides a similar case during the early free-trade period. It was largely contained within the church. Among those movements that were not contained were the "great dispute" in Scotland in 1843, the secession of "Old Lutherans" in Prussia, and the birth of the Christian Reformed Church in the Netherlands. In each instance these movements were predominantly populated by interest groups whose privileges were being undermined by the emergence of new patterns of international exchange.

The conditions leading to the rise of sects among the lower classes during these periods result in the largest sense from a lack of stable international monetary and political relations. These uncertainties precipitate and worsen domestic economic crises that create temporary unemployment and economic hardships for the lower strata. These deprivations are aggravated by the efforts of both rising and declining elites to maintain their share of scarce economic resources. In addition, the likelihood of new sects emerging among the lower strata is enhanced by their physical migration away from established moral communities due to economic difficulties and changing opportunities for employment. The kinds of movements that result are illustrated by the diffuse spread of what G. L. Mosse (1970) has termed "popular piety" among the peasants of England, Holland, and Germany during the early mercantilist period and by the efflorescence of Baptists, Methodists, and Adventists in the new grain-growing regions of North America and the new industrial workers of Britain during the early free-trade period. The diffusion of these movements is significantly enhanced by the presence of political and economic instability throughout the world-system during such transitional periods.

This instability, together with the fluctuating moral climates it produces, is also an important factor contributing to the radical and utopian sects that have frequently developed among intellectuals and students during these periods (e.g., the Cambridge Platonists and the Rosicrucians in England and the Socinians in Poland during the seventeenth century, the Christian Socialists in England and the Transcendentalists in America during the nineteenth century). In each case, consciousness among intellectuals of domestic injustices to the lower classes and of foreign struggles for political reform were significant factors in the inspiration of these movements.

THE PERIOD SINCE WORLD WAR II

One of the questions that initially motivated this effort to spell out some of the broad relations between ideological movements and patterns of world order was that of identifying social factors underlying the considerable ideological ferment that has been evident in the United States since World War II. Some observers—especially during the high point of unrest in the late 1960s and early 1970s—suggested that the present period signaled changes as sweeping as those of the Reformation or the Enlightenment. Others argued that there had always been ideological movements and that nothing special should be made of the contemporary ferment. Still others drew parallels between the 1960s and moments of unrest at earlier times in American history, such as the 1770s or the 1830s. The problem with most of these comparisons was that they were made without any consideration of the broader social context in which ideological movements had appeared. The present framework at least provides some crude dimensions along which such comparison cases can be selected. It suggests that the period since World War II has been characterized mainly by the transition from the world order that dominated the latter half of the nineteenth century to a new world order that has not yet become fully institutionalized. Some observers of the present world order, it should be noted, suggest a different scenario. They argue that the United States achieved a dominant position in the world economy immediately following World War II, much as Britain had in the nineteenth century, and that this world order flourished with few problems until the 1970s, when it finally began to be challenged by the growing economic power of rivals such as West Germany and Japan. According to this scenario, there will be increasing protectionism, economic and political rivalry, and eventually another major world war before another world order comes into being (barring nuclear annihilation). This model has the advantage of highlighting the importance of economic expansion in the American context. However, even within this context there has remained much domestic uncertainty and adjustment concerning the terms of domestic and world order. For purposes of understanding cultural change, these realignments appear to warrant the greatest emphasis.

Ever since World War II, the United States has experienced a great number of ideological movements. Contrary to predictions promising an "end of ideology," movements and countermovements have been the order of the day. Especially evident has been the unrest that has characterized American religion. In the 1950s, these movements included a broad revival in mainline denominations, a rebirth of pentecostalism and fundamentalism, and a renewed interest in ecumenism and church union. In the 1960s, religious unrest became more pronounced. That decade witnessed a movement away from organized religion, especially among young people, many of whom defected from the churches, first to campus religious centers, and later from those, too. It also saw the spread of religiously inspired civil rights movements among minorities and, in turn, of ethnic backlash. Among Catholics, it saw the initiation of the Vatican II reforms. And perhaps most visibly, the 1960s gave birth to a host of new religious movements, many of which harkened to traditions other than Christianity. In the 1970s, these movements survived for the most part, spread, splintered, and cross-fertilized to the extent that the number of local groups ran in the thousands and the number of followers ranged in the hundreds of thousands. By the end of that decade, a strong movement on the conservative end of the religio-political spectrum had also arisen. Consolidating its ideological claims around traditional positions on abortion, pornography, homosexuality, and communism, it attracted a large following, including disproportionate numbers from the South, from rural areas, and among the less educated and elderly.

Although many of the religious movements of the past few decades have deep historic roots, the postwar period is unique in several ways. It has produced a unique mixture of Judeo-Christian, Asian, tribal, cultic, and pseudoscientific movements. It has resulted in no single philosophy or liturgical reformation, but a diversity of competing movements and countermovements. These alternative movements have not crystallized into distinct, stable organizations, but have shown a great deal of fluidity in organizational style, teachings, and membership. Like religious movements of the past, many of the current organizations have attracted the downtrodden and disadvantaged, but other movements have been effective in attracting the privileged. The religious unrest of the postwar period has not been limited to America. If anything, it has been equally pronounced in Japan, Western Europe, and, though different in content, throughout large sections of the Third World.

A variety of social and cultural conditions has contributed to this ideological ferment. But these conditions do not explain it satisfactorily, either singly or in combination. The great increase in higher education since World War II has undoubtedly exposed people to new ideas, many of which have run counter to traditional beliefs. But there have been educational revolutions before, in the 1880s, for example, without similar repercussions, and even the best statistical studies have failed by and large to pin down a direct causal relation between higher education and religious experimentation. The postwar period has contributed prosperity and affluence. But religious movements in the past have more often occurred among the less affluent and in times of economic uncertainty. Science has mushroomed in the years since Sputnik, undoubtedly with some effects on worldviews. But the most dramatic scientific revolution in modern history, that of the late seventeenth century, did not produce such dramatic religious unrest. There has perhaps been enough tension and stress to inspire some to seek comfort in new religious movements. But this stress has been no greater than that associated with two world wars or the Great Depression. Some have suggested that religious pluralism in America has itself been the source of ever-expanding religious experimentation. But this explanation fails to account for the parallel experimentation that has occurred in countries as different as France, Japan, England, and Denmark. Others have seen a connection between the present religious turmoil and the demise of the small business in favor of the giant corporation. But this connection fails to explain the relative absence of religious turmoil in earlier periods of this economic transition, notably during the age of giant trusts, nor does it account for even earlier periods of religious unrest, such as in the early nineteenth century. Still other explanations emphasizing professionalization, ecology, the mass media, urbanization, trade and technology have been tendered. But they, too, fall prey to these limitations.

All these explanations are limited because they are not situated in a historical context. Each development has had some impact on religious communities, but an understanding of that impact requires knowledge of the broader context in which each has occurred—the broader transitional period in world order. This transition has directed such domestic social changes as rising levels of education, dependence on technology, and the growth of the state. Placed in the present international context, these changes have affected religious communities in ways that were not characteristic of other times and places.

A PERIOD OF TRANSITION

An understanding of the present transition in world order requires going back again briefly to the nineteenth century, when the world order we have inherited was constructed. That order rested principally upon the functioning of free trade within a self-regulating international market. From the middle of the century onward, the free-market system regulated trade, dominated international relations, benefited and maintained the power of principal interest groups, and provided unprecedented material welfare. Especially in Britain, where it was of obvious economic advantage, the free-trade system was looked on with near-religious devotion. For instance, the *Economist* editorialized in 1843:

Free trade is itself a good, like virtue, holiness and righteousness, to be loved, admired, honoured and steadfastly adopted, for its own sake, though all the rest of the world should love restrictions and prohibitions, which are of themselves evils, like vice and crime, to be hated and abhorred under all circumstances and at all times. (quoted in Amery, 1969:221)

In addition to the free market, the nineteenth-century world order rested on three supporting institutions. The first was the British-dominated balance-of-power system that maintained international peace throughout most of the century, a condition necessary for the successful conduct of international free trade. Second was the laissez-faire system of government that minimized domestic interference with the free functioning of the market. And third was the international gold standard that limited fluctuations in exchange rates, protected the value of foreign loans, facilitated the free flow of international commerce, and benefited the industrialized countries, mainly Britain, which were the leading exporters of goods and capital. These institutions, in turn, were legitimated by an underlying utilitarian philosophy that called for freedom of the will, freedom in trade, and freedom in civil matters, the combination of which was assumed to guarantee high levels of prosperity and social justice. Under this system, nearly all parts of the globe were incorporated into the Western world economy.

The free-market system operated as an integrated form of world order. Organized around a coherent philosophical worldview, the free-market system wedded the interests of dominant political and economic elites, provided stable assumptions for the governing of international relations, maintained the position of dominant nations, and effectively controlled the passions of subordinate nations and classes. It functioned effectively, however, only as long as Britain maintained the industrial supremacy that ensured it the advantages of open trade (cf. Hobsbawm, 1969). This advantage diminished greatly by the eve of World War I, as other European nations, especially France and Germany, developed their own industrial capacities. The economic competition that resulted led the European powers increasingly to expand their trade and investments into the developing world and ultimately to circumvent the free-trade process itself by partitioning the developing world into colonial enclaves.

With the outbreak of World War I, financial chaos befell the already weakened free-market system. The war hampered trade and investments. Country after country repudiated foreign debts or declared moratoria on their repayment and otherwise acted to halt international gold shipments, leaving the gold standard operational only in a trivial sense. The economic impact on Britain was devastating. After the war, Britain was forced to borrow heavily from the United States and liquidated much of her investments abroad. In 1931, Britain abandoned the gold standard, devalued the pound, and adopted protectionist trading policies, signaling the collapse of the free-market era. Other signs of its demise included the launching of the New Deal, the five-year plans in Russia, the rise of fascism in Germany, and the collapse of the League of Nations in favor of autarchist empires. Karl Polanyi (1944:23) has described the change in the international order in this way:

> While at the end of the Great War nineteenth century ideals were paramount, and their influence dominated the following decade, by 1940 every vestige of the international system had disappeared and, apart from a few enclaves, the nations were living in an entirely new international setting.

The international gold standard had been displaced both in practice and, following Keynes, in economic theory as well. Throughout Europe, currencies fluctuated wildly, bringing concomitant unemployment and economic uncertainty. The hegemony of Britain, and with it Britain's peacekeeping ability, had been permanently destroyed. The liberal nation-state had temporarily ceased to function throughout much of the world and was replaced either by totalitarian regimes or by new welfare state economies. And although the ideology and tactics of free trade were far from dead, a profound ideological revolution had been successfully institutionalized in the Soviet Union, one that challenged the basic premises of the free-trade system.

By the end of World War II, the realities of global politics precluded any possibility of reconstructing an international order along the principles of the nineteenth-century free-market system. Western Europe lay in disarray, and the United States was still reluctant to shoulder the responsibilities of world leadership that Britain had carried. The lessons of international finance during the preceding two decades had shown the impossibility of any single country stabilizing international monetary arrangements in the way that Britain had done during the previous century. The communist bloc had succeeded in establishing itself as a significant foe of the free world. China had ceased to be a hinterland for Japanese and American investment. The preoccupation of Europe with its own affairs during the war had created opportunities for numerous incipient nationalist movements to emerge throughout the colonized world. As a result, the postwar period emerged as one in which repeated efforts to create a new world order would be made.

These efforts have been made in the absence of an integrated system of international institutions and in the presence of a world divided ideologically between the successors of the Enlightenment and the successors of Marxist socialism. As a result, national and international policy since World War II has had to be formed in the face of frequently incompatible objectives without the benefit of well-established policy guidelines. American relations with Western Europe, for example, have vacillated between a policy of bilateralism, designed to keep Europe divided and economically subordinate, and a policy of multilateralism, designed to strengthen Europe as a buffer against the Soviet Union. As international power arrangements have shifted, often from year to year, the United States has found itself favoring first one and then the other of these contradictory policies toward Western Europe (cf. Calleo and Rowland, 1973). United States policy toward former colonial possessions of the European nations has demonstrated a similar ambivalence: on the one hand, American policymakers have wished to erode the privileges of Europe; on the other hand, they have wished to make sure that these possessions do not fall to hostile regimes, as in the case of French Indochina. In American eyes Third World nations have appeared alternatively as little brothers ready to imitate the modernity of their more mature siblings, as junior partners capable of offering new markets and sources of labor, and as potential enemies ever waiting to remind Americans of their own guilty consciences. The political instability of the Third World has only added to the ambiguities of U.S. policy.

International economic arrangements have also been in a transitional phase since World War II. Chronic inflation, defiant of all Keynesian solutions, has dramatized the instability of the international monetary system that had been forecast by the economic planners from forty-four nations who participated in the conference at Bretton Woods, New Hampshire, in July of 1944. Rather than being guided by long-term policies, responses to economic crises, such as the OPEC price increases of 1973, typically have come forth on a case-by-case basis. Often, each nation has acted unilaterally to protect its own economy, through currency devaluation, for example, and in so doing has neglected the interests of international economic well-being.

At a deeper level, economic policy remains ambivalently associated with the lingering principles of free trade. Given the changes in world economic conditions, a policy of free trade permits only two means of economic adjustment: (1) changing the level of domestic economic activity, or growth rate; and (2) changing the exchange rate, or productivity ratio, of currency. Both techniques are likely to have negative political repercussions. At the same time, economic policy is guided by principles of social planning, the application of which is likely to be perceived within the business community as restrictive of vital competitive prerogatives, as evidenced by the recent tensions between multinational corporations and their host governments. Of course, economic policy is a function of compromise in any era. But the capacity to achieve workable compromises in recent years has been complicated by the absence of both an underlying international monetary system and a coherent economic philosophy (cf. Block, 1977).

The construction of a stable world order has also been made difficult in the years since World War II because of (1) political problems associated with the management of large military forces and wartime economies in ways that are consistent with the prospects of world peace; (2) the fundamental instability of a nuclear weapons monopoly on the part of the superpowers as a key to world order; and (3) the comparative recency with which both the Soviet Union and the United States have assumed roles of world leadership. Despite frequent complaints about American imperialism, the United States has actually adapted slowly to its leadership role, lacking any deep philosophical rationale for taking an aggressive stance in international affairs, save perhaps the fear of communism. Having been critical of European imperialism and having been economically self-sufficient throughout most of its history, the United States has remained deeply sensitive to accusations of imperialism. And yet, as further evidence of the ironies of world politics in the postwar period, some of the most blatant U.S. imperialist activities, usually disguised as policies designed to protect national security, have been implemented by isolationists and internationalists alike.

In addition to the international uncertainties that these conditions have generated, an important consequence has been the politicization of domestic interest groups, including a nearly constant shifting of positions and alliances among these interest groups. The shifting state of world affairs has produced a proliferation of pressure groups to influence the domestic response. Labor has emerged as a politicized interest group, dependent on government goodwill (again in the absence of a firm international monetary order) to go slowly in the fight against inflation, rather than opposing it through recessionary policies that might reduce standards of living and create unemployment among workers. These concerns, together with fears of competition from foreign workers, have made U.S. labor a generally protectionist, patriotic supporter of national government, contrary to labor's more general tradition of internationalism and class consciousness across national boundaries. Agriculture has also been politicized but has found itself in an even more ambiguous position than labor. As political and climatic conditions fluctuate throughout the world, agriculture finds itself the supporter of protectionist nationalism in one instance and, in another instance, the supporter of open international markets. The professional and managerial staffs of large corporations that depend on multinational markets have adopted a more consistent live-and-let-live attitude toward international policy, even toward the Soviet Union and China insofar as it has benefited trade, but have been less eager to take such an attitude toward left-leaning countries in the developing world for fear of losing overseas investments. The universities have been placed in a similarly ambiguous position of benefiting materially from the development of advanced technology, including military and space technology inspired by the arms race and nationalist competition, while at the same time being committed to more humanitarian and universalistic values. Other examples could be added, but the important point is that domestic interest groups have increasingly become oriented to the vagaries of international politics, finding themselves frequently in the position of having to adopt orientations internally inconsistent or contradictory to more traditional positions and having to adjust these orientations with each new development in world affairs. The task of achieving stable relations among domestic interest groups, therefore, does not simply rest on domestic political consensus, but is deeply conditioned by the affairs of world politics.

RETROSPECTIVE COMPARISONS

The relevance of all this to the recent ideological unrest in American religion may in some ways be obvious. But it will help to see the connections in a more informed manner if, before considering them explicitly, we pause to examine briefly the religious response to the two similar periods of transition in world order in past centuries.

As mentioned before, there have been two previous periods bearing conditions structurally similar to the present one. The first was the early part of the seventeenth century. In these years, the European world lay in the midst of a major social transition. The imperial order that the Spanish

Hapsburgs had attempted to impose on Europe during the sixteenth century had been defeated militarily and economically by the rising states of northern Europe. The Reformation had played a significant role in undermining the universalistic assumptions on which the domination of the Hapsburg dynasty had been erected. In its wake followed a period of international wars that emancipated most of the Hapsburg imperial possessions. The resulting situation in the early seventeenth century was a period of domestic tension and instability as the English, Dutch, and French sought to reconstruct a normative order along mercantilist lines. The civil war between crown and country in England reflected the adjustments being made among interest groups across Europe.

The second period was the early and middle years of the nineteenth century, during which the Western world was undergoing a transition from the mercantilist system to the free-trade system, of which we have already spoken. These years followed a period in which the sovereign ideals associated with mercantilism had led to increasing international conflict among the core European powers, drastically increasing the costs of maintaining the entire system. In addition, the Industrial Revolution had brought about new modes of economic production, the Enlightenment had done much to undercut the protectionist principles of international exchange, and the American Revolution had largely destroyed the prevailing pattern of colonial relations. By the early nineteenth century, the old mercantilist system had ceased to provide a stable normative order. The following transition period was accompanied by unparalleled conflict within nations. New interest groups arose and replaced old interest groups, both looked to the polity for assistance, and the lower strata clamored for social reform. Between 1812 and 1865, Spain and Portugal (and their American colonies), Russia, Greece, France, Belgium, Italy, Poland, Germany, and the United States all experienced major revolts or civil wars.

What was common in both of these periods, as well as in the more recent period, was that the basic institutional structure of the prevailing world order had, for various reasons associated with the expansion of that order, broken down. As the core area of each prevailing world order was weakened, economic and political domination shifted to new areas formerly on the periphery of world politics. In each case, this shift was facilitated by a profound ideological revolution that undermined the sacredness of the dominant system of world order and gave legitimacy to its successor. But the transition to a new system of world order was not accomplished immediately or without difficulty. Each transition was followed by a period of domestic economic instability, itself the function of an ambiguous structure of international finance and exchange, and by a succession of civil conflicts brought on by the changing roles and strengths of nations and of interest groups within nations. Only gradually, through these series of domestic adjustments, were new patterns of world order forged and stabilized.

In these two historical periods, hindsight has shown a close connection between the general crisis in world order and the prevailing religious responses. Both periods were characterized by exceptional religious unrest and diversity. Rising interest groups developed new religious forms, often with strong moral and social welfare components that assisted in legitimating their new preeminence in social affairs, while declining interest groups were frequently led to reject prevailing values and to form splinter groups, often in response to changing relations between church and state. The rising power of the Puritans in England during the first period and of the New Light and so-called "popular" denominations in the United States during the second period are among the best known examples of the former; the latter are illustrated by the Oxford movement and sectarian divisions in the Reformed and Lutheran churches. Instabilities in moral climates produced corresponding shifts in the popularity of alternative religious persuasions. And unsettled political conditions motivated religious protest, persecution, and emigration. The net effect of each period was a proliferation of religious movements throughout the international system.

In an immediate sense, the source of each of these episodes of religious unrest was domestic turmoil. But to understand the pervasiveness and the complexity of this turmoil, it must be viewed in an international context. We have come to recognize more clearly the profound connections between the religious convictions of a people and their sense of national purpose.[10] But this sense is molded by the climate of world opinion and by the global milieu within which nations function. In times when there is an underlying structure of world order, national purposes are formed within a matrix of shared assumptions, whether these concern the defense of a universalistic religion and the authority of dynastic succession, as in the Hapsburg empire, or the sovereignty and mutual antagonism of states, as in the mercantilist system. In times of deep polarization and conflict in world order, nations continue to be guided by prevailing global assumptions, either through strong reaffirmation of these assumptions or in strong reaction against them. But in the aftermath of such polarization and transition, when the fundamental operating principles of world order are in question, the purposes of nations become subject to the vagaries of events and opinion. Interest groups adopt moral positions and root them in religious convictions. Religious bodies, in turn, derive moral positions in keeping with their role in society and the role of their members. As political and economic conditions change, both domestically and in the larger world, the fortunes of those associated with these moral positions also change, and the relevance of the moral positions themselves may change. Religious orientations are likely to alternate, conflict, and multiply with each nation's efforts to find its place in the international order.

MORAL CLIMATES AND RELIGIOUS UNREST

Since World War II, the multiplicity of U.S. religious movements has been conditioned by the deep uncertainty of world affairs. Moral climates have vacillated in response to the changing circumstances of world politics, and with them the legitimacy of alternative religious orientations has risen and fallen. A few examples will serve to illustrate some of these relations.

The freezing and thawing of the cold war and the uncertainties of detente have provoked direct religious responses from the American public, for we perceive rightly that communism represents not only an alternative political system but also a profoundly different interpretation of ultimate reality itself. As relations between the two superpowers have shifted, the plausibility of alternative religious positions has also varied. Whether we wish to acknowledge it or not, periods of moral conflict with the Soviet Union have always been associated with a reassertion of American religious traditions, and detente and peaceful coexistence have invariably required us to rethink those traditions. How closely linked our religious convictions as a people are with our sense of national purpose toward the communist bloc has been well evidenced in recent years, not only in President Ford's much-criticized remarks about Eastern Europe and in President Carter's campaign for human rights, but also in President Reagan's cultivation of anticommunist fears among evangelicals and fundamentalists. Yet the very reality of the Soviet Union and its growing importance as a vast export market for agricultural and industrial production have placed the religious convictions of many a farmer and factory worker at odds with their economic motivations. Is it not perhaps the accompanying sense of guilt and betrayal, however deeply subconscious, that has led to such violent denunciations of campus radicals and others who have openly admitted their Marxist leanings? The effect of a world divided between democracy and communism has not been simply to reinvigorate our civil religion, but to cast it into the depths of uncertainty.

The rise of China to world power has also contributed to the moral ambiguity of U.S. religious culture. The case of China has been especially revealing of the precarious framework of world order that has been constructed since World War II. To a great extent the postwar order has been predicated upon domination by the superpowers of the ultimate deterrent force, namely, nuclear weapons. When China exploded its own atomic bomb in 1964, a new reality was imposed on the superpowers. Within both China and the Soviet Union, the progress toward China's nuclear capability had been fraught with political conflict. Khrushchev fell from power the same day that China tested its bomb. For the United States, short-term alarm gradually gave way to long-term changes in foreign policy as the Sino-Soviet split deepened and as the United States became increasingly dependent on China to assist in extricating itself from Vietnam.[11] Although the religious responses to these events were less direct than they typically have been to the activities of the Soviet Union, the consequences reverberated widely. No longer could the world be divided as easily into the "just" and the "unjust." China's power represented an added peril, should its differences with the Soviet Union be healed, or a potential ally, should some common ground be found. Scholars and diplomats revived earlier reservoirs of fascination with the ancient culture and religions of China. Forward-looking American missionaries again began praying for the day when China's door would be reopened and took heart at reports of the number of indigenous Christians still living in China. "Yellow peril" fears that had crept into the churches during the 1950s (and before) came increasingly to be disrespectable, and groups that had flourished in these fears, of which Sun Myung Moon's Unification church was one of the most notable examples, became increasingly sectarian and suspicious of the new mood of the U.S. government.

The absence of stable relations between the United States and the Third World, too, has deeply affected the moral consciousness of the postwar period, particularly when these relations have involved Americans in morally questionable positions, as in Vietnam, Cambodia, Chile, Bangladesh, and Nicaragua. Each new failure to impose our American conceptions of stability and prosperity on the Third World has brought with it charges of imperialism and neocolonialism. Americans have been forced to reevaluate the moral basis of their motivations. The changes have come both from other nations and from domestic interest groups, and they have multiplied as policies are first initiated, then reversed, and then reinitiated. The effect on religion has been that the plausibility of the whole Western tradition, with its emphasis on modernity and rationality, can no longer be taken for granted quite as easily as it once was. This has not been the result of some mysterious philosophical reorientation, but the product of empirical relations between the West and the developing world. And in the *lacunae* of ultimate confidence, many have turned inward to reconstruct their own personal experiences of the sacred, often by borrowing heavily from the tribal, magical, and mystical religions previously relegated to the fringes of the Western tradition.

The relations between moral climates, religious movements, and the broader transition in world order were probably revealed most clearly by the crisis of the 1960s. That crisis, in an immediate sense, was the Vietnam war. It was also a crisis in world order and in the positions of domestic interest groups connected to that order. Insofar as the United States was concerned, the world order of the 1950s and early 1960s was oriented chiefly toward military containment of the communist bloc and the strengthening of America's stabilizing influence in the free world. This system was predicated upon the monopoly of effective nuclear strike capacities by the United States and by the Soviet Union, the dominance of the Soviet Union in the communist world and its ability to exert control over member nations, U.S. ability to maintain security within its sphere of influence, and the tacit agreement on the part of both superpowers as to the boundaries of their respective spheres.

The containment system also meshed neatly with the interests and ideologies of major U.S. power groups, even to the extent of limited wars. In the South, strong military commitments to the defense of the free world strengthened the political power of old-guard hawks, fed money into southern military training camps, provided career opportunities for both blacks and whites, and wedded the conservative religious orientations of the South to the national interest. For agriculture, the same forces that kept southern politicians strong also helped ensure a stable farm subsidy program that in the short run appeared better than the vagaries of an open international market, and again coincided with the religious and moral convictions of farmers and townspeople in the rural areas. For the largest corporations, containment politics were scarcely essential to their prosperity. But for many of the weaker corporations (and, in turn, labor), continuous demands for new weapons systems, the role of a large standing army in minimizing unemployment, and formal encouragement of foreign subsidiaries and joint ventures with Japan and Western Europe were by no means without importance. Even for the larger corporations, and certainly the universities, the scientific and technological efforts inspired by the arms race, and increasingly the space race, contributed significantly to their overall well-being.

Vietnam was both symptom and cause of the changes in world order that witnessed the demise of containment politics. These changes included the rise of China as a nuclear power, the Sino-Soviet split, economic tensions among the Western allies, and postcolonial instabilities in the Third World. Under these circumstances Vietnam became the catalyst that precipitated far-reaching realignments among domestic interest groups. For the South the increasing costs of the war, and hence its growing unpopularity, undermined the power of the old guard and facilitated the rise of the so-called new southern politician. Increasingly the war divided the interests of blacks, who saw the Great Society usurped by the costs of defense, from those of the white establishment, further eroding the traditional base of southern politics.

Ideologically, the war drove a wedge between the more liberal advocates of containment and the more conservative champions of a rollback policy. For the corporate community, the worsening balance of foreign payments as the war dragged on precipitated a reevaluation of its commitment to a firm containment orientation. In the universities, the war brought to a crisis the basic inconsistency of interests wedded to the export of military technology and ideology espousing universal humanitarian ideals. In short, the 1960s witnessed a major realignment of domestic interests, not just because of internal unrest, but also because of larger conditions in world affairs associated ultimately with the breakup of the free-trade system and the transition to a new pattern of world order.

In religion, the most immediate consequences of this realignment were the radical and utopian cults that emerged among intellectuals and students, generally espousing antiwar and antitechnological sentiments, and deriving popularity from their rejection of Western religious traditions. But the religious repercussions of Vietnam ran far deeper. The shifting moral climate and definitions of national purpose associated with the protests and realignments of the 1960s nourished liberalizing and social reform movements within the mainstream churches, including Christian-Marxist dialogue, civil rights activism, antiwar efforts, experiments in liturgy, and reevaluations of traditional political and moral postures. They also contributed to widespread defection from the

churches among the better educated classes for whom the events of the
1960s symbolized a growing gap between world conditions and the traditions of the church.

As in the past, religious accommodation of this sort brought forth
other movements as a reaction among those for whom the emerging pattern of world order meant declining power—new denominations in the
South and in the Midwest, such as the National Presbyterian church and
the reconstituted Missouri Lutherans; movements among Vietnam hard-
liners within the churches (the Presbyterian Laymen's Association, for
example); and diffuse defection from mainline denominations into the
more politically conservative evangelical churches. Although generalized affluence and the welfare state prevented the kind of extreme hardships that had given rise to widespread sectarianism among the lower
classes in the past, those caught at the margins of society during this
transitional period, particularly minorities and less privileged young people, followed predictable patterns in their attraction to movements such
as the Children of God, Pentecostalism, the Unification church, the
Black Muslims, and the Black Christian Nationalist movement.

Because the United States has been a nation of immigrants, the frontiers of American religion have always been exposed to the influences of
foreign affairs. But never before have these frontiers been as widely exposed as they have been in recent years. Not only has the postwar period suffered from the tensions of a world order in transition, but America's dominant role in world politics has also exposed it on all fronts to
world events. Accordingly, many of its new religious movements have
been directly or indirectly influenced by U.S. foreign relations. As in the
past, friendly relations with Britain and Western Europe have facilitated
the import and export of new religions. Devotees of groups such as the
Process and Scientology turned from Britain to the United States when
legal and economic restrictions became oppressive. The Children of
God turned to Britain when the same pressures developed against them
in the United States. Transcendental Meditation found its way west-
ward more easily because of the longstanding relations between India
and Britain and because of the use of those relations by such prominent
figures as the Beatles. Yet the tensions that have existed between the
United States and Western Europe since World War II as the United
States has exerted its dominant influence in world affairs have made
Americans somewhat less eager to borrow from the Europeans than
they may have been in the past. Certainly there has been less fascination
with European theology than with Asian religions. The protective and

commercial alliances between the United States and Japan have made it as easy to import Zen Buddhism and Nichiren Shoshu as Datsuns and Toyotas. Similarly, the ease with which Tibetan yoga has been implanted, and the degree to which American youth have been able to make pilgrimages to the fountains of Divine Light and Hare Krishna, are partly a function of U.S. relations with Asia. In short, American religion has experienced the consequences of the deep U.S. involvement in a global network of security and trade relations.

This network has created exposure to new religions, but the transitional state of world affairs has ultimately conditioned their legitimacy. Students, especially those on the nation's large cosmopolitan campuses, and young people more generally have grown up amid competing conceptions of national destiny. Their futures have been much influenced by the demands of foreign wars, by the varied fortunes of the space and arms races, by academic preoccupations with international studies, and by the economic consequences of currency fluctuations, inflation, and energy embargoes. This has been as true of students in Japan and Western Europe as in the United States. And the religious consequences have been much the same. For the churches, it has been the liberal mainline denominations, those most capable of and most committed to speaking out on world affairs, whose plausibility has been undercut by the shifting contingencies of national and international politics. The effect on these denominations was particularly evident during the 1960s when the rapid transition from support of the cold war to protest against the Vietnam war gave rise to criticism and defection among both conservatives and liberals. Rightly or wrongly, the preeminent orientation in foreign affairs has been an amoral realpolitik, rather than the moral principles devised by the churches in their quest for public relevance. Thus, the churches that have fared healthiest have generally been those among the fundamentalist and evangelical denominations that have sought only the salvation of souls and have skirted the practicalities of social policy pronouncements. Much the same kind of negative consequences seem likely to overtake their counterparts in the other wings of U.S. fundamentalism that have become mobilized in support of strong defenses, anticommunism, traditional sexual standards, and so on.

In the most general sense, the plausibility structure undergirding U.S. religious culture is one that encourages diversity and change. The most powerful gods we experience in our everyday lives—the sovereign nation-states of the modern world—function within a transitional international order ideologically fractionated and institutionally precarious. Indeed, the precariousness of international affairs has made governments reticent to espouse irrevocable moral positions or to encourage the formation of overweening interest groups whose support today may become burdensome tomorrow. Particularly in the democratic world, where public policy and public opinion are so closely linked, it has been in the interest of states to promote a climate of tolerance for diversity within broad limitations. This has redounded for the most part to the benefit of religious experimentation. As long as world affairs remain in their present transitional condition, there is no reason to suspect that religious movements and countermovements will cease to be born.

Yet suggesting that the current unsettledness in world order and in ideology is somehow an undesirable situation to be gotten through as quickly as possible would be rash. In the past, tightly consolidated world orders have been constructed only at a tremendous cost in human freedom and social resources. And when economic and political contingencies have gone beyond a certain point, the prevailing system of world order has itself given way to the challenges of new forces and new ideologies, as the failures of Spain, the Netherlands, and England at various times in the past have borne witness. What is perhaps more viable in the long run than a tightly consolidated framework of world order is a loose confederation of local, national, and regional communities that can respond with flexibility to changing global conditions. Religious pluralism, diversity, and toleration could contribute much to the strength and adaptability of such a confederation.

Implicit in the foregoing has been an assumption that ideology requires social resources and undergoes change depending on tendencies in the broader social environment. Ideologies respond, as it were, to the changing fortunes of the moral order, both domestically and internationally, and these responses help to dramatize the symbolic constructions on which moral order depends. These are the relations between ideology and moral order on which the dramaturgic approach to cultural analysis focuses. But ideologies clearly do not arise only in the context of loosely organized social movements, nor are they free-floating responses to social events. They become institutionalized and are produced and diffused within specific institutional settings: universities, churches, government agencies, scientific organizations. Consideration of these contexts requires shifting from a purely dramaturgic approach to an institutional level of cultural analysis.

CHAPTER EIGHT

The Institutionalization of Science

Cultural forms are produced, selected in different social environments, and institutionalized. The process of institutionalization increases the likelihood that a particular cultural form will continue to be reproduced even if the environment changes. Through this process, culture ceases to be merely a set of ideas and becomes a social institution.

People typically do not invent or adopt new ideas without the assistance of some institution that has disseminated these ideas. The relations between ideas and the social environment are thus mediated by institutions. In these institutions, social resources are channeled specifically into the creation, dramatization, and dissemination of ideas. These "means of cultural production," as they can be called, are like other organizations. First, they require a sufficient degree of *autonomy* (differentiation) from other organizations to be able to apply resources to the attainment of specified ends. Second, *social resources* must be available for the staffing of creative (productive) and administrative roles and for the payment of other costs incurred in developing and disseminating cultural forms. Third, an internal system of *communication and organization* must be present in order for the various activities involved in producing cultural forms to be coordinated. And finally, a degree of *legitimacy* is required in order to sustain favorable relations with centers of power, the state, potential clients or recruits, and other significant collectivities in the broader environment. When these conditions have been satisfied, a cultural form has become *institutionalized*.

The development of modern science provides an instructive example of the process by which a cultural form becomes institutionalized. Although the production and diffusion of scientific ideas now occurs on such a vast scale that the existence of science as a cultural form is often taken for granted, science nevertheless has gained prominence only through the process of becoming a social institution. The crucial period in this process is generally taken to be the seventeenth century. During this period science acquired the requisite position in relation to its social environment that allowed it to develop subsequently into the major cultural institution that it is today. Before (and even during) the seventeenth century, competition and selection influenced the relation that different scientific approaches came to have with particular social environments. But the significant accomplishment of the seventeenth century was science's achievement of sufficient autonomy, resources, communication and organization, and legitimacy for its development to become largely self-sustaining and in large measure self-guided. On each of these dimensions of institutionalization, science was furthered by the special conditions that existed in Europe at the time. Examining the relations between science and these conditions therefore provides a window for observing the process of cultural institutionalization more generally.[1]

Historians of science characteristically distinguish between internalist and externalist approaches to the development of science. Internalist approaches focus on the unfolding of ideas within science itself as the prime mover of its development. Externalist approaches emphasize interaction between science and the social environment. Although both approaches are necessary, internalist explanations have long had the upper hand. Because science has been responsible for a number of discoveries about the natural world and because many of these discoveries have contributed to technological development, it has been easy for scholars and the public alike to assume that science is uniquely suited to arrive at the truth. Although this assumption can be disputed, it has probably obscured understanding of the development of science by reinforcing the internalist perspective. In regarding science strictly as truth, one can be tempted to explain its development as the simple unfolding of an inner intellectual logic. According to Barry Barnes (1974), this point of view is in fact the one currently taken by most historians of science of both Popperian and Kuhnian persuasion.[2]

At present, therefore, efforts to examine the institutionalization of science with reference to larger social conditions run counter to the mainstream of historical explanation. Yet it seems hard to deny that institutionalization is a social process—even when it involves science. Joseph

Ben-David (1971), who has recognized this fact more clearly than most, puts it well when he says that certain aspects of science are "eminently sociological phenomena." To say this in no way jeopardizes the importance of examining the internal dynamics of scientific ideas. But it poses the importance of also investigating the institutionalization of science in relation to social conditions.

MERTONIAN AND MARXIST EXPLANATIONS

The two leading attempts to account for the institutionalization of modern science are those advanced by Robert K. Merton and by various Marxist writers. The "Merton thesis," as it has been called, was set forth in Merton's doctoral disseration, later published in 1938 as *Science, Technology and Society in Seventeenth-Century England*. The Marxist explanations were formulated about the same time. Neither theoretical approach was intended as a complete explanation for the development of science in Europe during the seventeenth century, but both have become prominent in the literature, and each represents a major application of one of the classical theorists' perspectives on culture.

Following a Weberian line of reasoning, Merton argued that certain values in English Puritanism had contributed legitimacy to the scientific role. These values included reason, service to humanity, and the glorification of God through study of his handiwork. The effect of these values, as they became increasingly pronounced in England during the second quarter of the seventeenth century, was to enhance the likelihood of science being chosen as a vocation. Like Weber, Merton assumed that motivation was an essential factor for any new social institution to come into being. He also recognized that culture is an institution that requires a commitment of social resources in order to develop and be maintained. In the case of science, a principal requirement was for individuals with the necessary talents and training to choose science as an occupation rather than engaging in other pursuits, such as theology, law, business, or the military. The values of Puritanism, he asserted, could have played a major role in legitimating science as an occupation.

This assertion, in fact, appeared to be supported by a considerable body of evidence that Merton was able to piece together. From materials on large numbers of prominent residents listed in the *Dictionary of National Biography,* it was possible to demonstrate that the numbers of persons choosing science as a career rose dramatically during the second quarter of the seventeenth century—precisely the time when Puritanism was gaining a large following among the elite. Shortly thereafter, in the 1660s, the number of scientific inventions also showed a dramatic increase. In addition, an examination of the founders of the first scientific academy, the Royal Society, revealed that most (forty-two out of sixty-eight) were Puritans. Other historical studies indicated that Protestantism and science seemed to go together generally (e.g., in New England, France, the Netherlands, and Germany). And materials from the writings and biographies of leading scientists suggested that they indeed were motivated by Puritan convictions about reason, service, and the glorification of God.

The Marxist approach, formulated by Edgar Zilsel (1951), J. D. Bernal (1971), Boris Hessen (1971), and others, was somewhat more complex as a result of its multiple originators. The essential idea, however, was that science had arisen in the seventeenth century primarily because of the increasing social role and needs of the bourgeoisie. The needs of the bourgeoisie in large measure consisted of new technological demands brought about by the growth of capitalism. Among these were problems of marine transport that had arisen as a result of the growth in international trade, military problems that had arisen indirectly from nations' increasing economic dependence on one another, and mining problems that had arisen because of the growing demand for precious metals and industrial ores. Not only the Marxists but also Merton argued that these technological needs had played an important role in guiding scientists' choice of problems. For example, Torricelli's discovery of the vacuum, Boyle's work on air pumps, and Huygens's experimentation with piston engines all reflected the growing need for pumps as a method of draining mines. Similarly, the need for improved navigational and transport technologies could be recognized behind such inventions as the pendulum clock and logarithms. Technological needs had another important effect on science as well. Not only did they contribute to the invention of new instruments; they also played a role in overturning traditional philosophical concepts and legitimating broad scientific views of the world. For example, the need for better astronomical calculations for navigation and the development of better lens-grinding techniques made possible the telescope, which in turn made possible Galileo's observation of Jupiter's moons and the terrain of the earth's moon, both of which were inconsistent with Aristotle's theory of a universe constructed of perfect spheres and therefore indirectly supported Copernican theory.

Beyond the effects of technology, capitalism also presumably encouraged science in several roundabout ways. One was by shifting the center of power from the aristocracy to the towns, thereby undermining the authority of traditional ideas and giving science freedom to grow. Another was by stimulating competition for economic goods, which eroded the power of the guilds, thereby encouraging individualism and greater freedom to think innovatively and independently. Still another was by eroding the medieval conception of a hierarchical society that had kept philosophers, as members of the educated aristocracy, from interacting with artisans. Theory was thereby allowed to interact with practical genius, resulting in new theories that combined logic and empirical evidence. Finally, the rise of the bourgeoisie was said to have stimulated broader interest in scientific discoveries because these new ideas helped legitimate the elite status of the bourgeoisie. (Newton, for example, was said to favor new concepts of gravitational force because they corresponded to his broader outlook as a member of the bourgeoisie.)

Here then were two theories, quite different on the surface, yet clearly influenced by the assumptions of the classical tradition (as discussed in Chapter 2). Both regarded science as a type of knowledge subject to the influences of other social institutions, whether religion or the economy. And both specified as the chief line of social influence a subjective or motivational factor: individual scientists were motivated to adopt scientific careers or to work on particular scientific problems because they were motivated by certain experiences, values, or interests. The two approaches did, however, depart significantly from the classical tradition in recognizing the institutional character of science. Rather than conceptualizing science purely as an individual belief system, the proponents of both approaches maintained that science developed because it was able to secure resources, chiefly individual talent, and to make useful discoveries.

A number of sympathetic readers have extended the Merton thesis in the half-century since it originally appeared. Some have argued that, in addition to its emphasis on reason, service, and God's glory, Puritanism also undermined the prevailing hierarchical picture of the world and the contemporary emphasis on unpredictable supernatural spirits, replacing them with a worldview that emphasized lawful order among interacting bodies. Others have suggested a more straightforward effect: science challenged the authority of the church, emphasized the individual's right to make private judgments, and thereby encouraged scholars to experiment with and make up their own minds about new scientific ideas.

Yet another argument has been advanced claiming that Puritanism encouraged science primarily by fostering a progressive, optimistic outlook on life. Finally, an empirical study of scientific discoveries confirmed the argument that Protestant countries had contributed a larger number of discoveries per capita than had Catholic countries.[3]

The Marxist literature has also been extended by arguments specifying additional causal links between capitalism and science. The role of capitalism as a source of rationality, for example, has been emphasized. The argument here is similar to Merton's except that the source of interest in reason has been identified as the economy rather than religion. Particularly, the emphasis on counting and calculation that capitalism required has been identified as a possible source of the new quantitative approach in science. A related argument has suggested a connection between increasing mechanization in the economy and the rise of mechanical and causal theories in science. The possibility that exploration, trade, travel, and increased wealth simply expanded people's horizons, giving them a thirst for novelty and new ideas, has also been considered.

WEAKNESSES OF THE TWO APPROACHES

Although both the Mertonian and Marxist theories have attracted large followings, each has nevertheless been seriously faulted by subsequent historical research. Even the harshest critics of the two theories have stopped short of suggesting that Puritanism and capitalism had *no effect* on the institutionalization of science. Puritanism and capitalism were such important social developments in the seventeenth century that science could scarcely have not been affected by them in some way, at least indirectly. But the accumulation of more detailed and more extensive historical information has led to two rather damaging conclusions.

First, neither the effects of Protestantism nor those of capitalism now appear to have been as direct or as straightforward as once thought. The Merton thesis has been reexamined in light of more extensive data on early members (not just founders) of the Royal Society and a comprehensive study of British scientists of the eighteenth century. The former revealed that only one-fourth of the members of the Royal Society were Puritans and that many had changed religious and political loyalties, seemingly more from expediency than from firm convictions (Mulligan, 1973). The latter discovered that less than 5 percent of eighteenth-century scientists had graduated from the Protestant dissenting academies (Hans, 1951). Intellectual historians have shown that the "elective affinity" between Puritan ideals and scientific values breaks down at a number of points upon closer scrutiny of these concepts (Hall, 1963; Greaves, 1969; Hooykaas, 1972). The country-by-country comparisons of scientific discoveries also fail to sustain an idea of Protestant dominance once more realistic controls for population differences are taken into account.[4]

The Marxist set of explanations has also come under attack. Recent work by economic historians has generally suggested that technological inventions in the seventeenth century owed little to scientific research and that scientific research was not greatly stimulated by technological problems. For example, John Nef (1964:320–321) concludes, "The more one considers the direct connections between the scientific and the early industrial revolution, the more they seem to be superficial." Sir George Clark (1970:63–64) has also questioned the connection between technology and science, asserting that "few of the inventions . . . owed anything to scientific inquiries." A. Rupert Hall (1967:154) has similarly argued that until well into the nineteenth century no evidence can be found of scientists being in any way consciously motivated by technological problems: "The men who followed science at all had done so either for the sake of its personal intellectual satisfactions or as an element in an educational scheme that was not directed towards technical or professional training" (cf. Hall, 1972; Braudel, 1973:321). Other evidence has challenged the assumption that scientists were recruited primarily from bourgeois backgrounds. Of a list of 186 scientists in seventeenth-century England, for example, only 22 had been reared by merchants and traders; even by the eighteenth century, only 84 out of 494 known scientists came from merchant backgrounds (Hans, 1951). Nor was the influence of the bourgeoisie particularly pronounced in the Royal Society: between 1660 and 1689, only 19 of its 108 members were from merchant or artisan backgrounds (Mulligan, 1973:108).

Second, it is now evident that neither theory accounts for some of the more interesting developments associated with the institutionalization of science. The Merton thesis fails to explain the significant degree of institutionalization that took place in Italian science prior to similar developments in England. The prosperity of French science also poses a particular embarrassment to the Merton thesis. Even if the Huguenots were a significant force in French science, their success amid presumably alien religious conditions and the continued success of French science after their expulsion remain to be explained. Nor will it do to argue that science on the Continent merely diffused there from England. Although there was substantial diffusion, there was equally as much infusion from the Continent to England. Dutch science presents an embarrassment of a different sort. Its marked decline after the middle of the seventeenth century squares poorly with the continued prominence of Calvinism there. The Merton thesis also falters, insofar as it is focused primarily on individual motivation, in accounting for the other social requisites that contributed to the emergence of science as an institution.

Spokesmen for the Marxist approach, for their part, have been noticeably silent about the virtual absence of scientific activity in the two countries where problems of transportation, metallurgy, and ballistics were particularly important—Spain and Portugal. Nor does the Marxian theory explain why other absolutist states—ones that remained very much in the hands of the aristocracy (as Perry Anderson [1974] has shown)—should have become major patrons of the fledgling sciences. The Marxist theory also proves unsatisfactory once comparisons are made between Europe and China. Until the end of the sixteenth century, China remained technologically superior to Western Europe in a number of important respects (Needham, 1954). Yet, contrary to the Marxist assumption that technology produces science, Chinese technology failed to promote anything like the institutionalization of systematic scientific experimentation that occurred in Western Europe.

These criticisms need not lead to the conclusion that the Mertonian and Marxist explanations should be abandoned—only that the last word on the institutionalization of science has not been spoken. As with any complex social process, the institutionalization of science in seventeenth-century Europe does not lend itself to monocausal explanations. The religious explanation yields considerable mileage in accounting for certain aspects of the institutionalization process in England, as does the economic explanation. But neither in itself, nor the two in combination, fully accounts for the connections that came to be established between science and its social environment. A large amount of historical research obviously remains to be done in examining these connections, but equally important is the need for new perspectives to guide this research.

AN ALTERNATIVE PERSPECTIVE

In this chapter use will again be made of the broad globalistic perspective on the social environment that was employed in the previous chapter. Borrowing from the work of Wallerstein and others who have made major contributions to the development of this perspective is not meant to rule out social factors on a smaller scale nor to imply agreement with the more specific assumptions in this literature about the development of the modern political economy. Nevertheless, certain general concepts emerge from viewing the European region as a single social system that correspond well with several of the important characteristics of seventeenth-century science. Before turning to specific considerations about the institutionalization of science, therefore, it is probably worthwhile to comment briefly on these points of correspondence.

In the first place, it can be argued that science in the seventeenth century was highly integrated across the European system. There were important differences in the character of science from one country to the next, to be sure, but science was European-wide, bound together by an international network of communication and concerned with problems that transcended national boundaries. In describing English science, A. Rupert Hall (1972:44) has remarked:

> The current problems in these various sciences tackled in England were the current problems over all Europe—science was international, critical, competitive in the seventeenth century as it is now. There was no separate little English world of science isolated from the universe and playing the game according to private rules, as though science were a form of cricket.

In both the Mertonian and Marxist approaches, science is implicitly acknowledged to have been distributed unevenly across Europe and, for this reason, to have been subject to social conditions that also differed from country to country. But the emphasis has clearly been on science *within* isolated national contexts, particularly England, rather than on science as a cultural institution that was an integral organization spanning national boundaries. Given this *transnational* character, the appropriate context in which to examine the institutionalization of science would appear to be one that emphasized the broader systemic nature of European social structure as well. In other words, science is one cultural institution, unlike many localized ideological movements, that seems to require a broad, transnational approach in relating it to the social environment.

Second, taking the entire European system as the relevant context forces the authority structure of seventeenth-century Europe to be viewed differently—again in a way that seems appropriate to an understanding of science. The shift of perspective here is away from an emphasis on centralized authority toward greater awareness of the decentralized structure of European authority. This shift is valuable because decentralized authority has received much attention in the literature on scientific development in other contexts. Generally speaking, decentralized authority has been regarded as a positive factor in the development of science and in intellectual innovation of other kinds as well. For example, Weber (1951:152) saw the importance of a lack of authoritarianism during the Period of Warring States in China, the first period in which "a hundred [intellectual] flowers bloomed," and likened it to the political conditions in antiquity that fostered Greek science and philosophy. More recently, for another example, Ben-David (1971) has stressed political decentralization as a factor in the institutionalization of science in Germany and the United States in the nineteenth century. Political decentralization has also been emphasized implicitly in discussions of the compatibilities between science and democracy.[5]

As far as the seventeenth century is concerned, it has been difficult to reconcile the growth of science with the prevailing political conditions of Europe because those conditions seemed more characterized by centralized than by decentralized authority. The traditional view, formulated by looking at individual societies, has been that the late sixteenth and early seventeenth centuries constituted an age of absolutism and oligarchy. In comparison with late medieval feudalism, the dominant feature of absolutism and oligarchy was their greater concentration of centralized authority. From the standpoint of the larger European system, however, the relevant comparison is with other territorially large social systems, of which the chief cases prior to the seventeenth century had been politically unified empires. In this comparison, the important thing about authority in Europe is not that it was centralized, but that it was decentralized—divided among competing sovereign states. Rather than having a single regime that imposed imperial authority over the entire social context in which science developed, Europe had a political system in which authority was divided territorially by France, England, Spain, and other countries. At the societal level, authority was often centralized; at the "world-system" level, it was decentralized.

These two views of authority are less incompatible than they may appear at first sight. Wallerstein (1974) has presented evidence suggesting that the growth of centralized authority within states was partly nurtured by the decentralization of authority between states—a fact to which we shall return later. But the important implication that derives from viewing Europe as a larger social system is that political decentralization may, after all, have contributed to the institutionalization of science in the seventeenth century, as it seems to have done in other periods. What this contribution may have been seems worthy of investigation.

The other conceptual advantage one gains by regarding Europe as an organic unit is probably less obvious. Some accounting has to be made for the fact that science became institutionalized in varying degrees in different parts of Europe—or at least did so at different times and, accordingly, grew at diverse rates. One of the reasons that the Mertonian and Marxian theories have enjoyed such prominence, despite the objections surveyed here, is probably that both predict a high degree of scientific institutionalization in England—where it did, in fact, occur. Yet if one takes the previously mentioned objections seriously, then some other manner of describing the variation in European social structure that better corresponds to the variation in scientific institutionalization must be sought. Without entering fully into the details at this point, we can argue that the distinction between "core" (or dominant) and "periphery" (or dependent) areas of territorially large social systems affords a useful way of doing this.[6]

Having hinted briefly at the relevance of the framework to be outlined, we can now turn to an examination of the institutionalization of seventeenth-century science from this perspective. Supplying empirical detail of the kind needed to fully test the utility of this perspective must be left to historians of science. But some tentative indications of this perspective's utility can be provided from even a cursory survey of the available historical material. Let us consider each of the four aspects of institutionalization previously listed: autonomy, resources, legitimacy, and internal communication and organization.

SCIENTIFIC AUTONOMY

Institutional autonomy, insofar as science is concerned, means autonomy from any body capable of arbitrarily restricting the freedom of scientific inquiry, which in nearly all practical instances means government. But no one would argue that autonomy implies total independence, let alone isolation, from government, for science has been heavily indebted to state protection and patronage. One might suggest, therefore, that scientific autonomy consists of a special form of relation in which science and the state interact for mutual gain, but where checks are present to limit the arbitrary extension of state control over science (cf. Shils, 1962; Price, 1965; Ravetz, 1971).

As previously mentioned, explaining how institutional autonomy for science could have developed during the age of absolutism and oligarchy is difficult because these highly centralized and expansive forms of political organization appear inimical to scientific autonomy. But if science is viewed in the context of the larger European "world economy," the presence of competing sovereign states emerges as a means by which the arbitrary intrusion of any single government could be circumvented or controlled.

AUTONOMY AND MIGRATION

How might this have worked in practice? One possibility is that scientists were able simply to migrate from one jurisdiction to another in order to escape politically undesirable conditions. There is indeed a great deal of evidence that this was the case. Kepler, for example, was persecuted in Tübingen but was able to escape to Austria. Descartes is alleged to have voluntarily exiled himself from France because of his disenchantment with the political conditions there. The scientific movement in Flanders was able to survive when the scientists fled north (Geyl, 1932:273–274). During the 1630s, large numbers of English students went to Leyden to study in order to escape the political turmoil in England (Hackmann, 1976:93). The entire group of scientists that had gathered around the Duke of Northumberland and that later became instrumental in the formation of the "invisible college" fled England during the revolutionary period and received patronage in France (Brown, 1934). Newton's mentor, Isaac Barrow, who was a firm supporter of the king, for which he felt certain of being excluded from becoming regius professor of Greek during the Cromwellian period, spent four years touring the Continent, returning to England only upon the restoration of Charles II. Joseph Priestly fled to America avowedly because of his political views. Countless other examples could be added. The obvious but not trivial point is that a politically centralized Europe would have made such freedom much more difficult to sustain.

Of course it is impossible to assess, except in individual cases, how much the political decentralization of Europe contributed to the political autonomy of scientists. However, the same conditions promoting autonomy in the larger European system seem also to have been present in the Italian city-state system. For example, Galileo's criticisms of an invention proposed by a member of the Medici family temporarily placed him in disfavor with the Grand Duke of Tuscany, who controlled his appointment at the University of Pisa. Fearing for his appointment, Galileo turned to the Venetian Republic, where he obtained an appointment at the University of Padua, avoiding an early termination of his career (Geymonat, 1965:15–16). For another example, Borelli found himself accused of sedition after an uprising at Messina. Rather than stand trial, the outcome of which seemed particularly uncertain, he took refuge in Rome, where he was received into the academy of Queen Christina of Sweden, who was residing there.

These examples may have been more the exception than the rule. But they illustrate that some of the same conditions that may have facilitated the institutionalization of science in seventeenth-century Europe may have also facilitated this process in Italian science. Insofar as this may have been the case, the hypothesis of a relationship between political decentralization and scientific autonomy appears to be at least somewhat generalizable. In contrast, the Mertonian theory, and to a lesser extent the Marxist theories, appear to be of limited applicability to the Italian situation.

POLITICAL COMPETITION

The other way in which political decentralization may have contributed to the autonomy of seventeenth-century scientists is by invoking political competition for their services, thereby enhancing the bargaining power of scientists with their particular governments. That there was such competition between governments seems to be well evidenced at least among the more prominent scientists of the period. A number of courts competed to attract the medical skills of Vesalius and Harvey. France competed successfully for Huygens, Homberg, Viviani, Cassini, and Roemer, among others, by offering handsome stipends in comparison to what they could have received in their native countries. The Dutch also competed actively to attract foreign scientists, offering high university salaries as incentives, apparently with considerable success, so that in the seventeenth century at Groningen, for instance, thirty-four of its fifty-two professors were foreign (Hackmann, 1976). And England drew a number of foreign scientists both through patronage and by promoting a climate of toleration and appreciation of scientific inquiry (Nef, 1964:324).

Clearly the fact that governments competed at all for the services of eminent scientists indicates that science already enjoyed a certain degree of respectability. This is not the point at issue. The point, as any scientist who has participated in the "job market" knows, is that one's autonomy goes up measurably if there are multiple sources of employment competing for one's talents. In the seventeenth century there was competition within countries as there is today (though on a smaller scale, of course). But the evidence suggests that there was also significant competition among countries.

The main comparison case that illustrates the importance of political centralization for scientific autonomy in the seventeenth century—by virtue of its absence—is the Hapsburg empire. Although Charles V, whom Napoleon came to admire greatly, nearly succeeded in bringing Europe under the central control of the Hapsburg regime in the early part of the sixteenth century, these ambitions lay unfulfilled and largely beyond hope of repair by the beginning of the seventeenth century. Castile was rapidly becoming incorporated into the larger European world economy as a peripheral member dependent on foreign exchange and foreign diplomatic agreements. Yet in domestic economic and political structure, Castile remained organized as a closed imperial state. Culturally it continued to be the most educated society in Western Europe. But unlike other areas having the necessary educational prerequisites, it developed no autonomous scientific tradition. According to Richard Kagan (1974), who has extensively studied seventeenth-century Castilian universities, the major cause of this failure was not so much Catholicism, as usually alleged (although this may have been an indirect factor), but the degree of government intervention in the selection of instructors, curricula, students' career choices, and academic standards (cf. Ortiz, 1971:235). Not only did the crown take a strong interest in salary raises, appointments, academic decisions, and student conduct, but books from the outside world were also strictly prohibited, and almost all students were forbidden to attend universities outside Castile. There was neither opportunity nor much incentive—given the reward system of the Castilian university—for scientists to bargain or migrate in hopes of gaining greater intellectual autonomy.

Of course, autonomy can be gained from even the most centralized empire if one is willing and able to emigrate. The difference with the decentralized European system was that one could emigrate but still remain within the larger system, where there was contact and communication with other scientists. In short, autonomy could be negotiated within the European social system itself.

Some evidence, then, appears to suggest that the institutional autonomy of science in the seventeenth century was facilitated by the political decentralization of the European world economy. However, the importance of autonomy and decentralization should not be overemphasized. At most, autonomy is but a passive condition in the development of a cultural institution. Other social and intellectual conditions no doubt played a much more active role in the overall growth of seventeenth-century science. Furthermore, the political autonomy that scientists enjoyed—to the extent that it was important—can be attributed only in part to political decentralization. Even if decentralization provided a lever against political interference, it must be asked why this lever was permitted to be used as it was. The role of autonomy, therefore, only partly explicates the effects of the European world economy on the institutionalization of science.

PATRONAGE

In the seventeenth century, science was infinitely less costly to maintain than it is now, but even then it had to obtain material resources in order to become established as a social institution. In particular, the livelihoods of interested and talented individuals had to be secured in order for them to devote time to scientific experimentation rather than to more gainful careers. Beyond this, support was also a frequent necessity for the procurement of expensive scientific apparatus.

FORMS OF PATRONAGE

In virtually every European country, scientists received financial assistance from persons of wealth and from those in positions of power. Tycho Brahe received assistance from Holy Roman Emperor Rudolf II. Kepler's observatory was built at the expense of the King of Denmark. Galileo received advances from the Medici and from the Florentine firm Giucciardi Corsi (Braudel, 1973:320). Benedetti, who was known primarily for his work in mathematics and physics, served as court mathematician to the Duke of Farnese in Parma and received financial support from the Duke of Savoy. Bonaventura was supported by the Duke of Urbino. In Italy the most consistent supporters of scientists were Ferdinand II, Grand Duke of Tuscany, and his brother Prince Leopold, founders of the Accademia del Cimento (Middleton, 1971). In France the Academy of Sciences provided royal pensions of 1,500 livres annually for fourteen scientists; in addition, a number received patronage from private sources (Hahn, 1962). In England similar sources of support were provided by a variety of individuals in private life.

Patronage was also bestowed indirectly in the form of public offices. In France these included the offices of tax collector (occupied by Lavoisier), treasurer (occupied by Montigny), postmaster general (occupied by d'Onsenbray), and director of the Royal Observatory, as well as numerous court physicians, apothecaries, surgeons, and tutors. Similarly, in England government positions were held by a number of the more prominent scientists, including Gilbert, Wilkins, Bacon, Newton, and Brouncker. One estimate has suggested that nearly one-third of the original members of the Royal Society were "high servants of the Crown and state officials" (McKie, 1960:35).

In addition to supporting scientists, a number of the nobility and officers of the state also took a personal interest in scientific experimentation. Rudolf II amassed a rich collection of scientific and artistic curiosities at his court in Prague (Holborn, 1976:284). Charles II had his own chemistry laboratory, as did Louis XIV's brother, the Duc d'Orléans. Other amateur scientists in France included the Duc de Luynes, the Duc de Roannes, and Melchisadec Thevenot (founder of the Academy Thevenot and patron of a number of scientists including Steno and Frenicle). Prince Rupert, according to his biographer, had an "inexhaustible interest in forge and laboratory." The ninth Earl of Northumberland earned the appellation "wizard of earl" for his experiments in anatomy, alchemy, and cosmography (Stone, 1967:326). Other amateur scientists in England who either had their own laboratories or took an active role in experimentation included the Earl of Cork, the Duke and Duchess of York, the Bishop of London, the second Earl of Cumberland, fifth Lord Dudley, the Duke of Buckingham, Lord Willoughby, Sir Robert Moray, and Sir Robert Hale.

As one survey suggests, patronage and direct involvement in science was a fact of life among the English elite by the early part of the seventeenth century:

> Noblemen and great officers promoted the rise of applied sciences, not only as patrons but sometimes also as active researchers. Cuthbert Tunstall, Master of the Rolls under Henry VIII and later Bishop of London and Durham, wrote a textbook on arithmetic (in Latin); in Thomas More's large household mathematics and astronomy were considered to be principal subjects of study, and the noted mathematician Nichols Katzer tutored More's children in astronomy. When John Dee in the third quarter of the sixteenth century assembled a large scientific library in his house near London, it became a center

not only for scholars and instrument makers who looked for advice, but also for the great merchants who sought his counsel before voyages, and for members of Elizabeth's court and council who came to study chemistry with him. Lord Burghley, Elizabeth's chief minister, tried to promote both the sciences and scientists. On his request, William Bourne wrote a short treatise on the properties and qualities of glasses for optical purposes. Digges, one of the greatest mathematicians of his time, was called into the service of his country as a military engineer, first to supervise the fortifications at Dover, later as Muster-Master-General of the English forces in the Netherlands. (Fischer and Lundgreen, 1975:544)

In Italy Ferdinand II and Prince Leopold were not only patrons of science but active experimenters as well, as were Count Federigo Cesi, founder of the Accademia del Lincei, and a number of other Italian notables (Burke, 1974:73–74). Members of both the Medici and Fugger families dabbled in science. Amateur scientists in Germany included the Duke of Magdeburg, Tschirnhausen, Hevelius, and Otto von Guericke. To the extent that scientists received patronage from persons of power, therefore, it seems reasonable to conclude that this patronage was given out of genuine interest in, and typically with some knowledge of, the nature and purposes of science.

In total amounts the patronage that scientists received was seldom a major expense on the part of its benefactors. For example, in France, where stipends were perhaps more generous than anywhere else, the total amount of pensions to scientists added up to approximately 30,000 livres a year during the 1670s and for the twenty-five-year period from 1664 to 1690 totaled 1.7 million livres, plus another 0.7 million livres if the cost of the royal observatory is included (King, 1948:289; Hahn, 1976:131). Yet during this period government receipts from the *taille* alone amounted to between 40 million and 50 million livres annually (Anderson, 1974:98). Thus the amount given over to scientific activities represented only a tiny fraction of the state's finances. However, this financial support was of considerable value to those receiving it, making it possible to devote time to experimentation that would otherwise probably have been spent in more gainful activities and providing instruments for the conduct of these experiments.

The importance of obtaining financial assistance was often evident in the activities of even the leading scientists. As Roger Hahn (1971:7) explains:

The financial problem became the central issue in the soliciting of governmental assistance by the more dedicated members of the learned circles. On one level, their needs stemmed from the cost of constructing improved instruments (especially the expensive ones for astronomical observations) and of purchasing raw materials to carry on chemical and biological experiments. Without substantial sums, it was also impossible to initiate large-scale enterprises such as scientific expeditions.

And in a similar vein, Martha Ornstein (1975:67) has argued that the high cost of instruments and laboratories was one of the important reasons why the aristocracy was so heavily represented among the early scientists and why gradually the scientists began to form organizations to allow greater cooperation in the procurement and use of instruments.

EXPLANATIONS FOR PATRONAGE

But why was patronage given to the sciences? The Mertonian theory offers no explicit explanation. One can perhaps infer from the Mertonian argument that patronage was granted because science was thought to be of value to the general welfare and that concern for the general welfare had been promoted by certain doctrines of the Protestant reformers. But this explanation fails to account for the extensive patronage that scientists received in Catholic countries and from Catholic monarchs. The Marxist discussions have also failed to give any explicit explanation of scientific patronage. It is not inconsistent with the Marxist approach to assume that the rise of commercial capitalism was an important stimulus to this patronage. Indeed, there are instances of patronage being given directly by members of the new commercial classes and of state-sponsored research connected with commercial ventures. What does not square well with the Marxist interpretation is the high involvement of the aristocracy and the absolutist state in providing patronage to the sciences.

Whatever their general limitations, the Mertonian and the Marxist theories do stress one motivation that seems to have been present among the early patrons of science. Both theories suggest that science was of utilitarian value, chiefly in promoting technological innovation. And there is certainly anecdotal evidence suggesting that science was patronized for this purpose. Bacon's utilitarian defense of science clearly seems to have been widely appealing. Charles II repeatedly admonished the Royal Society to study things that were useful. Colbert's interest in science rested heavily on utilitarian considerations. "Among the noblemen and gentlemen who were conspicuous as scientific dilettanti at this time," writes G. N. Clark (1970:9), "it is easy to see that the excitement of study was mixed with the hope of gain."

The case could probably be argued that both Protestantism and capitalism reinforced a general "ethos" in seventeenth-century Europe in which utilitarian interests in science could surface. But there also seems to be evidence that this utilitarian interest in patronizing the sciences, especially insofar as much of this patronage seems to have been associated with the state, may have been reinforced by the political and economic competition that prevailed among the leading members of the European world-system. More explicitly, one of the social conditions that probably helped to motivate patronage of the sciences in the seventeenth century was the decentralized character of the European world economy and the rivalry that existed among these multiple centers of power. This condition emerges as a dominant feature of the seventeenth century once one adopts a world-system perspective on the period.

By the end of the sixteenth century, it had become apparent to contemporary statesmen that Europe could not be politically unified but would consist of a system of multiple competing powers. Hopes of religious unification had been destroyed by the firm footholds that Protestantism had gained in the German states, the Low Countries, Scandinavia, and England. Militarily, the Hapsburg efforts to restore unity to Europe had dissipated with the defeat of the Spanish armada, the success of the revolt in the Netherlands, and the continuing effectiveness of France as a counterpoise against Hapsburg expansion.

The fact of political decentralization had also begun to be regarded as normative. Schemes emphasizing the doctrine of equilibrium or "balance" were evident in Machiavelli and later became pronounced in the writings of Harrington and Cromwell and in the Duke of Sully's "Great Design." "That Europe should be unified through the hegemony of any one power, be it Hapsburg or be it Bourbon," Geoffrey Barraclough (1963:28) has written, "was rejected on all sides as unthinkable." In place of unification, the new schemes argued that interdependence among the European powers was preferable, indeed, that it was inevitable because the various states were endowed with different abilities, climates, and resources. If interdependence was inevitable, the important problem was to maintain a balance of power among the major contending states sufficient to ensure a steady flow of exchange without any one state gaining an unfair advantage over the others.

Along with the political doctrine of equilibrium, the economic theory—later to be named "mercantilism"—stressed the necessity of each state cultivating its own unique resources and developing its full potential strength in relation to the others (see Schmoller, 1896; Knorr, 1944; Hecksher, 1955; Wilson, 1958). The assumption upon which this theory rested was that the European states, though interdependent, coexisted competively in what would now be called a "zero-sum game" in which one could gain only at the expense of another. As Bacon put it, "whatsoever is somewhere gotten, is somewhere lost" (quoted in King, 1948). If any one state failed to maintain its strength, it was thought that the result would be unwarranted gains on the part of other states, the ultimate consequence of which might be the destruction of the precarious European equilibrium. Thus, a politically and economically powerful corporate state was deemed to be important both for its own domestic security and for the well-being of the larger international system.

The situation in the seventeenth century therefore resembled in many respects the political situation in the contemporary world, especially in the importance attached to the power of competing states and in the degree to which this power was evaluated, perhaps less in terms of control over subject populations, but in comparison with other states occupying similar positions in the world-system. Both in reality and in normative understandings, the world economy of seventeenth-century Europe was characterized by competition among states to develop their political, social, and economic resources to the fullest possible extent.

Evidence has already been presented on the extent to which European states competed to attract and retain eminent scientists. In mercantilist theory, science was regarded, like material resources, as a storehouse of strength with which each country had been differently endowed, and it was up to the officials of each country to develop this potential. According to one authority on the period:

> Laffemas, the earliest of the French economic writers who attempted to work the scattered mercantilist ideas into a complete system, proposed the organization of *Chambres des manufactures* which should instruct youth in "sciences" and teach them to study scientific treatises. In his *Economies royales* . . . the Duc de Sully, who had been the principal finance minister of Henry IV, proposed an industrial museum like that suggested by Descartes; there should be set up in the Louvre a collection of models of machines used in industries. A. de Montchretien, who had traveled in Holland, Germany, and Switzerland, proposed the establishment in France of the sort of elementary industrial training which he had seen abroad. (Artz, 1966:24)

Not only the domestic good of the nation but also the collective good of the entire region depended on the responsible cultivation of the sciences. As one observer of the times wrote in 1646:

> Each climate receives its particular influences; these influences communicate divers qualities, and the qualities create divers talents of the mind, and by consequence divers kinds of sciences and industries among men. Some are suited for Philosophy, others for mechanics, others to some arts and particular exercises: the Author of nature distributing thus unequally his gifts and his talents to men, in order to render them reliant on one another, and to oblige them to share what they have in particular. (quoted in King, 1948:135)

It is difficult to know how much the political and economic competition of the mercantilist period may have contributed to the provision of patronage to the sciences. What does seem clear is that this competition carried over into the realm of science, as we have seen, and that it was typically the countries that provided the greatest patronage and resources, either in the form of royal stipends as in France or in the form of private support and state offices as in England, that attracted the most eminent scientists. The competitive spirit of the age was clearly not wholly lost on scientists themselves. For example, the undercurrent of this spirit is evident in the following appeal to Louis XIV on behalf of a proposal to found a national observatory in France:

> Its *Project* is so great, and may be so glorious for the state, and so useful for the public, if it is executed in all its details, that it is impossible not to be persuaded that Your Majesty, who has designs so vast and so magnificent, should not approve and favor it; and I can declare that all the neighboring nations have been for some time in an incredible expectation of so great an establishment. (quoted in Brown, 1934:145)

The observatory was built at a cost of 700,000 livres.

Although much of the incentive for patronizing the sciences may have been rooted in strictly utilitarian considerations, this patronage was probably also motivated by expressive or "ceremonial" concerns. The seventeenth century was the great age of ceremony. In the arts, in architecture, and in learning, it was the age of the baroque, of Versailles, of the richly ornamented facade and the ornamental garden, the heroic tragedy, great operas and orchestras, punctilious court etiquette, the King James Bible, and St. Paul's Cathedral (Ogg, 1972:36–38). The seventeenth century was also the age of high ceremony and protocol in diplomatic relations, and it was the age of what G. N. Clark (1947:139–

143) has called "speculative wars," which dramatized state boundaries by testing the military strength of opposing forces.

It is perhaps not surprising that ceremony should have been as pronounced as it was in the seventeenth century, given what has already been said about the European world economy. Lacking a central authority capable of defining and legitimating the membership and status of states in the European system, ceremonial activities may have served as an alternative means of dramatizing the strength and status of states to one another. These activities may have also served as a means of demonstrating each state's ability to maintain and defend its position in the European system and of manifesting each state's subscription to norms and expectations common to members of the system. In a somewhat parallel context, for example, Meyer and Rowan (1977) have observed that formal organizations in competitive environments often develop formal structures that, among whatever other functions they may fulfill, dramatize the status and purposes of the organization to its competitors.[7]

There are several reasons for suspecting that science may have been patronized, though perhaps not in any deliberate or systematic fashion, because of its ceremonial value. For one, the arts were just as likely as the sciences to be the recipients of patronage (Wolf, 1951; Foss, 1971)—something that one would not expect had utilitarian concerns been the sole motivation for patronage. For another, the scientists who received patronage and who were elected to the royal academies were more often men of eminence, whose sponsorship added prestige to the state, than men of proven practical accomplishments. For example, in describing the members of the French Academy of Sciences, Roger Hahn (1971:14–15) observes:

> Among them were men of considerable cultural attainments and erudition, such as Pierre Carcavi and Christian Huygens, the polymath Marin Cureau de La Chambre, the Oratorian theologian Jean-Baptiste Du Hamel, the magistrate Bernard Frenicle de Bessy, and Charles Perrault's equally famous brother, the architect and physician Claude Perrault. Though many were intimately concerned with the practical applications of scientific studies, none was selected for his technical prowess alone. . . . A tacit understanding almost seems to have existed that a sound liberal education rather than apprenticeship in a trade was a proper qualification for admission. Hence, from the outset, there was a certain social and intellectual bond in the Royal Academy which ran counter to the hopes of the framers of the Company. Artisans were clearly excluded.

A similar picture is given by Maurice Ashley (1973:156) in his description of the Royal Society in England:

One is particularly struck by the versatility of the members of the Royal Society. They included John Aubrey, the author of the *Brief Lives* of his contemporaries . . . John Evelyn, botanist and numismatist, and Samuel Pepys, the naval administrator . . . John Locke, metaphysician, educationist, political philosopher, theologian, physician, and man of affairs; Sir William Petty, who contends with Captain John Graunt for the distinction of being the first English statistician or "political arithmetician"; Dr John Wallis, who wrote books on arithmetic as well as English grammar; John Dryden, the poet; Wren, the architect; Dr John Williamson, the politician; the Duke of Buckingham and the Earl of Sandwich; Sir Kenelm Digby, the Roman Catholic, who collected book bindings and invented the "powder of sympathy" to heal wounds; and even the Moroccan ambassador who was admitted as an honorary member. Besides them stood scientists whose names are still universally honoured: Robert Boyle, the "father of modern chemistry" and inventor of Boyle's law; Isaac Barrow, the mathematician and clergyman; Robert Hooke, city surveyor, mathematician, physicist, and a great inventive genius; and Jonathan Goddard, one of the first English makers of telescopes.

Many of these individuals, as we shall see later, were also placed in diplomatic positions where their eminence could serve directly to dramatize the prestige of their sponsoring governments.

Patronage continued to be granted to the sciences even when it was evident that few scientists were especially concerned about practical problems and few practical solutions seemed to be directly attributable to their work. It seems doubtful that patronage would have been as consistent in the absence of more pronounced practical accomplishments had patronage been given only for utilitarian considerations. But even when science was not of practical value, it may have functioned as a locus of erudition. Thus, by supporting the sciences—even nominally as Charles II did in chartering the Royal Society—representatives of state could demonstrate their commitment to learning, rationality, and modernity.[8]

In short, the decentralized and competitive social structure of the larger European system in the seventeenth century may have contributed to the interest that representatives of state showed in patronizing the sciences, perhaps for both utilitarian and ceremonial reasons. Patrons also supported the sciences for a host of personal reasons; many probably supported the sciences simply because of personal fascination. Had it been strictly a matter of personal whim whether or not the sciences received patronage, however, this aspect of the institutionalization process might not have developed to the extent that it did. What the social structure of the larger European system did was to create a competitive situation, both practically and normatively, that encouraged the leading states to develop their national resources, among which was scientific experimentation.

LEGITIMATION

Traditional explanations have paid more attention to the legitimation of early scientific activities than to the other aspects of scientific institutionalization that have just been considered, and they have been relatively more successful at explaining legitimation than these other aspects. Protestant and capitalistic values, insofar as both stressed the practical realities of this life and of nature, probably helped legitimate science even beyond those specific areas in which Protestantism and capitalism were most successful. Also, Protestantism and capitalism were probably pervasive enough that their values "filtered down" sufficiently to individual scholars to have some direct motivating potential in the direction of scientific careers, as Merton in particular has stressed.

ROLE OF THE STATE

To this discussion of scientific legitimation can be added the suggestion that science may have also received a significant share of legitimation from its relation to the state. In an age when even religious claims were coming to be subordinate to the ideology of *raison d'état* and when enterprises ranging from trading ventures to societies of literature looked to the state for justification, it would be surprising if science did not also receive legitimation from the state. We have already seen that there was, indeed, a close relation between science and the seventeenth-century state: (1) in the numbers of scientists who received patronage from the state; (2) in the numbers of scientists who occupied positions within state bureaucracies; and (3) in the numbers of state officials who took a personal interest in science as amateur experimenters. Evidence also suggests that scientists, for their part, were aware of the importance of receiving official sanctioning of this nature.

It has been said that Galileo's willingness to recant his views to the church was less a sign of any weakness of character than an indication of his conviction that good relations with the church, as the most powerful authority in his immediate milieu, were crucial to the legitimacy and survival of the fledgling sciences (Geymonat, 1965). This same conviction allegedly motivated him to devote over twenty years of his life to a dialogue with representatives of the church on behalf of his discoveries and to make every effort to enlist the powerful Medici in his struggle.[9]

In England the members of the invisible college, though by no means of exclusive royalist persuasion, were quick to agree on the importance of soliciting a royal charter for their society from Charles II. It has been more generally argued that royal legitimation, even before the founding of the Royal Society, was one of the decisive influences that attracted scientists to England and permitted science to flourish there to the extent that it did:

> On the Continent, except perhaps in Holland and Denmark, there was no country where the learned man who wanted to try new methods of scholarship and research, without any practical purpose, could count as much as in England on sympathetic recognition and authoritative support. For several generations the universities and the ecclesiastical foundations, including the churches set up by the Reformers, had been generally hostile to revolutionary intellectual innovations. Queen Elizabeth's patronage of Gilbert was a symptom of a new attitude among the mighty toward the experimenter and his efforts. Isaac Casaubon (1559–1614), the French classical scholar, could not find satisfactory conditions for his work either at Geneva or at Paris, and in 1610 he finally sought asylum at the English court and became a naturalized Englishman. Casaubon's biographer, Mark Pattison, tells us that the court of James I, for all the king's pedantry, was the only court in Europe where the learned professions were in any degree appreciated. It is significant that Kepler, who must have known of James I's visit to the observatory of Brahe in Denmark in 1590, should have thought enough of the king's scientific interests to dedicate to him *De harmonice mundi*, a work published at Augsburg in 1619, in which the great scientist announced his third law of motion. During James I's reign, with Francis Bacon in office as solicitor-general and later as attorney-general, the outlook on experimental inquiry by learned men was more liberal in England than in other parts of Europe. So the English court provided new experimental work with official approval such as could be obtained almost nowhere else. (Nef, 1964:324)

The relation between this sort of legitimation and the decentralized character of the European world economy is indirect, of course. If it can be argued, as attempted in the previous section, that the actual and normative political competition that characterized the mercantilist world economy of the seventeenth century was an inducement to the patronage of science, both for utilitarian and for ceremonial reasons (although in varying degrees in different countries), then this aspect of the larger European social system also contributed indirectly to the legitimation that came with patronage from the state. It is perhaps useful to mention at least two specific consequences of this legitimation.

CONSEQUENCES FOR SCIENCE

First, to the extent that official approval of the sciences on the part of the state fulfilled ceremonial functions as well as strictly utilitarian interests, science was afforded an a priori form of legitimation that did not depend on the production of immediately useful knowledge. As we have seen, science continued to receive support even though its practical accomplishments were as yet of perhaps minimal importance in comparison with those being made outside of science. This support and approval was probably of special value when science was first becoming institutionalized—that is, before its legitimacy became independently rooted in discoveries and technological contributions.

The second consequence of receiving legitimation from the state that may have been of particular importance to the development of science was the fact that this legitimation gave science additional autonomy from the established universities. It was important for the state to function as a corporate unit, according to mercantilist philosophy, especially in the eyes of its rivals in the European system. As far as the universities were concerned, however, they had, following the decline of the church's influence, become a force increasingly associated with local interests (Lytle, 1974; Morgan, 1974; Stone, 1974). By supporting scientific activities outside the universities, the state was able to circumvent the power of the universities to some degree, and, in turn, science received from the state a strong voice in overcoming resistance from within the universities to the new methods and discoveries it sought to propound (cf. Ben-David, 1971).[10]

COMMUNICATION AND ORGANIZATION

The remaining aspect of institutionalization mentioned earlier has to do with the fact that any institution must manifest a minimal degree of communication among its members and must organize its activities into stable patterns of organization if it is to survive. The two most notable developments along these lines in seventeenth-century science were the institutionalization of an extensive international communication network among scientists and the organization of scientists into national academies. The latter has been carefully described in studies by Harcourt Brown (1934), Roger Hahn (1971), W. E. Knowles Middleton (1971), Martha Ornstein (1975), and others. The former has been studied less systematically, but there is ample evidence of the extensive communication that existed among European scientists from at least the middle of the sixteenth century onward.

INTERNATIONAL COMMUNICATION

For example, Henry Oldenberg carried on an extensive correspondence with scientists throughout Europe from his home in England. A similar network was established in France through the efforts of Mersenne. Galileo appears to have kept informed of Kepler's research through personal correspondence. Galileo is also alleged to have first learned of the Dutch telescope from correspondence with a French nobleman, Jacques Badovere (Drake, 1957:28–29). Besides correspondence, scientists also learned of one another's work through extensive foreign travel. For example, forty-four of the sixty-five eminent sixteenth- and seventeenth-century scientists discussed in Taton's *History of Science* had been educated abroad, had traveled extensively, or had worked in countries other than those in which they had been born.

Had Europe in the seventeenth century consisted simply of a set of relatively autonomous countries, as textbook history has often portrayed it, it would likely have been less conducive to the kind of international communication that developed within the scientific community. But the various countries of Europe by the seventeenth century had become highly interconnected economically and politically. Regular shipments of naval stores from the Baltic to the Mediterranean by way of the German trading cities, or grain from Poland to England via the Netherlands, or wool from England to the Netherlands in return for finished cloth had become commonplace, ensuring that correspondence and informal flows of information would occur on a routine basis (Wallerstein, 1974).

With increasing economic interdependence also came attempts to institutionalize diplomatic relations (Mattingly, 1955). These attempts especially appear to have augmented the flow of information among scientists. For example, most of the extensive international correspondence of the Accademia del Cimento was carried on by resident ministers of the Grand Duke of Tuscany, such as Lorenzo Magalotti in France, and other persons in diplomatic service (Middleton, 1971). For another example, Sir Francis Bacon spent four years in the retinue of the English ambassador at the French court, where he came into contact with a number of French scientists. William Harvey visited Germany in 1636 in the company of the English ambassador and made observations that served importantly in the writing of his *Anatomical Exercises on the Generation of Animals* (1651). Sir John Finch, a noted English astronomer, became the resident minister of Charles II in Florence. The French diplomat Frenicle, a protégé of Melchisadec Thevenot, is said to have been an important link between experimenters in Italy and experimenters in France. Thevenot himself, founder of one of the forerunning academies to the Academy of Sciences, was both scientist and diplomat and maintained close contact between scientists in France and Italy during the 1650s. Leibniz, of course, was also both scientist and diplomat. Perhaps Dorothy Stimson (1948:146) has described the situation most clearly:

> Though there were no newspapers as yet, even then a net-work of communications linked England with the European countries. Men went abroad on government or on private business and brought back European books as well as news. Students wandered from university to university in Italy, France, Holland. Men, exiled to foreign cities, when restored to favor, brought back with them new tastes, new ideas, new interests learned abroad.

RIVALRIES

Scientists, in a sense, were welded into a single transnational community through their correspondence, travel, and common interests. However, no single scientific body of the kind that might have eventually stifled creativity and diversity of opinion emerged. Instead, separate scientific academies developed in the various European states. The circumstances surrounding the founding of these academies have been studied extensively. What is of interest in the present context is that the political and economic competition that characterized the European state system in the seventeenth century also seems to have been reflected in the competition among the scientific academies themselves. The rivalry between the Royal Society and the Academy of Sciences is well known. Such rivalry, it appears, also characterized some of the earlier academies in Italy. Indeed, one theory concerning the founding of the Accademia del Cimento in Tuscany—the theory espoused by distinguished Italian historian Riguccio Galluzzi—suggests that its founding may have been at least partly motivated by the founding of an Academy of Belles Lettres in Vienna a year previously (1656).

Middleton (1971) discounts this theory on the grounds that the academy was short-lived and had nothing to do with scientific experimentation. Yet the founders of the Accademia del Cimento were aware of the other academy, and the two were organized along similar lines in their respective states. Middleton's research has also uncovered evidence in letters from the 1650s showing the rivalry then beginning to exist between the Montmor Academy in Paris and the scientists associated with Prince Leopold in Tuscany. For example, a letter from Constantyn Huygens to his brother Christiaan remarks:

> We have had a good laugh at that fine assembly at Monsieur de Montmor's, and what happened in that meeting of fools when you were there hardly makes us respect the intelligence of these academicians, who patiently listen to pedants jawing for hours on end about nothings. To tell you what I think, it seems to me that those gentlemen in Florence are worth much more than these Parisians and treat things with fore-thought and modesty. (Middleton 1971:298–299)

Rivalry such as that expressed in Huygens's letter may have contributed to the multiplicity of academies that developed across Europe in the seventeenth century, and these in turn may have afforded greater intellectual freedom than might have been present had a single academy, capable of imposing its opinion on all, developed. Rivalries between scientists in different states may have also reinforced skepticism and criticism of the kind useful for the advancement of scientific knowledge. For example, Wolf (1951:224) has suggested that there were probably not more than three or four people in all of Europe capable of understanding Newton's *Principia* at the time it was published. Among these were Halley in England, Huygens in France, and Leibniz in Germany. It may not be entirely coincidental that, of the three, only Halley accepted Newton's work without reservation; Huygens and Leibniz raised important criticisms, some of which were not answered until the middle of the nineteenth century.

These pieces of evidence suggest that the structure of the larger European world-system—integrated yet decentralized—was reproduced in the scientific community. Scientists not only interacted with one another across national boundaries but also organized themselves into competing bodies. There was within the scientific community already in the seventeenth century, therefore, the making of an integrated yet flexible institution capable of expanding and adapting as its own discoveries and the growth of modern political and economic conditions dictated.

DIFFERENCES BETWEEN CORE
AND PERIPHERY

Thus far, the important differences that existed among the various European countries in their contributions to scientific activity have been ignored in the interest of discussing some of the general implications for the institutionalization of science of the decentralized social structure of the European system. Against this background some suggestions can now be formulated from the same perspective about the sources of national differences and similarities in the production of scientific culture.

IMPLICATIONS FOR SCIENCE

An important distinction that informs work on the early modern world-system is that between core areas, which are politically and economically dominant, and periphery areas, which are politically and economically dependent. From the perspective of the world-system as a whole, core areas occupy structurally similar positions that differ from those occupied by the periphery. Core areas can be expected to generate some of the same kinds of activities, therefore, merely because of their structurally similar positions, despite differing greatly from one another on other political, religious, or economic characteristics. Similarly, certain activities would be expected to be common to periphery areas, despite other domestic differences in these areas.

The implication of this argument for the institutionalization of science is that scientific activity might be expected to manifest similarities in areas occupying structurally similar positions in the world-system, regardless of other differences in these areas. In particular, we might hypothesize that science should show similar overall patterns of growth in core areas of the world-system, despite political and religious or other differences, because of certain advantages accruing to core areas from their central position in the world-system. These advantages might include (1) the flow of economic resources toward the core, making it possible for the core to support a larger educated elite from whom scientists and patrons of science could be recruited and a larger state bureaucracy providing offices and patronage to scientists; (2) the central position of the core in relation to channels of trade, diplomacy, and communication, all of which might create more effective exposure to new ideas; and (3) the greater role of ceremonial activities for the purpose of legitimating the power and position of states in relation to one another in the core (cf. Shils, 1972; von Gizycki, 1973).[11]

It is possible to test this hypothesis, at least indirectly, not only by comparing the scientific activity of core and periphery areas, but also by examining the changes in scientific activity that occurred over time as countries moved into or out of the core of the world-system. Two generalized indicators of scientific activity are available for the period 1500 to 1850: the number of scientists living in selected countries as calculated from Marquis's *Who's Who in Science* and the number of discoveries in selected countries listed in Ludwig Darmstädter's *Handbuch zur Geschichte der Naturwissenschaften und der Technik*.[12]

SOME EVIDENCE

The data on numbers of scientists demonstrate the relative dominance of the Hapsburg domains (Spain, Italy, and Germany) in 1500—when the Hapsburg empire could be regarded as the core of the European system—and the increasing shift away from these domains as the core of the world economy moved to other parts of Europe. Of the ninety-three scientists who were living in 1500, for example, sixty-four resided in Spain, Italy, or Germany. By the beginning of the seventeenth century, this pattern had begun to alter. Although Italy still led (with fifty-eight scientists in 1600), England, France, and Germany had each become near-rivals for the leadership as well (with fifty, forty-seven, and forty-nine, respectively). During the course of the seventeenth century, these three countries solidified their position while Italy—paralleling the larger shift of economic power—gradually declined. In 1700, for example, France had one hundred six scientists, England had seventy-three, Germany had forty-nine, and Italy had only thirty-two. The Netherlands also showed an interesting pattern during this period. As its position among the core powers of the world-system increased, the numbers of scientists residing there also increased, rising from six in 1550 to seventeen in 1600 to twenty-three in 1650; after this date, however, the Netherlands' difficulties in rivaling England and France economically and politically were also evident in the numbers of scientists, which declined to fourteen in 1700. Other countries that were definitely peripheral in terms of economic and political power in the seventeenth century—for example, Poland, Denmark, Portugal, and Ireland—each registered fewer than five scientists at any point in the seventeenth century.

Finally, the differences between core and peripheral countries is also evident in these data for the eighteenth and early nineteenth centuries. During most of this period, the core countries consisted mainly of England, France, and Germany. For all three, numbers of scientists grew rapidly and in about the same absolute proportions. Thus by 1850, 480 scientists were listed for England, 510 for France, and 470 for Germany. By comparison, only 60 were listed in 1850 for Italy, 9 for the Netherlands, 12 for Poland, and 14 for Denmark. Only the United States, which was rapidly gaining strength as a core economic power, had begun to rival the leading European states, listing 408 scientists in 1850.[13]

The data on scientific discoveries, as might be expected, closely resemble those on numbers of scientists. Again, differences appear between core and periphery countries, and the longitudinal trends closely parallel movement into and out of the core. Spain and Italy are again prominent at the beginning of the sixteenth century, but Spain's position declines markedly after 1550, and discoveries in Italian science appear to level off after 1600. From 1600 onward, approximately the same number of discoveries are made in England, France, and Germany—with Germany taking a slight lead around 1850. Scientific discoveries in the Netherlands rank nearly equal to England, France, and Germany in 1600 and grow at nearly the same rates until 1700, after which they lag increasingly behind the numbers made in the core countries. Again, scientific discoveries are virtually absent in the periphery countries.[14]

These indicators, of course, mask important differences in the kinds of scientific work being done in the various countries at different times—differences in style, subject matter, and quality of research, owing to variations both in cultural traditions and in the talents of individual scientists. But they suggest a crude correspondence between levels of scientific activity and countries' positions in the larger European world economy. The reasons for this correspondence undoubtedly include social conditions indigenous to particular countries preceding both their position in the world economy and their level of scientific activity. Apart from these conditions, however, the similarities in levels of scientific activity in countries occupying similar positions in the larger European system suggest that influences of this larger system cannot be ignored.[15]

IMPLICATIONS FOR
CONTEMPORARY SCIENCE

In concluding, some implications for the analysis of contemporary science might be suggested. Although science has for several centuries been a highly institutionalized feature of modern culture, some of the same patterns in the broader social environment that contributed to its initial institutionalization also appear to have a continuing effect in promoting scientific productivity. Three influences in particular seem to remain evident today as much as in the seventeenth century.

First, there continue to be similarities in the scientific activities of countries occupying similar positions in the world-system, despite gross differences in the domestic structure of these societies. Contrary to the argument that science and totalitarianism are mutually exclusive, for example, the Soviet Union has emerged as a major competitor of the United States in scientific research. The achievements of both in science and technology serve not only to maintain their status as core nations in the modern world but also to dramatize this status to each other and to the other nations of the world. Manifestations of these achievements, whether in explorations of outer space, military hardware, or consumer products, dramatize the powers not only of science but also of the societies sponsoring them. Nobel prizes especially, as Harriet Zuckerman (1967, 1977) has shown, become cherished tokens of national wisdom in much the same way that Olympic medals symbolize national fitness or physical prowess. However different in domestic social structure, the core countries of the world have felt compelled to participate in this ceremonial scientific competition and have allowed this competition to influence their scientific activities.

Second, periods of intense national competition such as prevailed in the seventeenth century (although actual outbreaks of war appear to be an exception) appear to have been particularly conducive to the rapid development of science. The great steps forward in atomic research during World War II cannot be fully explained without taking account of the conflict present in the larger world-system, nor can the rapid buildup of scientific research in the 1960s be explained apart from the cold war competition between the two leaders of the postwar world. Despite the universalistic norms and the cosmopolitan attachments of the scientific community, science has frequently been the beneficiary of rivalries among core nations.

Finally, the foregoing discussion suggests certain continuities in the history of science. Contrary to popular arguments distinguishing between the contemporary problems associated with "big science" and the historic opportunities associated with "little science," there appear to be some similarities in the social factors conditioning the institutionalization of science throughout the entire modern era. In particular, the close relation between contemporary science and the state is not entirely new; it can be illustrated as early as the seventeenth century. Again, the state seems an especially important factor to consider in examining the institutionalization of cultural forms—a factor that will emerge again in the next chapter as a central issue.

The aim of this chapter has not been to present a thorough analysis of the relations between the European world economy and the institutionalization of science in the seventeenth century, but rather to suggest some of the relations between science and the broader social environment and to illustrate some of the ways in which the idea of "world-system" might be beneficial in examining these relations. There is no need to argue that the effect of international or transnational factors was *more* important than the effect of domestic factors; those were surely important as well. But the limitations of purely domestic arguments, such as those found in both the Mertonian and Marxist traditions with respect to England, indicate that some attention needs to be paid to broader social contexts as well.

CHAPTER NINE

State Structures and Cultural Reform

Although historical problems have been attracting renewed interest in sociology, many of the theoretical assumptions on which sociological models of historical processes are constructed still remain tenuous. This is particularly the case in studies of the relationship between social structure and ideology. Research on this topic often suffers from being rooted in subjective social psychological assumptions that are inappropriate or at best untestable with historical materials. These assumptions need to be reexamined for the historical sociology of ideology to advance. As a means to that end, this chapter reexamines a study that represents one of the most rigorous efforts to relate social structure and ideology in a historical setting. This discussion will afford an opportunity to consider further the institutional approach to ideology.[1]

Religion and Regime by Guy E. Swanson (1967) is in many ways one of the most ambitious attempts to demonstrate a strong relationship between social conditions and ideology using systematic comparative-historical data. The focal concern of the book—the Protestant Reformation—has occupied a prominent place in sociological theory (from Weber and Troeltsch to contemporary writers such as Habermas and Luhmann), but Swanson's study remains the only book-length effort by an American sociologist to provide a systematic theoretical interpretation of the social conditions facilitating the adoption of the Reformation in some parts of Europe and deterring its adoption in others. Indeed, no historical treatment of the subject has attempted to bring to bear on the Reformation the kind of theoretical and quantitative rigor reflected in

Swanson's study. Combining important theoretical concerns with a massive array of carefully analyzed data, *Religion and Regime* represents a model of systematic comparative methodology. Moreover, the volume purports to make a substantial contribution to the application of Durkheimian theory to the sociology of knowledge. Along with his *The Birth of the Gods* (1960) and numerous articles (1971, 1973, 1976, 1978a, 1978b, 1980), it stands as one of the central contributions in Swanson's extended quest to demonstrate the universality of the effects of political arrangements—specifically, variations in the structure of sovereign groups—on popular attitudes and beliefs. Although others have made significant applications of the Durkheimian tradition in a number of areas, Swanson's work is distinctive in the specificity of its hypotheses concerning the social determination of ideology and its attempts to subject these assertions to empirical test.

In the two decades since it was written, *Religion and Regime* has experienced a somewhat curious reception. Soon after its publication, historians devoted a great deal of attention to it, including two major review symposia in leading journals, where it was discussed by a number of prominent experts on early modern European history (Brodek, 1971; Bouwsma, 1968; Davis, 1969, 1971; Flint, 1968; Francois, 1972; Koenigsberger, 1971). Since then, however, historians have paid the book almost no attention, often failing even to include it among standard bibliographic sources on the Reformation. Sociologists, in contrast, have shown far more positive and sustained interest in the book, recommending it favorably in reviews, discussing it in textbooks on the sociology of religion and culture, and applying some of its major concepts in other studies (Bergesen, 1977, 1978, 1984; Robertson, 1970; Robertson and Lechner, 1984; Winter, 1983, 1984; O'Toole, 1984; Simpson, 1983). Judging from the reception it has been given, the book appears to have become a minor classic in some branches of sociology. This is not to say that it has been received uncritically. Sociologists, like historians, have raised questions about some of the book's conclusions. But neither group has attempted to replicate the study empirically or even to reexamine its major premises in light of more recent historical evidence—a fact that appears all the more surprising because a substantial amount of new evidence on the Reformation period has accumulated in recent years.

The purpose of this chapter is to reexamine part of the evidence on which Swanson's theory of the Reformation is based in order to clarify the intervening theoretical links relating regime structures to religious ideology. At a more general level, the chapter's goal is to suggest an alternative to the way in which the relations between social conditions and ideology have generally been conceived, using Swanson's study as a vehicle to illustrate this alternative. This effort should be seen neither as a full replication nor as an attempt to refute the conclusions of *Religion and Regime,* but as an attempt to transcend some of the limitations of the approach to the study of states and ideology that it exemplifies. The chapter begins with an attempt to situate Swanson's study in terms of its larger theoretical importance to the sociology of knowledge; criticisms of the study that suggest its chief shortcoming is a failure to specify a plausible set of intervening connections between state structures and ideology are then discussed; next, evidence on the Reformation in France and England is presented to illustrate the nature of these connections in two prominent European states where religious policies clearly differed; and finally, an alternative approach that stresses the institutional relations between state structures and ideological outcomes is proposed.

RELIGION AND REGIME

The theoretical thread integrating Swanson's work on ideology is the argument, suggested by Durkheim, that when human beings worship the gods, they really, unknowingly, worship society. Swanson argues that the critical dimension of society that generates variations in religious ideas is the arrangement of sovereign groups. These are the repositories of transcendent force that carry the immutable, constraining power that Durkheim regarded as the source of fear, trust, veneration, and other sentiments assigned to the gods. The way to verify the correctness of this assertion, Swanson recognized, was to examine societies differing in authority structures to determine if religious patterns varied accordingly. His work on primitive societies in *The Birth of the Gods* examined these structures, yielding powerful empirical results that demonstrated, among other things, that belief in "high" or monotheistic gods is more common in societies characterized by at least three levels of political authority where the highest authority's sovereignty is manifested by its rule over lesser authorities. The results of that study appeared to provide evidence for a strong, direct influence of political arrangements on the actual content of religious ideas.

Religion and Regime sought to extend the generalizability of this conclusion by examining a related set of hypotheses for early modern societies. Differences in ideology between Protestantism and Roman Catholicism provided the critical dependent variable. Swanson argued that the important operative distinction between the two lay in their differing conceptions of God's *immanence:* Catholics believed that God was actually (physically) present in the Eucharist, in the offices of the priest, in relics of the saints, and in the church; Protestants denied that God was immanent in these ways, adopting the view that God was in heaven and could be reached only through faith and prayer. These differences, Swanson hypothesized, bore a direct relation to the kind of regime structures present in the various European areas just prior to the Reformation. Specifically, Protestantism should have been adopted in areas where political authority was decentralized or shared by constituent interests, thus leading to a conception of political sovereignty that transcended any of these component bodies; Catholicism, in contrast, should have remained strongest in areas with centralized regimes (i.e., where sovereignty was vested in or "immanent" in the regime itself). In short, Swanson posited a direct resemblance or correspondence between how people experienced political authority and how they conceptualized God. If ultimate power in the political sphere resided in the central organs of the state itself, then people would be more likely to think of God's authority as being immediate and tangible. If political power was divided, so that sovereignty was in a sense higher or removed from any specific interest group, then God's authority would also be thought of as distant, removed, transcendent, separate from any particular religious ritual or object.

To test this hypothesis, Swanson developed a list of forty-one sovereign states (territorial states, principalities, duchies, and cantons) that were free of any kind of external rule by another power during the critical decades prior to the Reformation. Using a complex series of indicators, he classified these states into five types of regime, ranging from centralized to four types of decentralized structures. He then related these patterns to the type of religious ideology officially adopted in each state. With only two exceptions the predicted patterns held. Further, Swanson was able to predict subtypes of Protestant ideology (Lutheran, Anglican, Calvinist) from variations in the political arrangements of the decentralized states. As in his previous study, then, strong evidence seemed to emerge in support of the argument that the manner in which people experienced political sovereignty had a direct impact on the content of their religious ideas.

Not surprisingly, many sociologists have recognized the importance of this conclusion. The study has been characterized as one of the most elaborate and successful applications of Durkheimian theory (Robertson, 1970:151; Fallding, 1974:22–24); as an "important critique of Weber" (Budd, 1973:61); as "complex and painstakingly detailed" (Wilson, 1978:174); as a study that is "original, detailed, and thought-provoking" (Nottingham, 1971:319); and as "a major resource with which to deal with problems of comparative and intersocietal analysis" (Robertson and Lechner, 1984:187). Methodologically, the book demonstrates the value of systematic comparisons among large numbers of societies; substantively, it offers a distinctly sociological explanation of the Reformation. Its primary importance as a theoretical work, however, lies in its systematic examination of the hypothesis that popular knowledge tends to correspond with social experience.

IDEOLOGY AS A REFLECTION OF SOCIAL REALITY

That there is a determinate relation between ideology and social experience is the central premise on which the subdiscipline of sociology of knowledge is based. According to this premise, ideas are substantively conditioned by the social contexts in which they arise. In the Durkheimian formulation (as seen in Chapter 2), ideas symbolize or represent vital aspects of collective reality (such as the distribution of authority). As a result things are never quite what they seem as far as ideas are concerned. Beneath their surface content lies another level of meaning, shaped by and symbolic of social configurations. Moreover, in the strict interpretation of this relation, the content of ideas themselves directly reflects these configurations. Ideas are said to vary not only in the indeterminate sense of being conditioned by different cultural traditions, but also in the determinate sense of having fixed relations with particular social arrangements. Thus, the task of sociological inquiry as far as ideology is concerned is to discover these relations.

This theory, which might be termed the "correspondence theory of knowledge," though seldom formulated explicitly, has wide currency in social science. Specific applications range from studies in social psychology and anthropology, to theories of cultural evolution, to the so-called "strong program" in the sociology of science. For example, Foucault (1965, 1975, 1979) has argued that the modern concept of the individual developed in some ways as a reflection of the experience that became increasingly prominent in the eighteenth and nineteenth centuries of ordering individuals according to strict arrangements in military regiments, of treating individuals' bodies medically, of incarcerating them in separate cells, and later of organizing work into specialized tasks. Thomas (1979, 1986) has presented evidence suggesting that the experience of producing for the market as an individual entrepreneur was associated in the history of American agriculture with rivivalistic religions, such as Methodism, which gave prominence to the salvation of the individual. For an earlier period, LeGoff (1984) argues that the birth of purgatory in the twelfth century was a type of ternary logic that corresponded directly to ternary divisions among social orders. In science, various observers have suggested correlations between how earthly powers were experienced and how heavenly bodies were conceptualized and between individuation in social life and atomistic theories of matter (e.g., Olson, 1971). Extending these ideas, Bloor (1976) has attempted to show that even simple mathematical ideas may reflect common types of social experience.

The theoretical underpinnings of these arguments have often remained implicit. There are, however, two arguments as to why a direct correspondence might exist between social arrangements and ideology. One is the concept of "natural symbolization," which has been advanced most explicitly in the work of Mary Douglas (1966, 1970). This work suggests that certain kinds of symbols (or knowledge) are associated with certain social arrangements because the intrinsic structure or form of the two is so naturally similar that virtually anyone can recognize the correspondence. For example, bodily orifices often symbolize social boundaries because goods obviously pass through or across both. Or in other settings, patron saints are believed in because societies are actually structured around relations of patronage and clientage. Here, the connection between social structure and ideology is not only direct but also straightforward and is rooted in conceptions of individual cognition. Knowledge will be learned more readily if it consists of classifications that are also dramatized by social arrangements. Thus, over time, one should expect a certain correspondence between cultural classification schemes and underlying social arrangements.

The other implicit interpretation of correspondence theory is the idea of "isomorphic legitimation." Derivative in some respects from both Marx and Weber, this idea suggests (1) that ideologies that legitimate dominant institutions will be generated and (2) that the capacity to legitimate will be greater if the ideology's form is isomorphic with that of the institutions. Thus, a rational ideology will be likely to emerge in a rationally organized society, individualism will emerge in individuated institutions, and so forth. This is a more macroscopic perspective than the first, focusing on dominant institutions, but an implicit assumption about the importance of individual cognition is again present. Individuals are presumably more likely to credit an ideology with plausibility if its form reflects that of familiar institutions.

Both of these arguments rest on the classical subject-object form of dualism in which ideas are distinguished from objective elements of the social environment and are, moreover, regarded as having been properly "explained" by being related to the social environment. Because of an apparent tendency toward sociological reductionism in these approaches, theorists in the neoclassical tradition (Chapter 2) have called for greater attention to the phenomenological meanings of ideological constructs themselves (e.g., Bellah, 1970; Geertz, 1973).[2] This alternative, however, has not generated a research strategy that goes significantly beyond empirical description or that manages successfully to reintroduce the traditional concern of the sociology of knowledge with relations between social structure and ideology. At present, the most viable alternative in the sociology of knowledge to correspondence theory is the reality construction approach, as articulated in the work of Berger and Luckmann (1966). Although portraying knowledge as emergent, objectivated constructions of reality, this approach brings social arrangements into the picture through the concept of "plausibility structures," that is, settings of social interaction (especially "conversation") in which ideologies are made plausible by being verbally articulated and by being dramatized in the unspoken assumptions on which interaction is based. The problem with the reality construction approach, however, is that it specifies only an indeterminate role for social conditions in the shaping of knowledge and ideology. Plausibility structures are essential, but essentially indeterminate: any set of ideas can apparently be maintained in any type of social setting. Thus, correspondence theory remains the strongest attempt to specify *determinate* relations between social conditions and social knowledge. Swanson's work, therefore, acquires added significance as one of the few efforts to systematically operationalize and test hypotheses derived from the correspondence argument.

Although *Religion and Regime* is but one of the studies in Swanson's oeuvre that has examined the correspondence between social experience and ideology, it serves as a particularly valuable case for consideration. It is the study that deals most explicitly with the relation between state structures and ideologies. Among Swanson's major works, it also is the one that has been most neglected in terms of having not been subjected to empirical reexamination. *The Birth of the Gods,* for example, has been reexamined several times, with mixed results as far as the broader theory is concerned (e.g., Underhill, 1975, 1976; Simpson, 1979, 1984). Perhaps obviously, the importance of *Religion and Regime* is also magnified by the fact that its subject matter—the Protestant Reformation—is an event of major consequence for understanding the development of modern societies.

CONCEPTUAL AND METHODOLOGICAL CONSIDERATIONS

Criticisms of *Religion and Regime* have focused on both conceptual and methodological issues. The conceptual issues raised by historians have focused on questions about the clarity and appropriateness of key concepts such as "immanence" and "gubernaculum" (e.g., Bouwsma, 1968; Davis, 1971; Ozment, 1975). A close reading of Swanson is sufficient to set many of these objections aside, however. Although the terminology often fails to capture precise historical nuances, it is admirably well articulated in terms of the basic variables at issue. More serious is the criticism that the linkage among major concepts remains sufficiently unclear as to leave the theoretical argument somewhat less than convincing. Specifically, the question of *why* theological views should correspond with political structures remains open.

The assumption on which Swanson's argument rests is essentially Durkheimian in that the society is presumed to penetrate individuals' consciousness as they inevitably confront society through the personal experience of living in it (cf. Robertson and Lechner, 1984:195). In the Durkheimian formulation, ideas about society are thus molded directly, albeit not necessarily consciously, by the forces constituting society, chiefly through the informal socialization process and through subsequent enactment in collective rituals.[3] In applying this logic to early modern societies, it becomes imperative, however, to indicate more precisely the channels by which social experience becomes articulated as an influence on formal religious ideology. Both Durkheim and Swanson imply that the process is sufficiently complex that it cannot be assumed to operate strictly through the psychological processes of atomized individuals.[4]

In focusing on the problem of establishing an empirical correspondence between regime structures and Reformation outcomes, Swanson does not indicate explicitly who makes the connection between regime structures and religious ideas, or exactly how this connection is made. Occasionally, reference is made to "apologists," "the reformers," or simply "the people," but for the most part passive verbs, such as "are regarded as" and "will be considered," which have no identifiable subject as the actor, are chosen. Presumably, the assumptions about this connection are the same as in *The Birth of the Gods* because the study is presented as a further test of the theory developed there. But the social psychological processes are not as obvious in early modern nation-states as they are in small primitive societies, both because of the difference in scale and because of presumed differences in cultural and institutional differentiation. In more recent work, Swanson has related authority structures to ideology by examining socialization patterns within families. But again it seems less obvious that the same processes would have been at work in linking state structures to the Reformation.

To frame the problem more concretely, we may consider two possibilities of how the experience of state structures could have affected Reformation ideology. First is the possibility that "the people" were more receptive to Protestant teachings in some countries than in others because of having experienced a decentralized political structure and, for this reason, influenced Reformation outcomes by lending popular support or popular opposition. This interpretation fits either of the theoretical approaches mentioned earlier, as well as the logic of Swanson's primitive and socialization studies. In the case of the Reformation, however, it tends to break down because it presupposes too much about typical levels of political awareness and exposure. Literacy, public education, and publishing were increasing rapidly during the Reformation, but upwards of 80 percent of the population (and in most cases 90 to 95 percent) still remained illiterate. Perhaps more to the point, the vast majority had little, if any, contact with the state as a basis for forming opinions influenced by its structure: uniform legal codes existed hardly anywhere; taxes were generally channeled through local notables or tax farmers; military service still focused on fealty or mercenary obligations rather than directly on the state; itinerant courts, which touched some of the people directly, still touched relatively few; and in most countries, an extended franchise was still more than three centuries in the future. Nor does the argument of variations among social strata make sense. The nobility, for example, was in a position to be especially aware of state structures; yet during the first half of the sixteenth century, the nobility everywhere remained overwhelmingly resistant to the Reformation, despite differences in state structures—even in Poland, where a decentralized parliamentary system kept the crown from exercising virtually any centralized authority. Similarly, in the towns, where awareness of the state might have been higher, artisan classes often supported the Reformation as much as did the more literate and more cosmopolitan professional and merchant classes; this was as true in areas such as Poland, France, and Spain, which remained Catholic, as in England or the German and Swiss territories, which turned Protestant. For these reasons, historians of the period have generally been skeptical of Swanson's interpretation, arguing that more immediate contexts—family, community, and patron/client relations—were probably more significant molders of ideology than were political structures. Even historians who give some credence to the correspondence theory have pointed to correlations between ideology and guild structures, local communities, trade networks, and godparentage, rather than more remote influences of the state (e.g., Davis, 1981; Moeller, 1972).

The second possibility of linking state structures to the Reformation is through "reformers" and "apologists." Here the argument would have to be that authority patterns in existence prior to the Reformation shaped the reformers' ideas as they were originally developing (i.e., scholars living in decentralized areas were more likely to come up with nonimmanentist ideas of God). This argument is more compelling than the first because it can more readily be assumed that reformers themselves were aware of political conditions and of theories about these conditions. There are, however, several difficulties. One is that the humanist tradition, which partially preceded the Reformation and which also rejected immanentist conceptions of God, fails to follow this pattern; much of the important humanist scholarship occurred in areas classified as politically centralized, namely, France and Spain (including the Spanish Low Countries). Nor does the Anabaptist tradition fit easily with the argument that reformers were highly aware of political conditions because its leaders included many lay preachers from lower status origins. More important, though, is the fact that Swanson's thesis is explicitly concerned, not with the intellectual origins of the Reformation, but with Reformation "settlements," that is, with the official endorsement of the Reformation in different societies. This emphasis solves one problem (the problem of political awareness, because settlements were made by those in power), but it creates another: even if state agents were disposed one way or another toward the Reformation, what was the mechanism by which these attitudes were put into practice? In other words, is it sufficiently explanatory to attribute the Reformation to personal predispositions (which are now largely unknown and even at the time may not have been apparent to the actors involved), or do these predispositions need to be considered in relation to social conditions that made them more or less likely to be adopted? The conceptual weakness of the correspondence theory rests squarely on this problem—the problem of letting unobservable psychological states serve as the only mechanism linking social structure and ideology, rather than considering *social processes* mediating between social structure and the formation or adoption of ideology. In the present case it seems especially ironic that the connection between social structure and ideology should turn out to be primarily a hidden psychological process because Swanson's neo-Durkheimian approach has generally been praised for its distinctively *sociological* character.

The other set of—methodological—considerations concerns the manner in which the thesis of *Religion and Regime* (accepting its conceptual correctness) was tested. As noted before, the study focuses on forty-one autonomous states, of which accurate predictions are given for thirty-nine. But the forty-one represent only a small fraction of the number of states in Europe at the time. Central Europe alone contained approximately two hundred forty principalities, bishoprics, duchies, imperial cities, and other political units of varying size. Nor do the forty-one encompass the most sizable, populous, or influential states. For instance, all of the Holy Roman Empire, the Papal States, Flanders, Norway, Finland, and Russia are excluded; in contrast, more than a third of the forty-one cases are Swiss cantons. This means, of course, that minor principalities each count as much in the analysis as do dominant countries such as England, France, and Spain (and collectively, of course, count for far more). Because many of these minor principalities are geographically proximate to one another, the study also suffers from Galton's problem (i.e., cases are not strictly independent). The basis on which these forty-one cases were selected was the requirement that states be autonomous (sovereign) in order to test the theory of political structure. But on this criterion, questions can also be raised about the basis for including or excluding a number of the cases. Austria is included; the Holy Roman Empire was excluded, even though both were officially part of the Hapsburg dynasty. None of the sixty-five imperial cities was included, even though most had been granted sovereignty as early as the thirteenth century. All the Swiss cantons were included as separate cases, despite the fact that the Swiss Confederation (just as much as the United Provinces, treated as a single case) bound them into a single unity for most purposes. Ducal (East) Prussia was excluded, even though its autonomy from Poland was virtually complete. Florence was included, but Piedmont and Sicily were excluded, even though the latter enjoyed greater autonomy from Spain than the former. Hesse, which was included, was officially subject to the emperor and was in practice governed for significant periods by regents from neighboring Saxony. In short, doubtful selection criteria were employed in many of the cases.

Faced with problems of this kind, sociologists often construct an enlarged or more elaborate data base on which to perform statistical calculations. Similar criticisms aimed at *The Birth of the Gods*, for example, have resulted in several studies employing larger numbers of cases and more elaborate statistical procedures (e.g., Underhill, 1975; Simpson, 1979, 1984). In the present case, however, a strategy of this kind is not preferable. Adequate data on the political structure of many of the cases still remain nonexistent. For example, Swanson's coding for Appenzell was based on a brief passage in a single study; fairly extensive searching indicates that that source still remains the only one. In other instances, such as Hesse, Württemberg, and the imperial cities, a great deal of research has been done since Swanson's study, but the result has been to make Swanson's coding scheme more, rather than less, ambiguous. Even an enlarged number of cases would remain subject to Galton's problem and would remain insufficient to provide for adequate controls of other variables. An enlarged sample, even if possible, would still remain undesirable because the thrust of the foregoing considerations has dealt chiefly with the intervening processes connecting state structures and ideologies. For this purpose, a more detailed comparative investigation of a few cases is preferable to a statistical approach involving larger numbers.[5] For this reason, the following discussion focuses on a comparison of two cases: France and England. Both meet Swanson's criteria of being sovereign states; both are sizable and of considerable importance to the subsequent history of the Reformation and of Europe generally; and ample evidence is available for each; indeed, much evidence has become available since Swanson's study was published, thus providing an opportunity for an "update" as opposed merely to a critical reanalysis. As will be shown, the two countries also resembled each other in many respects, thus sharpening the importance of explaining why one adopted the Reformation and the other did not.

THE REFORMATION IN FRANCE
AND ENGLAND

The fact that the Reformation was adopted in England but not in France should not obscure the considerable similarities that also characterized the two countries. In both, reformed teachings spread to the major cities within a few years of Luther's break with Rome. London and Paris had groups of Lutheran devotees by 1520, and other cities in southeastern England and in northern and eastern France had pockets of evangelical activity by the same date. The new doctrines in each case were carried by merchants with commercial connections in central Europe and by students and clergy from German universities. If anything, there may have been more reform activity in France than in England during these years because it was easier to travel and to ship books, even after they were banned, between France and the Rhineland (Knecht, 1972).

At the popular level, evangelical activity was most common in the cities and relatively absent in rural areas in both countries. In England, London was the most visible center of reform interest, although there were also congregations in the smaller towns in Kent, Sussex, Essex, and neighboring areas (Clark, 1977; Cross, 1980; Manning, 1969; Parker, 1966). In northern France, adherents of the new doctrines were most evident in Rouen and to the east in Paris, Meaux, Beauvais, Senlis, and Soissons (Benedict, 1981; Bercé, 1980; Nicholls, 1980, 1983; Richet, 1977). Other towns where reforming sentiment was strong included Troyes, Nantes, Lyons, Montpellier, and Nîmes (Davis, 1975; Galpern, 1976; Vance, 1977:178–179). In all of these areas, merchant-traders and artisans were disproportionately involved in the new congregations relative to local shopkeepers, unskilled workers, and vagabonds (Davis, 1981; Rosenberg, 1978; LeRoy Ladurie, 1974:158–164). Among merchants and artisans, those involved in the textile industry in both countries appear to have been particularly well represented. These trades were more likely to have contact with Protestant areas, had higher rates of literacy, and were less tied to local markets or guild associations sponsored by the church.

Protestantism, therefore, was by no means absent at the grassroots level in France. During the first half of the sixteenth century, it experienced steady growth in the cities. By mid century, as many as one-third of Rouen's seventy thousand residents had converted, approximately the same proportion of Lyons's sixty thousand residents were Protestants, and perhaps as many as a fourth of Paris's two hundred thousand residents had adopted the new faith. In medium-sized towns, the proportions of Protestants were often equally high: 25 percent of Caen's fifteen thousand residents, 50 percent of Nîmes's ten thousand residents, 50 percent of LaRochelle's twenty-five thousand residents, and as many as 78 percent of Montpellier's ten thousand residents (Lamet, 1978). Overall, approximately two thousand Protestant congregations are known to have existed in France by 1559. Figures as high as one-quarter of the total population have been suggested for adherents, but at minimum at least 5 or 6 percent (totaling about 1.2 million) probably converted to Protestantism by this date (Spitz, 1985:194–203). It is difficult, consequently, to attribute the Reformation's failure in France strictly to a lack of popular appeal. If, as Swanson argues, the immanent conception of political sovereignty in France stripped Protestantism of legitimacy, this problem seems not to have deterred many of the more active, literate residents of its cities—those in a position to be aware of prevailing political conceptions—from adopting the new teachings. Judging from the extent of Protestantism's appeal, the immanent sense of political sovereignty supposedly present in France may have actually been as weak as it was in England.

If attitudes toward the Reformation among those at the highest levels of French and English government are examined, greater support for Swanson's thesis may be evident, at least on the surface, for Francis I threw his weight against the reforms, but Henry VIII became the Reformation's greatest defender. Yet closer consideration reveals a somewhat more complicated pattern. During the first decade or so of the Reformation, Henry VIII was largely opposed to it. Indeed, while his older brother was yet alive, Henry had been destined for the priesthood and thus had fairly well developed views on theology. In 1521, he wrote a treatise condemning Lutheranism that he sent to the pope, who, in gratitude, bestowed on Henry the honorific title "defender of the faith." Francis I, in contrast, was keenly interested in humanism, became known for both his tolerance and his defense of new ideas, and several members of his household were counted among the early converts to Protestantism (Knecht, 1981, 1982). In 1532, this erstwhile symbol of immanental sovereignty even concluded an agreement with Henry VIII in which he promised to exercise his influence with the pope on behalf of Henry's "great cause." Only after the *placards* affair in 1534 did Francis begin to actively oppose the reformers. Even two years later, John Calvin was sufficiently optimistic about the king's leanings to dedicate the *Institutes* to him. In England, however, even after the king was proclaimed head of the church, little progress was made toward instituting reforms in the actual conduct of religious worship. Not until the reign of Elizabeth does evidence suggest that reform ideas began to penetrate widely into popular practice (Bowker, 1981; Hey, 1974; Oxley, 1965; Haigh, 1975). During most of the sixteenth century, the major changes were in high levels of ecclesiastical administration, rather than in sacraments and belief; and for an even much longer time, Anglicanism did not depart radically (except in official treatises) from immanentist conceptions of God. In other words, here were two kings, the one supposedly in charge of a state with immanental sovereignty and the other heading a state lacking such sovereignty; yet their own views of religious immanence demonstrate little in the way of a straightforward correspondence with their experiences of political sovereignty. Thus, it appears difficult to account for the Reformation's success in England compared to France strictly on the basis of its intrinsic appeal to the two countries' rulers.

Nor are the differences entirely evident among other top officials. Members of the nobility who occupied high government offices were often opposed to the reforms in England just as in France, at least until revenues from the sale of church lands began to change their minds.[6] The Sorbonne's denunciation of Lutheran heresies in 1521 is no more intolerant than the campaigns against them led by Thomas More (Elton, 1963:118–119; Knecht, 1972:9–10; Hempsall, 1973). Nor was the Sorbonne itself beyond taking a liberal stance toward the church. By a narrow margin it actually came out on Henry's side in his contest with the pope (Knecht, 1978). In the same year, the English Parliament, although also supporting Henry, nevertheless passed the Heresy Act in an attempt to root out Protestantism once and for all through heavy fines, imprisonment, and death by fire. It is the case, of course, that Parliament lent a more sympathetic voice to the Reformation than did the Parlement of Paris or any of the regional parlements in France. But these differences raise questions less about religious attitudes than about differences in the distribution of power in the two countries—Swanson's independent variable. This variable bears closest examination.

For Swanson the principal grounds for characterizing England and France as different types of government appear to be formal (i.e., dependent on the formal nature of legitimate authority). England represented a "limited centralist" regime because of the division of sovereignty between the crown and Parliament and between the crown and local authorities. No such division existed in France; sovereignty adhered strictly in the crown; hence, it exemplified a "centralist" regime. As specific indicators, Swanson points to the fact that in England the king was bound by customs and laws of the realm, was dependent on Commons to originate money bills, and could be impeached by Commons. Moreover, nobles, gentry, and boroughs were represented in Parliament, and local justices remained capable of resisting royal law (Swanson, 1967: 129–133). In contrast, the French state was centralized in the hands of the monarch, who was in control of vast patronage and wealth that was meted out in the form of offices for the higher nobility. The Estates General had given up control of the public purse, parlement was not an effective check on royal policy, and the crown managed successfully to establish its own officers in titular control over every major division of local government (Swanson, 1967:77–85).

But this conception of the state in France and England has undergone a serious revision since Swanson's study was conducted, not in direct response to Swanson, but on the basis of more careful considerations of the actual functioning of the two regimes, including studies of both the processes of policy formation at the central level and policy execution as well as political representation at the community level. Historians have concluded that the French state under Francis I was in practice a weak, relatively decentralized regime in which authority was shared by special interests. England, rather than France, more nearly exemplified a strong, centralized regime with actual power concentrated in the crown. Not until well after the Reformation, particularly during the parliamentary period in England and the reign of Louis XIV in France, did the two countries assume the characterizations given them by Swanson. These conclusions require more careful explication.

CONTRASTING STATE STRUCTURES

In practice, the development of a strong regime in England that was capable of exercising central authority was greatly facilitated by economic developments of the period—a factor largely ignored in *Religion and Regime*. Commercial expansion worked primarily to the advantage of the state relative to its major rival, the landed aristocracy. Commercial expansion in England, as elsewhere, depended partly on rising demand from domestic population growth. This growth, though unspectacular in comparison with that in the Low Countries and many of the German areas, was nevertheless steady, giving the country a figure about 50 percent higher at the end of the century than at the beginning

(Cornwall, 1970; Grigg, 1980). But having a population only half the size of Spain, one-third the size of Germany, and one-sixth the size of France meant that England's economic fortunes had to be more closely associated with foreign trade than with the growth of its domestic market. On the whole, England's foreign trade tripled during the last half of the fifteenth century and multiplied several times again during the sixteenth (Postan, 1973:162). Cloth exports grew particularly rapidly, quadrupling between 1500 and 1550, both as a result of favorable treaties negotiated by the crown and as a result of royal loans (Bowden, 1962; Parry, 1967; Dietz, 1964; Postan, 1973:214–218). Unlike Poland and Spain, England's trade was not allowed to slip into foreign hands. Accordingly, London became a prosperous commercial center and a powerful lobby that the crown could exploit against the rural nobility (Myers, 1971:206; Ramsey, 1965:55; Zagorin, 1982:72).

By the beginning of the sixteenth century, the crown had become solvent as a result of rising customs revenues, better management of its estates, and a policy of frugality in military affairs and administration of the royal household (Batho, 1967a:257, 1967b; Wolffe, 1964, 1970). More important, the *structure* of crown revenues gave the state a degree of fiscal autonomy from the landed sector that was unparalleled at the time. According to estimates at the beginning of the reign of Henry VIII, 35 percent of the crown's revenues came from customs, another 35 percent came directly from the earnings of crown lands, and an additional 20 percent came from special sources such as revenues from the royal mint (Williams, 1979:58; Slavin, 1973:98–103; Alsop, 1982). Thus, only 10 percent was left to be raised from direct taxes on land or other properties. Although Parliament did control the public purse, therefore, this control posed little in the way of a real threat to the crown's sovereignty.

Administratively, the state also succeeded in emancipating itself in large measure from the landowners' control. The Tudors, unlike their counterparts in France, practiced a deliberate policy of excluding the nobility from high appointive office. Nor did they sell offices to the nobility in order to raise supplemental revenue. Instead, officeholders were selected from the royal family itself, from merchant and professional families, and from the lower strata. As a result, the king's advisory councils and ad hoc commissions were largely independent of noble connections (Elton, 1953). In some ways the ability to gain this degree of administrative autonomy also rested on broader economic conditions. Compared with France, where the economic plight of the nobility during most of the fifteenth century had reinforced its efforts to secure remunerative positions in the state, the English nobility had a wider variety of options available outside of the state, particularly as suppliers for the burgeoning trade in wool (cf. Heller, 1977b).

Like representative bodies in other European countries, the English Parliament still reflected the vested interests of men of wealth, including landowners. But by the reign of Henry VIII, the landowners' influence in Parliament was greatly reduced. Through strategic moves the crown gradually increased the representation of merchants and city officials, members of the clergy, and royal officeholders—all loyal to the crown or dependent on its patronage (Miller, 1970). Thus, the Parliament of Henry VIII—the Parliament that assisted him at every turn in advancing the Reformation—was an ally on whom he could generally depend rather than a foe ready to limit his sovereignty and defend the landowners' interests (Lehmberg, 1970).

The House of Commons in 1529 consisted of 74 knights of the shire and 236 burgesses. The former were landowners, all but a few with stronger ties to the gentry than to the crown. The burgesses, in contrast, physically resided in the towns, and most were engaged in commerce. Indeed, the majority participated in some aspect of the cloth trade. Of the remainder, many were local officeholders or professional people (e.g., lawyers, surveyors) with close connections to the crown. Thus, landed interests were outnumbered by a margin of as many as three to one.

In the same year, the House of Lords' dependence on the crown was also clearly in evidence. Nearly half its members were representatives of the church—a surprising fact in view of the ecclesiastical reforms they were to approve. But ecclesiastical appointments had for some time been made by the crown, and representatives voicing opposition to royal policy found the seats they vacated filled by appointees with more pliable views. Among the temporal lords, many were longtime servants of the crown, holding peerages created by the king in return for their services; others were members of the royal household itself. The crown also held traditional prerogatives giving it influence over the lords. It could command opponents not to attend or at least intimidate them, threaten the positions of ecclesiastical and royal officials, and appoint its own chancellor and other nonnoble servants of the House. Overall, the influence of the crown over the Lords was probably as great as, if not greater than, its influence over the Commons. Contrary to the supposition that Henrician England represented a decentralized state in which royal power was balanced by Parliament, therefore, it is probably more appropriate to conclude, as one historian does, that Parliament had still "not established itself as an effective and sufficient vehicle for the expression of opposition and for the resolution of political conflict" (James, 1970:70; McKenna, 1979).

The means by which the state administered local justice were also symptomatic of the crown's capacity to rule in a manner largely autonomous from the landed elite. Under the Tudors, the collection of local taxes did remain directly or indirectly under the influence of the local landed elite. But these collections were by no means the centerpiece of crown finances (as they were in France). Nor were the local clergy, who remained closely allied with the landowners, utilized to any significant extent in the administration of local justice, certainly not to the extent that they were in France. Gradually their role was modified toward little more than a hortatory function. Local justices of the peace were the primary officials concerned with local administration, and, although they were in effect selected by local landlords, they were increasingly subjected to the authority of royal lords-lieutenant. Courtier justices, crown lawyers, and special commissions—deliberately created on an ad hoc basis to prevent attachments from developing with local elites—were also used to extend the state's control (Williams, 1979:407–420; Clark, 1977:19–20). Finally, the Tudors were by no means above using intimidation and sheer force, including purges and treason charges, to keep the nobility in line (Williams, 1979:381–382; Elton, 1972).

The contrasting situation in France is readily apparent. Again, the state's power in actuality was heavily dependent on broader economic developments. After more than a century of war that had badly depopulated much of the country, France experienced a demographic recovery during the last two decades of the fifteenth century and first half of the sixteenth (Salmon, 1975:27–37). Demand for foodstuffs and necessities rose, stimulating vigorous trade in local markets and providing incentives for expansion in agriculture. Coastal cities such as Bordeaux, Nantes, and Rouen, as well as regional markets such as Troyes and Lyons, grew at a rapid pace. But the price inflation was generally not as severe in French towns as in England (Baulant, 1976). Nor did the topography of France lend itself to widespread or intensive involvement in commerce. Approximately nine of every ten persons remained closely tied to the land, and the majority of the nobility continued to derive their incomes from the land (Lütge, 1958:45–46; Fourquin, 1964; Wood, 1980). Generally, the seigneurial system intensified: landlords acquired stronger claims over common lands, peasants found themselves increasingly at the mercy of landlords, and both found themselves wedded to the other in a marriage of economic interdependence (Bloch, 1966; Teall, 1965; Galpern, 1976).

As for the state, certain powers had been arrogated by the crown, such as extending its powers of taxation and expanding venality of offices (Knecht, 1982). But the centralized absolutism that was to characterize the reign of Louis XIV was by no means that of Francis I (Wolfe, 1972:98). Instead of being powerful, centralized, or capable of engaging in autonomously determined policies, like England, the French state was "inherently weak, not strong"; its administrators "accepted the decentralization of the state and made little effort to centralize it" (Major, 1971:44). Separate provinces retained distinctive prerogatives in administering local justice; landowning magnates cultivated their own patronage networks, opposed centralization of tax administration, kept a rein on venality of office, objected to the garrisoning of troops, and retained regulatory control over the grain trade (Harding, 1978; Lewis, 1965, 1968; Shennan, 1969; Strayer, 1971:346–347). If the king was officially sovereign, his sovereignty was nevertheless shared in practice with the powerful Parlement of Paris. This body, permanently located in the capital city, in contrast to the king's peripatetic court, often had greater command over public affairs than the king himself. During the king's imprisonment in Spain in 1525, it clearly held the upper hand. It also held legal right to pass remonstrances against the king and used this right on several occasions to express severe indictments of royal policy. Particularly in matters of religious heresy, this body, along with the ecclesiastical courts, established policies and executed final jurisdiction (Knecht, 1978). Compounding these problems, the central bureaucracy was understaffed and ineffective in implementing royal policy (Anderson, 1974:87); the treasury continued to function as an aggregation of private accounts; military strength remained almost exclusively in the hands of the wealthier nobles; and the financial condition of the crown steadily deteriorated, from the fiscal crisis of 1522 to its eventual bankruptcy in 1559 (Thompson, 1967:2; Edelstein, 1974; Guéry, 1978). Henry VIII had gained sufficient control over Parliament that he could risk asking for—or, perhaps better, demanding—increases in customs rates and taxes. Francis, in contrast, knew better than to attempt to convene the Estates General for this purpose. In consequence, state revenues in England multiplied more than tenfold during Henry's reign; those in France little more than doubled, causing the king increasing difficulties in implementing either foreign or domestic policies (Miskimin, 1977:160). If, as Swanson (1967:84) asserts, Francis I "went from one military and diplomatic success to another, constantly strengthening his house," these successes were not evident in most of the state's operations.

It was instead the landed nobility who expanded their control over the state to the point that "the crown had become the archpatron and a number of powerful noble factions had created networks of their own influence" (Salmon, 1975:92; cf. Major, 1964). Rather than exercising autonomous sovereignty over the nobility, the state served as an institution for the protection of the nobility's interests. Just as in Poland, the nobility continued to dominate Parlement, provincial governorships, and local jurisdiction (Major, 1960:115; Neuschel, 1982:42; Wood, 1980:170). Financially, the landowners held close rein over the state. At the start of the sixteenth century, only one-fifth of the king's revenue was supplied by crown lands, with the remaining four-fifths having to be raised from taxation and borrowing (Shennan, 1969:50; Wolfe, 1972:11). As for taxation, the nobility claimed broad prerogatives for itself, including exemption from major taxes and control over the officials who supervised the administration of local taxes (Major, 1980; Mandrou, 1974; Bonney, 1981:1–21). But taxes alone failed to be adequate for the king's needs: expenditures consistently outstripped revenues by a sizable margin (Guéry, 1978). Intermittent wars with the Hapsburgs, including Francis's defeat, capture, and ransom in 1525, required extensive borrowing. Between 1522 and 1547, this borrowing, in fact, tripled, and most of it came from the wealthier landowners who held provincial offices, either in the form of payments for office or direct loans (Salmon, 1975:76–77; Wolfe, 1972:93; Knecht, 1981:24–33). The nobility also became the state's chief beneficiaries. Comprising less than 2 percent of the population, they received more than half of the state's total outlays, the largest share consisting of stipends for venal and military offices (Heller, 1977b). Administratively, the largest share of offices in the bureaucracy and in the Estates General was held by the nobility. In contrast with England, the French monarchy had been constrained by economic expediency to grant the largest number of offices to the nobility rather than gaining autonomy from the nobility by selecting officials from professional or artisan classes (Pegues, 1962; Autrand, 1974; Stocker, 1978). The fact that many of these offices were sold when the crown was in desperate financial need also meant that offices generally went to anyone who could be persuaded to take them, rather than (again in contrast with England) being used to reshape the bureaucracy or gain greater autonomy from the nobility (cf. Perroy, 1959). As time progressed, the *noblesse de robe* emerged as a distinct class, although even in the eighteenth century its distinctness from the older nobility should not be exaggerated. In the sixteenth century, however, the landowning nobility appears to have retained its authority even among those holding government office (Heller, 1977b; Guenne, 1963; Contamine, 1972). Even explicit conceptions of the state recognized its function as a preserver and protector of its aristocratic subjects' interests (Stocker, 1971).

If the actual structure of power (as opposed to formal authority) means anything, therefore, France seems to provide a better candidate for Swanson's category of "limited centralist" regime, and England seems to have functioned more effectively as a "centralist" regime. France had a more immanental sovereign state in principle because the Estates General was infrequently convened and a national assembly similar to Parliament had not emerged. But in practice the king shared authority with the judiciary and regional parlements, the members of which acted as representatives of their constituent estates, and the nobility exercised strong influence over the financial and administrative functions of the state. The experience of political authority in England, comparatively, came much more directly and totally from the crown, which embodied not only the state but, after 1534, the church as well. Perhaps those who framed policies toward the Reformation were more deeply influenced by political theory than by political practice, but if ideas were to reflect their experience of the distribution of political authority, France rather than England should have abandoned immanentist conceptions of God and supported the Reformation. The manner in which power was actually structured does, however, provide a clue to the mechanism that was probably at work linking state structures to Reformation outcomes.

IMPLEMENTING RELIGIOUS POLICIES

That clue is the degree of relative autonomy that the state in England enjoyed vis-à-vis the ruling aristocracy, as compared with the high degree of dependence on the rural elite in the case of France. Virtually everywhere in Europe the church was deeply integrated into the moral economy of rural life. Religious rituals mirrored the patron-client relations on which rural society depended, physical arrangements in churches and in religious festivals dramatized the status of landlords in relation to peasants, the church provided public goods from which peasants could draw in times of exceptional hardship as well as offices for

the absorption of younger sons of the nobility, and fiscal relations between the church and the state played an important role in maintaining
tax exemptions for the nobility (e.g., see Burguière, 1978; Bossy, 1973,
1975, 1981; Febvre, 1977; Tazbir, 1975; Christian, 1981; Kagan,
1981; Mousnier, 1979). In return, the nobility generally contributed
heavily to the maintenance and defense of the church (Addy, 1970; Dickinson, 1979; Goubert, 1973; Cipolla, 1976). For the state to adopt policies that threatened this structure as radically as did the teachings of
many of the reformers, the structure of power obviously had to give
state actors a high degree of autonomy relative to the landed ruling
class. The importance of this relation can be seen clearly in the different
policies pursued by the state toward the Reformation in England and
France.

Virtually every account of the Reformation in England emphasizes
the decisive role of the state (cf. Elton, 1958:226; Parker, 1966:47;
Cross, 1976:53; Slavin, 1973:117–152; Dickens, 1964). Although religious unrest was in evidence at the popular level as well, it was the state
that succeeded in imposing the Reformation, as it were, "from above."
Incentive for the state's action came, of course, from Henry's famous divorce case (Elton, 1958; Heal, 1980; Smith, 1953). Had it not been for
a favorable arrangement in the structure of power, however, Henry
probably would not have been able to carry out successfully the policies
he initiated. Nor does the English Reformation appear to have been
strictly the result of a rationally calculated strategy on the part of high
officials. Rather, solutions to immediate problems were developed on a
piecemeal basis but within the constraints and opportunities provided
by the structure of the state. Thus, in 1534 (a year after the secret marriage to Anne Boleyn) Henry was proclaimed head of the church, placing the entire jurisdiction of ecclesiastical affairs under the state's control. Having accomplished this with only minor resistance, he launched
a general investigation of the monasteries the next year, culminating in a
series of dissolutions that included virtually all monastic lands by 1539.
In 1540, all church wealth and property was declared vested in the
crown.

In initiating these reforms, the crown received strong assistance from
Parliament (Lehmberg, 1970). As already shown, Parliament had ceased
to function as a political voice for the landlords and was temporarily
dominated by a coalition of cloth merchants, burgesses, and royal officials closely allied to the crown. In 1529, the "Reformation Parliament"
canceled the king's debts, providing greater room to maneuver in nego-

tiations with the pope. In 1531, it imposed an indictment and fine on the clergy for acting without respect for the king's rights. The next year it forced the clergy to surrender ecclesiastical law to the jurisdiction of the crown and forbade the granting of papal annates. A year later the Act of Restraint of Appeals to Rome prohibited appeals from domestic courts to courts outside the realm, and in 1534, the Act of Supremacy named the king as supreme head of the Church of England.

Merchants and burgesses played a significant role in the Reformation Parliament's actions. A number of interests were reflected in their decisions, not the least of which were the facts that the church had long been accused of restricting trade and that popular support for reformed teachings was relatively widespread in the towns (Lehmberg, 1970:81–82; Palliser, 1979:233–234; Clark, 1977:40; Cross, 1980:210; Manning, 1969:243; Parker, 1966:19; Brigden, 1981:286). Nevertheless, the crown was by no means the dependent partner in this alliance. Merchants were personally beholden to the crown for trading privileges and for the crown's promotion of favorable foreign relations. In addition, the crown had strong support from ecclesiastical appointees, royal officials, and temporal lords as well as merchants.

Predictably, the rural nobility opposed the reforms. Uprisings developed in 1536 and again in 1549 at least partly in response to the crown's religious policies (Cross, 1976:83; Dodds and Dodds, 1915; Dickens, 1964; Davies, 1968; James, 1970). Nothing symbolized the crown's expanding influence in the countryside quite as dramatically as the sight of local religious treasures being loaded onto royal wagons for shipment to London. By this time, however, the crown's control was sufficiently complete to quash incipient rebellions. Family alliances, patronage and royal office, as well as a centralized army, provided what was needed to carry out the reforms. As elsewhere, danger always lay in the possibility of leading nobles entering directly into alliances with foreign powers and receiving financial and military assistance against the king in return. Some intrigue of this sort did develop between the nobility and agents of the French and Spanish kings. However, Henry's political and economic strength was largely successful at minimizing these risks through diplomatic agreements with France and Spain.

In contrast, the Reformation in France was unable to secure ratification even in the cities where its popular support was strongest. One of the inhibiting factors was the continuing strength of the landlords relative to the local merchant classes and agents of the state. What Protestantism depended on, as elsewhere, was sponsorship from the state or from municipalities that had sufficient autonomy from the landed sector to risk such actions. Where this autonomy was at least partially present, as in Lyons, Protestantism experienced a degree of success. In other areas it either failed to take root initially (as in Bordeaux) or else ran into trouble in attempting to gain official support (Benedict, 1981; Major, 1964). In Rouen, for example, the parlementaires were largely of rural landowning stock, even though they maintained residences in the city, and most had extensive landholdings from which the greatest share of their incomes derived (Dewald, 1980). These elites also loaned considerable sums of money to the crown. When religious unrest broke out in Rouen, they immediately supported neighboring landlords in suppressing it (Benedict, 1981; Nicholls, 1980). In Lyons, a similar uprising was also forcibly suppressed; in Reims, Troyes, and Toulouse, town councils' policies were also heavily influenced by the landed elite (Galpern, 1976:123–140; Mentzer, 1973).

At the level of central regime, religious policies also reflected the deep influence of the nobility over the state. Gallicanism had given the king considerable power over the church, and the Concordat of 1516 had extended these privileges. In material terms the king benefited from his share of the tithe and from loans granted by the church (Salmon, 1975:79–89). Yet the nobility benefited to an even greater extent than the king by protecting the church. Of the 129 appointments to ecclesiastical office made as a result of the Concordat of 1516, for example, 123 went to the nobility (Edelstein, 1974). By mid century virtually all appointments to high ecclesiastical office were under the control not of the crown but of the Guise faction among the nobility. In local and provincial assemblies the nobles also managed to bring the clergy more completely under their control by securing appointments to these assemblies for members of the middle clergy (whom they could influence) while excluding members of the upper clergy (Major, 1960:136).

During the religious wars that broke out during the latter half of the sixteenth century, a significant number of the nobility did become supporters of the Protestant cause. But by this time the regime had become sufficiently weakened that power was effectively being contested by different factions of the nobility itself. Protestantism served as an oppositional ideology for the less powerful of these factions (Galpern, 1976; Wood, 1980; Kingdon, 1956; Harding, 1978). During the formative period of the Reformation itself, it was chiefly the lack of autonomy in relation to the nobility that restricted the state's options in dealing with the reformers and their supporters. Much in the same way in which the state in Poland and in Spain remained closely tied to the nobility, the state in France was unable to seriously pursue a policy of active support for the Reformation. England, in contrast, experienced a greater degree of separation between the state and the rural elite, just as in Sweden and Denmark and in many of the imperial cities in central Europe, which expanded its options in dealing with the Reformation.

For the Reformation to be carried out successfully in England, certainly to a greater extent than in Scandinavia or the German territories, given the institutional scale of the church in England, an effective bureaucracy was also imperative. The task of dissolving the monasteries was no mean achievement. Assessments of ecclesiastical lands and treasuries had to be undertaken, those that were acquired and retained by the state had to be efficiently managed, and the remainder had to be disposed of in a timely and profitable manner. The mere task of surveying properties and crops was immense, let alone the task of dealing with litigation, the resettlement of clergy, and claims of tenets. In this period state officials often did not act in ways that clearly maximized the state's interests, but they seldom engaged in projects that were totally beyond the grasp of existing organizational capacities or that would be of obviously greater benefit to rival groups than to the state itself. In the case of the monastic dissolutions, it seems doubtful that state officials would have been as ready to promote the Reformation as they were had the organizational means of doing so not already been in existence. These means, however, had gradually come into being as a result of the reforms put into practice in managing the crown's extensive lands, in dealing with local justice, in creating ad hoc commissions for special projects, and in organizing the state's fiscal matters (Elton, 1953). Studies of the revenues derived from sales of monastic lands do indicate that these properties were often disposed of at lower than market values and to purchasers who did, in fact, manage to increase their influence in local affairs as a result (Knowles and Hadcock, 1971; Youings, 1954; Habakkuk, 1958; Trevor-Roper, 1953; Nef, 1964:215–239). Nevertheless, the crown did succeed to a large extent in minimizing these problems through systematic division and reorganization of monastic holdings and by developing an efficient system of settling legal disputes. Overall, the potential for ecclesiastical properties to be exploited by members of the bureaucracy for private gain or to cultivate personal patronage networks appears to have been minimized (Elton, 1953:206). In France, by comparison, it seems unlikely that the central bureaucracy could have sustained a similar enterprise. Anderson (1974:90), for example, argues that one of the principal reasons for the continuing regional autonomy in provincial government in general was simply the central bureaucracy's incapacity to manage affairs on a national scale. In short, the execution of the Reformation depended not only on relative state autonomy but also on an autonomy that had developed into an effective organizational structure.

STATE STRUCTURES AND IDEOLOGY

This interpretation of the Reformation in England and France does not entirely rule out the possibility that some correspondence may have also existed between immanent or transcendent concepts of the state and of the divine in the two societies. The degree of centralization actually present in the English state as compared with the fragmentation of power in France casts some doubt on this possibility. In terms of actual authority, the state in England was experienced as highly powerful and centralized, and this authority was clearly symbolized in the person of the king, so much so that contemporaries often described him as "the most sovereign king England ever had" (Pickthorn, 1934). In France the actual experience of authority consisted of competing regional, representative, judicial, and executive bodies that clearly functioned on behalf of their constituencies, especially the nobility, in ways that seriously constrained the implementation of royal policy. The evidence also casts doubt on the clarity of the distinction between immanence and transcendence in the two societies. England appears to have backed itself into the Reformation, almost unwittingly, by contesting the pope's authority over the state and by taking action against the economic power of the church, rather than directly challenging the immanental view of the supernatural; indeed, those who actively did so were punished for religious heresy. France, on the other side, witnessed a striking amount of support for the reformed teachings both at the popular level and among certain segments of the state itself.

But the main purpose of reviewing the historical evidence has been to suggest an alternative perspective that highlights the role of social resources in bringing about ideological change. An advantage of this approach is that hidden psychological affinities need not be posited as the primary connection between social arrangements and ideologies. The Reformation was clearly more than a set of beliefs: it constituted a far-reaching restructuring of the moral order, and this restructuring appears to have required a highly favorable set of social circumstances in order to have been carried out successfully. The nature of these institutional arrangements is readily observable in the historical material. In contrast, the difficulties faced in attempting to establish a direct attitudinal link between authority and belief seem nearly insurmountable. A closer look at one specific episode—the *placards* affair—will serve to illustrate this point.

According to most accounts, the *placards* affair marked a significant turning point in the history of the French Reformation. Before this event, reformed teachings seem to have had some chance of succeeding in France; after it, this chance seems to have been virtually nil. The episode itself consisted simply of a number of posters, denouncing the Mass in quite outspoken terms, being posted in Paris and in a number of other French cities, including one allegedly attached to the door of the king's bedchamber. In many respects the *placards* affair offers evidence that seems to support Swanson's interpretation. First, the *placards'* message directly attacked the sacredness of the elements of the Mass, thus attesting to the importance of Swanson's emphasis on the idea of immanence. Second, the king and other officials of state appear to have been infuriated by the *placards,* suggesting that they may have at least intuitively felt the correspondence between an attack on immanence in the Mass and their own authority. Third, a relatively widespread popular uprising broke out in Paris in reaction against the *placards,* suggesting that high state officials may not have been the only ones to sense the connection between immanence in the Mass and public authority. Finally, the king himself only a few days later led a public processional to restore order in which his sovereignty was dramatically reassociated with the Mass, particularly as he stopped at numerous points along the way to partake of the Mass at temporary altars that had been erected for this purpose. From this series of events, a close connection between the sovereign conception of the state and the immanent sense of sacredness in the church's central sacrament is apparent. When Protestant heretics challenged this sense of immanence, their attack was perceived as a deep defilement of the state itself, which in turn lent both its ceremonial and coercive powers to restoring the moral order.

A closer consideration of the *placards* affair, however, casts a relatively broad shadow across this interpretation. At no time did the perpetrators of the affair point any of their attacks at the state itself, a fact that seems surprising if the association between the Mass and the state was as close as it has been alleged to be. They may have refrained from attacking the state on grounds of expediency; yet they clearly stood to lose as much by challenging the church as the state. Even the *placard* attached to the king's door turns out to have been apocryphal, in all likelihood, because many of the early accounts fail to mention it. Moreover, the intent of the affair seems to have been to challenge the Mass itself rather than anything about the state because the posters were put up so that devout Catholics would see them the next morning on their way to Mass. The event was not timed to coincide with any public ceremony of state; indeed, the king and much of his retinue were away from Paris at the time. The perpetrators, of course, simply may have been unaware of the implicit political message in their attack on the Mass. Yet the official reaction is also puzzling. Although reports of the king's anger seem to be fairly well substantiated, action against the perpetrators was not initiated by the sovereign himself but, without consulting him, by the theological faculty of the Sorbonne and then by the ecclesiastical members of the Parlement of Paris. The king actually sought to downplay the event (and did later reduce some of the sentences), but found the wheels of justice already in motion by the time he returned to Paris. Indeed, the king's reaction to the attack on the Mass can hardly be taken as evidence of an implicit connection between political sovereignty and divine immanence, for at the very time of the affair the court was engaged in negotiations with some of the reformers to reach a conciliar compromise on the very meaning of the sacrament (Knecht, 1978). Finally, very much cannot be made of the fact that a popular uprising occurred in defense of the Mass. Similar reactions occurred in England, Holland, and in many of the German towns during this period as well. Iconoclasm never went unopposed. Nor was the uprising in Paris entirely representative of public sentiment. As already noted, as many as a quarter of the population seems to have been sympathetic with Protestantism around this time. The question in the case of Paris, therefore, should focus not on the popular uprising, but on why the state was constrained to favor this reaction rather than place itself behind the reforms.

The ambiguities involved in interpreting the *placards* affair illustrate the difficulty in pinning down the intervening processes supposedly operating in the correspondence approach to ideology. Ultimately the process depends on implicit connections that may not be evident even to the actors involved in the situation and that may be contradicted by their own behavior. Even if a formal correlation can be demonstrated, little can be said about why this correlation exists. Closer examination of the actors involved is likely to reveal a variety of orientations and competing motives. In addition, the presence of a motivational predisposition toward a particular ideology does not in itself tell anything about the conditions under which these predispositions can be realized.

TOWARD A SOCIOLOGICAL FOCUS

The correspondence hypothesis offers a plausible approach to ideology if ideology is depicted as simply the atomized beliefs of individuals. In developing their particularistic worldviews, individuals may be predisposed toward certain ideas because of affinities between personal experience and these ideas (e.g., favoring paternalistic images of God in paternalistic families). But this is an extremely limited view of ideology. Rather than being depicted as sets of subjective beliefs, ideology needs to be recognized as a constitutive feature of social order itself. Ideology requires social resources to be produced and maintained, it defines moral obligations that influence the distribution of social resources, and it becomes institutionalized in organizations, in professional roles, in collective rituals, and in relations with the state. Neither the Catholic church nor the Protestant opposition was simply a set of subjective beliefs, available for individual adoption in the free market of ideas; both were ideological institutions of sufficient magnitude that specific characteristics of the state were required for their institutionalization to be protected or eroded.

Emphasizing the role of social resources shifts the burden of explanation from psychological processes to sociological variables. Rather than accounting for the presence of ideology in terms of its subjective appeal, a structural approach emphasizes the embeddedness of ideology in social arrangements. To institutionalize a new ideology, therefore, requires a set of social conditions that permits resources to be expended in ways that further ideological innovation. In the present case, these conditions consisted chiefly of relative autonomy on the part of the state, financially and administratively, from the landed ruling class. This autonomy gave agents of the state in England certain options in dealing with religious reforms that were not open in France. This is not to say that officials in either country were favorably disposed toward the Reformation or that they set out on a rationally calculated course of support or opposition. In both countries officials did what was their chief responsibility to do: maintain public order, protect the society from external threat, and protect their own power from being interfered with or dissipated. In responding to immediate problems along these fronts, Henry VIII had options available that gradually favored the Reformation; Francis I had options available that increasingly shut the door on reform.

In neither case was the relation between state structures and ideological *content* strictly determinate. Even to suggest that a single factor such as state authority could have determined the essential content of a movement as vast and as complex as the Reformation strains the bounds of credibility. In terms of the correspondence hypothesis itself, it is difficult to defend consistently the idea that experiences of state sovereignty alone were the determining factor because many other kinds of social experience could also have conceivably conditioned religious ideas. The present emphasis on structural conditions affecting the availability of resources focuses more on the timing and social location of ideology than on its specific content. The Reformation became institutionalized at about the same time under roughly equivalent conditions in a number of different sections of Europe, but its content even within particular countries was highly diverse. What an institutional approach offers is a means of highlighting the social resources that become available directly or indirectly to ideological movements. These resources shape the social location an ideological movement comes to occupy, and this location in turn may have decisive consequences for some of the specific ideological forms that become emphasized. In the Reformation, for example, the moderation of the reforms in England as opposed to many of the urban reforms in central Europe appears to have been influenced by the fact that the king's control, however extensive, was nevertheless limited at the local level by other constituencies, whereas in central Europe many of the more extreme reforms took place in limited urban contexts where the magistracy had fewer competing power groups with which to contend. Or in a different context, as noted previously, Fulbrook (1983) has suggested that much of the difference in the political orientations that came to be associated with Puritanism and Pietism, which were quite similarly theologically, can be accounted for by the different arrangement of power groups in seventeenth-century England as opposed to eighteenth-century Prussia.

It remains to draw together several threads of a more general nature that bear on the relation between states and ideologies. Implicit in the approach taken here is an attempt to reformulate the relation between states and ideologies in a way that deemphasizes the idea of legitimation. This idea is clearly important to the understanding of modern states, but its weaknesses as an analytic tool are sufficiently apparent that it should not be the only way of conceiving the relation between states and ideologies. One of the, albeit avoidable, problems to which discussions of legitimation often fall victim is the tendency to assume that the existence of an ideology implies it has a positive legitimating function in relation to the state or ruling class. Another, perhaps more serious, problem is the tendency to attribute the existence of an ideology to the fact that it seems to fulfill a legitimating function. What the present example illustrates is a different causal model in which certain state structures make more or less likely the possibility of a given ideology becoming institutionalized. Having attained the resources to become institutionalized, an ideology *may* or *may not* work to the benefit of the state. In the case of England, for example, the Reformation provided Henry with substantial sums of money, which postponed the fiscal problems of his administration, but it is arguable whether or not the Reformation contributed stability to the throne at any point during the next two centuries.

Finally, the issue of state autonomy warrants comment. The manner in which this concept has been used here differs from its usage in several prominent discussions. Generally, state autonomy has been conceived in terms of *interests* (i.e., as conditions under which the state pursues its own interests rather than those of a ruling class or external interest group). The difficulty with this formulation has been identifying the state's interests as opposed to the interests of other groups (especially when these interests may overlap). Here, state autonomy has been conceptualized in terms of a specific *relationship* (i.e., its relationship administratively and financially to the landed ruling class). No asssumptions were made about the state's intrinsic interests as opposed to those of the landed elite. Rather, it was argued that a degree of fiscal and administrative autonomy from the landed elite gave the state certain options that it otherwise may not have had. In some cases these options clearly favored the rising commercial classes; in others, holders of bureaucratic office; and in others, the longer term growth of the economy as a whole. But for the institutionalization of a major ideological reform, such as Protestantism, state autonomy clearly played an important role. It essentially supplied a concentrated pool of resources that were not under the control of the landed ruling class, thus providing the reformers with a means of institutionalizing their claims. This function, it should be noted in concluding, does not appear limited to the sixteenth century. As the state expanded both functionally and administratively, it has in fact provided an increasingly important pool of resources that influence the institutionalization of ideology.

CHAPTER TEN

Conclusion

At the outset, distinctions were drawn among four levels of cultural analysis: subjective, structural, dramaturgic, and institutional. In the explorations that have been presented these distinctions have served as general guidelines. It remains to consider explicitly what has been discovered about the uses and limitations of each. These considerations will also serve as a basis for some broader conclusions about the purposes of cultural analysis and the problem of meaning and moral order.

LEVELS OF ANALYSIS: USES AND LIMITATIONS

To review briefly, it was suggested in Chapter 1 that culture has often been approached in the social sciences with a strong emphasis on the subjective. Beliefs, attitudes, internalized norms and values, subjective predispositions, moods, motivations, meanings, and mentalities have constituted the definitional components of culture. Participant observers have sought to gauge the deeper meanings of their subjects' outlooks; survey researchers have probed the patterns of attitudes and orientations; theoreticians have posited subjective states as the key variables linking ideas and experience. At the core of subjective analyses has lain the problem of meaning—personal meaning and well-being, the capacity to construct reality in a meaningful way, the subjective meanings of symbols and events. The broader theoretical and epistemological underpinnings of this emphasis on meaning (as shown in Chapter 2) are firmly rooted in both the classical and neoclassical traditions.

The structural level of analysis, in contrast, pays relatively little attention to the individual or the problem of meaning. Its emphasis is on the objectified social presence of cultural forms. Symbols—utterances, acts, objects, and events—are assumed to exist in some ways independent of their creators and to take forms not entirely determined by the needs of individuals. That is, patterns among symbols cannot be understood with reference alone to the requirements for meaning, security, or personal integration of individuals. Rather, the elements of culture are arranged in relation to each other, forming identifiable patterns. Understanding the structure of culture, therefore, requires paying attention to the configurations, categories, boundaries, and connections among cultural elements themselves. Although this level of analysis has been less commonly incorporated into sociological investigations of culture, its theoretical foundations are firmly established in the poststructuralist literature, and some of the classical theories contain ideas that point as much to this approach as they do to the subjective approach.

The dramaturgic level builds on the structural by adding considerations about the relations between patterns of symbols and broader social relations. Although it remains important at this level to examine the patterns among symbols that give them coherence, these patterns are assumed to play an expressive role in dramatizing and affirming the moral obligations on which social interaction depends—the moral order. It is again assumed at this level of analysis that cultural elements are not exclusively (and perhaps not even primarily) shaped by individual motives and meanings. Rather, the *sociological* importance of cultural elements arises decisively from the fact that they take place within a matrix of moral obligations and are, in turn, shaped by the structure of social relations. From this perspective, the kinds of cultural elements likely to be of greatest interest are those that are objectified in concrete social settings. Ideologies and ideological movements, therefore, acquire special significance, as do the ritual aspects of social behavior. In both cases, the degree of uncertainty present among moral obligations is a significant consideration in attempting to understand the conditions giving rise to cultural forms.

At the institutional level of analysis, all of the foregoing assumptions remain in effect, but greater emphasis is given to the role of social resources in producing and maintaining cultural forms. In a direct sense, time and money are required for ideas to become part of the culture.

Less directly perhaps, the very moral obligations that ideologies articulate are concerned with the control of social resources and are likely to be influenced by the type and amount of resources to be controlled. Because the connection between ideas and resources is always precarious, those ideas that survive and that gain social importance are likely to be the ones that become institutionalized. Regular and well-organized means of extracting resources from the broader environment and of channeling these resources into specified types of cultural production greatly enhance the chances of survival of any given ideological form. As the preceding two chapters in particular have shown, this process typically depends on constraints and opportunities built into the structure of the broader society. The likelihood of any cultural form becoming institutionalized, it has been argued, depends especially on conditions affecting its autonomy; its access to political, social, and economic resources; its legitimacy in relation to broader cultural patterns; and a degree of internal communication and organization.

In much of the foregoing the structural, dramaturgic, and institutional levels of analysis were emphasized. The subjective level was given less attention because it already represents a well-established tradition in the study of culture. As a matter of strategy, it appeared more useful to point out the limitations of the subjective approach and to explore ways of applying the other three. In the process, only the advantages of the structural, dramaturgic, and institutional approaches were considered, and even these were often dealt with implicitly rather than explicitly. Any conceptual or methodological tool brings its own weaknesses as well as its strengths. Some candid reflections on the uses and limitations of each of the four levels of cultural analysis, therefore, would seem to be in order.

SUBJECTIVE ANALYSES

The criticisms of the subjective approach that were raised in Chapters 1 and 2 dealt mainly with the problem of meaning. It was suggested that, for all its intrinsic interest, the problem of meaning may have become more of a detriment than an asset to the analysis of culture. Implicit in that assertion, of course, is an emphasis on *culture* as a focus of inquiry. One can obviously choose to investigate the problem of meaning for its own sake. The difficulty lies in the fact that so much of what passes as cultural inquiry has actually focused on the problem of meaning that the two have often become synonymous. There are exceptions,

of course. Especially at the institutional level, studies that have had little
to do with the problem of meaning have been made. But the more common tendency has been a strong infusion of questions about meaning
into the very theoretical and methodological assumptions of cultural
analysis.

The limitations associated with emphasizing the subjective, perhaps
not surprisingly, have both theoretical and methodological counterparts. That is, certain biases are built in with respect to the investigator's
choice of problems and concepts, including the assumptions typically
made about the processes shaping cultural patterns. In addition, these assumptions produce operative problems as soon as the investigator attempts to study culture in accordance with the accepted canons of social
research.

The methodological limitation posed by the subjective approach
arises principally from the difficulties associated with making verifiable
claims about subjective phenomena. As argued in Chapter 2, the subjective meanings evoked in a person's mind by any given symbol or complex of symbols are likely to be highly idiosyncratic and at least margin-
ally unstable, because of their contingency on the immediate context,
and are also likely to be richly interwoven with the person's biographi-
cal and intellectual experience. If an investigator sets out with the task
of providing a complete, rich description of some symbol or event's
meaning to an individual, it will be necessary, first, to do an incredible
amount of probing into the individual's experiences, background, cognitive frameworks, and emotional states of which the individual may not
even be fully aware. Second, it will be necessary the very next day to re-
peat the entire process because new experiences, contexts, and memo-
ries (including those of having been a research subject) will all alter the
meanings the person constructs to at least some small, or possibly large,
extent. Finally, one must not assume that the information gained can be
generalized exactly to any other individual or situation. To engage in a
phenomenological or hermeneutic analysis of these meanings, therefore,
is unlikely to result in any readily verifiable or compellingly cumulative
type of knowledge.

Social scientists have not been unmindful of this problem. Several leading ways of resolving it have in fact been evident in the literature. One is
to draw a sharp distinction between the interpretive sciences that focus
on meanings and the more positivistic sciences that are devoted to the pursuit of objectified, cumulative knowledge. A second is to diminish the
problems of probing subjective meanings by arguing for the possibility of

a kind of empathic or intuitive understanding of these meanings. A third is to deemphasize their subjectivity and variability by demonstrating the existence of shared or "intersubjective" meanings.

But none of these alternatives is entirely satisfactory. Differentiating sharply between the interpretive and the positivistic sciences gives up too much too quickly. Many aspects of culture can be treated as observable data and can be investigated with rigorous, replicable methods. Even if cultural analysis is regarded as an interpretive science, the need remains to put its claims on as solid an empirical footing as possible. (Nor should it be assumed that other phenomena in the social sciences simply conform more readily to the positivistic model.)[1] Interpretation, it appears, should be acknowledged as the epistemological stance from which all sociological investigation is conducted, not just the investigation of culture; but interpretation should not provide an excuse for bad methods, subjectivism, and analyses lacking a strong evidentiary base. Relying on empathic or intuitive methods may work in some cases, for example, where the objects of investigation are either widely and consensually understood or where they are completely esoteric.[2] But in most instances, skeptics are unlikely to be satisfied. Some imaginative insights that strike a resonant chord with the sensitive reader may be gained, but such insights need to be received cautiously in light of any broader claims that may be offered about "the meaning" of an event or about the subject's "worldview" or mode of "constructing reality." If it can be shown that the materials at issue are not really subjective but rather that they are shared (intersubjective), these problems are less serious. In that case, however, it can legitimately be asked what the level of analysis actually is. The very basis for making claims about the shared quality of meanings is likely to have shifted to the level of discourse and symbolic behavior. Thus it may be well simply to acknowledge that the level of analysis has shifted away from the problem of subjective meaning.

As noted earlier, one of the symptoms that seems particularly indicative of the methodological problems faced at the subjective level is that investigators typically do not have much to say about subjective meanings, despite their claims, and often appear to rely more on other kinds of evidence. Studies of cat massacres, coronations, and Balinese cockfights are interesting because they provide us with an interpretation of the event, because they put it in a set of cultural contexts that enhances its meaningfulness, but they do not actually tell us what "the meaning" of the event is. Although the stated objective may be to interpret the "meaning" of an idea or event, what is usually presented is only an assessment in terms of broader cultural or social patterns. The investigator develops his or her interpretation by describing a context or framework of events, but actually does not reveal what actors in the situation may have thought or felt.[3] In other instances—especially ones involving firsthand interviewing or participation—stronger claims may be made, but here too the results need to be regarded with caution. Although words such as "moods" and "motivations" are likely to be employed, the account actually consists of discourse—both the subjects' and the observer's—and requires an effort to identify underlying patterns or relations with behavior. Seldom does it genuinely exhaust the subjects' own subjectively held meanings.

At the theoretical level, the limitations inherent in the subjective approach consist mainly of underestimating the significance of social, as opposed to psychological, processes and of attributing too much to the needs and interests of the individual. As previous chapters have shown, almost every topic that cultural analysts have addressed—from religious rituals to witch-hunts, to the origins of millenarian movements, to the cultural factors giving rise to modern science, to the sources of geographic variation in the Reformation—has been subjected to an essentially psychological interpretation. Characteristically, the theoretical connection seen between social structure and cultural outcomes has been one involving moods and motivations: religious movements arise from subjective deprivation, ritual enactments occur because of subjective anxieties, science developed in the seventeenth century because Englishmen were properly motivated, and the Reformation was adopted because it corresponded with people's experience of the polity. In each case, some subjective state has served as a kind of mysterious process relating social structure to cultural patterns. Sociologists, it appears, have had a marvelous propensity to advance psychological interpretations of culture rather than focus on the collective variables of their own stock and trade. Rather than examining what could be observed at the social level itself—discourse, dramatic acts, resource arrangements, means of cultural production—investigators have simply posited a "black box"— a subjective state that could not be observed directly.

In other instances, these kinds of arguments have been carried further, influencing the *substance* of theoretical interpretations as well. That is, not only do subjective states serve as a theoretical link between social conditions and cultural phenomena, but a specific kind of cultural pattern is also emphasized as a result of assumptions being made about the nature of these subjective states. The clearest example of this kind of reasoning is the wholistic view of culture in many of the neoclassical theories (discussed in Chapter 2). Assuming a need for personal integration, these theories went on to argue by analogy that cultural systems provided meaning and integration for whole institutions in much the same way that meaning was provided at the personal level. In some of the more extreme Marxist theories of culture—for example, Hessen's interpretation of Newton—assumptions about personal experience have also been allowed to color the entire interpretation given for a cultural development. These interpretations may at times have value, but they tend generally to obscure the communicative aspects of culture that derive from its broader location in the society. Usually there is a lot more going on than just the "objectification" of the reality constructions of individuals or the shaping of attitudes by the experiences of many disaggregated individuals.

It should be apparent, therefore, that the subjective level of cultural analysis—taken alone—is constrained by rather serious methodological and theoretical limitations. As in any other approach, this is only to be expected. The purpose of pointing out these limitations is not to generate defensive arguments between the users and opponents of a particular perspective, but to clarify costs and benefits likely to be associated with adopting a research strategy. The benefits—or uses—associated with the subjective approach also need to be appreciated. Two such uses, in particular, warrant consideration.

The first of these uses is as an exploratory tool of inquiry. Many of the objections that can be raised about the subjective level of cultural analysis focus on matters of evidence, proof, and replicability. Ideally, arguments need to be based on rigorous, observable cultural materials rather than assertions about unobservable inner conditions. In exploratory stages of cultural research, however, efforts to gain an intuitive feeling for what is happening are likely to be of considerable value. The researcher may not know what all the subjective meanings present in a situation are. But some effort to elicit these meanings and to develop empathy can be a valuable aid to the research process. Among other things, such subjective impressions can orient one to the complexities of cultural patterns and can yield valuable clues about what is important in the situation or transferable to other situations. Ideas about what is being communicated suggest what cultural patterns may be most important to investigate. This, of course, has been the principal argument behind the explicit use of such tools as *verstehen* or ethnographic immersion in the social sciences. Analyses of culture can benefit greatly from these methods. At the same time, cultural research should be pressed as much as possible toward the use of other kinds of evidence as well.

The second use is as a vehicle for examining commitment. In many cases the object of inquiry is not culture alone, or even culture in relation to social conditions, but culture in relation to the person. Problems pertaining to what might be referred to as the "social psychology of culture" are indeed quite prominent. They arise in studies of religious belief; in research on self-concepts, stress, alienation, and personal adjustment; in surveys of political opinions and voter preferences; and in any number of inquiries in which ideas are assumed to bear on individuals' uses of time and energy. In all of these cases, what is at issue is the question of a relationship between particular cultural elements and the person. Whether a person is "committed to" an idea or belief is the heart of the matter. From the standpoint of the individual, commitment is important because it reveals something about how one is likely to think and behave. From the standpoint of the cultural element, commitment is also important because it signifies a kind of resource that may enhance the viability of that cultural form (i.e., people who are willing to defend, disseminate, and enact an ideological pattern). With a relatively slight modification in perspective, the subjective level of analysis can be a useful tool for examining commitment. That modification is to think of commitment not primarily as a subjective state or inward predisposition, nor as "the meaning" of a cultural element, but as a relatively discrete and observable relation between a symbolic statement and the person. As suggested in Chapter 2, one aspect of the conditions that make any symbolic statement meaningful is a relation of sincerity between the statement and the person who utters it. Something that demonstrates the speaker's sincerity is likely to be built into the statement. What this consists of is actually quite close to the usual idea of commitment (i.e., the speaker is committed to or "really believes in" the statement that has been uttered). The virtue of this reformulation of the problem is that it renders as an issue worthy of investigation the very means by which commitment is expressed. Rather than assuming that commitment is simply an expression of some internal state of the individual, the researcher now must consider the cultural repertoire of utterances and actions that can be used to demonstrate commitment. Under different conditions, the same subjective propensity is likely to find expression in quite different ways. For example, whether a commitment to public service takes the form of defending capitalism, being a responsible parent, or engaging in volunteer work is obviously a matter of cultural definition. The subjective level serves quickly to move one toward cultural questions. Again, little may actually be learned about subjective meanings. But commitment, after all, is more than merely a subjective condition.

STRUCTURAL ANALYSES

This way of thinking about commitment actually comes close to suggesting the importance of moving from a subjective to a structural level of analysis. If both the person and a given symbolic statement are conceived of as cultural categories, then one way of thinking about commitment is as the relation between these two categories. Both the boundary separating them and the connections that allow them to be related are cultural constructions. The individual by no means drops out in structural analyses of culture. Rather, the individual is regarded as an entity about which discourse takes place. The relation between the individual as a cultural category and other cultural categories, therefore, can be examined. More generally, the structural approach is concerned with dissecting relations of this kind.

The main limitation of this approach is a dearth of theoretical propositions. Much of the theoretical literature has emphasized the idea of symbolic boundaries between opposites or the notion that such boundaries are often revealed by opposites (e.g., deviance/normality, male/female, etc.). The theoretical rationale for emphasizing opposites has in some of the structuralist literature been linked to ideas about binary structures in the brain and to assumptions of parallelism among pairs of opposites. It is not essential to adopt these extreme limiting assumptions, however, to recognize the importance of opposing symbolic categories as aspects of cultural order. In the discussion of moral codes (Chapter 3), some use was made of a looser conception of symbolic boundaries to suggest some of the conceptual distinctions on which moral commitments may depend. In general, however, little has been offered in the theoretical literature as guidelines to the kinds of structure that may be worthwhile investigating.

Another limitation of this approach is that applications seem to be particularly susceptible to the kinds of untestable psychological assumptions that have been criticized in conjunction with the subjective approach. The reason for this problem may lie in the fact that symbolic structures, as manifested in categories of discourse, are still largely presumed to reflect the cognitive or emotive processes of individuals. In discussing moral codes, for example, some strong assumptions were made about individuals' requirements for self-worth, absolution from guilt, and so on. These assumptions may have seemed necessary there, because issues of moral commitment were at stake, to a greater extent than they might in dealing with, say, categories of discourse about the state. In any case, such assumptions may not prove to be entirely dispensable even in deliberate efforts to shift away from the subjective. If so, they should at least be presented as *presuppositions* rather than empirical concepts that can actually be observed in cultural data.[4]

The structural approach, at present, must also be regarded as subject to limitations of established methods and, indeed, of clear canons of evidence. As with the subjective approach, efforts to document structural patterns in cultural materials often appear to succeed purely because the materials presented are from esoteric contexts, and the ethnographic depth of these materials gives the investigator a dispensation from skeptical criticisms. In more ordinary settings, the fact that cultural materials are readily observable may in some ways also mitigate this problem. In selecting cases to illustrate the ingredients of moral codes, for example, attention was deliberately restricted to these kinds of materials. Nevertheless, the problem that remains largely unresolved is how to establish the existence of a particular cultural category or symbolic boundary.

Established methods can go part way toward resolving this problem. For example, "content analysis" techniques can be used to establish the existence and frequency of relatively straightforward cultural categories and to demonstrate empirical correlations among the distributions of these categories. Survey data, analyzed with standard statistical techniques, can also be of value in determining whether various utterances tend to cluster together (as shown by the material concerning "Holocaust" in Chapter 4). These methods remain most limited in examining the nature of symbolic distinctions and connections themselves. Often the sheer presence of categories in the same contexts reveals little about how these categories are related. Imaginative analyses of these kinds of symbols generally cannot be reduced to a simple formula or be derived directly from reading a text or observing a ritual. They require the investigator to draw on a wider body of knowledge and experience. They are, again, essentially acts of interpretation. But the kinds of evidence used to create these interpretations still need to be disclosed as fully as possible. As suggested in Chapter 3, these relations are often precarious, fraught with ambivalence, and in need of periodic reaffirmation. Heroes and villains, connections with cultural authorities, poignant examples, deviance, and other symbolic violations are all likely to be important considerations in determining how symbolic categories are related.

It also bears noting that the paucity of formalized methods for examining cultural structures in the social sciences does not exhaust the possibilities of identifying such methods more broadly. Major advances have been made in recent years in disciplines such as artificial intelligence, cognitive psychology, and musicology, from which ideas might usefully be borrowed. To cite only one example, a study by Cerulo (1985) has presented a highly sophisticated method, drawing on insights from musicology, for comparing the structures of musical codes. Using these measures, the study was able to provide rigorous tests of propositions derived from Bernstein (1975) about the relations between social structure and elaborated or restricted codes. In a broader sense, the study suggested rich possibilities for developing mathematical measures of the form, complexity, and variability of such musical properties as melody, harmony, and rhythm.

The uses to which structural analyses of culture can be put are clearly limited, therefore, by the relative novelty of this approach in relation to established social scientific theories and methods. Nevertheless, at least four promising areas of application seem worthy of mention.

The first of these is deviance, the one area of study in which considerable use has already been made of the structural approach. As many of the examples presented in the chapters on moral codes and rituals suggested, deviance has often been recognized as one of the ways in which moral boundaries are expressed. Kai Erikson, as well as Mary Douglas, Foucault, and others, has seen this relation between deviance and symbolic structures. Other approaches, such as the familiar "labeling theory" of deviance, have also paid close attention to this relation. Often the thrust of this work has been more concerned with understanding deviance than with understanding culture. But the basis for further work paying greater attention to culture has been laid. The essential insight is that symbolic boundaries are often maintained by litanies of deviant events that reveal normality by their very violations of it.

Cultural change is the second area. Because the structural approach focuses on patterns among symbols themselves, it is especially appropriate for comparing differences in these patterns from one time period to another. A clear distinction must be drawn, however, between the structural approach and the ways in which cultural change has most often been examined. The usual method has been to trace the development of

particular ideas (e.g., race, death) or the evolution of broader cultural
abstractions (e.g., universalism, nationalism). Where the structural approach differs is in emphasizing categories, boundaries, relations, and
the symbols that express these structures. For example, rather than pursuing a study of church-state relations by tracing arguments about
church and state, a structural approach to cultural change would begin
by regarding both the concepts of "church" and of "state" as problematic cultural constructions, and then proceed by examining what was
categorized with each, how the boundary between the two was negotiated, and how symbolic events contributed over time to changes in these
definitions. Underlying this kind of study is the assumption that ideas
have a distinctly objective existence as cultural categories and that the
structural relations among these categories are at least as important to
examine as their content.

A third promising area of application is moral order. If, as argued in
a number of the foregoing chapters, uncertainties or ambiguities in the
moral order are likely sources of rituals, ideologies, or other cultural productions, then the nature of these uncertainties is clearly a problem
worth investigating. The structural approach is one method by which
these uncertainties might be examined. Assuming that moral obligations
constitute a kind of cultural code (as suggested in Chapter 3), then the
components of this code might be examined to discover points of uncertainty or ambiguity. What may loosely be termed "uncertainty" may,
on closer inspection, turn out to have its own decipherable patterns. The
loci of ambiguity may actually consist of disputes over the classification
of specific acts into broader categories, of problems in relating categories to one another, or of difficulty in maintaining the objectivity of certain categories. This kind of analysis, it has been suggested, can also be
applied to more traditional questions about the self or about commitment by comprehending these as cultural categories as well.

Finally, as an application of a more general kind, the structural approach seems well suited to the task of making culture a more objective
focus of inquiry. Much of the literature that deals with culture continues
to "look past" it, not so much (as Geertz suggested) by looking to the interests being served or to class relations, but by concentrating on the
meanings conveyed. Rather than treating culture as an object, to be investigated from the outside, studies have shown a preference for delving
into the midst of culture, exploring it from the inside. There is value in
doing this. But much is missed as well. The problem is somewhat akin to
participating in a conversation. The participant becomes so engrossed in

the content of the conversation that little awareness remains of the underlying rules by which the conversation is governed. A bystander, taking a more distanced perspective, may be in a better position to analyze what the participants are taking for granted. So it is with culture. The structural approach requires that a degree of distance be established.[5] The elements of culture must be treated almost as if they were tangible objects—building blocks—to be arranged, rearranged, and scrutinized in order to determine how they are put together. From such a process, greater awareness of the rules of communication (as Habermas has suggested) is the desired result. Such awareness can also play a valuable role as a foundation for relating cultural elements to other aspects of the social order.

DRAMATURGIC ANALYSES

From a sociological perspective, a key virtue of the dramaturgic level of analysis is that it incorporates an explicit *social* dimension into the study of culture. In suggesting that culture dramatizes something about the moral order, one necessarily raises questions about the broader social milieu in which culture exists and the influences that this milieu may have on culture. The foregoing chapters have implicitly adopted this perspective at a number of points. Although these explorations have touched on only a few of the many facets of analysis possible at this level, four important uses have been illustrated.

First, at a very general theoretical level, dramaturgic analyses of culture offer a distinct alternative to the kinds of social psychological explanations that have fallen into disrepute for lack of empirical confirmation. Deprivation as a source of ideological movements and anxiety as a source of ritual are two examples that have been considered at some length. The assumptions about psychological needs in these models have been widely challenged in the empirical literature as an inadequate basis for explaining the connections between cultural outcomes and social conditions. The dramaturgic approach substitutes the idea of moral order as the intervening link in these models. It suggests that ideologies, rituals, and other cultural phenomena may arise in response to social rather than psychological conditions. The role of symbolism, according to this view, may be less to resolve personal anxieties than to clarify the nature of social relations and expectations. In many cases, this type of argument seems at least worthy of serious consideration.

Second, a focus on the dramaturgic aspects of culture offers a theoretical extension of the conditions outlined by Habermas under which symbolic acts are likely to be meaningful. As discussed in Chapter 2, Habermas's formulation represents a significant recasting of the general problem of meaning. Shifting attention away from the subjective meaning of symbols, Habermas has attempted to emphasize instead the conditions under which a symbolic act is likely to be meaningful, where "meaningful" becomes a central theoretical concept in predicting the use, existence, survival, or distribution of a given symbolic act. It was seen that Habermas specified four types of conditions, each marked by a relation between the symbolic act and a relevant aspect of its environment: a relation with the speaker or actor, marked by sincerity or truthfulness; a relation with the external or factual world, marked by truth; a relation with language, marked by comprehensibility; and a relation with the social milieu, marked by legitimacy. The last of these clearly represents the domain of greatest interest to sociologists. However, Habermas's own specification of this relation is somewhat less than satisfactory. His view of the social milieu (in this context) emphasizes norms and values that give substantive legitimacy to a given symbolic act (e.g., like democratic values giving legitimacy to the act of voting). This kind of legitimacy is obviously important but does not exhaust the relations between symbolic acts and their social environments that may contribute meaningfulness. The dramaturgic emphasis on moral order broadens the relevant types of social conditions that may affect the meaningfulness of a symbolic act. In this conception, symbolic acts are likely to be meaningful if they articulate the nature of social relations. Articulation may occur through substantive legitimation or, more likely, by clarifying the positions and interests of actors in relation to one another.

A third important use is the role of uncertainty. In a more specific sense, several of the preceding explorations have pointed to the importance of uncertainty in the moral order as a source of cultural production. The idea on which this observation rests is that cultural forms dramatize (articulate, clarify, reaffirm) the character of moral obligations. Thus these dramatizations are likely to be in greater demand whenever the character of moral obligations becomes uncertain. If other things remain constant, uncertainty is likely to be increased by an addition of new actors, by greater numbers of available choices, and by more complex relations among actors. This kind of argument seems to have some empirical support in studies of the conditions under which rituals arise or attract interest and in studies of the origins of new ideological movements. Obviously, a great deal more needs to be done toward specifying and applying this type of argument to other areas.

Finally, in addition to simply articulating ideas about moral obligations, ideologies also reinforce these obligations. In this sense, ideologies exercise influence or control over the ways in which social resources may be distributed or expended. It was suggested in the context of discussing the relations between ideologies and social environments (Chapters 5 and 6) that one way of assessing the survival possibilities of an ideology is to consider its implications for controlling the moral order. If resources are quite heterogeneous, for example, an ideology that decouples moral obligations, permitting individuals a high degree of diversity, may have a high survival value. Here, the formal properties of an ideological system are said to bear an important relation to the kinds of moral obligations that are most conceivable. Again, this is little more than a suggestive hypothesis that stands in need of further elaboration.

The principal limitation that confronts the dramaturgic approach, as presently conceived, is a lack of theoretical specification concerning the core concept of moral order. Several competing conceptualizations of this idea are currently available in the sociological literature. One conceives of moral order as a kind of internalized set of norms or expectations. Another conceives of it as a set of intrinsic or deep commitments that are somehow more enduring or less instrumental than social exchange of a purely utilitarian variety. A third posits moral order as a kind of analytic element of any social relation (i.e., as the ordinary relation that may exist analytically independent of any goods and services that are exchanged).

Clearly, none of these conceptions seems entirely satisfactory. The idea of internalized expectations again introduces subjective elements that may be difficult to examine empirically. The idea of noninstrumental commitments obscures the fact that even instrumental commitments contain moral connotations and are dramatized ideologically (as seen in considering market behavior as a moral code). Conceiving of moral order as an analytic distinction may be most useful, but greater clarity is needed about how this distinction is to be made and what purpose it serves.

Lacking this kind of conceptual specificity, the dramaturgic approach remains subject to considerable theoretical ambiguity. It can be argued, perhaps compellingly, that cultural forms dramatize something about the character of social relations (i.e., that culture plays a communicative role). Yet any number of alternatives remains open for conceptualizing this aspect of culture. What seems essential, at minimum, is the idea that social relations require some degree of organization and that this organization is not supplied in all cases either by totally coercive power structures or by totally self-interested exchanges of goods and services. Even in coercive and self-interested relations, signals need to be sent about actors' positions and the courses of action they are likely to take. These signals constitute, on the one hand, the moral order and are, on the other hand, supplied by cultural forms such as ideologies and rituals.

INSTITUTIONAL ANALYSES

At the institutional level, cultural forms are regarded as having not only structural and dramaturgic qualities but also relations of dependence with social resources. Thus the role of social factors becomes particularly important to examine. Whereas dramaturgic approaches emphasize the symbolic messages about social relations that are often communicated unintentionally, institutional analyses focus mainly on social resources that are deliberately devoted to cultural production. This type of analysis obviously has close ties with fields of inquiry devoted to the study of specific cultural institutions, such as science, religion, education, and the mass media. For this reason, many of its applications have already become widely developed. However, to draw the contrast with other levels of cultural analysis, three of its more general uses can be enumerated.

The first is social resources. More than any of the others, the institutional level stresses the importance of social resources to the production and maintenance of cultural forms. In the preceding chapters, several models for considering the role of these resources were utilized. In Chapters 5 and 6, inferences about the general relations between such properties of social resources as quantity, heterogeneity, and stability and the selection of alternative cultural forms were developed from a population ecology model. In Chapter 7, some implications were drawn from world-system theory about the general effects of changes in social resources, such as expanding economic conditions or declining political positions, on the origins of various types of ideological movements. In Chapter 8, a similar set of theoretical assumptions was used to provide an interpretation of the conditions surrounding the early institutionalization of modern science. And in Chapter 9, more attention was given to the role of the state as a significant actor in the control of resources affecting cultural production. In all of these cases, it was assumed that cultural forms depend on an appropriate mix of social, economic, and political resources. Attention was also directed to the fact that these resources were linked to broader social patterns. Thus it was important to look not only at the internal dynamics of particular cultural movements, but also at their larger social environment.

Establishments and movements are the second general use. As suggested in Chapter 5, ideologies often appear to undergo a process of production, selection, and institutionalization. The last phase in this process generates sensitivity to the fact that ideological movements do not simply compete with one another on a more-or-less equal basis. New movements continually confront well-established ideological institutions that have vast resources at their disposal. These ideologies do not prevail on the basis of being attractive alone—of fulfilling individuals' needs for meaning and purpose—or because their "hegemony" is implicitly taken for granted.[6] They prevail because they have a systematic relation with organizations, because they are routinely enacted in rituals, and because they are closely linked with a power structure that channels them resources in return for tangible and intangible rewards. This fact bears repeating here because more attention needs to be devoted to how ideological movements confront these established cultural forms. Some examples were given in the discussion of ideological revolutions in Chapter 7, but this is an area that clearly needs more detailed consideration.

The third general use is the role of the state. It was also suggested in several of the preceding chapters that alternatives to the usual formulations of state-ideology relations need to be entertained. The problem with many traditional formulations is that they deal only with the idea of legitimation—at their worst, leading to teleological explanations for the origins of political ideologies. An emphasis on the resources involved in ideological institutionalization points to the possibility that ideologies may come into being for quite different reasons than the functions they eventually serve. Thinking of the state as having a limited array of options for dealing with ideological movements, because of their relations with elites who control fiscal and administrative resources (as argued in Chapter 9), may be one useful way of conceptualizing the state's role in cultural production.

The limitations of institutional analyses of culture arise mainly from the fact that cultural institutions, like other institutions, are sufficiently complex to require detailed investigations of everything from budgets to leadership styles, from publishing practices and attendance records to communication networks and personnel policies. Thus what is usually of greatest interest as culture—the form and content of the ideas them-selves—becomes easy to neglect. The institutional analysis of science in Chapter 8, for example, provides some insight into the development of science as a general cultural form, but offers little with respect to particu-lar theories or inventions. What needs to be specified in dealing with cul-tural institutions are sublevels of analysis at which particular cultural variations can be examined in greater detail. Also needed are deliberate efforts to link matters of organization, leadership, participation, and so on with the form and content of culture itself.

Institutional analyses of culture run the danger of focusing too heav-ily on deliberately produced cultural forms—on official ideologies and explicit efforts to communicate systematic ideas and to cultivate commit-ment to formal creeds. As it has been argued, culture also needs to be considered more broadly as the symbolic-expressive dimension of social life generally, as an aspect of behavior that communicates implicitly as well as explicitly. Keeping in mind the structural and dramaturgic levels of analysis is, therefore, likely to be a useful corrective in pursuing insti-tutional analyses of culture.

MEANING AND MORAL ORDER

In the present period, it is perhaps vaguely sentimental to be con-cerned with meaning and moral order. These concepts, having legacies in the classical theories of the nineteenth century, can arguably be re-placed in mainstream social science by concerns of greater contempo-rary relevance, such as the structuring of market relations, the triumph of technology and science over religion, the pursuit of rational communi-cation systems, and the functioning of the bureaucratic state. Yet it has been seen that all of these seemingly hard and dry topics—from the mar-ketplace to the bureaucratic state—have cultural dimensions that raise significant questions about meaning and moral order. These questions, it has been argued, need not remain the domain of subjective analyses or of humanistic exhortations alone. They require careful consideration, in-cluding efforts particularly devoted to examining the internal structure of cultural forms, their relations to the moral order, and the role of so-cial resources in producing and sustaining them.

Cultural analysis, like other social scientific investigations, can be di-rected toward various ends. At one extreme, it can be concerned simply with the technical maintenance of prevailing cultural institutions—with the collection and tabulation of statistics on members, leaders, products, revenues, and so forth. It can be devoted to matters that are largely descriptive or to studies aimed at revealing the significance of events by relating them to larger cultural patterns. For the social sciences, developing theoretical models has always been of higher priority than purely technical, descriptive, or even interpretive applications. The selection of theoretical models, moreover, can itself be influenced by broader critical objectives—by a search for knowledge that promotes discourse about collective purposes and the common good. This is the point at which meaning and moral order properly cease to be entirely matters of detached investigation and fold back into the process of inquiry itself. This is the goal that inspired the classical theorists to be interested in meaning and moral order and that continues to inspire much of the best in social science—work that becomes an influential part of the culture itself.

If the present treatment of meaning and moral order has been self-consciously programmatic, it is because the task of cultural analysis clearly deserves to be advanced by every means that it can. It has been said, in a different context, that self-consciousness—consciousness of one's feet—is a hindrance to dancing. Maybe so. It is, nevertheless, an indispensable step toward learning how.

Notes

CHAPTER ONE

1. Hammond (1985) has recently edited another survey of the field that draws much more optimistic conclusions.

2. The wide differences in orientation are evident in the contrasting approaches provided by such volumes as Harris (1979), Borhek and Curtis (1975), and Geertz (1973).

3. For a recent study of considerable merit that nevertheless reflects the abstract philosophical orientation toward the analysis of culture, see Thompson (1984). Much of the secondary literature generated by the work of writers such as Habermas and Foucault (cited in Chapter 2) also reflects this tendency.

4. The idea of dramaturgy in the social sciences has been associated particularly with the work of Erving Goffman. Using the term "dramaturgic" here implies no attempt to follow the intricacies of Goffman's approach, which was oriented more toward questions about the dramatization of the self than about the dramaturgic character of culture more generally.

5. Gilbert and Mulkay (1984) provide a valuable discussion of scientific discourse that generally follows the structural approach.

CHAPTER TWO

1. The term "poststructuralism" will not be used to refer to the specific, small, Paris-based school of literary criticism sometimes known as "poststructuralism," but will be given a broader definition in the course of the discussion that follows.

2. There is, for example, a much more pronounced tendency in American sociology than in European sociology to emphasize the subjective aspects of some of the classical theorists' conceptions of culture.

351

3. Ollman (1971:131) remarks that Marx's theory of alienation is "the intellectual construct in which Marx displays the devastating effect of capitalist production on human beings, on their physical and mental states and on the social processes of which they are a part." Ollman's study provides a particularly valuable explication of Marx's theory of alienation.

4. For a useful discussion of Weber's idea of the iron cage, see Mitzman (1971).

5. In comparison with Marx and Weber, Durkheim is usually credited with taking a more objective approach to religion insofar as he emphasizes the role of collective rituals. If we pay closer attention to this description of the functions of these rituals, however, we see clearly the basis, again, of a conception of culture rooted in subject-object dualism.

6. These ways of conceptualizing the relations between the individual and society are examined critically in Giddens (1971).

7. From Durkheim's argument about men's true object of worship and from his discussion of the rules of sociological method, a number of writers have drawn a more general perspective on the social sources of knowledge; for example, Hamilton (1974:105) interprets Durkheim as suggesting that "concepts and the categories of understanding are not given, but are created by the facts of social life; in short, the forms which thought takes are constructed as *representations* of social organization in terms of its collective nature." Many of the empirical studies of Guy E. Swanson have, of course, explored the validity of this argument. For more on this, see Chapter 9.

8. On Berger's approach to religion, see Wuthnow (1986a).

9. Although Berger and Luckmann's version of phenomenology differs significantly from Heidegger's (cf. Wuthnow et al., 1984:21–76), there is nevertheless a significant degree of borrowing from Heidegger as well. Among the concepts Heidegger emphasized are those of the linguistic construction of reality, the nature of everyday reality, the concept of facticity, and, above all, the importance of examining meanings. As Steiner (1979:82) observes: "To question *Sein* is to question its *Sinn*—its 'sense,' its 'meaning,' its 'purpose.' "

10. For an introduction to the hermeneutic method in social science, see Bleicher (1980).

11. Cf. Bibby (1979). On the broader question of research approaches to meaning systems versus research approaches to worldviews, see Aidala (1984).

12. Cf. Fingarette (1963), who describes the therapeutic process as one of "meaning-reorganization." He writes: "What the patient 'reads' are the bits and pieces of his life. He brings these fragments of his life to the therapist who then suggests a meaning-scheme in terms of which to reorganize and unify the patient's experience" (p. 21). At a more philosophical level, Barrett (1978:141), who contrasts the modern search for meaning with that of Descartes, suggests that we have developed a "coherence theory of truth, according to which truth is a matter of our ever-widening and self-integrating consciousness."

13. In contrast to research that suggests low levels of consistency in worldviews, empirical findings generally support the idea of a widespread concern for *coherence*. For example, 70 percent of the respondents in a California survey claimed they thought a lot or some about the purpose of life (Wuthnow,

1976); 90 percent of the respondents in a Gallup survey of the U.S. population said they thought at least a fair amount about living a worthwhile life, and 83 percent said they thought this much about basic values in life; and the same survey indicated that seven of ten respondents attempt to tie together the different spheres of their lives rather than keeping them separate (Gallup Organization, 1982).

14. The essentially subjective character of the hermeneutic method is stressed by Bleicher (1980:9), who writes: "Understanding, then, is motivated by our interest in partaking in the inner life of somebody else and is both necessary and rewarding."

15. In discussing Ricoeur's understanding of the hermeneutic method, Bleicher (1980:220), who is basically sympathetic to the approach, nevertheless observes its open-ended quality: "The object of interpretation, the text, furthermore, takes on an autonomous character once produced, so that it is no longer adequate to merely refer to its original meaning; instead of containing a fixed meaning, a text invites plural reading and interpretation. It is on this basis an open, unlimited process."

16. See especially Lévi-Strauss (1963). Leach (1974) provides a useful introduction to the work of Lévi-Strauss; several useful essays of a critical nature are found in Leach (1967).

17. The essay titled "Myth Today" in Barthes (1972) provides a useful overview of Barthes's method; for greater detail, see Barthes (1967).

18. See especially Chomsky (1957, 1965) and Searle (1969). For more general overviews of structural linguistics, see Pettit (1977) and Leiber (1975). Habermas (1979a) is a particularly vivid demonstration of his borrowing from Searle.

19. The contrast between the subjectivism of the neoclassical approaches and the reorientation toward the problem of meaning evident in poststructuralism is aptly summarized by Barrett (1978:170), who writes: "Meanings are first and foremost not in the mind but in the world, in the linkings and interconnections of things we find there." Barrett, in focusing primarily on European writers, perceives a greater degree of continuity between writers such as Heidegger and Wittgenstein and the poststructuralists than is typical among American writers. Among European writers the discontinuity is nevertheless evident in the major debates that have taken place between Gadamer and Habermas; see, especially, Gadamer (1975), Habermas (1977), and Misgeld (1976, 1977).

20. For a fuller discussion of the contributions to the analysis of culture of Douglas, Foucault, and Habermas, see Wuthnow et al. (1984). Among the many secondary sources on Foucault, Major-Poetzl (1983) and Dreyfus and Rabinow (1982) are particularly useful in explicating his methodological approach; the latter also emphasizes Foucault's differences with hermeneutics and classical structuralism. On Habermas, one of the most useful secondary sources remains that of McCarthy (1978), which emphasizes the problem of communication. A brief but highly useful discussion of Habermas's work on ideology (more from a philosophical than a sociological perspective) is found in Geuss (1981); Held (1980) is valuable for situating Habermas in the broader context of critical theory.

21. Darnton's account is not presented as an attempt to examine the meanings of the French Revolution, but it provides a rich example of historical analysis at its best.

CHAPTER THREE

1. Some of these studies of voting records and public opinion polls are referred to more specifically in Chapter 4. Recent issues of *Public Opinion* and the *Gallup Opinion Index* provide useful general sources. For a valuable nonquantitative sampling of opinions on many of these topics, see Bellah et al. (1985).

2. Marvin Harris's (1979:47) injunction against reifying the idea of cultural *systems* is appropriate here: "The systemic nature of such conjunctions and arrangements is not something to be taken for granted. Rather, it is a strategic assumption that can be justified only by showing how it leads to efficacious and testable theories."

3. Fundamentalism as a cultural system is discussed at greater length in Chapter 6.

4. For examples of observations of and conversations with randomly chosen families, see Sennett and Cobb (1972) and Terkel (1974).

5. Examples of qualitative evidence from people in the human potential movement include Tipton (1982), Westley (1983), and Downton (1979).

6. More generally, discourse about "doing my best" or "trying hard"—presumably common constructions in American culture—removes action from pragmatic criticisms based on performance criteria. Thus, as long as one "tries hard," one's moral obligations have been satisfactorily discharged, even though one may not have achieved a specific objective.

7. Sennett (1976:263) makes this point about the separateness of the self and the worker in discussing what he regards as a prevailing emphasis on interiority in modern concepts of the self: "The self no longer concerns man as actor or man as maker; it is a self composed of intentions and possibilities."

8. The distinction between selves and actors is analogous to that between "competence" and "performance" in Chomsky's and Habermas's discussions of language (Chapter 2). The self remains morally competent, even though the actor's performances sometimes deviate from this standard.

9. These observations concerning the "real self" and roles obviously have implications for Habermas's argument (as discussed in Chapter 2) that meaningful speech acts must communicate a relation of sincerity between the act and the speaker. Clearly, there are layers of sincerity and multiple relations between the speech act and the speaker. In commenting on one's own speech acts, one implicitly raises doubts about their sincerity (were they in fact the product of an actor rather than the self?). But in making such comments one also realigns a speech pattern by indicating that it had gone in a wrong direction and that one's "true self" now realizes the mistake.

10. Some of the evidence discussed in the next chapter on Nazi villainy and vulnerability to evil produces a further example of the pattern typified by heroes and villains.

11. Victims also play an important symbolic role in relation to the boundary between inevitability and intentionality. In the case of Jim Jones's followers (or in the case of victims of racial discrimination or of the Nazi Holocaust), victims symbolize the power of the inevitable to penetrate and control those who would otherwise presumably act according to their own good intentions. Counterarguments against victims—the proverbial "welfare chiseler," for example—aim to demonstrate that persons were really not subject to a realm of inevitability but acted intentionally and could, therefore, be held morally responsible for their own fate. Arguments and counterarguments over victims have great cultural importance because they define symbolic boundaries between the inevitable and the intentional.

12. Goffman's (1974:28–37) discussion of "primary frameworks" provides a useful basis for identifying other ways in which the boundary between the inevitable and the intentional may be dramatized. His terms "natural" and "social" connote a similar distinction. He identifies five kinds of activities that in different ways deal with this symbolic boundary: (1) the "astounding complex," in which (in our terms) the intentional miraculously penetrates the inevitable; (2) "stunts," in which the intentional is heroically maintained against seemingly insuperable constraints presented by the inevitable; (3) "muffings," in which the intentional or controllable is temporarily lost control of, allowing the inevitable to take over; (4) "fortuitousness," in which the inevitable happens to coincide with or cooperate with the intentional, leading to either good or ill consequences; and (5) "tension," in which the boundary between the intentional and the inevitable is artificially confused, generally with either comic (the intentional knowingly masquerading as the inevitable) or tragic (the intentional unknowingly being made into the inevitable) effects.

13. A negative example that perhaps reveals the importance of removing the moral object from empirical observation is the frustration that came to many parents during the 1960s as a result of children—who had become quite tangible moral objects to which many parents were sacrificially devoted—adopting different ideas or seeking independence, thus denying parents the opportunity of serving them and thereby achieving a sense of moral worth.

14. An effective moral obligation assumes that the object of that obligation in fact desires or needs the acts performed (e.g., God wants our obedience, humanity needs us to make it better). The object may or may not desire or need the acts performed; the important thing is that the actors are able to assume that it does. When the object is an individual or group, even minimal evidence that it desires or needs certain performances may be sufficient to maintain moral commitment as long as reinforcement occurs. In other cases, the possibility of receiving information to the contrary must be avoided. Accordingly, a vague or unobservable definition of the moral object renders an important service in making the connection between performances and the moral object secure against empirical disconfirmation.

15. A more systematic discussion of rationality as an ideological form is presented in Chapter 6.

16. The boundary between self and actor essentially prevents guilt that results from incompetent role performances from becoming associated with the

self. This distinction suggests a basis for interpreting Heidegger's claim that the "they-self" of everyday life is inauthentic in that it knows no ethical guilt. The they-self is objectified culturally and separated from the active self; only the active self can be made to know guilt. There is, however, an irony here. Heidegger describes the condition of engaging in actions from which a sense of moral worth can be derived as one of "fallenness." That is, the basic existential problem arises precisely at that point at which a person attempts to achieve a sense of moral worth. Evil, therefore, does not represent a turning away from moral action, but the pursuit of it. And this problem appears inevitable. The more one tries to convince oneself that one is acting morally, the more "fallen" (estranged, divided) one will become—in the sense of reinforcing the division between (moral) self and actor.

17. Religious teachings on charitable works are interesting because they often provide secondary arguments to counteract problems of bureaucratization. For example, the feeling that one's efforts make no difference is countered by the "bread upon the waters" argument that asserts the possibility of indirect, even unknown, effects and by an antipragmatic argument that asserts the importance of obeying religious injunctions whether they seem to have practical effects or not.

18. Some insight into the contemporary problem of alienation may also be gained from considering the boundary between self and actor. Alienation from public institutions can function symbolically as a means of reaffirming the boundary between self and actor. In withdrawing emotional investment from the roles one plays, one protects the self from compromises, failures, and other problems of performance associated with these roles. As Sennett and Cobb (1972:197) suggest, "The divorce of the real person from the institution's individual is a way to ward off becoming an 'institutional man.' "

19. Charles Y. Glock has developed the idea of science adding to ambiguities in several essays; see, for example, Glock (1976) for a discussion of the corrosive effects of science as a possible factor leading to social unrest and experimentation with alternative life-styles and new religions.

20. Although Barrington Moore's (1978) discussion of moral codes goes in a direction quite different from that presented in the text, he also assumes that moral codes are fundamental to an understanding of society and that certain regularities of structure may be identified. He writes, for example, that "there are grounds for suspecting that the welter of moral codes may conceal a certain unity of original form, as well as a discernible historical drift in a single direction, and that variations from this pattern of a single basic form undergoing prolonged historical modification are explicable in general terms" (1978:4). Moore's discussion also overlaps with the present formulation in emphasizing the importance of the distinction between controllable and uncontrollable realms of behavior. Another useful discussion of moral codes, but one that stays primarily with the conception of morality as normative orientation, is that of Little and Twiss (1978).

21. Reference to the problem of separation of the self and one's roles is also made in the discussion of individualism in Chapter 6.

22. The idea of *sacrifice* is, of course, a prominent theme in discourse about

behavior in the marketplace. Both the moral significance of this theme and its potential for perversion have been usefully examined by Sennett and Cobb. For example, they write:

> Sacrifice, then, legitimizes a person's view of himself as an individual, with the right to feel anger—anger of a peculiar, focused sort: In setting you off as an individual, a virtuous person compared to less forceful others, self-denial makes possible the ultimate perversion of love; it permits you to practice that most insidious and devastating form of self-righteousness where you, oppressed, in your anger turn on others who are also oppressed rather than on those intangible, invisible, impersonal forces that have made you all vulnerable. (1972:140)

23. Dumont (1970) argues that the Western concept of freedom as individual automony was virtually unknown in India until recent times.

24. Based on analysis of Detroit Area Survey data for 1958 and 1971, Blackwood (1979) found a major decline in responses indicating intrinsic attachment to the importance of work among professionals and managers, a moderate decline among skilled workers, and only a modest decline among service workers.

25. Insofar as social institutions sometimes appear to be organized around distinct moral codes (e.g., the marketplace, fundamentalist churches, human potential movements), decoupling and recoupling may become major sources of organizational restructuring as well. For example, schisms in American religious denominations in the twentieth century sometimes appear to have been closely associated with a shift in real programs for serving God—from an emphasis on biblical knowledge and personal morality to an emphasis on altruistic or social reform activities. The presence of a symbolic "fault line" between moral objects and real programs, again, may have adaptive value in permitting these forms of restructuring to take place without negative repercussions for the moral objects themselves.

CHAPTER FOUR

1. For an extensive bibliography of empirical studies of ritual, see Grimes (1985).

2. For examples of writers who link ritual and emotion, see Van Gennep (1960), Gluckman (1962), and Turner (1977).

3. Malinowski (1925:32) writes:

> An interesting and crucial test is provided by fishing in the Trobriand Islands and its magic. While in the villages on the inner lagoon fishing is done in an easy and absolutely reliable manner by the method of poisoning, yielding abundant results without danger and uncertainty, there are on the shores of the open sea dangerous modes of fishing and also certain types in which the yield varies greatly according to whether shoals of fish appear beforehand or not. It is most significant that in the lagoon fishing, where man can rely completely upon his knowledge and skill, magic does not exist, while in the open-sea fishing, full of danger and uncertainty, there is extensive magical ritual to secure safety and good results.

Malinowski's view was challenged by Radcliffe-Brown (1939), who argued that the function of ritual was not so much to alleviate anxiety as to evoke it so that it could be displayed publicly. In both cases, however, the idea was that the essential quality of ritual was one of expressing individual anxiety. Also see Homans (1941) for a discussion of this dispute.

4. The brief conceptual remarks on ritual in Leach (1964) remain as some of the clearest allusions to the communicative nature of ritual. He suggests that ritual should be understood as a "symbolic statement about social order" (p. 14), as an activity that "makes explicit the social structure" (p. 15), and as "a language of signs in terms of which claims to rights and status are expressed" (p. 278).

5. See especially Goffman (1967).

6. Lane (1981:11) makes a similar point in suggesting that the activities making up social relations "can be entirely symbolic, or [social relations] can have both a symbolic and an instrumental or expressive aspect."

7. Several important contributions to this literature on rationality and nonrationality have been reprinted in Wilson (1970a).

8. Further discussion of this period of European reintegration and consolidation is presented in Chapters 7 and 8.

9. An excellent discussion and criticism of the anthropologist's role in interpreting ritual is found in Skorupski (1976), especially part 2.

10. Survey No. 4036 was conducted by Response Analysis Corporation, Princeton, New Jersey, in May 1978. Telephone interviews were conducted with 411 randomly selected adult viewers and 411 randomly selected adult nonviewers. Data from this survey were made available by Response Analysis. A summary of results from the study is available in a report entitled "Americans Confront the Holocaust: A Study of Reactions to NBC-TV's Four-Part Drama on the Nazi Era" (New York: American Jewish Committee, Institute on Human Relations, 1978).

11. Data were collected from clergy under a grant to the author from the Anti-Defamation League of B'nai B'rith by means of a mailed questionnaire sent to nationally representative samples of pastors from five religious bodies: Unitarian, United Presbyterian Church U.S.A., Lutheran Church in America, Reformed Church in America, and Roman Catholic. These bodies were chosen in order to represent a broad spectrum of theologian orientations, including liberal (Unitarian), moderate (Presbyterian, Lutheran, and Catholic), and conservative (Reformed), as well as both large and small denominations and Protestants and Catholics. The samples were selected by choosing names randomly from clergy directories from each of the five denominations. Questionnaires were mailed to each pastor in the sample in mid June, approximately eight weeks after the television broadcast. A follow-up letter including a second copy of the questionnaire was mailed to nonrespondents approximately three weeks after the initial mailing. A third reminder letter was mailed about a month later. In all, 1,144 completed questionnaires were returned, a response rate of 68 percent.

12. Data from teachers were collected, also under a grant to the author from the Anti-Defamation League, through the cooperation of the National Council for Social Studies, a national voluntary organization with a membership of approximately twenty thousand teachers drawn mainly from specialists in high school social studies. Although the membership of NCSS cannot be assumed to be representative of all high school social studies teachers, it does provide a

broad cross-section of teachers with a variety of orientations on a nationwide basis, as well as representing those educators most likely to be in charge of instruction in their high schools dealing with issues such as those raised by the "Holocaust" program. A random sample of teachers was drawn from the complete NCSS membership list. Questionnaires were mailed in mid September to coincide with teachers' return to regular fall schedules. Follow-up letters and questionnaires were mailed approximately three weeks later, and, as with clergy, a final follow-up letter was mailed about a month later. A total of 1,344 completed questionnaires was returned, a response rate of 72 percent.

13. A questionnaire designed by the author and administered by a local staff representative of the Anti-Defamation League was administered to 326 seniors (the entire senior class) in a suburban community high school in the Midwest in the fall of 1978. The project originally called for data to be collected in other parts of the country as well, but cooperation could not be obtained from local school boards in the time period necessary for making valid comparisons of responses to the program. The results of the student study largely parallel those of the clergy and teacher surveys and, for this reason, will be referred to only when they afford additional information.

14. A study of more than twenty-two thousand high school students (sophomores and juniors) from twenty-seven different schools in the Pittsburgh area explored viewing and attitudes toward the program (summarized in Burnstein, 1979). A second study was conducted among 668 tenth grade social studies students from five schools in the Miami area to measure attitudes before the Holocaust program was shown and to make comparisons with attitudes from a subsample of 289 respondents given questionnaires again after the telecast (Greenberg et al., 1978).

15. National surveys were conducted in West Germany and Austria. The West German data are summarized in Ernst (1979). The Austrian data are discussed in Markovits and Hayden (1980). "Holocaust" was televised in West Germany in January 1979 to an audience of 15 million viewers, more than a third of the total viewing public. In Austria more than half of all viewers watched the program when it was shown in March 1979.

16. Of all the "Holocaust" viewers surveyed, 73 percent had watched the first evening, 75 percent had watched the second evening, 76 percent had watched the third evening, and 80 percent had watched the final evening. In West Germany the same pattern developed, even though the program was aired on different evenings of the week than in the United States.

17. Most viewers in other countries also watched "Holocaust" with other members of their household. In Austria, 61 percent of the viewers had discussed the film with their families, 49 percent had discussed it with friends, and 35 percent had discussed it with people at work. In West Germany, 64 percent had discussed the program with members of their family, 40 percent had discussed it with friends, acquaintances, and colleagues, and only 23 percent had discussed it with no one.

18. Viewers were given three options to choose from as well as the option of saying they did not recall.

19. The six items and the correct answer for each were (1) "Jews were killed

in Germany, but not in Poland" (false); (2) "The Nazis permitted Jews to migrate to America until 1944" (false); (c) "The Nuremberg Laws denied Jews the
right to vote" (true); (4) "Although the Nazis killed Jews, they did not destroy
synagogues" (false); (5) "The Nazis killed people who they thought were mentally ill" (true); (6) "Himmler was Hitler's field marshal in North Africa"
(false). The percentage of clergy and teachers, respectively, giving the correct answer to each question were (1) 94 and 95 percent; (2) 60 and 68 percent; (3) 25
and 42 percent; (4) 76 and 83 percent; (5) 78 and 78 percent; and (6) 78 and 85
percent. The average percentage correct for all the questions was 74 percent
among clergy who had watched the entire series, 67 percent for clergy who had
watched some of the series, 63 percent for clergy who had not watched but had
heard a lot about the program, and 57 percent for clergy who had heard little
about the show. For teachers the respective figures were 81, 73, 67, and 60 percent. Measured at only one time after the show, these patterns of course do not
indicate whether the program led to an increase in knowledge or whether it was
the more knowledgeable who watched in the first place. Several of the other
studies, however, did incorporate longitudinal designs. In West Germany,
where 51 percent said they had learned something new about the Holocaust
from the program, "before" and "after" comparisons of responses given by the
same persons showed significant changes. For example, before the program 15
percent had thought Nazi crimes should continue to be prosecuted; after the program this figure had risen to 39 percent. Austrian responses also showed a
change in this attitude, although somewhat smaller, from 17 percent to 24 percent. In the Miami study, before and after comparisons showed that the percentage who felt Nazi atrocities should continue to be discussed went up from
slightly over half to about two-thirds of the respondents.

20. Additional questions asked only in the clergy survey showed that 78 percent of the clergy viewers had been bothered a lot by "the fact that Jews were innocent victims," and 75 percent had been bothered a lot by "the way Germans
blindly followed their leaders." Only 6 percent of the clergy and 4 percent of the
teachers had been bothered a lot by the "feeling that the Holocaust was cheap-
ened by being shown on TV."

21. Not surprisingly, the response in West Germany and Austria was also
highly emotional. In West Germany, 64 percent of the viewers questioned said
they had found the show deeply upsetting, 41 percent said the show was an important experience for them personally, 39 percent felt shame that Germany
had committed such crimes and tolerated them as well, and 22 percent said
there were scenes that made them almost cry. In Austria, 82 percent of the viewers indicated that the film had been truly moving.

22. The question read, "There have been a number of TV specials lately dealing with the great tragedies of history—the Holocaust, slavery, assassinations,
war. Which one of these statements comes closest to your own view of these programs?" Seventy-four percent of the clergy and 81 percent of the teachers selected the response "I definitely think they should be shown, no matter how
shocking they may be." Fifteen percent and 9 percent, respectively, selected the
response "As long as they tone down the violence, it's OK to show them."
"Somehow I tend to dislike shows like this, although I can't exactly say why"

was the response of 5 and 3 percent, respectively. "Shows like this are definitely in bad taste and should not be shown on TV" was the response of only 2 and 0 percent, respectively. Five percent in both studies opted for none of the responses listed.

23. This question pertained to the Holocaust as a historical event, rather than the television program: "Which one of the following comes closest to your view of the Nazis' campaign against the Jews during World War II?" The response "It definitely raises some profound moral questions that we need to ponder very carefully" was chosen by 87 percent of the clergy and 85 percent of the teachers. "I agree that it raises moral questions, but we shouldn't dwell on it too much" was chosen by 4 and 7 percent, respectively. "Although it was certainly tragic, Hitler is dead and there are other problems for us to be concerned about now" was the response of 5 and 4 percent, respectively. Only a few (2 and 1 percent) chose "I honestly feel that it has been given too much attention," and the remainder (2 and 2 percent) opted for none of the responses provided.

24. Fifty percent of the teachers and 37 percent of the clergy said they had learned a lot about the Holocaust during the past few years from reading books. Another 38 and 44 percent, respectively, said they had learned a little from this source. Books, it turned out, were the largest single source of information for these groups. The second most common source was television programs. Thirty-six percent of the teachers and 20 percent of the clergy had learned a lot from television programs; another 51 and 59 percent had learned a little. Publications for teachers appeared to be a fairly important source of information: 24 percent of the teachers had learned a lot from this source and 47 percent had learned a little. By comparison, church publications were important to relatively fewer of the clergy: 10 percent had learned a lot and 52 percent a little from this source. Classes, lectures, and speeches were another source of information. Fifteen percent of the teachers and 8 percent of the clergy indicated that classes in school had been a source of a lot of information about the Holocaust. Another 31 and 23 percent, respectively, said they had learned a little from this source. Other classes, lectures, or speeches were the source of a lot of information for 15 percent of the teachers and 9 percent of the clergy. Thirty-one percent and 39 percent, respectively, had learned a little from this source. Finally, a majority of each group had learned something about the Holocaust from friends—another indication of the role played by social interaction. Fifteen percent and 12 percent, respectively, said they had learned a lot from this source, and 47 percent and 50 percent said they had learned a little.

25. National Data Program for the Social Sciences, *Cumulative Codebook for the 1972–1980 General Social Surveys* (Chicago: National Opinion Research Center, 1980).

26. Eighty-four percent of the public said they had only some or hardly any confidence in the leaders running Congress. Sixty-seven percent gave these responses concerning the Supreme Court.

27. Quoted in Lipset and Schneider (1978:43); also cited are Harris polls showing a drop in the proportion of the public expressing confidence in "major companies" from 55 percent in 1966 to 23 percent in November 1977.

28. A Yankelovich poll showed that 67 percent of the public thought the

country was in "deep and serious trouble." According to a Gallup poll, 69 percent were "dissatisfied with the way things are going in the U.S. at this time." In a national poll conducted by Patrick Caddell for President Carter in 1978, one person in three listed himself or herself as being "pessimistic" about the nation's future. By 1979 this proportion had risen to one in two. A Gallup poll in 1978 showed that just under a third of the public (32 percent) thought America's power would decline during the following year. Using a different question, a study conducted by CBS showed that 56 percent of the public felt America was less powerful than it had been a decade before.

29. "Transcript of President's Address to Country on Energy Problems," *New York Times* (July 16, 1979), p. A10.

30. The two samples were asked, "How much of a problem would you say each of the following is in our country?" "Dishonesty in the government" was marked as an extremely serious problem by 35 percent of the clergy and 32 percent of the teachers and as a serious problem by another 56 and 53 percent, respectively. "Corruption in big business" was considered extremely serious by 32 and 27 percent, respectively, and serious by an additional 54 and 53 percent. "People feeling that they can't affect what goes on in the society" was regarded as an extremely serious problem by 51 percent of both groups and as a serious problem by 41 percent of the clergy and 39 percent of the teachers.

31. "Racial inequality" was regarded as an extremely serious problem by 30 percent of the clergy and 23 percent of the teachers and as a serious problem by 57 and 56 percent, respectively. "Prejudice toward ethnic groups" was listed as extremely serious by 19 and 21 percent, respectively, and as serious by 56 and 51 percent. Two additional problems also elicited expressions of concern by many of the pastors and teachers. "Doctors charging too much for medical care" was listed as an extremely serious problem by 25 and 22 percent, respectively, in the two groups and as a serious problem by 46 and 41 percent. "Too much power in the hands of the military" was regarded as an extremely serious problem by 20 percent of the clergy and 9 percent of the teachers; 38 and 28 percent, respectively, thought it was a serious problem.

32. The question asked, "Do you think that any of the following could happen within, say, the next 25 years?" Fifty-five percent of the clergy and 47 percent of the teachers thought that "new outbreaks of racial violence in the United States" "definitely could" happen, and almost all of the remainder (42 and 49 percent) thought this "possibly could" happen. The proportions who felt that "violence and social unrest like we had during the Sixties" could definitely happen were 46 and 39 percent, respectively. Large proportions also felt that "police harassing innocent citizens in the United States" was something that could definitely happen (46 and 40 percent).

33. Clergy and teachers who said they had any interest in the Holocaust at all were asked to indicate, for a list of reasons, whether each was a major reason for their interest, a minor reason for their interest, or not a reason. For clergy and teachers, respectively, the percentages listing each as a major reason were 13 and 16 percent for "People keep writing books and making TV shows about it," 12 and 10 percent for "It's mostly because Israel is in the news so much," 28 and 23

percent for "I know people who experienced it personally," and 28 and 46 percent for "I can't understand how something like that could have happened."

34. "Holocaust Keeps Memory Alive" (April 28, 1978). The editorial went on to say, "This may be impossible for many to believe. But right today in many parts of the world—in the Middle East, in Africa, Asia, Latin America, Ireland and elsewhere—people are killing, persecuting, torturing or threatening one another because of their race, religion, political views or other causes." Other newspapers also drew contemporary implications from the program. For example, the Columbia, South Carolina, *State* described the program as "a symbolic story of the tyranny that still stalks mankind." Ellen Goodman wrote in the *Boston Globe* (April 25, 1978) that the experience of watching the program was like "a confrontation with Evil. Pure Evil. Irrational Evil. What Martin Buber once described as 'the eclipse of the Gods.' " William F. Buckley, Jr., in a more critical vein, wrote that the world could benefit from the program only "by resolving that such a thing shall not happen again" (April 20, 1978, *Worcester Telegram*). The *Christian Science Monitor* (May 8, 1978) highlighted another contemporary lesson implicit in the Holocaust story, noting that the "Holocaust has become a rallying point through which religious leaders—Christian and Jewish—are expressing mutual concern about global violations of human rights."

35. The figures for clergy were 73 percent and for teachers 57 percent fearing that something like the Holocaust could recur.

36. Interest in the Holocaust, rather than having watched the program, was used as a measure for making these comparisons because watching appeared to be more contingent on personal time schedules than was interest. In all, 39 percent of the clergy and 47 percent of the teachers said they had a lot of interest in the Holocaust. As evidence of the relationships between interest in the Holocaust and concerns about contemporary social problems, 45 percent of the clergy who felt that corruption in big business was extremely serious said they had a lot of interest in the Holocaust, compared to 37 percent of those who thought corruption was just a serious problem, and only 34 percent of those who thought it was a small problem. The comparable percentages for teachers were 57 percent, 46 percent, and 39 percent. For the question about dishonesty in government, the percentages having a lot of interest were 44 percent among clergy who thought the problem was extremely serious, compared with 38 percent among those who thought it was only a small problem. For teachers, the comparable percentages were 54 and 45. Similar comparisons, using the question on alienation, showed differences of 42 percent versus 34 percent for clergy and 50 percent versus 36 percent for teachers. Although these differences are generally small, they are consistent with and in the expected direction for both clergy and teachers. Perceptions of problems having directly to do with issues of justice and inequality were somewhat more strongly related to differences of interest in the Holocaust. For example, 48 percent of the pastors who thought racial inequality was extremely serious said they had a lot of interest in the Holocaust, compared with only 26 percent of those who thought racial inequality was a small problem. The differences among teachers on this question were 61 percent versus 39 percent. Substituting questions about military power, preju-

dice, or doctors charging too much produced patterns of similar magnitude. Translating these percentage differences into "odds" of having a lot of interest produces ratios on the order of 1.2 to 1.5 for persons concerned about social problems compared with persons not concerned about these problems.

37. Among conservatives, 34 percent of those who regarded corruption in business as an extremely serious problem (using this as a measure of perceived threat in the moral order) said they had a lot of interest in the Holocaust, compared with 23 percent of those who thought corruption in business was only a small problem. Among moderates the comparable figures were 36 and 29 percent. Among liberals the figures were 53 versus 46 percent. Each relationship was significant at or beyond the .05 level.

38. Among conservative clergy, 35 percent of those who thought declining moral standards were an extremely serious problem had a lot of interest in the Holocaust, compared with only 17 percent of those who said that declining morals were "serious" (too few thought declining morals were a small problem to permit comparisons with this category). Among liberal clergy, exactly the same percentages (48 percent) were interested in the Holocaust in all three categories of perceptions about moral decline. Among moderate clergy, there was a weak relation between perceptions and interest (36 percent, 28 percent, and 29 percent, respectively, for the three levels of perception). The comparable figures for teachers were 48 versus 18 percent for conservatives (again, too few said moral decline was only a small problem to allow comparisons); 49, 38, and 41 percent for moderates; and 66, 53, and 52 percent for liberal teachers. A comparison of gamma statistics confirmed that the relations were stronger in both cases among conservatives than among liberals.

39. Comparing the percentages who had a lot of interest in the Holocaust for those who thought corruption in business was extremely serious with those who thought it was only a small problem revealed the following: 54 versus 43 percent for clergy who said the Holocaust happening again was a major reason for their interest, 19 versus 23 percent for clergy who said this was a minor reason, and 12 versus 9 percent for clergy who said this was not a reason for their interest. For teachers, the comparable figures were 65 versus 53 percent, 45 versus 28 percent, and 30 versus 29 percent.

40. Theologically liberal denominations included Presbyterian, Lutheran, and Roman Catholic, in which 57 percent, 54 percent, and 60 percent of the pastors, respectively, listed their theological views as liberal or neoorthodox. The Reformed Church in America was classified as theologically conservative because 60 percent of its pastors listed their theological views as conservative or fundamental. Unitarians were not included in these comparisons because there were no conservative or fundamental pastors in the sample from this denomination. The percentages indicating a lot of interest in the Holocaust were 38 percent among conservatives in liberal denominations, 36 percent among liberals in conservative denominations, 33 percent among consistent liberals, and 27 percent among consistent conservatives. These differences were statistically significant beyond the .05 level.

41. Of the 326 high school seniors who filled out the questionnaires, 28 percent said they were bothered a lot by "problems with school," 44 percent said

they were bothered a little, and 28 percent said they were not bothered. Thirteen percent said they were bothered a lot by "feeling lonely," 39 percent said they were bothered a little, and 48 percent said they were not bothered. Forty-nine percent said they were bothered a lot by "deciding what you want to do in life," 30 percent were bothered a little, and 20 percent were not bothered. Among those bothered a lot by school problems, 58 percent indicated a lot of interest in the Holocaust, compared with 41 percent among those bothered a little and 35 percent among those not bothered. Among those bothered a lot by loneliness, 53 percent had a lot of interest, compared with 41 percent of those bothered a little, and 44 percent of those not bothered. And among those bothered a lot by deciding what to do in life, 51 percent had a lot of interest, compared with 34 percent among those bothered a little and 38 percent among those not bothered.

42. See Lukes (1977) for an excellent discussion of the potential in political ritual for exacerbating social conflict and a critique of the civil religion literature from this perspective.

43. A useful discussion of the traditional problem in the civil religion litera- ture is found in Schoffeleers and Meijers (1978); see especially pp. 13–50.

44. Exact figures for clergy indicating that each option would help a lot and that it would help most of all are as follows: having students learn about it in school (41 and 16 percent); showing stories about it on TV (26 and 3 percent); teaching people about democracy (41 and 11 percent); making sure that every- one has a good job and a decent living (32 and 16 percent); teaching people to be better Christians (55 and 38 percent); strict laws against political extremists (5 and 1 percent); limiting the power of big business and big government (21 per- cent and 7 percent); can't decide (8 percent). For teachers the respective figures were as follows: students (41 and 21 percent); stories (31 and 5 percent); democ- racy (40 and 18 percent); decent living (37 and 25 percent); better Christians (27 and 12 percent); strict laws (5 and 1 percent); limiting power (14 and 7 per- cent); and can't decide (6 percent).

45. The only answer that varied significantly was that concerned with show- ing stories on TV. Thirty-four percent of the clergy who had watched all of the program said this would help a lot, compared with only 11 percent of the clergy who had not watched and had not heard much about the program. The percent- ages for teachers were, respectively, 39 and 15. Viewers were also somewhat less likely to check "better Christians" as the best solution than were nonviewers among clergy and, among teachers, were somewhat more likely to check "students." Otherwise, the percentages were nearly identical for viewers and nonviewers. Favored solutions were also examined to determine if reading books about the Holocaust might have a significant influence on the kinds of so- lutions adopted. Clergy were again somewhat less likely to choose "better Chris- tians" if they had learned a lot about the Holocaust from books than if they had learned little or nothing from this source. And teachers were more likely to choose "students" if they had learned a lot than if they had learned nothing from this source. The other responses did not vary.

46. For clergy the exact percentages choosing each option as a very or fairly important reason for the Holocaust and as the most important reason of all were as follows: the Nazis were mentally disturbed (23 and 9 percent); times

were so hard in Germany that people would have done almost anything (35 and 16 percent); the Germans were taught to obey orders no matter what (73 and 27 percent); Hitler created such a huge bureaucracy that nobody could oppose it (59 and 20 percent); the Jews brought it on themselves by not leaving when they still could (2 and 1 percent); there was no democracy in Germany (47 and 10 percent); it was part of God's plan, although we don't know why it had to happen (7 and 3 percent); and can't decide (15 percent). For teachers these are the comparable figures: mentally disturbed (20 and 7 percent); hard times (52 and 25 percent); taught to obey (72 and 24 percent); huge bureaucracy (61 and 18 percent); Jews (3 and 0 percent); no democracy (47 and 12 percent); God's plan (4 and 1 percent); and can't decide (7 percent).

47. Clergy who watched all of the program were slightly less likely to select "mentally disturbed" and slightly more likely to choose "hard times." Otherwise the responses were almost identical for viewers and nonviewers. Nor did the extent of reading books about the Holocaust seem to affect these explanations. Usually only a couple of percentage points distinguished the explanations of those who had learned a lot about the Holocaust from books from those who said they had learned nothing from this source.

48. Theological conservatism was measured by an item that asked, "Which of the following would come closest to describing your theological views?" Thirty-five percent of the pastors said "liberal," 24 percent said "neo-orthodox," 32 percent said "conservative," 2 percent said "fundamental," and 7 percent said "other." Teachers were asked, "Which of the following would come closest to describing your religious views?" Forty-four percent said "liberal," 27 percent said "conservative," 18 percent said "nonreligious," and 10 percent said "other." Denominational conservatism (pastors only) was measured by classifying denominations into liberal (Unitarian, Presbyterian, Lutheran, and Catholic) or conservative (Reformed) according to the proportions of clergy from each who listed themselves as liberal (including neoorthodox) or conservative. Emphasis on doing God's will was measured by an item in both surveys phrased "following God's will." Seventy-four percent of the clergy said this was of "great importance" to them, as did 34 percent of the teachers. Of clergy who preferred making people better Christians as the best preventive measure, 53 percent listed themselves as theological conservatives, 33 percent were from a conservative denomination, and 93 percent valued following God's will a great deal. Of teachers who selected this option, 54 percent were religiously conservative, and 68 percent valued following God's will a great deal.

49. Forty-one percent of the total clergy sample and 42 percent of the total teacher sample listed their political orientations as liberal or radical. By comparison, 65 percent of the clergy and 51 percent of the teachers who felt good jobs would be the best preventive measure listed themselves as liberals or radicals.

50. The distinction between ikonic and conceptual symbolism is from Bruner, Oliver, and Greenfield (1966:1–66). The distinction here is also similar to that between presentational and discursive forms, as drawn by Langer (1951:75–93).

51. Of clergy who thought the Holocaust "was part of God's plan, although we don't know why it happened," 69 percent were theologically conservative,

46 percent were denominationally conservative, and 94 percent valued following God's will a great deal (compared with 32 percent, 15 percent, and 74 percent for the total clergy sample). Of teachers who gave this response, 63 percent were religiously conservative, and 75 percent valued following God's will a great deal (compared with 27 and 34 percent for all teachers).

52. Of clergy who thought hard times were the main reason for the Holocaust, 50 percent listed their political orientations as liberal or radical, compared with 41 percent of all clergy; respective figures for teachers were 45 and 42 percent. By comparison, only 34 percent of each group who felt that Hitler's bureaucracy was the main cause of the Holocaust listed themselves as liberals or radicals. These relations were relatively weaker in general than were the relations for preventive measures.

53. A higher percentage of the students who selected the option of "strict laws against political extremism" had watched the program (79 percent) than the percentage of those who had watched among students in general (73 percent). Slightly more of the former than of the latter also expressed a lot of interest in the Holocaust (46 versus 43 percent).

54. Exactly the same proportion (67 percent) of those who favored strict laws gave correct answers on the average to the factual questions as did the whole student sample. Seventy-eight percent of each group said they had learned about the Holocaust from classes in school.

55. The figures for students favoring strict laws and the figures for the entire student sample on each item are as follows: B− to D grade point average (50 and 34 percent); spend one-half hour or less a day on homework (67 and 47 percent); value keeping up to date on national news little or none (54 and 36 percent); value helping solve social problems little or none (63 and 41 percent); value helping people who are in need little or none (42 and 25 percent); racial inequality is only a small problem or not a problem (71 and 48 percent); doctors charging too much is only a small problem or not a problem (63 percent and 40 percent); agree there are countries in the world today similar to Nazi Germany (42 and 60 percent).

56. Of clergy who thought "good jobs" were the best prevention, 67 percent thought racial violence could definitely happen in the next twenty-five years, 62 percent thought social unrest and violence could break out, and 64 percent thought police harassment was likely. These were higher than the figures for clergy who favored teaching democracy (53, 40, and 50 percent, respectively) or who favored making better Christians (50, 41, and 32 percent, respectively). For teachers the differences were smaller but in the same direction. Of those who thought "good jobs" were best, 47 percent expected racial violence, 44 percent expected social unrest, and 43 percent expected police harassment. Comparable figures for those favoring the teaching of democracy were 48, 35, and 36 percent and for those favoring making better Christians, 41, 30, and 32 percent. In other words, there was a relation between the kind of solution preferred to prevent another Holocaust and the propensity to see various problems in the society. Other questions showed similar patterns. Fifty percent of the clergy who favored "good jobs" thought racial inequality was extremely serious, compared with 32 percent of those who favored teaching democracy and 21 percent of

those who favored making better Christians. Comparable figures for teachers were 31, 18, and 16 percent. Similar patterns were evident for the perception that doctors were charging too much and that the military had too much power.

57. Comparing clergy who favored teaching democracy with clergy who favored making people better Christians, 50 percent of the former compared with 32 percent of the latter felt that police harassment could definitely happen. For teachers, the comparable figures were 36 and 32 percent.

58. Sixty-three percent of the clergy who favored making people better Christians as the best solution thought declining moral standards were an extremely serious problem, compared with only 34 percent of those who favored teaching democracy and 33 percent of those who favored good jobs. The respective figures for teachers were 53, 36, and 29 percent.

59. In a much quoted passage, Durkheim writes, "The believer who has communicated with his god is not merely a man who sees new truths of which the unbeliever is ignorant; he is a man who is *stronger*. He feels within him more force, either to endure the trials of existence, or to conquer them" (quoted in Bellah, 1973:189).

60. The question read, "Suppose you had lived in Germany during World War II. Do you think you might have gone along with the Nazis in their effort to wipe out the Jews?" The percentages of clergy and teachers, respectively, giving each response were as follows: "I'm afraid I'd have probably gone along with it just like everyone else" (5 and 6 percent); "I'm not sure, but I might have" (35 and 32 percent); "No, I definitely would not have gone along with it" (38 and 43 percent); and "No, I would have actively resisted the Nazis" (23 and 17 percent).

61. Forty-four percent of the clergy who had watched all of the program said they might have gone along with the Nazis, compared with 39 percent of those who had watched some of the program and 32 percent of those who had not watched the program. This pattern did not hold among teachers. Perceptions of personal vulnerability did not vary by levels of viewing.

62. The question concerning following orders even if one injured another was prompted by Stanley Milgram's research using laboratory techniques. Milgram's findings suggested that otherwise conscientious people might be convinced under laboratory conditions to deal out electrical shocks that they believed to be painful to other experimental subjects. See Milgram (1974). Subsequent research has both challenged and confirmed Milgram's findings. For example, see Bickman and Zarantonello (1978), Hamilton (1978), Miller et al. (1974), and Zimbardo (1974). The intent of the question was to see whether or not clergy and teachers agreed with Milgram's conclusions. It read, "Some people claim that many Americans would do exactly what they're told to do, even if it hurt someone else, just like the Nazis. Do you think this is true or not true?" Fifteen percent of the clergy and 13 percent of the teachers thought it was "definitely true," 54 and 48 percent, respectively, thought it was "probably true," 26 and 31 percent thought it was "probably not true," and 5 and 7 percent thought it was "definitely not true."

63. Of those who thought the statement was definitely or probably true, 43 percent in both the clergy and teacher studies said they might have gone along with the Nazis, compared with 26 percent of the clergy and 28 percent of the

teachers who felt the statement was probably or definitely not true. These findings were replicated in the student study, in which 53 percent of those who thought the statement was true said they might have gone along, compared with 30 percent of those who thought the statement was not true. Here, the sense of vulnerability was also more pronounced among students who saw the Holocaust as a product of broad social forces than among those who thought it had been the result of only a few mentally disturbed leaders. For example, among those who thought the main reason for the Holocaust was the economic hard times in Germany, 55 percent felt they might have gone along; by comparison, only 26 percent of those who thought the main reason was the Nazis being mentally disturbed said they might have gone along. The student data included a question that allowed another dimension of the sense of vulnerability to be explored as well. The study asked, "To what extent do you think most Germans knew what the Nazis were doing to Jews," in response to which 21 percent said "knew a lot," 54 percent said "knew something," and 25 percent said "knew little or nothing." The expectation was that those who felt the Germans had known a lot about what was going on would be more likely to say that they themselves might have gone along with the Nazis. The results showed just the opposite. Among those who thought the Germans knew a lot, only 30 percent said they might have gone along, compared with 53 percent of those who thought the Germans knew little or nothing. This finding seems to suggest that the feeling of vulnerability represents a fear of unknowingly getting "caught up" in something, rather than willingly taking part in atrocities.

64. Thirty percent of those who thought Americans would definitely blindly obey orders had preached a sermon on the Holocaust, compared with 21 percent of those who thought Americans would probably blindly obey orders, 18 percent of those who thought they probably would not do so, and 21 percent of those who thought Americans would definitely not blindly obey orders. The proportions who had mentioned the Holocaust in a sermon also varied in this manner. The respective figures were 87 percent, 79 percent, 76 percent, and 71 percent.

65. Forty-six percent of the teachers who thought Americans would definitely obey orders blindly said they favored devoting at least five hours of instruction to the Holocaust, compared with 41 percent of those who thought Americans would probably do so, 38 percent of those who thought Americans would probably not do so, and 22 percent of those who thought Americans would definitely not blindly obey orders. This question—support for instruction—was used as an indicator of activity among teachers instead of actual classroom instruction because a number of the teachers were not employed in full-time classroom situations.

66. Thirty-five percent of the clergy who had preached a sermon on the Holocaust thought they would have actively resisted the Nazis, compared with 19 percent of those who had not preached a sermon on it; 25 percent of those who had mentioned the Holocaust in a sermon gave this response, compared with 15 percent of those who had not mentioned it. Among teachers, 34 percent of those who favored twenty-five or more hours of classroom instruction about the Holocaust said they would have actively resisted, compared with 25 percent of those

who favored between ten and twenty-five hours, 17 percent of those who favored between five and ten hours, 13 percent of those who favored between one
and five hours, and 11 percent of those who favored less than one hour.

67. The question read, "Suppose the government asked you to do something
you felt was wrong. Which of the following do you think you would actually
do?" Twenty-one percent of the clergy and 13 percent of the teachers said, "I'd
do what I felt was right, no matter how much the government tried to stop me."
Forty-six and 44 percent, respectively, responded, "Frankly, it would be a hard
decision, but I honestly feel that I'd do what I felt was right." Thirty-two and 42
percent said, "I hope I would do what was right, although one never knows for
sure what he'll do until the time comes." Less than 1 percent of each group responded, "If it wasn't very serious, I really think it would make more sense to go
ahead and do it rather than get into trouble with the government." Among
those who felt they could have actively resisted the Nazis, 41 percent of the
clergy and 31 percent of the teachers felt they would do what was right if the
government asked them to do something that was wrong, compared with 24
and 14 percent, respectively, among those who said they probably wouldn't
have gone along with the Nazis, 8 and 5 percent of those who said they might
have gone along with the Nazis, and 6 and 4 percent of those who said they
probably would have gone along.

CHAPTER FIVE

1. A discussion of the sources of ideological movements is included in Chapter 7.

2. These four conditions are discussed in greater detail in Chapter 8 in conjunction with the institutionalization of science.

3. A third concept—cult—is often introduced as well. By one set of criteria,
a cult differs from a sect chiefly by virtue of originating as an independent organization rather than as a splinter group from an established organization; in
other treatments, cults are simply less stable or more dependent on a charismatic
leader than are sects. It would appear preferable to retain these questions about
the origins and evolutions of religious movements as empirical matters rather
than prejudge them by the definitional process. On the debate over terminology,
see especially Stark and Bainbridge (1985).

4. "Civil religion" may fit this category; however, civil religion in modern
societies, although appealing to a large environment, generally does not appear
to evoke *intense* commitments.

5. Representatives of the perspective concentrating on the growth of institutional differentiation between religion and the state include Donald Eugene
Smith (1970). For a critique, see Levine (1979, 1981:24–25).

6. On Latin America, see especially Levine (1980, 1981), Smith (1982),
Dussel (1981), Bruneau (1982); also see Levine (1985) for a wide-ranging review of the literature; studies of religion and politics in the Middle East include
Esposito (1983), Arjomand (1984a, 1984b), Piscatori (1982), Voll (1982), Haddad (1982), Fischer (1980), Keddie (1983), and Pipes (1983). Recent work has
also focused on Poland (Pomian-Srzednicki, 1982), Italy (Kertzer, 1980), Ire-

land (Bowen, 1983; Gallagher and Worrall, 1982), and Israel (Elazar, 1983; Liebman and Don-Yehiya, 1983, 1984). Work on the United States has been somewhat more scattered, often dealing with specific religiopolitical movements or with the relations between religion and voting. Several studies of more general use include Kelly (1983), Benson and Williams (1982), Mechling (1978), Sorauf (1976), Bourg (1980), and Robertson (1981). Earlier works that are still valuable include Stokes and Pfeffer (1964), Pfeffer (1967), and Stroup (1967). An excellent source for more specific studies is the *Journal of Church and State*.

7. For an extensive review of the literature on civil religion, see Gehrig (1979); also see Hammond (1976) and John F. Wilson (1979). Most of the work on civil religion has been limited to the American case, but several valuable studies that provide comparisons are also available; see especially Moodie (1975), Liebman and Don-Yehiya (1983), and the essays in Bellah and Hammond (1980).

8. Further examples of increased interest in and access to national agendas on the part of religions are given in Chapter 7.

9. Further evidence on this point concerning the retention of Roman Catholicism for France and England is presented in Chapter 9.

CHAPTER SIX

1. Some of the more interesting of these studies, by subject matter, include the following: Middle Ages: Lerner (1972), Moore (1975); early modern Europe: Bruckner (1968), Thomas (1971), LeRoy Ladurie (1979); Third World: Wilson (1973); American rural south: Browne (1958), Rickles (1965), Genovese (1974); Amish: Hostetler (1968); Hutterites: Peters (1965), Hostetler and Huntington (1967); Judaism: Trachtenberg (1970), Poll (1969), Friedman (1975).

2. For some statistical studies, see Greeley (1975), Gallup (1982), Wuthnow (1978), Krarup (1983), and Towler (1983). On holidays, see Caplow and Williamson (1980), Caplow (1982), and Caplow, Bahr, and Chadwick (1983); and on sports and other media events, see Owens (1980) and Goethals (1981).

3. For a mathematical proof of this assertion regarding the ability of a disconnected system to withstand external shocks, see May (1973). I am indebted to James R. Beniger for this insight; see Beniger (1981).

4. Among the relatively large number of discussions of the common experiences with which the dominant social institutions fail to deal adequately, several that bear on the subject of religion include Parsons (1951:297–321; 1978:264–299, 331–351), Cook and Wimberley (1983), Ariès (1981), and Hochschild (1978).

5. The relationship suggested by Bernstein's (1975) research appears to have gained empirical confirmation in a wide variety of settings; see, for example, Bergesen (1979) and Cerulo (1985).

6. For example, core tenets are variously combined with widely differing teachings about the so-called charismatic gifts, about prophecy, about baptism, and about church government. For an interesting discussion of the ways in

which theological tenets among evangelicals have adapted to contemporary culture, see Hunter (1987).

7. The argument here about individual freedom is the same as that developed in Chapter 3.

8. As suggested in Chapter 3, the boundary between self and actor is of particular importance in this conception of individuality.

9. Recent contributions to the debate on rationality and cultural relativism include Geertz (1984) and the essays in Hollis and Lukes (1982).

CHAPTER SEVEN

1. The following sections draw on material from Wuthnow (1980, 1982).

2. The flexibility associated with these cultural developments is often increased as well by an added emphasis on the individual (i.e., individualism becomes a decoupling ideological mechanism that favors the adaptive potential of new ideologies and ultimately contributes to the adaptability of the cultural system at large). However, the role of individualism can be overemphasized. Doing so reinforces the linear evolutionary assumptions of the modernization perspective by suggesting that individualism is simply the long-term (perhaps inevitable) tendency of modern culture. This assumption is contradicted by the fact that many revitalization movements as well as some aspects of ideological revolutions have scarcely been individualistic in character. The flexibility added to modern culture by these movements has not been a function simply or even primarily of a tolerant, "do your own thing" attitude. Rather, it must be seen, again by adopting a globalistic perspective, as resulting from opposition to established cultural systems and the rise of regionally diverse ideological movements that "block" the cultural system into an increasing number of loosely connected subsystems.

3. See, for example, the following analyses of religious movements in the United States, all of which use ideas about the effects of changing positions in the broader world order: Anthony and Robbins (1978), McGuire (1982), Wuthnow (1978), Thomas (1986), and Hunter (1987).

4. For example, studies of price fluctuations have resulted in various models that depict change occurring in regular cycles lasting approximately fifty years each; research on colonial expansion, in contrast, has divided the past half-millennium into roughly two periods, each characterized by initial expansion followed by contraction.

5. England, for example, appears to have mostly achieved the reintegration process involved in the rise of the free-market system by the end of the 1830s, whereas France underwent a series of domestic crises that lasted until 1871.

6. Variations in these generalizations concerning groups whose power increases and decreases again need to be allowed for because of differences in societal structure. In later periods of capitalist development, one of the mechanisms that appears to have maintained the core position of societies like England and France was a relatively flexible economic structure in which new elites were able to increase power and even reinvigorate established elites rather than having to operate in different societies altogether. Also, the periphery of the world econ-

omy during expansionary periods may in certain areas be gaining political power or growing economically at a more rapid pace than the core itself. England, for example, although "peripheral" with respect to the Mediterranean economy of the late Middle Ages, was nevertheless developing more rapidly by the end of the fifteenth century than many parts of the Mediterranean. The same was true of the United States relatively early in the nineteenth century. Though peripheral to the core of the mercantilist world economy of the eighteenth century (England, France, and the Low Countries), the United States rapidly became a more dynamic sector of the nineteenth-century world economy than many sectors of the earlier core. In short, peripheral status is often more clearly defined for present purposes in relation to the preceding form of world order that is being transcended than with respect to simple calculations of contemporary economic strength.

7. The Anabaptist movements are another case in which the immediate social sources of an ideological movement are domestic, even local; yet taking the broader picture into account helps illuminate why these cleavages occurred when they did.

8. Diversity is also a function of prevailing religious cultures; for example, millenarianism appears to be more common in areas exposed to the Judeo-Christian tradition, and tribal cultures without this exposure are more likely to generate spiritualistic and thaumaturgic movements.

9. Another feature of revitalization movements that has often seemed curious is why these otherwise apolitical, often pacifist, groups should arouse such violent hostility from their host environments. Part of the explanation (besides the obvious threat of religious nonconformity to established traditions) may lie in the fact that their emergence often coincides with periods of rapid expansion in which there is an exceptionally strong demand for labor. In retreating from the world, as many of these groups do, they also sometimes withdraw their labor from available markets, preferring instead to depend on subsistence incomes and communal bases of mutual support.

10. This awareness of the connection between national purpose and religious convictions has been heightened especially by the literature on "civil religion."

11. An excellent discussion of these relations among China, the Soviet Union, and the United States is found in Schurmann (1974).

CHAPTER EIGHT

1. This chapter is a revision of an article originally published in Bergesen (1980).

2. A distinction is often drawn between the Popperian and the Kuhnian perspectives because the former emphasizes gradual evolutionary development, and the latter emphasizes abrupt revolutionary changes in science. Both perspectives, however, focus almost exclusively on the internal development of scientific ideas rather than considering the relations between science and its external environment.

3. Thorner (1952) and Hooykaas (1972) are particularly interesting exten-

sions of the Merton thesis. For a useful survey of the literature, see Greaves (1969); see also the essays in Marsak (1964).

4. Thorner's (1952) study simply divided the total number of scientific discoveries in each country by total population. This strategy seriously weights the results against Catholic countries, however, because the most populous were France, Spain, and Italy. Nor does any plausible reason to divide by total population seem evident. Scientists (and therefore scientific discoveries) were by no means drawn from a national talent pool; only those with access to higher education could generally qualify; and in no case did more than fifty persons (out of total populations ranging from 5 million to 20 million in the larger countries) devote their major energies to science.

5. For example, see the discussions of science and democracy in Barber (1962), Polanyi (1964), and Merton (1973). Much of this literature can, of course, be criticized in light of advances in science under totalitarian regimes, such as Nazi Germany or Stalinist Russia. With the rise of large-scale, state-administered research and development (R&D) systems involved in scientific work on "collective goods" problems, the relation of decentralization to innovation has also become problematic (see, for example, Shrum, Wuthnow, and Beniger, 1985).

6. The concepts of "core" and "periphery," as employed in the text, derive mainly from Prebisch (1959), Shils (1972:355–371), and Wallerstein (1974). Wallerstein's intermediate concept of semiperiphery may also have applications to the study of science, but for present purposes does not appear to require separate attention.

7. Other examples also suggest that ceremony is particularly important for dramatizing membership "in good standing" in decentralized systems. For instance, athletic contests, colors, mascots, and so forth dramatize membership in loosely coupled systems such as the Ivy League or among major cities. Membership in these systems is often problematic, depending largely on recurring ritual dramatizations because a single authority capable of defining membership is generally lacking. In contrast, membership in bureaucratic organizations is generally determined and legitimated simply by a hierarchical chain of command.

8. The peculiar manner in which some of the European states patronized science makes more sense from the ceremonial perspective than from the utilitarian perspective. Had science truly been regarded as a promising endeavor for strictly utilitarian purposes, it seems surprising that Charles II gave no money to support it and Louis XIV gave relatively modest amounts in comparison with the larger resources at the state's disposal. From the ceremonial perspective, this kind of minimal support still fulfilled its function. Science was not supported adequately enough to achieve any major utilitarian goals, but supporting it even nominally created the necessary ceremonial tie between science and the state.

9. On behalf of the Medici, Galileo named the moons of Jupiter after members of their household.

10. As observed in Chapter 6, the close relation that developed between science and the state also tended to legitimate the adoption of a rational style of discourse in science (which in turn dramatized the mercantilist state's commitment

to rationality). The early scientific academies typically borrowed parliamentary modes of deliberation and reporting directly from established practices in legislative and bureaucratic agencies.

11. There is, of course, considerable support in the social network literature for the relation between centrality in communication systems and greater scientific productivity. Some of these studies are limited to relatively small samples of scientists (e.g., Breiger, 1976; Crane, 1972), but others show similar results on networks of organizations at least as large as that of the scientific academies in seventeenth-century Europe. For example, several colleagues and I have studied communication and research productivity in two national R&D networks devoted to energy problems, each involving more than three thousand scientists scattered among more than fifty major organizatons across the United States. Our findings show strong relations at both the organization and individual levels between various measures of centrality in communication networks and scientific productivity (as indicated both by bibliographic counts and by network assessments of the quality of contributions). For example, see Wuthnow, Beniger, and Shrum (1982) and Shrum, Wuthnow, and Beniger (1985). The hypothesis that core states may have used science to a greater degree for ceremonial purposes than peripheral states is more open to dispute. On theoretical grounds, it could also be argued that peripheral states might have made even greater use of this tactic because their membership may have been more in doubt. In the twentieth century it appears, for example, that Third World countries have often developed formal scientific and educational programs well beyond what their economic and political resources might warrant in order to dramatize their status as "modern" countries. Contrary to this pattern, however, the empirical evidence from the seventeenth century suggests that greater ceremonial use was made of organizational affairs in general by core states than by peripheral states. Part of the reason appears to be the fact that economic and political theory recognized that core states were more crucial to the equilibrium of the larger system and therefore paid more attention to the "balance of power" among these than among the peripheral states.

12. Darmstädter's volume was originally published in Berlin in 1908. A brief description of the material is contained in Merton (1970). I made the calculations from both sources.

13. The numbers in each case refer to all scientists listed in the Marquis volume who were living in a particular country in the year indicated. The Marquis volume does not purport to provide an inclusive listing of all known scientists, only those who had achieved some degree of eminence. It does, however, list far more names than any other single source (for example, than the multivolume *Dictionary of Scientific Biography*). The numbers for England are consistent over the entire period in that Scottish scientists are listed separately (one in 1550, four in 1600, four in 1650, eleven in 1700, twenty-two in 1750, forty-six in 1800, and eighty-two in 1850). Germany is, of course, a statistical fiction for this period, because it was not politically unified until 1871. Prussia was by far the leading German state both politically and scientifically. During much of the mercantilist era, many of the German states functioned to some degree as an eco-

nomic unit because of the *Zollverein.* Data were tallied only through 1850 because the volume after this date appears to become decreasingly representative as the numbers of scientists began to increase dramatically.

14. The numbers of discoveries calculated for each country for the half-century preceding each date, beginning in 1500 and extending through 1850, are as follows: England, 3, 6, 32, 44, 121, 141, 341, 843; France, 4, 15, 33, 55, 75, 134, 290, 801; Germany, 19, 38, 35, 49, 93, 107, 257, 1,026; Italy, 23, 47, 67, 62, 49, 21, 44, 82; Netherlands, 8, 33, 31, 32, 65, 51, 42, 64; Switzerland, 1, 7, 5, 10, 7, 13, 22, 20; Spain, 15, 20, 8, 5, 2, 6, 6, 5; Portugal, 9, 6, 1, 0, 0, 0, 0, 1; Scandinavia, 0, 5, 13, 3, 9, 11, 13, 29; United States, 0, 0, 0, 0, 0, 4, 20, 137.

15. It is possible to speculate that some of the differences in the content or style of scientific work in these countries are also associated with their position in the larger European social system. Specifically, scientific work in core areas may differ systematically from scientific work in periphery areas, given differences in access to communication and legitimacy. Core areas, in particular, seem more likely to be conducive to *theoretical* innovations, along with other types of discoveries; periphery areas seem more likely to be limited to making *empirical* and *technical* innovations. Although it is difficult to distinguish precisely among these kinds of work, scientists commonly use the three terms to characterize their own work. In rough contrast, theoretical innovations are concerned with ordering phenomena (i.e., finding a general order of things, a pattern, system, or unifying explanation, such as Boyle's Law). Empirical activity involves observing phenomena and making new descriptions (e.g., Leeuwenhoek's discovery of bacteria). Technical activity consists of inventing tools or methods (e.g., the invention of the telescope). Reasons for expecting greater concentrations of theoretical activity in core areas include the resources in these areas for (1) chartering scholars with the task of ordering culture in a general way, (2) providing the confidence and legitimacy to innovate (as in the case also of "center" concepts in primitive cultures that define areas from which supernatural revelations can arise), (3) providing the confluence of information channels necessary for constructing new integrative models, (4) providing material resources to sustain a larger critical mass of scientists in one place, from which cross-fertilization and specialization can develop, (5) providing the communication channels necessary for disseminating a new theory to all parts of the scientific community, and (6) legitimating new ideas simply because they come from core areas. For the seventeenth century, some support for the hypothesis comes from an examination of the geographical origins of the forty-four scientific discoveries given greatest attention in several leading histories of science. Of the seventeen discoveries that could be classified as theoretical innovations, eleven originated in the core areas of England, France, and Germany; of the seventeen discoveries that could be classified as empirical discoveries, only four originated in these countries; and of the ten technical inventions, only three originated in these areas.

CHAPTER NINE

1. An earlier version of this chapter was published in the *American Sociological Review* 50 (December 1985): 799–821.

2. For a useful argument that interprets Swanson in a way that circumvents the two criticisms, see Robertson and Lechner (1984).

3. Bergesen (1977, 1984), for example, in applying Swanson's concept of immanence to the study of state structures and deviance, suggests that the mechanism by which political experience influences ideology is collective rituals, specifically political witch-hunts, in which the nature of collective purposes is actually dramatized.

4. Winter (1984) also raises the problem of the complexity of the process but resolves it in a way that seems unsatisfactory for understanding the influence of state structures on ideology in complex societies. His argument is that social forces represent an example of Mead's "generalized other" and are thus internalized by the individual according to principles of functional psychology.

5. Although the problems involved in Swanson's choice of specific cases remain, some of the original study's lack of representativeness can be excused on the same grounds, namely, that Swanson was chiefly concerned with theoretically strategic comparisons rather than an effort either to generalize to a larger population of cases or to provide an empirically satisfactory explanation for the Reformation.

6. Powerful factions in the court itself also opposed the reforms, of course, and remained loyal to Catholicism for a number of decades (e.g., Ives, 1972).

CHAPTER TEN

1. Part of the reason why the distinction between the interpretive and positivistic sciences is unsatisfactory is that the positivistic approach is now generally regarded as an overly simplistic orientation in the social sciences.

2. Several writers have suggested that Erving Goffman's work on the rituals of everyday life is compelling because the evidence is so completely in the domain of shared experience. At the other extreme, anthropological work sometimes succeeds, even on the basis of sketchy evidence, because it deals with societies about which little is known.

3. For an example of an investigator interpreting by describing an event's context or framework, see Hunter (1987), who employs the question "What do these things mean?" more as a device for reflecting on their broader social significance than for actually probing the subjective meanings attached to them.

4. It is, of course, possible in many cases to obtain and examine cultural data consisting of discourse about subjective concepts (such as guilt, anxiety, etc.), but these kinds of data should not be confused with direct measures of subjective conditions.

5. This requirement of distance is why anthropological studies of other cultures often succeed to a greater extent than analyses of one's own culture.

6. The term "hegemony" is, of course, from Gramsci's writings, but has gained wider currency in the literature advancing the idea of a "dominant ideology."

Bibliography

Addy, Sidney Oldall.
    1970.   *Church and Manor: A Study in English Economic History.* New York: Augustus M. Kelley.

Aidala, Angela A.
    1984.   " 'The Consciousness Reformation' Revisited." *Journal for the Scientific Study of Religion* 23: 44–59.

Alsop, J. D.
    1982.   "The Theory and Practice of Tudor Taxation." *English Historical Review* 97: 1–30.

Amery, Julian.
    1969.   *The Life of Joseph Chamberlain,* vol. 5. London: St. Martin's.

Ammerman, Nancy Taton.
    1983.   "The Fundamentalist Worldview: Ideology and Social Structure in an Independent Fundamental Church." Ph.D. dissertation, Yale University.

Anderson, Perry.
    1974.   *Lineages of the Absolutist State.* London: Humanities Press.

Anthony, Dick, and Thomas L. Robbins.
    1978.   "The Effect of Detente on the Growth of New Religions: Reverend Moon and the Unification Church." In *Understanding the New Religions,* edited by Jacob Needleman and George Baker, 80–100. New York: Seabury.

Antoun, Richard, and Mary Hegland, eds.
    1986.   *Religious Resurgence in Comparative Perspective.* Syracuse, N.Y.: Syracuse University Press.

Apostle, Richard A., Charles Y. Glock, Thomas Piazza, and Marijean Suelzle.
    1983.   *The Anatomy of Racial Attitudes.* Berkeley and Los Angeles: University of California Press.

Ariès, Philippe.
    1981.   *The Hour of Our Death.* New York: Knopf.
Arjomand, Said Amir.
    1984a.   *The Shadow of God and the Hidden Imam: Religion, Political Order, and Societal Change in Shi'ite Iran from the Beginning to 1890.* Chicago: University of Chicago Press.
    1984b.   *From Nationalism to Revolutionary Islam.* Albany: State University of New York Press.
Artz, Frederick B.
    1966.   *The Development of Technical Education in France, 1500–1850.* Cambridge, Mass.: MIT Press.
Ashley, Maurice.
    1973.   *England in the Seventeenth Century.* London: Penguin Books.
Ault, James M., Jr.
    1983.   "The Shawmut Valley Baptist Church: Reconstructing a Traditional Order of Family Life in a Fundamental Community." Unpublished paper, Pembroke Center, Brown University.
Autrand, Françoise.
    1974.   *Pouvoir et société en France XIVe–XVe siècles.* Paris: Presses Universitaires de France.
Bainbridge, William Sims.
    1978.   *Satan's Power: A Deviant Psychotherapy Cult.* Berkeley and Los Angeles: University of California Press.
Barber, Bernard.
    1962.   *Science and the Social Order.* New York: Collier Books.
Barnes, Barry.
    1974.   *Scientific Knowledge and Sociological Theory.* London: Routledge and Kegan Paul.
Barraclough, Geoffrey.
    1963.   *European Unity in Thought and Action.* Oxford: Basil Blackwell.
Barrett, William.
    1978.   *The Illusion of Technique: A Search for Meaning in a Technological Civilization.* Garden City, N.Y.: Doubleday.
Barthes, Roland.
    1967.   *Elements of Semiology.* New York: Hill and Wang.
    1972.   *Mythologies.* New York: Hill and Wang.
Batho, Gordon.
    1967a.   "Landlords in England: The Crown." In *The Agrarian History of England and Wales,* vol. 4, edited by Joan Thirsk, 256–276. Cambridge: Cambridge University Press.
    1967b.   "Landlords in England: Noblemen, Gentlemen, and Yeomen." In *The Agrarian History of England and Wales,* vol. 4, edited by Joan Thirsk, 276–306. Cambridge: Cambridge University Press.

Baulant, Micheline.
  1976.   "Prix et salaires à Paris au XVIe siècle: Sources et résultats." *Annales: Economies, sociétés, civilisations* 31: 954–995.
Beckford, James.
  1975.   *The Trumpet of Prophecy: A Sociological Study of the Jehovah's Witnesses.* New York: Wiley.
  1986.   *Cult Controversies.* London: Tavistock.
Bell, Daniel.
  1976.   *The Cultural Contradictions of Capitalism.* New York: Basic Books.
  1977.   "Beyond Modernism, Beyond Self." In *Art, Politics, and Will: Essays in Honor of Lionel Trilling,* edited by Quentin Anderson, Stephen Donadio, and Steven Marcus, 213–253. New York: Basic Books.
Bellah, Robert N.
  1970.   *Beyond Belief: Essays on Religion in a Post-Traditional World.* New York: Harper and Row.
  1973.   "Introduction." In *Emile Durkheim on Morality and Society,* edited by Robert N. Bellah, ix–lv. Chicago: University of Chicago Press.
  1975.   *The Broken Covenant.* New York: Seabury.
  1982.   "Cultural Pluralism and Religious Particularism." In *Freedom of Religion in America: Historical Roots, Philosophical Concepts, and Contemporary Problems,* edited by Henry B. Clark II, 33–52. New Brunswick, N.J.: Transaction Books.
Bellah, Robert N., and Phillip E. Hammond.
  1980.   *Varieties of Civil Religion.* New York: Harper and Row.
Bellah, Robert N., Richard Madsen, William M. Sullivan, Ann Swidler, and Steven M. Tipton.
  1985.   *Habits of the Heart: Individualism and Commitment in American Life.* Berkeley and Los Angeles: University of California Press.
Ben-David, Joseph.
  1971.   *The Social Role of the Scientist.* Englewood Cliffs, N.J.: Prentice-Hall.
Ben-Yehuda, Nachman.
  1980.   "The European Witch Craze of the Fourteenth to Seventeenth Centuries: A Sociologists's Perspective." *American Journal of Sociology* 86: 1–31.
Bender, Lauretta.
  1970.   "The Maturation Process and Hallucinations in Children." In *Origins and Mechanisms of Hallucinations,* edited by Wolfram Keup, 95–101. New York: Plenum.
Bendix, Reinhard.
  1977.   *Nation-Building and Citizenship,* rev. ed. Berkeley and Los Angeles: University of California Press.

Benedict, Philip.
    1981.   *Rouen During the Wars of Religion.* Cambridge: Cambridge
                 University Press.
Beniger, James R.
    1981.   "Ideology as a Dynamic System: Complexity Versus Stability."
                 Unpublished paper, Department of Sociology, Princeton Univer-
                 sity.
    1986.   *The Control Revolution: Technological and Economic Origins
                 of the Information Society.* Cambridge, Mass.: Harvard Univer-
                 sity Press.
Benson, Peter L., and Dorothy L. Williams.
    1982.   *Religion on Capitol Hill: Myths and Realities.* New York:
                 Harper and Row.
Bercé, Yves-Marie.
    1980.   *Révoltes et révolutions dans l'Europe moderne.* Paris: Presses
                 Universitaires de France.
Berger, Peter L.
    1969.   *The Sacred Canopy: Elements of a Sociological Theory of Reli-
                 gion.* Garden City, N.Y.: Doubleday.
Berger, Peter L., and Thomas Luckmann.
    1966.   *The Social Construction of Reality.* Garden City, N.Y.: Double-
                 day.
Bergesen, Albert.
    1977.   "Political Witch-Hunts: The Sacred and the Subversive in Cross-
                 National Perspective." *American Sociological Review* 42: 220–
                 233.
    1978.   "A Durkheimian Theory of Political Witch-Hunts with the Chi-
                 nese Cultural Revolution of 1966–1969 as an Example." *Jour-
                 nal for the Scientific Study of Religion* 17: 19–29.
    1979.   "Spirituals, Jazz, Blues, and Soul Music: The Role of Elaborated
                 and Restricted Codes in the Maintenance of Social Solidarity."
                 In *The Religious Dimension,* edited by Robert Wuthnow, 333–
                 350. New York: Academic Press.
    1980.   *Studies of the Modern World-System.* New York: Academic
                 Press.
    1984.   *The Sacred and the Subversive: Political Witch-Hunts as Na-
                 tional Rituals.* Storrs, Conn.: Society for the Scientific Study of
                 Religion Monograph Series.
Bernal, J. D.
    1971.   *Science in History,* 4 vols. Cambridge, Mass.: MIT Press.
Bernstein, Basil.
    1975.   *Class, Codes and Control.* New York: Schocken.
Bibby, Reginald W.
    1979.   "Religion and Modernity: The Canadian Case." *Journal for the
                 Scientific Study of Religion* 18: 1–17.

Bibby, R., and M. Brinkerhoff.
1973.   "The Circulation of the Saints." *Journal for the Scientific Study of Religion* 12:273–285.
1983.   "Circulation of the Saints Revisited: A Longitudinal Look at Conservative Church Growth." *Journal for the Scientific Study of Religion* 22: 253–262.

Bickman, L., and M. Zarantonello.
1978.   "The Effects of Deception and Level of Obedience on Subjects' Ratings of the Milgram Study." *Personality and Social Psychology Bulletin* 4: 81–85.

Blackwood, Larry.
1979.   "Social Change and Commitment to the Work Ethic." In *The Religious Dimension,* edited by Robert Wuthnow, 241–256. New York: Academic Press.

Bleicher, Josef.
1980.   *Contemporary Hermeneutics: Hermeneutics as Method, Philosophy and Critique.* London: Routledge and Kegan Paul.

Bloch, Marc.
1966.   *French Rural History: An Essay on Its Basic Characteristics.* Berkeley and Los Angeles: University of California Press.

Block, Fred L.
1977.   *The Origins of International Economic Disorder: A Study of United States International Monetary Policy from World War II to the Present.* Berkeley and Los Angeles: University of California Press.

Bloor, David.
1976.   *Knowledge and Social Imagery.* London: Routledge and Kegan Paul.

Bonney, Richard.
1981.   *The King's Debts: Finance and Politics in France, 1589–1661.* Oxford: Clarendon Press.

Borhek, James T., and Richard F. Curtis.
1975.   *A Sociology of Belief.* New York: Wiley.

Bossy, John.
1973.   "Blood and Baptism: Kinship, Community and Christianity in Western Europe from the Fourteenth to the Seventeenth Centuries." In *Sanctity and Secularity: The Church and the World,* edited by Derek Baker, 129–144. Oxford: Basil Blackwell.
1975.   "The Social History of Confession in the Age of the Reformation." *Transactions of the Royal Historical Society* 25: 21–38.
1981.   "Essai de sociographie de la masse, 1200–1700." *Annales: Economies, sociétés, civilisations* 36: 44–70.

Bottomore, T. B.
1964.   *Karl Marx: Selected Writings in Sociology and Social Philosophy.* New York: McGraw-Hill.

Bourg, Carroll J.
    1980.   "Politics and Religion." *Sociological Analysis* 41: 297–315.
Bouwsma, William J.
    1968.   "Swanson's Reformation." *Comparative Studies in Society and History* 10: 486–491.
Bowden, Peter.
    1962.   *The Wool Trade in Tudor and Stuart England*. London: Macmillan.
Bowen, Kurt.
    1983.   *Protestants in a Catholic State: Ireland's Privileged Minority.* Montreal: McGill-Queens University Press.
Braudel, Fernand.
    1973.   *Capitalism and Material Life, 1400–1800*. New York: Harper and Row.
Breiger, Ronald L.
    1976.   "Career Attributes and Network Structure: A Blockmodel Study of a Biomedical Research Specialty." *American Sociological Review* 41: 117–135.
Brigden, Susan.
    1981.   "Tithe Controversy in Reformation London." *Journal of Ecclesiastical History* 32: 285–301.
Brodek, Theodor V.
    1971.   "Socio-Political Realities in the Holy Roman Empire." *Journal of Interdisciplinary History* 1: 395–406.
Brown, Harcourt.
    1934.   *Scientific Organization in Seventeenth Century France (1620–1680)*. Baltimore: Johns Hopkins University Press.
Browne, Ray B.
    1958.   *Popular Beliefs and Practices from Alabama*. Berkeley and Los Angeles: University of California Press.
Bruce, Steve.
    1983.   "Social Change and Collective Behaviour: The Revival in Eighteenth-Century Ross-shire." *British Journal of Sociology* 34: 554–572.
Bruckner, Wolfgang.
    1968.   "Popular Piety in Central Europe." *Journal of the Folklore Institute* 5: 158–174.
Brummer, Vincent.
    1982.   *Theology and Philosophical Inquiry*. Philadelphia: Westminster.
Bruneau, Thomas C.
    1982.   *The Church in Brazil: The Politics of Religion*. Austin: University of Texas Press.
Bruner, Jerome S., Rose R. Oliver, and Patricia M. Greenfield.
    1966.   *Studies in Cognitive Growth*. New York: Wiley.
Budd, Susan.
    1973.   *Sociologists and Religion*. London: Collier-Macmillan.

Burguière, A.
1978.   "Le rituel de mariage en France: Pratiques ecclésiastiques et pratiques populaires (XVIe–XVIIIe siècles)." *Annales: Economies, sociétés, civilisations* 33: 637–649.

Burke, Peter.
1974.   *Venice and Amsterdam: A Study of Seventeenth-Century Elites.* London: Temple Smith.

Burnstein, Barbara.
1979.   "Television, the Schools and the Problem of Communicating the Holocaust." Unpublished paper, University of Pittsburgh, Center for International Studies.

Calleo, David P., and Benjamin M. Rowland.
1973.   *America and the World Political Economy: Atlantic Dreams and National Realities.* Bloomington: Indiana University Press.

Caplow, Theodore.
1982.   "Christmas Gifts and Kin Networks." *American Sociological Review* 47: 383–392.

Caplow, Theodore, and Margaret Holmes Williamson.
1980.   "Decoding Middletown's Easter Bunny: A Study in American Iconography." *Semiotica* 32: 221–232.

Caplow, Theodore, Howard M. Bahr, and Bruce A. Chadwick.
1983.   *All Faithful People: Change and Continuity in Middletown's Religion.* Minneapolis: University of Minnesota Press.

Carroll, Michael P.
1983.   "Visions of the Virgin Mary: The Effect of Family Structures on Marian Apparitions." *Journal for the Scientific Study of Religion* 22: 205–221.
1986.   *Ave Maria, Gratia Plena: The Social Origins of the Mary Cult.* Princeton, N.J.: Princeton University Press.

Cerulo, Karen A.
1985.   "Music as Symbolic Communication: The Case of the National Anthem." Ph.D. dissertation, Princeton University.

Chase-Dunn, Christopher.
1975.   "The Effects of International Economic Dependence on Development and Inequality: A Cross-National Study." *American Sociological Review* 40: 720–738.

Chirot, Daniel.
1977.   *Social Change in the Twentieth Century.* New York: Harcourt Brace Jovanovich.

Chomsky, Noam.
1957.   *Syntactic Structures.* The Hague: Mouton.
1965.   *Aspects of the Theory of Syntax.* Cambridge, Mass.: MIT Press.

Christian, William A., Jr.
1981.   *Local Religion in Sixteenth-Century Spain.* Princeton, N.J.: Princeton University Press.

Cipolla, Carlo M.
1976.   *Before the Industrial Revolution: European Society and Economy, 1000–1700.* New York: W. W. Norton.

Clark, G. N.
1947.   *The Seventeenth Century.* London: Oxford University Press.
1970.   *Science and Social Welfare in the Age of Newton.* Oxford: Clarendon Press.

Clark, Peter.
1977.   *English Provincial Society from the Reformation to the Revolution: Religion, Politics and Society in Kent, 1500–1640.* Sussex: Harvester Press.

Contamine, Philip.
1972.   *Guerre, état et société à la fin du moyen age: Etudes sur les armeés des rois de France, 1337–1494.* Paris: Presses Universitaires de France.

Converse, Philip E.
1964.   "The Nature of Belief Systems in Mass Publics." In *Ideology and Discontent,* edited by David E. Apter, 206–261. New York: Free Press.

Cook, Judith A., and Dale W. Wimberley.
1983.   "If I Should Die Before I Wake: Religious Commitment and Adjustment to the Death of a Child." *Journal for the Scientific Study of Religion* 22: 222–239.

Cornforth, Maurice.
1955.   *The Theory of Knowledge.* New York: International Publishers.

Cornwall, J.
1970.   "The English Population in the Early Sixteenth Century." *Economic History Review* 23: 32–44.

Crane, Diana.
1972.   *Invisible Colleges: Diffusion of Knowledge in Scientific Communities.* Chicago: University of Chicago Press.

Cross, Claire.
1976.   *Church and People, 1450–1660: The Triumph of the Laity in the English Church.* Atlantic Highlands, N.J.: Humanities Press.
1980.   "Priests into Ministers: The Establishment of Protestant Practice in the City of York, 1530–1630." In *Reformation Principle and Practice: Essays in Honour of Arthur Geoffrey Dickens,* edited by Peter Newman Brooks, 203–226. London: Scholar Press.

Cuddihy, John.
1978.   *No Offense: Civil Religion and Protestant Taste.* New York: Seabury.

d'Aquili, Eugene G., Charles D. Laughlin, Jr., and John McManus, eds.
1979.   *The Spectrum of Ritual: A Biogenetic Structural Analysis.* New York: Columbia University Press.

Darnton, Robert.
1984.   *The Great Cat Massacre and Other Episodes in French Cultural History.* New York: Basic Books.

Davies, C. S. L.
   1968.   "The Pilgrimage of Grace Reconsidered." *Past and Present* 41:
                54–76.
   1977.   *Peace, Print and Protestantism, 1450–1558*. London: Paladin.
Davis, Natalie Zemon.
   1965.   "Strikes and Salvation at Lyons." *Archiv für Reforma-
                tionsgeschichte 56*: 48–64.
   1969.   "Deforming the Reformation." *New York Review of Books* 7
                (April 10): 35–38.
   1971.   "Missed Connections: Religion and Regime." *Journal of Inter-
                disciplinary History* 1: 381–394.
   1975.   *Society and Culture in Early Modern France*. Stanford, Calif.:
                Stanford University Press.
   1981.   "The Sacred and the Body Social in Sixteenth-Century Lyon."
                Past and Present 90: 40–70.
Dewald, Jonathan.
   1980.   *The Formation of a Provincial Nobility: The Magistrates of the
                Parlement of Rouen, 1499–1610*. Princeton, N.J.: Princeton
                University Press.
Dickens, A. G.
   1964.   *The English Reformation*. New York: Schocken.
Dickinson, J. C.
   1979.   *The Later Middle Ages: From the Norman Conquest to the Eve
                of the Reformation*. London: Adam and Charles Black.
Dietz, Frederick C.
   1964.   *English Government Finance, 1485–1558*. London: Frank
                Cass.
Dodds, M. H., and R. Dodds.
   1915.   *The Pilgrimage of Grace and the Exeter Conspiracy*. Cam-
                bridge: Cambridge University Press.
Dohrenwend, Bruce P., and Barbara S. Dohrenwend, eds.
   1974.   *Stressful Life Events: Their Nature and Effects*. New York:
                Wiley.
Douglas, Mary.
   1966.   *Purity and Danger: An Analysis of Concepts of Pollution and
                Taboo*. London: Penguin.
   1967.   "The Meaning of Myth, with Special Reference to 'La Geste
                d'Asdiwal.' " In *The Structural Study of Myth and Totemism*,
                edited by Edmund Leach, 49–70. London: Tavistock.
   1970.   *Natural Symbols*. New York: Vintage.
   1979.   *The World of Goods*. New York: Basic Books.
   1980.   "Theories of Pollution." Unpublished lecture, Christian Gauss
                Seminar in Criticism, Princeton University.
   1982.   *Risk and Culture*. Berkeley and Los Angeles: University of Cali-
                fornia Press.
   1984.   *Food in the Social Order: Studies of Food and Festivities in
                Three American Communities*. New York: Russell Sage.

Downton, James V., Jr.
  1979.   *Sacred Journeys: The Conversion of Young Americans to Divine
             Light Mission*. New York: Columbia University Press.
Drake, Stillman.
  1957.   *Discoveries and Opinions of Galileo*. Garden City, N.Y.: Dou-
             bleday.
Dreyfus, Hubert L., and Paul Rabinow.
  1982.   *Michel Foucault: Beyond Structuralism and Hermeneutics*. Chi-
             cago: University of Chicago Press.
Dumont, Louis.
  1970.   *Homo Hierarchicus: The Caste System and Its Implications*. Chi-
             cago: University of Chicago Press.
  1977.   *From Mandeville to Marx*. Chicago: University of Chicago
             Press.
Durkheim, Emile.
  1933.   *The Division of Labor in Society*. New York: Free Press.
  1951.   *Suicide*. New York: Free Press.
  1956.   *Education and Sociology*. New York: Free Press.
  1958.   *Professional Ethics and Civic Morals*. New York: Free Press.
  1961.   *Moral Education*. New York: Free Press.
  1962.   *Socialism*. New York: Collier.
  1965.   *The Elementary Forms of the Religious Life*. New York: Free
             Press. [Originally published 1915]
  1973.   *On Morality and Society*. Chicago: University of Chicago Press.
Dussel, Enrique.
  1981.   *A History of the Church in Latin America: Colonialism to Lib-
             eration*. Grand Rapids, Mich.: Eerdmans.
Edelstein, Marilyn Manera.
  1974.   "The Social Origins of the Episcopacy in the Reign of Francis I."
             French Historical Studies 8: 377–392.
Eisenstadt, S. N., and Louis Roniger.
  1980.   "Patron-Client Relations as a Model of Structuring Social Ex-
             change." *Comparative Studies in Society and History* 22: 42–
             77.
Elazar, Daniel J., ed.
  1983.   *Kinship and Consent: The Jewish Political Tradition and Its
             Contemporary Uses*. Washington, D.C.: University Press of
             America.
Elton, G. R.
  1953.   *The Tudor Revolution in Government: Administrative Changes
             in the Reign of Henry VIII*. Cambridge: Cambridge University
             Press.
  1958.   "The Reformation in England." In *The New Cambridge Mod-
             ern History*, vol. 2: *The Reformation, 1520–1559*, edited by
             G. R. Elton, 226–250. Cambridge: Cambridge University Press.
  1963.   *Reformation Europe, 1517–1559*. New York: Harper and
             Row.

1972.   *Policy and Police: The Enforcement of the Reformation in the Age of Thomas Cromwell.* Cambridge: Cambridge University Press.

Erikson, Kai T.
1966.   *Wayward Puritans: A Study in the Sociology of Deviance.* New York: Wiley.
1976.   *Everything in Its Path: Destruction of Community in the Buffalo Creek Flood.* New York: Simon and Schuster.

Ernst, Tilman.
1979.   "Holocaust and Political Education: Selected Results of a Representative Empirical Survey." Unpublished paper, Federal Central Office of Political Education (Berlin), Department of Planning and Development.

Esposito, John L., ed.
1983.   *Voices of Resurgent Islam.* Oxford: Oxford University Press.

Fallding, Harold.
1974.   *The Sociology of Religion.* Toronto: McGraw-Hill Ryerson.

Farb, Peter.
1973.   *Word Play.* New York: Bantam.

Febvre, Lucien.
1977.   *Life in Renaissance France.* Cambridge, Mass.: Harvard University Press.

Fieldhouse, D. K.
1966.   *The Colonial Empires from the Eighteenth Century.* New York: Delta.

Fingarette, Herbert.
1963.   *The Self in Transformation: Psychoanalysis, Philosophy and the Life of the Spirit.* New York: Harper and Row.

Firth, Raymond.
1984.   "The Plasticity of Myth: Cases from Tikopia." In *Sacred Narrative: Readings in the Theory of Myth,* edited by Alan Dundes, 207–216. Berkeley and Los Angeles: University of California Press.

Fischer, Michael M. J.
1980.   *Iran: From Religious Dispute to Revolution.* Cambridge, Mass.: Harvard University Press.

Fischer, Wolfram, and Peter Lundgreen.
1975.   "The Recruitment and Training of Administrative and Technical Personnel." In *The Formation of National States in Western Europe,* edited by Charles Tilly, 456–561. Princeton, N.J.: Princeton University Press.

Flint, John T.
1968.   "A Handbook for Historical Sociologists." *Comparative Studies in Society and History* 10: 492–509.

Foss, Michael.
1971.   *The Age of Patronage: The Arts in Society, 1660–1750.* London: Hamilton.

Foucault, Michel.
 1965.   *Madness and Civilization: A History of Insanity in the Age of Reason.* New York: Random House.
 1970.   *The Order of Things: An Archeology of the Human Sciences.* New York: Random House.
 1972.   *The Archeology of Knowledge.* New York: Random House.
 1975.   *The Birth of the Clinic: An Archeology of Medical Perception.* New York: Random House.
 1979.   *Discipline and Punish: The Birth of the Prison.* New York: Vintage.
Fourquin, Guy.
 1964.   *Les campagnes de la région parisienne à la fin du moyen age du milieu du XIIIe siècle au début du XVIe siècle.* Paris: Presses Universitaires de France.
Francois, M.
 1972.   "Reformation and Society: An Analysis of Guy Swanson's Religion and Regime." *Comparative Studies in Society and History* 14: 287–305.
Friedman, Milton.
 1962.   *Capitalism and Freedom.* Chicago: University of Chicago Press.
Friedman, Norman L.
 1975.   "Jewish Popular Culture in Contemporary America." *Judaism* 24: 263–277.
Fulbrook, Mary.
 1983.   *Piety and Politics: Religion and the Rise of Absolutism in England, Württemberg, and Prussia.* Cambridge: Cambridge University Press.
Gadamer, H. G.
 1975.   "Hermeneutics and Social Science." *Cultural Hermeneutics* 2: 307–316.
Gager, John G.
 1975.   *Kingdom and Community: The Social World of Early Christianity.* Englewood Cliffs, N.J.: Prentice-Hall.
 1983.   *The Origins of Anti-Semitism: Attitudes Toward Judaism in Pagan and Christian Antiquity.* Oxford: Oxford University Press.
Gallagher, Eric, and Stanley Worrall.
 1982.   *Christians in Ulster, 1968–1980.* Oxford: Oxford University Press.
Gallup, George, Jr.
 1980.   "Looking Ahead to the 1980s." *Religion in America, 1979–80.* Princeton, N.J.: Princeton Religion Research Center.
 1982.   *Adventures in Immortality: A Look Beyond the Threshold of Death.* New York: McGraw-Hill.
Gallup Organization.
 1982.   *Faith Development Study.* Princeton, N.J.: Gallup Organization.

1983.   *Self-Esteem Study*. Princeton, N.J.: Gallup Organization.
1984.   *Religious Television in America*. Princeton, N.J.: Gallup Organization.

Galpern, A. N.
1974.   "Late Medieval Piety in Sixteenth-Century Champagne." In *The Pursuit of Holiness in Late Medieval and Renaissance Religion*, edited by Charles Trinkaus, 141–176. Leiden: E.J. Brill.
1976.   *The Religions of the People of Sixteenth-Century Champagne*. Cambridge, Mass.: Harvard University Press.

Geertz, Clifford.
1968.   *Islam Observed: Religious Development in Morocco and Indonesia*. Chicago: University of Chicago Press.
1973.   *The Interpretation of Cultures*. New York: Basic Books.
1984.   "Distinguished Lecture: Anti Anti-Relativism." *American Anthropologist* 86: 263–278.

Gehrig, Gail.
1979.   *American Civil Religion: An Assessment*. Storrs, Conn.: Society for the Scientific Study of Religion Monograph Series, No. 3.

Genovese, Eugene D.
1974.   *Roll, Jordan, Roll: The World the Slaves Made*. New York: Random House.

Geraets, Thomas, ed.
1979.   *Rationality Today*. Ottawa: University of Ottawa Press.

Gerlach, Luther P., and Virginia Hine.
1970.   *People, Power, Change: Movements of Social Transformation*. Indianapolis, Ind.: Bobbs-Merrill.

Geuss, Raymond.
1981.   *The Idea of a Critical Theory: Habermas and the Frankfurt School*. Cambridge: Cambridge University Press.

Geyl, Pieter.
1932.   *The Revolt of the Netherlands, 1555–1609*. London: Williams and Norgate.

Geymonat, Ludovico.
1965.   *Galileo Galilei: A Biography and Inquiry into His Philosophy of Science*. New York: McGraw-Hill.

Giddens, Anthony.
1971.   *Capitalism and Modern Social Theory: An Analysis of the Writings of Marx, Durkheim, and Max Weber*. Cambridge: Cambridge University Press.

Gilbert, G. Nigel, and Michael Mulkay.
1984.   *Opening Pandora's Box: A Sociological Analysis of Scientists' Discourse*. Cambridge: Cambridge University Press.

Glock, Charles Y.
1973.   "On the Origin and Evolution of Religious Groups." In *Religion in Sociological Perspective*, edited by Charles Y. Glock, 207–220. Belmont, Calif.: Wadsworth.

1976.   "Consciousness Among Contemporary Youth: An Interpreta-
             tion." In *The New Religious Consciousness*, edited by Charles
             Y. Glock and Robert N. Bellah, 353–356. Berkeley and Los An-
             geles: University of California Press.
Glock, Charles Y., and Phillip E. Hammond, eds.
1973.   *Beyond the Classics? Essays in the Scientific Study of Religion.*
             New York: Harper and Row.
Glock, Charles Y., and Rodney Stark.
1965.   *Religion and Society in Tension.* Chicago: Rand McNally.
Gluckman, Max.
1962.   "Les rites de passage." In *Essays on the Ritual of Social Rela-
             tions,* edited by Max Gluckman, 1–52. Manchester: Manches-
             ter University Press.
Goethals, Gregor T.
1981.   *The TV Ritual: Worship at the Video Altar.* Boston: Beacon
             Press.
Goffman, Erving.
1967.   *Interaction Ritual.* Garden City, N.Y.: Doubleday.
1974.   *Frame Analysis: An Essay on the Organization of Experience.*
             New York: Harper and Row.
Goubert, Pierre.
1973.   *The Ancien Régime: French Society, 1600–1750.* New York:
             Harper and Row.
Greaves, Richard L.
1969.   "Puritanism and Science: The Anatomy of a Controversy." *Jour-
             nal of the History of Ideas* 31: 345–368.
Greeley, Andrew M.
1975.   *The Sociology of the Paranormal: A Reconnaissance.* Beverly
             Hills, Calif.: Sage.
Greenberg, Barry, Barbara Bader, Steve Fain, and Marshall Farkas.
1978.   "An Overview and Preliminary Findings of 'A Study of the Im-
             pact of the Television Show "Holocaust." ' " Unpublished pa-
             per, Florida International University.
Griffiths, Gordon.
1974.   "The State: Absolute or Limited?" In *Transition and Revolu-
             tion: Problems and Issues of European Renaissance and Refor-
             mation History,* edited by Robert M. Kingdon, 13–31. Minne-
             apolis: Burgess.
Grigg, David.
1980.   *Population Growth and Agrarian Change: An Historical Per-
             spective.* Cambridge: Cambridge University Press.
Grimes, Ronald L.
1982.   *Beginnings in Ritual Studies.* Washington, D.C.: University
             Press of America.
1985.   *Research in Ritual Studies: A Programmatic Essay and Bibliog-
             raphy.* Metuchen, N.J.: Scarecrow Press.

Guenne, Bernard.
  1963.   *Tribunaux et gens de justice dans le bailliage de Senlis à la fin du moyen age*. Paris: Presses Universitaires France.
Guéry, Alain.
  1978.   "Les finances de la monarchie français sous l'ancien régime." *Annales: Economies, sociétés, civilisations* 33: 216–239.
Habakkuk, H. J.
  1958.   "The Market for Monastic Property, 1539–1603." *Economic History Review* 10: 362–380.
Habermas, Jürgen.
  1976.   *Legitimation Crisis*. Boston: Beacon Press.
  1977.   "A Review of Gadamer's *Truth and Method*." In *Understanding and Social Inquiry*, edited by F. Dallmayr and T. McCarthy, 335–363. Notre Dame, Ind.: Notre Dame University Press.
  1979a.   *Communication and the Evolution of Society*. Boston: Beacon Press.
  1979b.   "History and Evolution." *Telos* 39: 5–44.
Hackmann, W. D.
  1976.   "The Growth of Science in the Netherlands in the Seventeenth and Early Eighteenth Centuries." In *The Emergence of Science in Western Europe*, edited by Maurice Crosland, 89–110. New York: Science History Publications.
Haddad, Yvonne Yazbeck.
  1982.   *Contemporary Islam and the Challenge of History*. Albany: State University of New York Press.
Hadden, Jeffrey, and Charles Swan.
  1981.   *Primetime Preachers: The Rising Power of Televangelism*. Reading, Mass.: Addison-Wesley.
Hahn, Roger.
  1962.   "The Fall of the Paris Academy of Sciences During the French Revolution." Ph.D. dissertation, Cornell University.
  1971.   *The Anatomy of a Scientific Institution: The Paris Academy of Science, 1666–1803*. Berkeley and Los Angeles: University of California Press.
  1976.   "Scientific Careers in Eighteenth Century France." In *The Emergence of Science in Western Europe*, edited by Maurice Crosland, 111–128. New York: Science History Publications.
Haigh, Christopher.
  1975.   *Reformation and Resistance in Tudor Lancashire*. Cambridge: Cambridge University Press.
Hall, A. Rupert.
  1963.   "Merton Revisited: Science and Society in the 17th Century." *History of Science* 11: 1–16.
  1967.   "Scientific Method and the Progress of Techniques." In *The Cambridge Economic History of Europe*, vol. 4: *The Economy of Expanding Europe in the Sixteenth and Seventeenth Centu-*

ries, edited by E. E. Rich and C. H. Wilson, 96–154. Cambridge: Cambridge University Press.

1972.   "Science, Technology and Utopia in the Seventeenth Century." In *Science and Society, 1600–1900,* edited by Peter Mathias, 101–123. Cambridge: Cambridge University Press.

Hamilton, Peter.
1974.   *Knowledge and Social Structure: An Introduction to the Classical Argument in the Sociology of Knowledge.* London: Routledge and Kegan Paul.

Hamilton, V. L.
1978.   "Obedience to Authority: A Jury Simulation." *Journal of Personality and Social Psychology* 36: 219–235.

Hammond, Phillip E.
1976.   "The Sociology of American Civil Religion: A Bibliographic Essay." *Sociological Analysis* 37: 169–182.

1985.   *The Sacred in a Secular Age.* Berkeley and Los Angeles: University of California Press.

Hammond, Phillip E., and James Davison Hunter.
1984.   "On Maintaining Plausibility: The Worldview of Evangelical College Students." *Journal for the Scientific Study of Religion* 23: 221–239.

Hannan, Michael T., and John Freeman.
1977.   "The Population Ecology of Organizations." *American Journal of Sociology* 82: 929–964.

Hans, Nicholas.
1951.   *New Trends in Education in the Eighteenth Century.* London: Routledge and Kegan Paul.

Harding, Robert R.
1978.   *Anatomy of a Power Elite: The Provincial Governors of Early Modern France.* New Haven, Conn.: Yale University Press.

Harris, Marvin.
1979.   *Cultural Materialism: The Struggle for a Science of Culture.* New York: Random House.

Heal, Felicity.
1980.   *Of Prelates and Princes: A Study of the Economic and Social Position of the Tudor Episcopate.* Cambridge: Cambridge University Press.

Hecksher, Eli F.
1955.   *Mercantilism.* 2 vols. London: Allen and Unwin.

Heinz, Donald.
1983.   "The Struggle to Define America." In *The New Christian Right,* edited by Robert C. Liebman and Robert Wuthnow, 133–149. New York: Aldine.

Held, David.
1980.   *Introduction to Critical Theory: Horkheimer to Habermas.* Berkeley and Los Angeles: University of California Press.

Heller, Henry.
  1977a.   "Famine, Revolt and Heresy at Meaux, 1521–1525." *Archiv*
             für Reformationsgeschichte 68: 133–157.
  1977b.   "The French Nobility and the State in the Late Middle Ages."
             Canadian Journal of History 12: 1–18.
Hempsall, David S.
  1971.   "The Languedoc 1520–1540: A Study of Pre-Calvinist Heresy
             in France." *Archiv für Reformationsgeschichte* 62: 225–244.
  1973.   "Martin Luther and the Sorbonne, 1519–1521." *Bulletin of the*
             Institute of Historical Research 46: 28–40.
Hessen, Boris.
  1971.   *The Social and Economic Roots of Newton's "Principia."* New
             York: Howard Fertig.
Hey, David G.
  1974.   *An English Rural Community: Myddle Under the Tudors and*
             Stuarts. Leicester: Leicester University Press.
Hilke, John C.
  1980.   "Voluntary Contributions and Monitoring Efforts: Revealed
             Preference for the Services of Religious Organizations." *Journal*
             for the Scientific Study of Religion 19: 138–145.
Hine, Virginia H.
  1974.   "The Deprivation and Disorganization Theories of Social Move-
             ments." In *Religious Movements in Contemporary America,* ed-
             ited by Irving I. Zaretsky and Mark P. Leone, 646–664. Prince-
             ton, N.J.: Princeton University Press.
Hirschfeld, Lawrence A.
  1986.   "Hermeneutics and Some Lessons from Anthropology." *Con-*
             temporary Sociology 15: 34–36.
Hirschman, Albert O.
  1977.   *The Passions and the Interests.* Princeton, N.J.: Princeton Uni-
             versity Press.
Hobsbawm, Eric J.
  1962.   *The Age of Revolution, 1789–1848.* New York: New American
             Library.
  1969.   *Industry and Empire.* London: Penguin Books.
Hochschild, Arlie Russell.
  1978.   *The Unexpected Community: Portrait of an Old Age Subcul-*
             ture. Berkeley and Los Angeles: University of California Press.
Holborn, Hajo.
  1976.   *A History of Modern Germany,* vol. 1: *The Reformation.* New
             York: Knopf.
Hollis, M., and S. Lukes, eds.
  1982.   *Rationality and Relativism.* Cambridge, Mass.: MIT Press.
Homans, George C.
  1941.   "Anxiety and Ritual: The Theories of Malinowski and Rad-
             cliffe-Brown." *American Anthropologist* 43: 164–172.

Hooykaas, R.
1972.   *Religion and the Rise of Modern Science*. Grand Rapids, Mich.:
             Eerdmans.
Horsfield, Peter G.
1984.   *Religious Television: The American Experience*. New York:
             Longman.
Hostetler, John A.
1968.   *Amish Society*. Baltimore: Johns Hopkins University Press.
Hostetler, John A., and Gertrude Enders Huntington.
1967.   *The Hutterites in North America*. New York: Holt, Rinehart
             and Winston.
Hunter, James Davison.
1980.   "The New Class and the Young Evangelicals." *Review of Reli-
             gious Research* 22: 155–169.
1983.   *American Evangelicalism: Conservative Religion and the Quan-
             dary of Modernity*. New Brunswick, N.J.: Rutgers University
             Press.
1985.   "Conservative Protestantism." In *The Sacred in a Secular Age*,
             edited by Phillip E. Hammond, 150–166. Berkeley and Los An-
             geles: University of California Press.
1987.   *Evangelicalism: The Coming Generation*. Chicago: University
             of Chicago Press.
Hunter, James Davison, and Stephen C. Ainlay, eds.
1986.   *Making Sense of Modern Times: Peter L. Berger and the Vision
             of Interpretive Sociology*. London: Routledge and Kegan Paul.
Inverarity, James M.
1976.   "Populism and Lynching in Louisiana, 1889–1896: A Test of
             Erikson's Theory of the Relationship Between Boundary Crises
             and Repressive Justice." *American Sociological Review* 41:
             262– 280.
Ives, E. W.
1972.   "Faction at the Court of Henry VIII: The Fall of Anne Boleyn."
             History 57: 169–188.
Jaffe, Steven.
1966.   "Hallucinations in Children at a State Hospital." *Psychiatric
             Quarterly* 40: 88–95.
James, M. E.
1970.   "Obedience and Dissent in Henrician England: The Lin-
             colnshire Rebellion 1536." *Past and Present* 48: 3–78.
Jarvie, I. C.
1983.   "Rationality and Relativism." *British Journal of Sociology* 34:
             44–60.
Johnson, Paul E.
1978.   *A Shopkeeper's Millennium: Society and Revivals in Rochester,
             New York, 1815–1837*. New York: Hill and Wang.
Kagan, Richard L.
1974.   "Universities in Castile, 1500–1810." In *The University in Soci-*

ety, vol. 2: *Europe, Scotland and the United States from the 16th to the 20th Century*, edited by Lawrence Stone, 372–385. Princeton, N.J.: Princeton University Press.

1981.   *Lawsuits and Litigants in Castile, 1500–1700.* Chapel Hill: University of North Carolina Press.

Kammen, Michael.

1970.   *Empire and Interest: The American Colonies and the Politics of Mercantilism.* New York: Lippincott.

Keddie, Nikki R., ed.

1983.   *Religion and Politics in Iran: Shi'ism from Quietism to Revolution.* New Haven, Conn.: Yale University Press.

Kelley, Dean M.

1972.   *Why Conservative Churches Are Growing.* New York: Harper and Row.

Kelly, George Armstrong.

1983.   *Politics and Religious Consciousness in America.* New Brunswick, N.J.: Transaction.

Kertzer, David I.

1980.   *Comrades and Christians: Religion and Political Struggle in Communist Italy.* New York: Cambridge University Press.

King, James E.

1948.   *Science and Rationalism in the Government of Louis XIV, 1661–1683.* Baltimore: Johns Hopkins University Press.

Kingdon, Robert M.

1956.   *Geneva and the Coming of the Wars of Religion in France, 1555–1563.* Geneva: Librairie E. Droz.

1968.   "Review of Religion and Regime." *American Sociological Review* 33: 843.

Knecht, R. J.

1971.   "The Concordat of 1516: A Reassessment." In *Government in Reformation Europe, 1520–1560,* edited by Henry J. Cohn, 91–112. New York: Macmillan.

1972.   "The Early Reformation in England and France: A Comparison." *History* 57: 1–16.

1978.   "Francis I, 'Defender of the Faith'?" In *Wealth and Power in Tudor England,* edited by E. W. Ives, R. J. Knecht, and J. J. Scarisbrick, 106–127. London: Athlone Press.

1981.   "Francis I and Paris." *History* 66: 18–33.

1982.   *Francis I.* Cambridge: Cambridge University Press.

Knorr, Klaus E.

1944.   *British Colonial Theories, 1570–1850.* Toronto: University of Toronto Press.

Knowles, David, and R. Neville Hadcock.

1971.   *Medieval Religious Houses: England and Wales.* London: Longman Group.

Koenigsberger, H. G.
  1971.   "The Unity of the Church and the Reformation." *Journal of In-
               terdisciplinary History* 1: 407–418.
Kohlberg, Lawrence.
  1981.   *Essays on Moral Development,* vol. 1. New York: Harper and
               Row.
  1984.   *Essays on Moral Development,* vol. 2. New York: Harper and
               Row.
Krarup, Helen.
  1983.   " 'Conventional Religion and Common Religion in Leeds' Inter-
               view Schedule: Basic Frequencies by Question." *Religious Re-
               search Papers* (University of Leeds, Department of Sociology).
Kroll-Smith, J. Stephen.
  1980.   "The Testimony as Performance: The Relationship of an Expres-
               sive Event to the Belief System of a Holiness Sect." *Journal for
               the Scientific Study of Religion* 19: 16–25.
Kuhn, Thomas S.
  1970.   *The Structure of Scientific Revolutions.* 2nd ed. Chicago: Univer-
               sity of Chicago Press.
Kurtz, Lester R.
  1983.   "The Politics of Heresy." *American Journal of Sociology* 88:
               1085–1116.
Kuznets, Simon.
  1966.   *Modern Economic Growth.* New Haven, Conn.: Yale Univer-
               sity Press.
Lamet, Maryelise Suffern.
  1978.   "French Protestants in a Position of Strength: The Early Years
               of the Reformation in Caen, 1558–1568." *Sixteenth Century
               Journal* 9: 35–55.
Lane, Christel.
  1981.   *The Rites of Rulers: Ritual in Industrial Society—the Soviet
               Case.* Cambridge: Cambridge University Press.
Langer, Susanne K.
  1951.   *Philosophy in a New Key.* New York: Mentor.
Lasch, Christopher.
  1978.   *The Culture of Narcissism: American Life in an Age of Dimin-
               ishing Expectations.* New York: Norton.
Laski, M.
  1961.   *Ecstasy: A Study of Some Secular and Religious Experiences.*
               London: Cresset.
Lauderdale, Pat.
  1976.   "Deviance and Moral Boundaries." *American Sociological Re-
               view* 41: 660–676.
Leach, Edmund.
  1964.   *Political Systems of Highland Burma.* Boston: Beacon Press.
  1967.   *The Structural Study of Myth and Totemism.* London:
               Tavistock.

1974.   *Claude Lévi-Strauss.* London: Penguin.
Lechner, Frank J.
1983.   "Fundamentalism and Sociocultural Revitalization in America: A Sociological Interpretation." Paper presented at the annual meeting of the Association for the Sociology of Religion, Detroit.
LeGoff, Jacques.
1984.   *The Birth of Purgatory.* Chicago: University of Chicago Press.
Lehmberg, Stanford E.
1970.   *The Reformation Parliament, 1529–1536.* Cambridge: Cambridge University Press.
Leiber, Justin.
1975.   *Noam Chomsky: A Philosophic Overview.* New York: St. Martin's Press.
Lenski, Gerhard.
1963.   *The Religious Factor.* Garden City, N.Y.: Anchor.
Lerner, Robert E.
1972.   *The Heresy of the Free Spirit in the Later Middle Ages.* Berkeley and Los Angeles: University of California Press.
LeRoy Ladurie, Emmanuel.
1974.   *The Peasants of Languedoc.* Urbana: University of Illinois Press.
1979.   *Montaillou: The Promised Land of Error.* New York: Vintage.
Levere, Trevor H.
1970.   "Relations and Rivalry: Interactions Between Britain and the Netherlands in Eighteenth-Century Science and Technology." *History of Science* 9: 42–53.
Lévi-Strauss, Claude.
1963.   *Structural Anthropology.* New York: Basic Books.
Levine, Daniel H.
1979.   "Religion and Politics, Politics and Religion: An Introduction." *Journal of Interamerican Studies and World Affairs* 21: 5–29.
1980.   *Churches and Politics in Latin America.* Beverly Hills, Calif.: Sage.
1981.   *Religion and Politics in Latin America: The Catholic Church in Venezuela and Colombia.* Princeton, N.J.: Princeton University Press.
1985.   "Religion and Politics: Drawing Lines, Understanding Change." *Latin America Research Review* 20: 20–39.
Lewis, P. S.
1965.   "France in the Fifteenth Century: Society and Sovereignty." In *Europe in the Late Middle Ages,* edited by J. R. Hale, J. R. L. Highfield, and B. Smalley, 276–300. Evanston, Ill.: Northwestern University Press.
1968.   *Later Medieval France: The Polity.* New York: St. Martin's Press.

Liebman, Charles S., and Eliezer Don-Yehiya.
1983.   *Civil Religion in Israel: Traditional Judaism and Political Culture in the Jewish State*. Berkeley and Los Angeles: University of California Press.
1984.   *Religion and Politics in Israel*. Bloomington: Indiana University Press.
Lindblom, Charles E.
1977.   *Politics and Markets*. New York: Basic Books.
Lipset, Seymour Martin, and William Schneider.
1978.   "How's Business? What the Public Thinks." *Public Opinion* 1: 41–47.
Lipset, Seymour Martin, and Ben J. Wattenberg.
1979.   "A Report from the Editors on the 'Crisis of Confidence.' " *Public Opinion* 2: 2–4, 54–55.
Little, David, and Sumner B. Twiss.
1978.   *Comparative Religious Ethics: A New Method*. New York: Harper and Row.
Luckmann, Thomas.
1967.   *The Invisible Religion: The Transformation of Symbols in Industrial Society*. New York: Macmillan.
Luker, Kristin.
1984.   *Abortion and the Politics of Motherhood*. Berkeley and Los Angeles: University of California Press.
Lukes, Steven.
1977.   *Essays in Social Theory*. New York: Columbia University Press.
Lütge, Frederich.
1958.   "Economic Change: Agriculture." In *The New Cambridge Modern History*, vol. 2: *The Reformation, 1520–1559*, edited by G. R. Elton, 23–49. Cambridge: Cambridge University Press.
Lytle, Guy F.
1974.   "Patronage Patterns and Oxford Colleges, c. 1300–1530." In *The University in Society*, vol. 1: *Oxford and Cambridge from the 14th to the Early 19th Century*, edited by Lawrence Stone, 151–166. Princeton, N.J.: Princeton University Press.
MacCulloch, Diarmaid.
1979.   "Kett's Rebellion in Context." *Past and Present* 84: 36–59.
Major, J. Russell.
1955.   "The Payment of the Deputies to the French National Assemblies, 1484–1627." *Journal of Modern History* 27: 217–230.
1960.   *The Deputies to the Estates General in Renaissance France*. Madison: University of Wisconsin Press.
1964.   "The Crown and the Aristocracy in Renaissance France." *American Historical Review* 69: 631–645.
1971.   "The French Renaissance Monarchy as Seen Through the Estates General." In *Government in Reformation Europe, 1520–1560*, edited by Henry J. Cohn, 43–57. New York: Macmillan.

1980.   *Representative Government in Early Modern France.* New Haven, Conn.: Yale University Press.

Major-Poetzl, Pamela.
1983.   *Michel Foucault's Archeology of Western Culture: Toward a New Science of History.* Chapel Hill: University of North Carolina Press.

Malinowski, Bronislaw.
1925.   "Magic, Science, and Religion." In *Science, Religion and Reality,* edited by James Needham, 17–92. New York: Macmillan.

Mandrou, Robert.
1974.   *Introduction à la France moderne; essai de psychologie historique 1500–1640.* Paris: Editions Albin Michel.

Manning, Roger B.
1969.   *Religion and Society in Elizabethan Sussex: A Study of the Enforcement of the Religious Settlement, 1558–1603.* Leicester: Leicester University Press.

Markovits, Andrei S., and Rebecca S. Hayden.
1980.   " 'Holocaust' Before and After the Event: Reactions in West Germany and Austria." *New German Critique* 19: 53–80.

Marks, Stephen R.
1974.   "Durkheim's Theory of Anomie." *American Journal of Sociology* 80: 329–363.

Marsak, Leonard M., ed.
1964.   *The Rise of Science in Relation to Society.* London: Macmillan.

Marsden, George M.
1980.   *Fundamentalism and American Culture: The Shaping of Twentieth Century Evangelicalism.* Oxford: Oxford University Press.

Marx, Karl, and Friedrich Engels.
1964.   *On Religion.* New York: Schocken.

Mattingly, Garrett.
1955.   *Renaissance Diplomacy.* Boston: Houghton Mifflin.

May, Robert M.
1973.   *Stability and Complexity in Modern Ecosystems.* Princeton, N.J.: Princeton University Press.

McCarl, Robert S., Jr.
1979.   "Smokejumper Initiation: Ritualized Communication in a Modern Occupation." *Journal of American Folklore* 89: 49–66.

McCarthy, Thomas.
1978.   *The Critical Theory of Jürgen Habermas.* Cambridge, Mass.: MIT Press.

McGuire, Meredith B.
1982.   *Penecostal Catholics: Power, Charisma, and Order in a Religious Movement.* Philadelphia: Temple University Press.

McKenna, J. W.
1979.   "The Myth of Parliamentary Sovereignty in Late-Medieval England." *English Historical Review* 94: 481–506.

McKie, Douglas.
  1960.   "The Origins and Foundation of the Royal Society of London."
              In *The Royal Society: Its Origins and Founders*, edited by Har-
              old Hartley, 95–116. London: The Royal Society.
Mechling, Jay, ed.
  1978.   *Church, State, and Public Policy: The New Shape of the
              Church-State Debate*. Washington, D.C.: American Enterprise
              Institute.
Mentzer, Raymond A.
  1973.   "The Legal Response to Heresy in Languedoc, 1500–1560." *Six-
              teenth Century Journal* 4: 19–30.
Merton, Robert K.
  1968.   *Social Theory and Social Structure*. New York: Free Press.
  1970.   *Science, Technology and Society in Seventeenth-Century En-
              gland*. New York: Harper and Row. [Originally published
              1938]
  1973.   *The Sociology of Science*. Chicago: University of Chicago Press.
Meyer, John W., and Brian Rowan.
  1977.   "Institutionalized Organizations: Formal Structure as Myth and
              Ceremony." *American Journal of Sociology* 83: 340–363.
Middleton, W. E. Knowles.
  1971.   *The Experimenters: A Study of the Accademia del Cimento*. Bal-
              timore: Johns Hopkins University Press.
Milgram, Stanley.
  1974.   *Obedience to Authority: An Experimental View*. New York:
              Harper and Row.
Miller, A. G., B. Gillen, C. Schenker, and S. Radlove.
  1974.   "The Prediction and Perception of Obedience to Authority."
              Journal of Personality 42: 23–42.
Miller, H.
  1970.   "London and Parliament in the Reign of Henry VIII." In *Histori-
              cal Studies of the English Parliament*, vol. 2: *1399–1603*, edited
              by E. B. Fryde and Edward Miller, 125–146. Cambridge: Cam-
              bridge University Press.
Miner, Horace.
  1956.   "Body Ritual Among the Nacirema." *American Anthropologist*
              58: 503–507.
Misgeld, Dieter.
  1976.   "Hermeneutics and Critical Theory: The Debate Between
              Habermas and Gadamer." In *On Critical Theory*, edited by J.
              O'Neill, 164–184. New York: Seabury.
  1977.   "Discourse and Conversation: The Theory of Communicative
              Competence and Hermeneutics in the Light of the Debate Be-
              tween Habermas and Gadamer." *Cultural Hermeneutics* 4:
              321–344.

Miskimin, Harry A.
1977.   *The Economy of Later Renaissance Europe, 1460–1600.* Cambridge: Cambridge University Press.
Mitzman, Arthur.
1971.   *The Iron Cage: An Historical Interpretation of Max Weber.* New York: Grosset and Dunlap.
Moeller, Bernd.
1972.   *Imperial Cities and the Reformation.* Philadelphia: Fortress Press.
Moodie, T. Dunbar.
1975.   *The Rise of Afrikanerdom: Power, Apartheid, and the Afrikaner Civil Religion.* Berkeley and Los Angeles: University of California Press.
Moore, Barrington, Jr.
1978.   *Injustice: The Social Bases of Obedience and Revolt.* White Plains, N.Y.: M.E. Sharpe.
Moore, R. I.
1975.   *The Birth of Popular Heresy.* London: Edward Arnold.
Morgan, Victor.
1974.   "Cambridge University and 'The Country,' 1560–1640." In *The University in Society,* vol. 1: *Oxford and Cambridge from the 14th to the Early 19th Century,* edited by Lawrence Stone, 31–49. Princeton, N.J.: Princeton University Press.
Mosse, G. L.
1970.   "Changes in Religious Thought." In *The New Cambridge Modern History,* vol. 4: *The Decline of Spain and the Thirty Years War, 1609–1648/59,* edited by J. C. Cooper, 169–201. Cambridge: Cambridge University Press.
Mousnier, Roland.
1979.   *The Institutions of France Under the Absolute Monarchy, 1598–1789,* vol. 1: *Society and the State.* Chicago: University of Chicago Press.
Mulligan, Lotte.
1973.   "Civil War Politics, Religion and the Royal Society." *Past and Present 59:* 92–116.
Mullins, Nicholas.
1973.   *Theories and Theory Groups in Contemporary American Sociology.* New York: Harper and Row.
Myers, A. R.
1971.   *England in the Late Middle Ages.* 8th ed. Baltimore: Penguin.
Needham, Joseph.
1954.   *Science and Civilization in China,* vol. 1: *Introductory Orientations.* Cambridge: Cambridge University Press.
Nef, John U.
1964.   *The Conquest of the Material World.* Chicago: University of Chicago Press.

Neuhaus, Richard John.
    1984.   *The Naked Public Square: Religion and Democracy in America.*
                Grand Rapids, Mich.: Eerdmans.
Neuschel, Kristen B.
    1982.   "The Picard Nobility in the Sixteenth Century: Autonomy and
                Power." *Proceedings of the Annual Meeting of the Western Soci-
                ety for French History* 10: 42–49.
Nicholls, David J.
    1980.   "Social Change and Early Protestantism in France: Normandy,
                1520–1562." *European Studies Review* 10: 279–308.
    1983.   "The Nature of Popular Heresy in France, 1520–1542." *Histori-
                cal Journal* 26: 261–275.
Nottingham, Elizabeth K.
    1971.   *Religion: A Sociological View.* New York: Random House.
Novak, Michael.
    1982.   *The Spirit of Democratic Capitalism.* New York: Simon and
                Schuster.
    1984.   *Freedom with Justice: Catholic Social Thought and Liberal Insti-
                tutions.* New York: Harper and Row.
Ogg, David.
    1972.   *Europe in the Seventeenth Century.* New York: Collier.
Ollman, Bertell.
    1971.   *Alienation: Marx's Conception of Man in Capitalist Society.*
                Cambridge: Cambridge University Press.
Olson, Mancur.
    1971.   *The Logic of Collective Action: Public Goods and the Theory of
                Groups.* Cambridge, Mass.: Harvard University Press.
Ornstein, Martha.
    1975.   *The Role of Scientific Societies in the Seventeenth Century.* Chi-
                cago: University of Chicago Press.
Ortiz, Antonio D.
    1971.   *The Golden Age of Spain, 1516–1659.* New York: Basic Books.
O'Toole, Roger.
    1984.   *Religion: Classical Sociological Approaches.* Toronto: Mc-
                Graw-Hill Ryerson.
Owens, Virginia Stem.
    1980.   *The Total Image: Or Selling Jesus in the Modern Age.* Grand
                Rapids, Mich.: Eerdmans.
Oxley, James E.
    1965.   *The Reformation in Essex to the Death of Mary.* Manchester:
                Manchester University Press.
Ozment, Steven E.
    1975.   *The Reformation in the Cities: The Appeal of Protestantism to
                Sixteenth-Century Germany and Switzerland.* New Haven,
                Conn.: Yale University Press.

Palliser, D. M.
    1979.   *Tudor York*. Oxford: Oxford University Press.

Parker, T. M.
    1966.   *The English Reformation to 1558*, 2nd ed. London: Oxford University Press.

Parry, J. H.
    1967.   "Transport and Trade Routes." In *The Cambridge Economic History of Europe*, vol. 4: *The Economy of Expanding Europe in the Sixteenth and Seventeenth Centuries*, edited by E. E. Rich and C. H. Wilson, 155–222. Cambridge: Cambridge University Press.

Parsons, Talcott.
    1951.   *The Social System*. New York: Free Press.
    1978.   *Action Theory and the Human Condition*. New York: Free Press.

Pegues, F. J.
    1962.   *The Lawyers of the Last Capetians*. Princeton, N.J.: Princeton University Press.

Perroy, Edouard.
    1959.   *The Hundred Years War*. London: Eyre and Spottiswoode.

Peters, Victor.
    1965.   *All Things Common: The Hutterian Way of Life*. New York: Harper and Row.

Pettit, Philip.
    1977.   *The Concept of Structuralism: A Critical Analysis*. Berkeley and Los Angeles: University of California Press.

Pfeffer, Leo.
    1967.   *Church, State, and Freedom*. Boston: Beacon Press.

Pickthorn, Kenneth.
    1934.   *Early Tudor Government: Henry VIII*. Cambridge: Cambridge University Press.

Pipes, Richard.
    1983.   *In the Path of God: Islam and Political Power*. New York: Basic Books.

Piscatori, James P., ed.
    1982.   *Islam in the Political Process*. New York: Cambridge University Press.

Polanyi, Karl.
    1944.   *The Great Transformation*. Boston: Beacon Press.
    1977.   *The Livelihood of Man*. New York: Academic Press.

Polanyi, Michael.
    1964.   "The Republic of Science: Its Political and Economic Theory." In *Criteria for Scientific Development: Public Policy and National Goals*, edited by Edward Shils, 43–61. Cambridge, Mass.: MIT Press.

Poll, Solomon.
    1969.   *The Hasidic Community of Williamsburg: A Study in the Sociol-
                 ogy of Religion*. New York: Schocken.
Pomian-Srzednicki, Maciej.
    1982.   *Religious Change in Contemporary Poland: Secularization and
                 Politics*. London: Routledge and Kegan Paul.
Popenoe, Cris, and Oliver Popenoe.
    1984.   *Seeds of Tomorrow: New Age Communities That Work*. New
                 York: Harper and Row.
Postan, M. M.
    1973.   *Medieval Trade and Finance*. Cambridge: Cambridge University
                 Press.
Powis, Jonathan K.
    1980.   "Order, Religion and the Magistrates of a Provincial Parlement
                 in Sixteenth-Century France." *Archiv für Reformations-
                 geschichte* 71: 180–197.
Prebisch, Raul.
    1959.   "Commercial Policy in the Underdeveloped Countries." *Ameri-
                 can Economic Review Papers and Proceedings* (May).
Price, Don K.
    1965.   *The Scientific Estate*. Cambridge, Mass.: Harvard University
                 Press.
Radcliffe-Brown, A. R.
    1939.   *Taboo*. Cambridge: Cambridge University Press.
Rambo, Lewis R.
    1982.   "Current Research on Religious Conversion." *Religious Studies
                 Review* 8: 146–159.
Ramsey, Peter.
    1965.   *Tudor Economic Problems*. London: Gollancz.
Ravetz, Jerome.
    1971.   *Scientific Knowledge and Its Social Problems*. Oxford: Oxford
                 University Press.
Redfield, Robert.
    1956.   *Peasant Society and Culture*. Chicago: University of Chicago
                 Press.
Ribeiro de Oliveira, Pedro A.
    1979.   "The 'Romanization' of Catholicism and Agrarian Capitalism
                 in Brazil." *Social Compass* 26: 309–329.
Richardson, James T.
    1982.   "Financing the New Religions: Comparative and Theoretical
                 Considerations." *Journal for the Scientific Study of Religion* 21:
                 255–267.
Richet, Denis.
    1977.   "Aspects socio-culturels des conflits religieux à Paris dans la
                 seconde moitié du XVI siècle." *Annales: Economies, sociétés,
                 civilisations* 32: 764–789.

Rickles, Patricia K.

    1965.   "The Folklore of Sacraments and Sacramentals in South Louisiana." *Louisiana Folklore Miscellany* 2: 27–44.

Ricoeur, Paul.

    1973.   "The Task of Hermeneutics." *Philosophy Today* 17: 112–129.

Robbins, Thomas.

    1985.   "Government Regulatory Powers and Church Autonomy: Deviant Groups as Test Cases." *Journal for the Scientific Study of Religion* 24: 315–331.

Robbins, Thomas, and Dick Anthony, eds.

    1981.   *In Gods We Trust: New Patterns of Religious Pluralism in America.* New Brunswick, N.J.: Transaction.

Robertson, Roland.

    1970.   *The Sociological Interpretation of Religion.* New York: Schocken.

    1981.   "Considerations from Within the American Context on the Significance of Church-State Tension." *Sociological Analysis* 42: 193–208.

Robertson, Roland, and Frank Lechner.

    1984.   "On Swanson: An Appreciation and an Appraisal." *Sociological Analysis* 45: 185–204.

Roof, Wade Clark.

    1978.   *Community and Commitment: Religious Plausibility in a Liberal Protestant Church.* New York: Elsevier.

Rosenberg, David.

    1978.   "Social Experience and Religious Choice: A Case Study, the Protestant Weavers and Woolcombers of Amiens in the Sixteenth Century." Ph.D. dissertation, Yale University.

Rothenberg, Stuart, and Frank Newport.

    1984.   *The Evangelical Voter: Religion and Politics in America.* Washington, D.C.: Institute for Government and Politics.

Rubinson, Richard.

    1976.   "The World-Economy and the Distribution of Income Within States: A Cross-National Study." *American Sociological Review* 41: 638–659.

Safire, William.

    1978.   "Silence is Guilt." *New York Times* (April 31).

Salmon, J. H. M.

    1975.   *Society in Crisis: France in the Sixteenth Century.* New York: St. Martin's Press.

Saussure, Ferdinand de.

    1959.   *Course in General Linguistics.* New York: McGraw-Hill.

Schluchter, Wolfgang.

    1981.   *The Rise of Western Rationalism: Max Weber's Developmental History.* Berkeley and Los Angeles: University of California Press.

Schmoller, Gustav.
1896. *The Mercantile System and Its Historical Significance.* New York: Macmillan.

Schoffeleers, Matthew, and Daniel Meijers.
1978. *Religion, Nationalism and Economic Action: Critical Questions on Durkheim and Weber.* Atlantic Highlands, N.J.: Humanities Press.

Schurmann, Franz.
1968. *Ideology and Organization in Communist China.* Berkeley and Los Angeles: University of California Press.
1974. *The Logic of World Power: An Inquiry into the Origins, Currents, and Contradictions of World Politics.* New York: Pantheon.

Schwartz, Gary.
1970. *Sect Ideologies and Social Status.* Chicago: University of Chicago Press.

Scott, James C.
1976. *The Moral Economy of the Peasant: Rebellion and Subsistence in Southeast Asia.* New Haven, Conn.: Yale University Press.
1977. "Protest and Profanation: Agrarian Revolt and the Little Tradition." *Theory and Society* 4: 1–38, 211–246.

Searle, John R.
1969. *Speech Acts: An Essay in the Philosophy of Language.* Cambridge: Cambridge University Press.

Seliger, Martin.
1977. *The Marxist Conception of Ideology.* Cambridge: Cambridge University Press.

Sennett, Richard.
1976. *The Fall of Public Man: On the Social Psychology of Capitalism.* New York: Vintage.

Sennett, Richard, and Jonathan Cobb.
1972. *The Hidden Injuries of Class.* New York: Vintage.

Shapiro, Sheldon.
1973. "Patterns of Religious Reformations." *Comparative Studies in Society and History* 15: 143–157.

Shaughnessy, James D., ed.
1973. *The Roots of Ritual.* Grand Rapids, Mich.: Eerdmans.

Shennan, J. H.
1969. *Government and Society in France, 1461–1661.* London: George Allen and Unwin.

Shils, Edwards A.
1962. "The Autonomy of Science." In *The Sociology of Science,* edited by Bernard Barber and Walter Hirsch, 71–95. New York: Free Press.
1972. "Metropolis and Province in the Intellectual Community." In

The Intellectuals and the Powers, edited by Edward A. Shils, 276–295. Chicago: University of Chicago Press.

Shils, Edward, and Michael Young.

1953. "The Meaning of the Coronation." *Sociological Review* 1: 63–81.

Shrum, Wesley, Robert Wuthnow, and James R. Beniger.

1985. "The Organization of Technology in Advanced Industrial Society: A Hypothesis on Technical Systems." *Social Forces* 64: 411–424.

Simpson, John H.

1979. "Sovereign Groups, Subsistence Activities, and the Presence of a High God in Primitive Societies." In *The Religious Dimension: New Directions in Quantitative Research,* edited by Robert Wuthnow, 299–310. New York: Academic Press.

1983. "Power Transfigured: Guy Swanson's Analysis of Religion." *Religious Studies Review* 9: 349–352.

1984. "High Gods and the Means of Subsistence." *Sociological Analysis* 45: 213–222.

Skocpol, Theda.

1979. *States and Social Revolutions.* Cambridge: Cambridge University Press.

Skorupski, John.

1976. *Symbol and Theory: A Philosophical Study of Theories of Religion in Social Anthropology.* Cambridge: Cambridge University Press.

Slavin, Arthur Joseph.

1973. *The Precarious Balance: English Government and Society.* New York: Knopf.

Smith, Brian H.

1982. *The Church and Politics in Chile: Challenges to Modern Catholicism.* Princeton, N.J.: Princeton University Press.

Smith, Donald Eugene.

1970. *Religion and Political Development.* Boston: Little, Brown.

Smith, Lacey Baldwin.

1953. *Tudor Prelates and Politics, 1536–1558.* Princeton, N.J.: Princeton University Press.

Smith, R. B.

1970. *Land and Politics in the England of Henry VIII: The West Riding of Yorkshire, 1530–46.* Oxford: Clarendon Press.

Smith, Wilfred Cantwell.

1979. *Faith and Belief.* Princeton, N.J.: Princeton University Press.

Solzhenitsyn, Aleksandr I.

1978. *A World Split Apart.* New York: Harper and Row.

Sorauf, Frank J.

1976. *The Wall of Separation: The Constitutional Politics of Church and State.* Princeton, N.J.: Princeton University Press.

Spitz, Lewis W.
  1985.   *The Protestant Reformation, 1517–1559.* New York: Harper
               and Row.
Stark, Rodney, and William Sims Bainbridge.
  1985.   *The Future of Religion: Secularization, Revival and Cult Forma-
               tion.* Berkeley and Los Angeles: University of California Press.
Starr, Paul.
  1982.   *The Social Transformation of American Medicine.* New York:
               Basic Books.
Steiner, George.
  1979.   *Martin Heidegger.* New York: Viking.
Stimson, Dorothy.
  1948.   *Scientists and Amateurs: A History of the Royal Society.* New
               York: Henry Schuman.
Stocker, Christopher.
  1971.   "Office as Maintenance in Renaissance France." *Canadian Jour-
               nal of History* 6: 21–43.
  1978.   "Public and Private Enterprise in the Administration of a Renais-
               sance Monarchy: The First Sales of Office in the Parlement of
               Paris (1512–1524)." *Sixteenth Century Journal* 9: 4–29.
Stokes, Anson Phelps, and Leo Pfeffer.
  1964.   *Church and State in the United States.* New York: Harper and
               Row.
Stokes, Kenneth E., ed.
  1982.   *Faith Development in the Adult Life Cycle.* New York: Sadlier.
Stone, Lawrence.
  1967.   *The Crisis of the Aristocracy, 1558–1641.* Oxford: Oxford Uni-
               versity Press.
  1974.   "The Size and Composition of the Oxford Student Body, 1580–
               1909." In *The University in Society,* vol. 1: *Oxford and Cam-
               bridge from the 14th to the Early 19th Century,* edited by Law-
               rence Stone, 3–110. Princeton, N.J.: Princeton University Press.
Strayer, Joseph.
  1971.   *Medieval Statecraft and the Perspectives of History.* Princeton,
               N.J.: Princeton University Press.
Stroup, Herbert.
  1967.   *Church and State in Confrontation.* New York: Seabury.
Swanson, Guy E.
  1960.   *The Birth of the Gods: The Origin of Primitive Beliefs.* Ann Ar-
               bor: University of Michigan Press.
  1967.   *Religion and Regime: A Sociological Account of the Reforma-
               tion.* Ann Arbor: University of Michigan Press.
  1971.   "Interpreting the Reformation." *Journal of Interdisciplinary His-
               tory* 1: 419–446.

1973.   "The Search for a Guardian Spirit: A Process of Empowerment in Simpler Societies." *Ethnology* 12: 359–378.

1976.   "Orpheus and Star Husband: Meaning and Structure of Myths." *Ethnology* 15: 115–133.

1978a.   "Trance and Possession: Studies of Charismatic Influence." *Review of Religious Research* 19: 253–278.

1978b.   "Travels Through Inner Space: Family Structure and Openness to Absorbing Experiences." *American Journal of Sociology* 83: 890–919.

1980.   "A Basis of Authority and Identity in Post-Industrial Society." In *Identity and Authority: Explorations in the Theory of Society,* edited by Roland Robertson and Burkart Holzner, 190–217. New York: St. Martin's Press.

Sweet, Leonard I.
1984.   "The 1960s: The Crises of Liberal Christianity and the Public Emergence of Evangelicalism." In *Evangelicalism and Modern America,* edited by George Marsden, 29–45. Grand Rapids, Mich.: Eerdmans.

Tai, Hue-Tam Ho.
1983.   *Millenarianism and Peasant Politics in Vietnam.* Cambridge, Mass.: Harvard University Press.

Taylor, Mark C.
1984.   *Erring: A Postmodern A/theology.* Chicago: University of Chicago Press.

Tazbir, Janusz.
1975.   "The Cult of St. Isidore the Farmer in Europe." In *Poland at the 14th International Congress of Historical Sciences in San Francisco,* 99–111. Warsaw: Polish Academy of Sciences, Institute of History.

Teall, Elizabeth S.
1965.   "The Seigneur of Renaissance France." *Journal of Modern History* 37: 131–150.

Terkel, Studs.
1974.   *Working.* New York: Avon.

Therborn, Goran.
1980.   *The Ideology of Power and the Power of Ideology.* London: Verso.

Thoits, Peggy A.
1981.   "Undesirable Life Events and Psychophysiological Distress: A Problem of Operational Confounding." *American Sociological Review* 46: 97–109.

Thomas, George M.
1979.   "Rational Exchange and Individualism: Revival Religion in the U.S., 1870–1890. In *The Religious Dimension: New Directions in Quantitative Research,* edited by Robert Wuthnow, 351–372. New York: Academic Press.

1986.   *Christianity and Culture in the 19th-Century United States: The Dynamics of Evangelical Revivalism, Nationbuilding, and the Market.* Berkeley and Los Angeles: University of California Press.

Thomas, Keith.
1971.   *Religion and the Decline of Magic.* New York: Scribner's.

Thompson, James Westfall.
1967.   "The Domination of Political Motives." In *The French Wars of Religion,* edited by J. H. M. Salmon, 1–5. Boston: D.C. Heath.

Thompson, John B.
1984.   *Studies in the Theory of Ideology.* Berkeley and Los Angeles: University of California Press.

Thorner, Isidor.
1952.   "Ascetic Protestantism and the Development of Science and Technology." *American Journal of Sociology* 58: 25–33.

Tilly, Charles.
1969.   "Collective Violence in European Perspective." In *Violence in America,* edited by Hugh David Graham and Ted Robert Gurr, 4–44. New York: Bantam.

Tipton, Steven M.
1982.   *Getting Saved from the Sixties: Moral Meaning in Conversion and Cultural Change.* Berkeley and Los Angeles: University of California Press.

Towler, Robert.
1983.   "Conventional Religion and Common Religion in Great Britain." *Religious Research Papers* (University of Leeds, Department of Sociology).

Trachtenberg, Joshua.
1970.   *Jewish Magic and Superstition: A Study in Folk Religion.* New York: Antheneum.

Trevor-Roper, H. R.
1953.   "The Gentry, 1540–1640." *Economic History Review,* Supplement 1.
1967.   *The European Witch-Craze of the Sixteenth and Seventeenth Centuries.* New York: Harper and Row.

Troeltsch, Ernst.
1960.   *The Social Teaching of the Christian Churches.* New York: Harper and Row. [Originally published 1911]

Turner, Bryan S.
1983.   *Religion and Social Theory.* London: Heinemann.

Turner, Victor.
1974.   *Dramas, Fields, and Metaphors: Symbolic Action in Human Society.* Ithaca, N.Y.: Cornell University Press.
1977.   *The Ritual Process: Structure and Anti-Structure.* Ithaca, N.Y.: Cornell University Press.

Underhill, Ralph.
    1975.   "Economic and Political Antecedents of Monotheism: A Cross-Cultural Study." *American Journal of Sociology* 80: 841–861.
    1976.   "Economy, Polity and Monotheism: Reply to Swanson." *American Journal of Sociology* 82: 418–421.

Van Baaren, T. P.
    1984.   "The Flexibility of Myth." In *Sacred Narrative: Readings in the Theory of Myth*, edited by Alan Dundes, 217–224. Berkeley and Los Angeles: University of California Press.

Van Gennep, Arnold.
    1960.   *The Rites of Passage.* Chicago: University of Chicago Press.

Vance, James E., Jr.
    1977.   *This Scene of Man: The Role and Structure of the City in the Geography of Western Civilization.* New York: Harper's College Press.

Voll, John Obert.
    1982.   *Islam: Continuity and Change in the Modern World.* Boulder, Colo.: Westview Press.

von Gizycki, Rainald.
    1973.   "Centre and Periphery in the International Scientific Community." *Minerva* 11: 474–494.

Vrijhof, Pieter Hendrik, and Jacques Waardenburg, eds.
    1979.   *Official and Popular Religion: Analysis of a Theme for Religious Studies.* The Hague: Mouton.

Wacker, Grant.
    1984.   "Uneasy in Zion: Evangelicals in Postmodern Society." In *Evangelicalism and Modern America*, edited by George Marsden, 17–28. Grand Rapids, Mich.: Eerdmans.

Wallace, Anthony F. C.
    1956.   "Revitalization Movements." *American Anthropologist* 58: 264–281.

Wallerstein, Immanuel.
    1974.   *The Modern World-System.* New York: Academic Press.
    1979.   *The Capitalist World-Economy.* Cambridge: Cambridge University Press.

Wallis, Roy.
    1984.   *The Elementary Forms of the New Religious Life.* London: Routledge and Kegan Paul.

Warner, W. Lloyd.
    1961.   *The Family of God: A Symbolic Study of Christian Life in America.* New Haven, Conn.: Yale University Press.
    1974.   "An American Sacred Ceremony." In *American Civil Religion*, edited by Russell E. Richey and Donald G. Jones, 89–111. New York: Harper and Row.

Weber, Max.
    1951.   *The Religion of China.* New York: Free Press.

1958.   *The Protestant Ethic and the Spirit of Capitalism.* New York: Scribner's.

1963.   *The Sociology of Religion.* Boston: Beacon Press. [Originally published 1922]

Westie, Frank R.

1965.   "The American Dilemma: An Empirical Test." *American Sociological Review* 30: 527–538.

Westley, Frances.

1983.   *The Complex Forms of the Religious Life: A Durkheimian View of New Religious Movements.* Chico, Calif.: Scholars Press.

White, O. K., Jr.

1972.   "Constituting Norms and the Formal Organization of America's Churches." *Sociological Analysis* 33: 95–109.

Wilensky, Harold.

1964.   "Mass Society and Mass Culture: Interdependence or Independence?" *American Sociological Review* 29: 173–197.

Williams, George H.

1962.   *The Radical Reformation.* Philadelphia: Westminster Press.

Williams, Penry.

1979.   *The Tudor Regime.* Oxford: Clarendon Press.

Williams, Peter W.

1980.   *Popular Religion in America: Symbolic Change and the Modernization Process in Historical Perspective.* Englewood Cliffs, N. J.: Prentice-Hall.

Wilson, Bryan.

1970a.   *Rationality.* London: Basil Blackwell.

1970b.   *Religious Sects: A Sociological Study.* New York: McGraw-Hill.

1973.   *Magic and the Millennium.* London: Heinemann.

1979.   "The New Religions: Some Preliminary Considerations." *Japanese Journal of Religious Studies* 6: 193–216.

Wilson, Charles.

1958.   *Mercantilism.* London: Routledge and Kegan Paul.

1976.   *The Transformation of Europe, 1558–1648.* Berkeley and Los Angeles: University of California Press.

Wilson, John.

1978.   *Religion in American Society: The Effective Presence.* Englewood Cliffs, N.J.: Prentice-Hall.

Wilson, John F.

1979.   *Public Religion in American Culture.* Philadelphia: Temple University Press.

Winter, J. Alan.

1983.   "Immanence and Regime in the Kingdom of Judah: A Cross-Disciplinary Study of a Swansonian Hypothesis." *Sociological Analysis* 44: 147–162.

1984.   "Toward a Fuller Version of Swanson's Sociology of Religion." *Sociological Analysis* 45: 205–212.

Wittgenstein, Ludwig.
    1974.   *Tractatus Logico-Philosophicus*. Atlantic Highlands, N.J.: Humanities Press.

Wolf, Eric.
    1959.   *Sons of the Shaking Earth*. Chicago: University of Chicago Press.

Wolf, John B.
    1951.   *The Emergence of the Great Powers, 1685–1715*. New York: Harper and Row.

Wolfe, Martin.
    1972.   *The Fiscal System of Renaissance France*. New Haven, Conn.: Yale University Press.

Wolffe, B. P.
    1964.   "Henry VII's Landed Revenues." *Economic History Review* 79: 253–264.
    1970.   *The Crown Lands, 1461–1536*. London: George Allen and Unwin.

Wood, James B.
    1980.   *The Nobility of the Election of Bayeux, 1463–1666: Continuity Through Change*. Princeton, N.J.: Princeton University Press.

Worsley, Peter.
    1968.   *The Trumpet Shall Sound*. New York: Schocken.

Wuthnow, Robert.
    1976.   *The Consciousness Reformation*. Berkeley and Los Angeles: University of California Press.
    1978.   *Experimentation in American Religion*. Berkeley and Los Angeles: University of California Press.
    1980.   "World Order and Religious Movements." In *Studies of the Modern World-System*, edited by Albert Bergesen, 57–75. New York: Academic Press.
    1982.   "Cultural Crises." In *Crises in the World-System*, edited by Albert Bergesen, 57–72. Beverly Hills, Calif.: Sage.
    1983.   "The Political Rebirth of American Evangelicals." In *The New Christian Right: Mobilization and Legitimation*, edited by Robert C. Liebman and Robert Wuthnow, 168–185. New York: Aldine.
    1985.   "The Growth of Religious Reform Movements." *Annals of the American Academy of Political and Social Science* 115: 121–130.
    1986a.   "Religion as Sacred Canopy." In *Making Sense of Modern Times: Peter L. Berger and the Vision of Interpretive Sociology*, edited by James Davison Hunter and Stephen C. Ainlay, 117–135. London: Routledge and Kegan Paul.
    1986b.   "Towns, Regimes, and Religious Movements in the Reformation." In *Geographic Perspectives in History*, edited by Eugene Genovese and Leonard Hochberg, 36–50. London: Basil Blackwell.

Wuthnow, Robert, James Beniger, and Wesley Shrum.
    1982.   "Networks of Scientific and Technological Information Ex-
                 change in the Technical Innovation Process: Final Report." Na-
                 tional Science Foundation, Washington, D.C. (Grant PRA-
                 7920573).
Wuthnow, Robert, James Davison Hunter, Albert Bergesen,
    and Edith Kurzweil.
    1984.   *Cultural Analysis: The Work of Peter L. Berger, Mary Douglas,
                 Michel Foucault, and Jürgen Habermas.* London: Routledge
                 and Kegan Paul.
Yankelovich, Daniel.
    1982.   *New Rules: Searching for Self-Fulfillment in a World Turned
                 Upside Down.* New York: Bantam.
Youings, Joyce.
    1954.   "The Terms of the Disposal of the Devon Monastic Lands,
                 1536–58." *English Historical Review* 69: 18–38.
Zablocki, Benjamin.
    1980.   *Alienation and Charisma: A Study of Contemporary American
                 Communes.* New York: Free Press.
Zagorin, Perez.
    1982.   *Rebels and Rulers, 1500–1660.* 2 vols. Cambridge: Cambridge
                 University Press.
Zald, Mayer N.
    1982.   "Theological Crucibles: Social Movements in and of Religion."
                 Review of Religious Research 23: 317–336.
Zilsel, Edgar.
    1951.   "The Sociological Roots of Science." *American Journal of Soci-
                 ology* 47: 544–562.
Zimbardo, P. G.
    1974.   "On 'Obedience to Authority.' " *American Psychologist* 29:
                 566–567.
Zuckerman, Harriet.
    1967.   "The Sociology of Nobel Prizes." *Scientific American* 217: 25–
                 33.
    1977.   *Scientific Elite.* New York: Free Press.

Name Index

Addy, Sidney Oldall, 321
Aidala, Angela A., 165, 352n.11
Ainlay, Stephen C., 43
Alger, Horatio, 83
Allen, Woody, 73
Alsop, J. D., 315
Althusser, Louis, 2, 6, 8, 57
Amery, Julian, 251
Ammerman, Nancy Taton, 44, 192
Anderson, Perry, 272, 281, 318, 324
Anthony, Dick, 160, 372n.3
Antoun, Richard, 192
Apostle, Richard A., 197
Ariès, Philippe, 371n.4
Aristotle, 268
Arjomand, Said Amir, 370n.6
Artz, Frederick B., 284
Ashley, Maurice, 286
Aubrey, John, 287
Ault, James M., Jr., 192
Autrand, Françoise, 319

Bacon, Francis, 280, 282, 284, 289, 291
Badovere, Jacques, 291
Bahr, Howard M., 371n.2
Bainbridge, William Sims, 152, 171, 370n.3
Barber, Bernard, 374n.5
Barnes, Barry, 266
Barraclough, Geoffrey, 283
Barrett, William, 352n.12, 353n.19
Barrow, Isaac, 276, 287

Barthes, Roland, 6, 50, 353n.17
Batho, Gordon, 315
Baulant, Micheline, 317
Beckford, James, 153, 160
Bell, Daniel, 67, 79, 202
Bellah, Robert N., 1, 2, 5, 20, 22, 26, 31, 36, 37, 39–40, 41, 42, 43, 44, 47, 50, 53, 133, 178, 197, 201, 203, 209, 215, 304, 354n.1, 371n.7
Ben-David, Joseph, 267, 274, 290
Bender, Lauretta, 190
Bendix, Reinhard, 198
Benedetti, Vincent, 279
Benedict, Philip, 311, 323
Beniger, James R., 205, 371n.3, 374n.5, 375n.11
Benson, Peter L., 371n.6
Bercé, Yves-Marie, 311
Berger, Peter L., 5, 9, 19, 20, 22, 36, 37–39, 42, 44, 46, 47, 49, 50, 53, 119, 189, 304, 352nn.8, 9
Bergesen, Albert, 118–119, 300, 371n.5, 373n.1, 377n.3
Bernal, J. D., 268
Bernstein, Basil, 190, 205, 341, 371n.5
Bibby, Reginald, 352n.11
Bickman, L., 368n.62
Blackwood, Larry, 92, 357n.24
Bleicher, Josef, 352n.10, 353nn.14, 15
Bloch, Marc, 318
Block, Fred L., 228, 254
Bloor, David, 304
Boleyn, Anne, 321

417

Subject Index

Abolition movement, as moral crusade, 84

Abortion, symbolic aspects of, 93

Academies, scientific. *See* Science

Acquisitive spirit, and rise of capitalism, 28

Actors, and selves in moral codes, 72–73

Adventists, 247

Alienation: in Berger's work, 36; in Marxism, 23–24; from work, 80

Ambiguity. *See* Uncertainty

Ambivalence, and modernity, 24

Anabaptists: early development of, 168; and economic conditions, 168, 235; and serfdom, 237

Annie Hall, 73

Anthropology: and language development, 37; priorities in, 3; and study of ritual, 97–98, 105

Antinomian controversy, 115

Anxiety, and ideological movements, 152–153

Aristocracy: and conflict with bourgeoisie, 245; decline of power of, 269; and Marxist theory of science, 272; and Protestant Reformation, 322–324

Artisan classes, and science, 269

Arts, patronage of, 286

Asceticism. *See* Protestant ethic

Assembly lines, and individualism, 87

Atheism, 240

Attitudes: changes in, 68; consistency among, 45–46; as defining elements

of culture, 7; toward Holocaust, 125–145; political, 130; racial, 63–64

Authority, 30, 54, 66–69. *See also* Power

Baptists, 247

Belief: contrasted with faith, 46; personalization of, 197; religious, 29–30; study of, 34–35; and utterances, 146; view of, in neoclassical theory, 36–42

Belief systems. *See* Worldviews

Bereavement, 189

Birth cohorts, among cultural theorists, 21

Blocking, of ideological systems, 207–211

Body ritual, 103–104

Bolshevism, 227

Boundaries. *See* Symbolic boundaries; Symbols

Bourgeoisie, and scientific development, 268, 271

Brainwashing, 74

Bureaucracy: and core countries, 241; in early modern England, 324; and freedom, 87; and individualism, 197–198, 202; in Nazi Germany, 133–134; and political development, 181–182; as symbol, 74

Business: alienation from, 80; in classical economic theory, 82; limits on power of, 133; organizational change in, 250; pessimism toward, 128; separa-